I0748870

# A Life in Three Acts

Solomon K. Samuels was born in Rangoon, Burma, prior to World War II. He and his family endured the hardships of Japanese occupation during the war and Burma's tumultuous journey toward independence and cruel military dictatorship. He obtained a medical degree in Burma, advanced education in the USA and Canada, and ran his own private medical practice in Michigan for thirty years before retiring to Arizona. He has published four previous books (www.sksent.com):

- *Imperial Jade of Burma and Mutton-fat Jade of India: Mining, Trade, and Use from Antiquity to the Present* (2014)
- *Rangoon 1941. A Novel Based on True Events* (2013)
- *Jade and Maw Sit Sit of Burma* (2004, 2009)
- *Burma Ruby: A History of Mogok's Rubies from Antiquity to the Present* (2003)

www.sksent.com
www.facebook.com/sksenterprises

# A Life in Three Acts

## My Journey from Wartime Burma to America

by

**Solomon K. Samuels**

SKS Enterprises, Inc.
Tucson, Arizona, USA
www.sksent.com
www.facebook.com/sksenterprises

Publisher's Cataloging-in-Publication data

Names: Samuels, Solomon K., author.
Title: A life in three acts : my journey from wartime Burma to America / Solomon K. Samuels.
Description: Includes bibliographical references and index. | Tucson, AZ: SKS Enterprises, Inc., 2021.
Identifiers: ISBN: 978-0-9725323-5-8
Subjects: LCSH Samuels, Solomon K. | East Indians--Burma--Migrations. | World War, 1939-1945--Personal narratives, Burmese. | Physicians--Biography. | Immigrants--United States--Biography. | BISAC BIOGRAPHY & AUTOBIOGRAPHY / Personal Memoirs | HISTORY / Military / World War II | HISTORY / Asia / Southeast Asia
Classification: LCC D767.6 .S26 2021 | DDC 959.1/092--dc23

Printed in the United States of America

Cover Art: Win Thein, "Nimbus" (portrayal of Sagaing, Shwebo Plain, Burma), watercolor on paper. Personal collection.

*Author's Note: The verdant countryside with clouds overhead, depicted in the painting on this book's cover, can be seen as emblematic of the current state of affairs in Burma, where uncertainty and fear cloud the country's beauty and promise.*

This book is dedicated to my father, my half-sister Margaret I, and my little sister Uku, who died during World War II in Burma.

I believe they would have encouraged me to pursue my dreams and would have been proud of my accomplishments as doctor, husband, and father.

# Contents

## Part Three
## Life in America



## Afterword
## Observations on the Current Situation in Burma

# Maps and Figures

# Acknowledgments

Traffic was heavy on the Pittsburgh high bridge. We reached the top of the bridge when the powerful sirens went off. I quickly looked skyward, scanning for aircraft. My first inclination was to jump out of the car and seek shelter. Then it dawned on me that I was no longer in Burma.

That episode made me pause to think of my life experiences, which I had told myself were not that extraordinary, that most people had similar experiences. But of course that was not so. My experiences were unique. That evening over a glass of beer, I started to put the facts together.

World War II in Burma defined my young years with fear, loss, deprivation, and uncertainty. I was in the fifth standard when the war began, with no advanced grammar, writing, or math skills. The immediate postwar years were consumed with getting an education. The American Baptist Mission school never returned, the Catholic schools refused to accept me because I was not of their religion, and the deadline set by the British government for matriculation was nearing. I found a Kashmiri brother and sister who had set up a school for desperate students like me. With their tutoring and much hard study, I passed my school-leaving-certificate exam, then matriculation, then came university and medical school. There was no time to pause and reflect.

Years later, in the USA, colleagues, friends, girlfriends, young fresh-faced girls whom I dated and who asked about myself and my family prompted me to share what little I remembered. The long hours spent being on call and lying on a cot or sitting in the empty call room provided time to reflect. I began to think of my past life, probing and wracking my brain to bring to light the frightful and dark moments of life during the war and its aftermath. Two Japanese residents whom I queried were obtuse and in denial about Japan's actions during the war.

There was an abundance of books on the war, but these typically focused on generals Patton, Bradley, and Nimitz; they had no information on *my* war. It was on my first visit to Australia and its War Museum in Canberra that I found material on war in Asia in general and Burma in particular. The first book that caught my eye was Louis Allen's *The Longest War.* I cut short my plans to see the city and instead spent time at the book shop. It was an awakening. I wanted to buy all the books on display! That would have been impossible. I had to prioritize if I wanted to carry them to America, so settled on about a dozen. I then went back to the hotel. To make room in my luggage, I threw out what I could replace in America. I came home with a list of titles of additional books I wanted, the most important being the five-volume *War Against Japan* by Major-General S. Woodburn Kirby. It was the most complete and comprehensive history of the war, printed by Her Majesty's Printing Press.

Then I met my second wife, an American of German extraction who, unlike many other women, loved Asia, its food, its culture, and history. She insisted on going to the battlefields and historical sites to go over the stories. We met my cousins Peter, Florence, Dorothy, and Lizzie and grilled them on what they remembered. Now I had enough material to collate and sift through. My research next extended to the British Archives and to Burmese and Japanese books from the other side, although there were few from Burmese authors. After going over the material with a fine-tooth comb, I started to put the facts down on paper. It has been a years-long effort and adventure.

Needless to say, I have many people to thank: my teachers and professors at all levels of schooling; Mr. Crozier and Mr. Comer who wrote kind letters of reference; friends and colleagues in Mawchi and Kengtung; my many mentors during my internships and residencies. Operating room and recovery room nurses at all hospitals helped answer many questions and provided information about cultural and local norms. Sometimes colleagues and patients in Kalamazoo provided new insights into wartime life. I made many friends in Burma who selflessly provided information and insights and shared their own stories: gemologists, taxi drivers, and so many others too numerous to mention. Finally, I thank my beautiful and talented daughters who kept asking me about my past.

# Prologue

It was summer in Ohio, deceptively warm. After traveling halfway around the world, I arrived at Youngstown Hospital on July 18, 1960, ready to begin my internship duties. My first posting would be to the north unit, which catered to an upper-class and nearly all-white clientele (and was therefore nicknamed "the country club"). The hospital grounds were clean, surrounded by acres of green grass, a wonderful setting. The red brick building was relatively new, the lawn freshly cut. I was greeted by a senior resident, a Filipino, who helped me check in and finish the paperwork, then took me on a walking tour of the hospital. He mispronounced my name, calling me Samwells. I was shown the floors I was to cover and work, the labs, and the surgical suite. Coming from the third world, I was surprised by many things I saw. Notably, there were no open wards: along the central walkway there were comfortable two-person rooms and a small number of single rooms. Next I was taken to my room in the intern's quarters. It was a small but comfortable bedroom, with a common bathroom one door away and a nearby recreation room with a TV. It would be the first time I would get a chance to see American TV. I would make up for all that I had missed in childhood and would become enamored of the cartoons.

In the following pages I tell the story of my life journey: a South Asian Indian born in British colonial Burma; a young boy surviving the bombing, occupation, and devastation of World War II in Burma; a young man enduring the subsequent rebellions and economic decline of the country that would drive me to emigrate to the US. My experiences in Burma have informed nearly every aspect of my life in the US—through my years of internship, residency, and private medical practice in the US; my personal life as a husband and father; my perspectives on politics and finances; and my assessment of the country I left behind. Here is a broad and sweeping tale—part history, part memoir, and part reflection on current twenty-first-century life.

# Part One

# Early Years in Burma

# Chapter 1
# Burma as a British Colony

Britain acquired Burma as a colony in stages, typically marked by the First, Second, and Third Anglo-Burmese Wars. The First, fought in 1824, brought Burma's Arakan and Tenasserim provinces under British control and gave them a foothold in Rangoon. The Second, ending in 1853, resulted in British control of Rangoon and all of Lower Burma. Total annexation of Burma by Britain was the result of the Third Anglo-Burmese War in 1885.[1] In this Third War, the inept Burmese king, Thibaw, under the thumb of his ambitious mother-in-law, foolishly went to war with the British Army and sepoys of the Madras presidency. It was an uneven fight, a misadventure rather than a war. It lasted less than a week.[2]

Before 1824, the town of Rangoon was livable only from October to March. The rest of the year, the monsoons rendered the town swampy, flooded, and uninhabitable. There were no all-weather roads. Travel and commerce were by river-craft, which limited movement and distribution of goods. Burma's economy was small.

After the First Anglo-Burmese War, the British set about making the city more livable and to that end built an escarpment and bund above the flood plain and drained the swamp. To the few wood and bamboo buildings already built on high ground, the British added new colonial-style buildings. They hired a brilliant

---

[1] See George Bruce, *The Burma Wars: 1824–1886* (London: Granada Publishing, Ltd., 1973) for details about the Wars.

[2] The hapless king, talking about the invasion of Burma by the British, is alleged to have made the following "humorous" statement: "The Kalaphyu or white strangers of the West, fastened a quarrel on the lord of the golden Palace. They landed at Rangoon, took that place, and were permitted to advance as far as Yandabo. For the king, from motives of piety and regard to life, made no effort to oppose them. The strangers had spent vast sums of money in their enterprise; and by the time they reached Yandabo, their resources were exhausted and they were in great distress. They petitioned the king, who, in his clemency and generosity, sent them vast sums of money to pay them back, and ordered them out of the country." Maung Htin Aung, *Burmese History before 1287: A Defense of the Chronicles* (Oxford: The Asoka Society, 1970). Experts are not unanimous in its interpretation, but it is emblematic of Burma's recorded history.

young engineer named Fraser (British) from Calcutta. He was given a broad outline and freedom to plan, but his charge was constrained by the geography, against which he must have chaffed. Extension to the north was limited by the Pagoda; to the east was the large (Pazundaung) creek and fishing village; and beyond was the swamp and the Rangoon River. So Fraser went westward and north, beyond the pagoda and around the man-made lake.[3] The center of the city, between the railroad and the Rangoon River, was laid out in a grid. But it was not a vast expanse, only five blocks north–south; the rest of the city was long, east–west. Pagoda Hill dominated the city. Built hundreds of years ago, the pagoda sat atop the hill overlooking the city. Due to its peculiar geography, the city was to remain small. But Rangoon now became a year-round city and busy trading center.

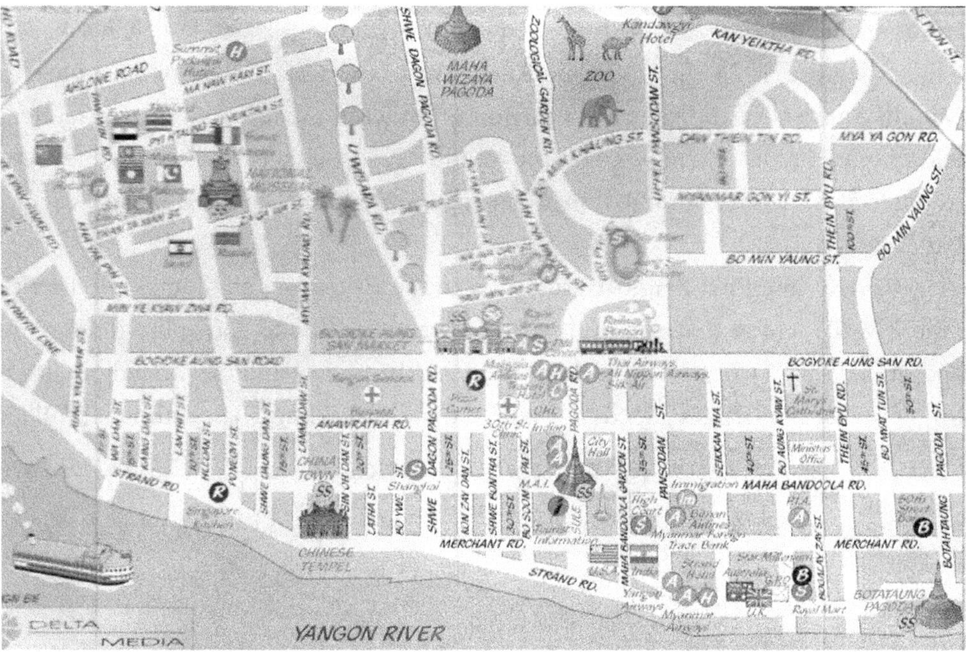


Figure 1. Map of downtown Rangoon. From tourist map.

[3] Prior to this there was a creek in this area, mostly dry, which would flood in the monsoon. To control the flooding, the British built a bund across the southern end of the creek, thereby creating Inya Lake, which would afford prime real estate in later years.

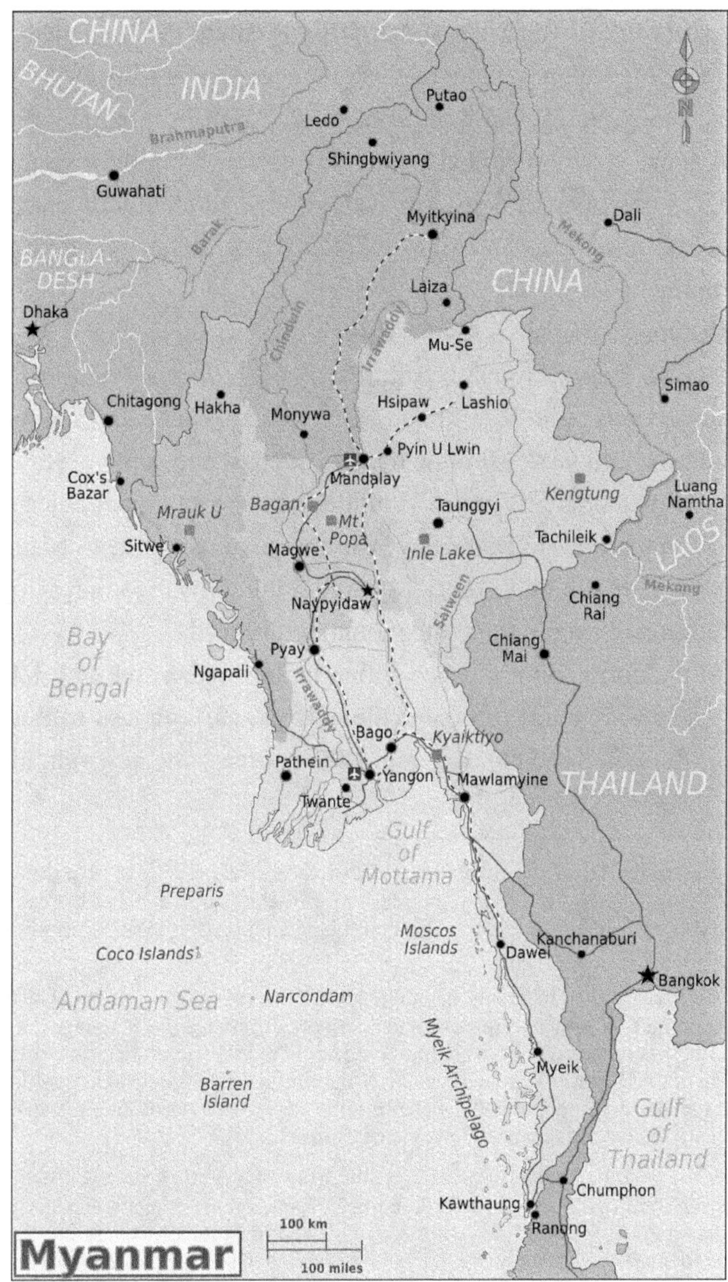


Figure 2. Burma regions map [https://commons.wikimedia.org/wiki/ File: Burma_Regions_Map.png] by Burmesedays, amendments by Globe-trotter and Joelf, CC BY-SA 3.0, via Wikimedia Commons.

The rest of the country, from the littoral south to the U-shaped hilly north, is different, not only in topography but also with respect to its people. The north is mountainous, more subtropical than tropical, and rich in mineral deposits, jade, and precious gems. It was inhabited by people different from the lowland Burmans in language, culture, and ethnicity;[4] its people were ethnically diverse. Generally speaking, the Burmese people are of Mongolian stock, different from people of the Indian subcontinent.[5]

With typical British zeal, the British expanded roads and in 1905 completed a single rail line to Prome, west of Rangoon, a distance of about 100 miles. The local railroad was built from Rangoon to Insein.[6] A second Rangoon to Moulmein railroad was built next. Moulmein lay to the east and south of Rangoon. Kipling the poet wrote eloquently about Moulmein, but he took poetic license, talking of flying fish on the road to Mandalay; Kipling never traveled to Mandalay. The British would eventually build roads to parallel the railway (a narrow-gauge rail) in littoral Burma and extending to the mountainous north.

After the north country was pacified in the wake of the Third Anglo-Burmese War,[7] plans were made to expand there. By 1930, with new rolling stock and locomotives—built in Scotland and shipped to Burma—the new rail line ran from

---

[4] In common usage, the all of the inhabitants of Burma are referred to as "Burmese." The word "Burman" or "Bamar" is used to refer to the majority Buddhist population of the country. "Ethnic peoples" or "hill tribes" refers to the non-Burman inhabitants of Burma, who mostly reside in the northern regions.

[5] Burmese politicians are fond of saying that there are 135 "races" in the country. This is confusing. There is only one race of humans: homo sapiens. Slight differences in language, skin color, and religious or cultural practices do not constitute a separate "race." These are ethnic differences. The genetic make-up of the Burmese people has yet to be determined by ongoing genetic studies. Previous assertions that the Burmese people had Tibetan origins are now being disputed, and it seems more likely that they are related to the Nancho people of China.

[6] In 1877, after the Second Anglo-Burmese War, the Irrawaddy Valley State Railway, under Commissioner Johnson, built a narrow-gauge railroad from Rangoon to Prome, a distance of 163 miles. The engine, named AO1, was built by Dübs & Co., based in Polmadie, Glasgow, Scotland. After 1885, when the annexation was complete, the railway expanded service to Mandalay and Myitkyina. As a youngster, I was captivated by Engine 612, YC class, which was introduced by Dübs in 1933.

[7] For details on this, see Sir Charles Crosthwaite, *The Pacification of Burma* (1912; London: Frank Cass & Co., Ltd., 1968).

Rangoon to Mandalay, then to Mogoung in the Kachin State, and finally to Myitkyina, a distance of almost 700 miles.

The Kingdom of Burma before 1885, like most of Southeast Asia, was mostly agrarian. Rice was its chief product; next was timber, especially teak, padauk, and other hardwoods; also pulses; then some minerals. Lumber was abundant: the great teak trees grew to a height of more than 150 feet, and even before the British annexation there was a brisk trade in hardwoods. Seafarers came from Portugal, the Netherlands, and Britain to trade in this commodity. Rangoon emerged as the port city for these traders, where goods ferried from agrarian hinterlands of the country, via the Irrawaddy River, were loaded onto merchant ships for transport. Rangoon had little or no industry to speak of beyond this.

People in the West generally knew little about Burma, although they may have been vaguely aware of the legendary ruby and sapphires mines of Mogok and its jade.[8] Local people had worked the mines for centuries. When the French challenged the British for dominance of this trade, it was not well received. The French king Louis XIV spent more than 100,000 livres and commissioned a ruby necklace that became part of his country's crown jewels.[9] Not only the French but also Indian rulers like the Nizam of Hyderabad were collectors of fabled Burma rubies.

The Bamar (Burma's dominant ethnic group, also called Burmans) never treated the ethnic peoples well; they regarded themselves as a master "race," superior to all others. Over the eons there was much strife between the mountain and lowland peoples. Relations between various ethnic people were also troubled and would be the cause of endless conflict. Among the minorities were Karens, who were predominantly Christian and served the British well; likewise the Kachins, but animism was also widely practiced. The country's population also included Hindus, Muslims, Christians, and even Arabs and Armenians, primarily in Rangoon. In spite of annexation by the British, there would be endless tension between these different groups. Riots would break out between Hindus and Muslims: Muslims would frequently throw portions of a cow into a Hindu temple; and the Hindus

[8] Not only rubies and sapphires but also peridot, spinel, and assorted colored gems were and are mined around Mogok.

[9] French Bourbon kings were noted for their collections of ruby jewelry.

would throw pig entrails into a mosque; that would start a riot. The Burmese Buddhists hated both groups, and whenever they got a chance, they killed both groups, but they reserved a visceral hatred for fundamentalist Muslims. What particularly incensed the Burmese was the clothing that Muslim women wore. The Muslim imams did not object to Muslims marrying Burmese women as long as the women converted to Islam, but they did not allow Muslim men or women to convert to the other's religion. This would anger Buddhists and would result in riots between the Muslims and the Burmese, with severe repercussions in later years; it is a source of violence even today.[10]

After the British consolidated their conquest post-1885, Britain formally annexed Burma to her Indian Empire, mostly so that India would be responsible to pay for the war. Queen Victoria reveled in her empire. She knew little about Burma yet prevailed upon Benjamin Disraeli, her favorite Tory P.M., to make her Queen Empress of the Indian Empire, and that is how she became Queen Empress of Burma as well. Under Tory rule the empire expanded. One of the instruments for this expansion was the Indian Army, which was a separate entity from the British Army in England. New Delhi became the seat of power and military operations throughout Southeast Asia.

British writ (India) extended from Southeast Asia to Hongkong to Iraq. People came to Burma from the far corners of the empire, not only from India but also from Palestine and Mesopotamia and Armenia. Armenians would invest and build the premier hotel in Rangoon, the Strand Hotel, and also invested in Singapore (Raffles hotel) and Hongkong. As the British administration strove to modernize and develop Burma, it needed skilled labor to build roads, railways, and industry. To that end, they encouraged movement of labor from one part of the empire to another. That is how my ancestors moved from their native India to Burma without the need for passports and travel papers. The Indian diaspora spread to Britain's Asian and African colonies as well. India had been colonized for almost 300 years; Burma would be a colony for fewer than sixty.

---

[10] Even as a young boy I felt that the imams were a special breed whose rigid religious practices would inevitably bring conflict.

# Chapter 2
# My Family Arrives in Burma

*"Luck is what happens when preparation meets opportunity."*
*—The Stoic Philosopher Seneca*

Father was born some time in the late nineteenth century, in coastal Andhra in the Telugu-speaking corner of India. Both Father and his first wife were Christians (Southern Baptists). Not much is known of the family, but it is clear that Grandfather was dedicated to the education of his children, for two sons were doctors, and two were civil servants. This was remarkable given India's caste-ridden and non-egalitarian society; in some respects it was the most destructive type of society known to the world.[1] In spite of being of the Christian minority, Father's family did well. In colonial times, not many Indians went to school or to college. The British colonial educational system called for nine years of schooling, then came the school-leaving-certificate exam, which allowed a young man to start work at the civil bureaucracy and with effort climb the ladder of bureaucracy. After ninth standard came Matriculation, which allowed one to go to college.

In 1892 India was going through difficult times economically. My grandfather worked for the Indian (Great) Peninsular Railway, and his son, my father, wanted to continue in that line of work. With a basic education, my father sought employment in the new colony of Burma and found it in the expanding Burma Railways. The British encouraged and helped people emigrate within the empire. Although ethnically different from the Burmese, many Indians migrated to Rangoon.

Who are we genetically? That is a question often asked. Indians are part of the out-of-Africa migration some 40,000 years ago. The first migrants stayed in what is now known as the fertile crescent for many generations, then broke up into groups and went their separate ways. One group migrated to the Indo-Gangetic plain, representing the earliest migrants; others went further south. This is India of

---

[1] The country still struggles with inequality and persecution, seventy-two years after adopting a secular constitution.

the pre-Hindu era.[2] I think of myself as of pre-Hindu Indian ancestry. Genetically, present-day people from India have a strong affinity to ancient Iranian farmers, suggesting that the expansion of Near Eastern farming spread eastward to the Indus Valley, 9,000 years ago. They adapted to the new land. Geneticists say that the second wave came later; this group was mostly Eurasians (a different Haplogroup) and settled primarily in what is called Ancestral North India. They interbred with the already settled southern Indians, so there was an admixture of later migrations with older migrants.

Along with Father, the extended family migrated with him, which included his three brothers and one sister.[3] Members of his close-knit family differed phenotypically, with variation in skin color and height. Aunt Ava was of medium height, with brown skin. She was kind and gentle. She had gone to school but could not read or write English. My Uncle Sam was a huge man, 6 feet 2 inches, and dark skinned; he was a full-fledged physician (MBBS, the equivalent of MD). Father was a handsome man of medium build, with curly hair and dark brown skin. His progeny showed the wide variations seen among his siblings. Uncle James—a handsome, portly man, not as tall as Uncle Sam, with a handlebar moustache and light skin—looked more like middle-eastern potentate; like my father, he was employed by the Burma Railways. The youngest brother, Uncle Rao, was also a doctor although his was a colonial degree called LMP (Licentiate in Medicine and Surgery); he was probably the smallest (physically) of the brothers. Father and his brother James married two sisters.

The new country had little infrastructure. All commerce was dependent on the great Irrawaddy River; at any distance from the river, travel was by bullock cart.

---

[2] Homo sapiens is more than 150,000 years old. Most religions are no more than 7,000 years old. So for 95 percent of human history, we do not know what gods we believed in. David Reich, *Who we are and how we got here: Ancient DNA and the New Science of the Human Past* (New York: Pantheon Books, 2018), 149. The Hindu religion is no more than 5,000 years old.

[3] Birth order was Ava, Samuel, Joseph (my father), James, Rao; surname was Kella. As he emigrated from India to Burma, my father was named Samuel on paperwork. Then, the American Baptists in Burma had difficulty grasping the Telugu naming protocol by which surname precedes forename, so the families came to be known as—and referred to themselves as—the Samuel family, the James family, etc.

There were no all-weather roads, and the rail service was in its infancy. Father and his siblings came not as labor but as part of a civil bureaucracy. The Indian civil service was a much-admired institution. My father did not pursue that route; instead, he found work for the budding Burma Railways. It was a good job, keeping the inventory of coal used by the locomotives. Uncle James worked for the railway as well, but I do not know in what capacity, as he died when I was just five years old.

Father's life was upended by the untimely death of his wife, leaving him with three young children. Initially his sister helped, but he had to find a new wife. So he went back to India to look for a wife. The search led him to a mission school, where he found a fifteen-year-old woman named Elizabeth. Her father had died suddenly, and her mother (whose immediate ancestors were goldsmiths; what caste she belonged to is no interest to me) was on a quest to marry off her daughter. Without any means, desperate, this woman who would become my grandmother had approached a mission run by Christian missionaries, who took her and my mother in and sheltered them. My father had heard of my mother's plight through church connections. In March of 1920, when she was just sixteen, my mother married my father in Srikakulum,[4] a scenic city about twenty miles north of Vizakhapatam (Vizag), the future naval base on the Bay of Bengal and the fastest growing city in the south.[5] After the marriage, my father brought my mother and my grandmother back to Rangoon and set up housekeeping. Mother spoke Telugu, understood some English, but could not read or write English.

It is hard to believe that my entire extended family packed their meager belongings to set sail to this unknown land. They traveled by steamship, a five-day journey in good weather. I took this sea journey myself in 1950, and it was not a cruise: rough seas in third class made me sick, and I constantly threw up. You took a bed roll and did your best to find a spot. My mother told me about the voyage when I was still a boy. Not knowing anything about the new country, its language,

---

[4] According to an affidavit Mother completed years later when I was getting a passport.

[5] Vizag was once a vassal city of the Sultanate (Muslim) of Golconda, noted for the great diamond mines and the Hope Diamond. The Sultan appointed a governor to rule over a good-sized Muslim community.

culture, and religion, it must have taken much perseverance to adapt to the new world. Nonetheless, my family survived, adjusted to the new land, and did well.

To my mother, Burma was a very different place than her native land, and it must have been not only strange but also frightful to her. She talked about how hard it was to adjust. The summers were wet, hot, and humid, with vibrant green and dense tropical vegetation. The long monsoon season was so hot, she often said, "that you could see water vapor rise from the ponds and creeks." When the rains came, they came with great gusto, sheets of rain drenching everything. Sometimes the sheets of rain fell sideways, and an umbrella was more a prop than a useful item. During the full moon and new moon, the rains fell for days and would flood the streets.

Burma was mostly Buddhist and, unlike India, did not have a caste system. Even in the twenty-first century, the overriding concern of people in India on a social basis is what caste and sub group you belong to. My mother must have been surprised to see that the Burmese women had a lot more freedom than Indian women. Burmese women were freer to own property and run shops. The people looked different too, and they spoke a different language. Rangoon was a city whose people were, in numbers, Indian, Burmese, and Chinese; there also was a sizable Japanese community in Rangoon, which kept to itself. Sitting on top of society were the British. The major ethnic group was the Bamar, who lorded it over various hill people. These differences caused tension and endless violence. The Burmese believe in astrology (a pseudoscience), that it controls your life and determines your destiny. Hindus believe in Karma, that life is preordained by your past and that your caste is preordained as well. The Burmese accepted this Vedic myth, even though evolution has basically debunked this insane belief system. We now know that probability theory and randomness of events is operative.

My father's first family consisted of three children (a son named Danam, born in February of 1913; and two girls, both named Margaret). The older Margaret was a gentle, hard-working girl. Her younger sister Margaret was the exact opposite; she turned out to be a problem child, a holy terror. She was very difficult to handle, as Mother would say.

My mother's first-born died shortly after birth; then she had three daughters (Emily, Kamala, Lily). I was the fourth-born, born in 1932 (the year is in question)[6] in the midst of the world-wide depression.[7] I was born at our home near a small rail station called Hume Road. It is no longer on the map, and I have no memory of the place. I was told that the railway home was in a blockish little apartment painted black and consisted of a front room, a bedroom, a small kitchen, and an outhouse. That stay lasted only a few years. With his growing family, Father went looking for a larger home. His work with the Burma Railways was going well despite the depression. He was promoted to coal supervisor, assuring adequate supplies of coal for the railways. He told of working hard, he said, "moving up the ladder." The railway was growing rapidly, especially to the north to Mandalay and to Lashio, close to the China border. His was, by standards of that time, a solid job with job security, and he saved enough money to buy land and build a home.

His quest led him about two miles north of Hume Road, to a place called Kamayut, where he was entranced by a parcel of land owned by the Sassoon family. Mr. Sassoon, a Jewish gentleman from Palestine, came to the country at the turn of the nineteenth century and, being an entrepreneur, bought swathes of empty wetlands and developed them. He built a realty company that, after his death, his daughter inherited, and it was from her that Father bought the land. Rangoon was growing and becoming ever more diverse. These diverse people brought capital and management skills and intellectual skills as well. George Orwell came to Burma with the Imperial Police; he was posted to Katha[8] in northern Burma, and it was here that he wrote and wrote, profusely.

Father obtained a loan from the Railway Provident Fund to buy land and build a house. In front and to the east of the plot he chose was a huge Mogul palace,

---

[6] All of the family papers were destroyed or stolen in 1942. A rigorous examination of my college entrance papers show that I was born in 1930 although other affidavits give the date of 1932. Four more siblings were born after me: Jason, Merlyn, Katherine, and Olive. The last-born, Uku, died of pneumonia during World War II, in my arms.

[7] Like all countries, Burma suffered through the depression. The price of paddy had fallen precipitously on the world market, causing a depression and giving rise to political unrest.

[8] Most of the buildings in Katha are in disrepair; the Burmese take no pride that the great man lived there.

built on the lines of majestic Mogul architecture from India. It was a beautiful marble palace, with a very large and beautiful dome, huge columns dominating the entrance, marble floors within, and the usual Mogul gardens. The estate was surrounded by a high bamboo fence. Surprisingly, the estate was already was in decline; to the best of my recollection, nobody lived there permanently. To the west of the house was a beautiful, large meadow that ended at the railroad tracks. At high tide, the Hlaing River glimmered to the west. To the northeast was a large parcel of land that was privately owned, with two large houses owned by a wealthy Anglo-Indian family; more about this estate later. Father deliberately picked a lot close to the rail station, halfway between the rail station and the main Rangoon–Insein Road. There were few houses in the neighborhood, and they were typically built of wood. Our house was an exception in that it was an all-brick bungalow, with prospect for expansion, and had provision for running water.

In typical Indian fashion, Grandmother lived with us. Already past sixty, she was active even at her age. She was a small, slightly built woman, but she was feisty and resourceful. She was also a good farm woman; she raised chickens, ducks, goats, and even a milk cow.[9] My mother was a small woman, about five feet tall, possibly a few inches taller. She was olive-skinned with delicate features. She grew up in a Christian household. Given her age when she was married, she had limited education.

Our life revolved around the rail station, which was within walking distance (many years later I would see the same pattern in the suburbs of London).[10] Small towns grew up around the rail stations. Cars were few at that time. Tea shops, pastry shops, "mom and pop" shops selling sundries, and small savory shops crowded around the station. One savory shop was notable: it was run by a one-legged man, a veteran, who made wonderful savories. A short distance from the station was the residential area. There were no zoning laws here: large modern homes were interspersed among more modest homes and hutments. Most of the

[9] From an early age, I loved animals. I helped Grandmother raise chickens, cows, and a goat in the back yard. At sunset I helped her gather the chickens and the goat, which would be a great help during the dark days of the war.

[10] Our station was Kamayut, and our main means of transport was the railroad.

houses were of Burmese design, with a lower level of bricks and mortar and an upper level made of teakwood—which was plentiful in Burma. Father wanted to buy another parcel but did not have sufficient savings at the time. Our house was more modern than many others; Father was going to dig a well and wanted to have running water. Months after the house was completed, an earthquake damaged part of the house. Although it was still livable, plans were delayed.

Our neighbors were a mixed lot. Burmese Buddhists predominated, then came Hindus, and Muslims from the subcontinent, and there was a small community of Anglo-Indians.[11] We all got along, respected one another, and celebrated each other's festivals with one another. For example, Aunty Nyunt, a Burmese Buddhist, lived around the corner from us. Her husband, like Father, had worked for the railways but had died years ago, leaving her with a boisterous son. She allowed us to fetch water from her well. In a big house across the street from Aunty Nyunt lived another Burmese family. Although they were very close-knit and their son went to a Burmese school, Ko Pe Thein and I became good friends. Mr. Patel, an ethnic Indian, lived just west of us; he was married to a Burmese woman, and I got along well with their middle son as well. Beyond the Patel house and across the street, at the bend in the road, was a large estate owned by a wealthy Anglo-Indian family, and just beyond lived a middle-class Anglo-Indian family whose daughter was named Shirley. Across from Shirley's house lived the family of Muslim Pir Mohammed and his Burmese wife. Englishmen[12] were rarely seen in our neighborhood; they lived in cantonments and at the government house. My earliest recollections of the Brits are rather vague. I saw them from a distance. There were red-faced, sun-burnt, burly policemen with their khaki shorts and putties. Their leather belt and boots were always polished to a fine shine, and they all wore the ubiquitous pith helmet.

---

[11] For the British, the term "Anglo-Indian" was reserved for children born to two British parents in India. Children of mixed parentage were called "Eurasians." In colonial Burma, however, Eurasians were referred to as "Anglo-Indians" or "Anglo-Burmese," often abbreviated simply to "Anglo."

[12] I did not know the difference between an Englishman and a Scotsman. As someone who survived the war, I like to watch parades. The most impressive regiments, in my view, are the Argyle and Sutherland Highlanders.

# Chapter 3
# Early Family Life in Kamayut

As in most Indian families, Father was distant. I hardly saw him, except on Sundays. Mother never addressed him by his name or, for the most part, directly. It was a peculiar Indian custom; she addressed him indirectly. If there was pillow talk, we the children were not aware. Most days he came home after dark and ate separately, late in the evening, as is the custom in the east, and he stayed up late.

Danam, my half-brother, was much older than I. He was of medium build, with stiff black hair. He was light brown in color, with a broad face. Like my Uncle Rao, he was an LMP so was allowed to practice limited general medicine.

My oldest half-sister Margaret was tall (for an Indian girl) and beautiful, with chiseled features and beautiful eyes, a pleasant personality and easy-going nature. She was hard working and took her responsibility seriously in caring for the younger siblings. I liked her dearly. She was also a good cook. I once overheard her say that she was going to cook my favorite rooster for dinner. I became so distressed that I chased her around the house. Finally she cornered the bird and hid it under her sari; after a short search I finally lost track of it ... and enjoyed supper. After she married, when I was still a pre-teen, she left home, as it was the custom for her to live with her in-laws.

Margaret's younger sister was lazy and self-absorbed, concerned only about herself. She did not play the half-sister role but instead was disruptive, resulting in frequent quarrels. We called her "chin-na-ka," meaning little sister. She was quite ordinary looking, given to intimidating others and making every effort to live by her wits rather than by hard work or good deeds. She suffered histrionic personality disorder (a psychoses and psychoneuroses). She went to school like the rest of us, but when she had to take her school-leaving exam, she failed it, feigning an asthmatic attack, probably self-induced. This angered Father. In spite her failure, however, she still claimed that she was well educated and could speak English well. Yet she was indolent, whiling away her time reading *True Romance* and *True*

*Life* pulp magazines and doing little to contribute to the housework. She could never hold a job for long. She was highly opinionated and turned to religious extremism, soon becoming a rabid evangelical. She hated the Hindu caste system, saving her greatest scorn for the higher-caste Brahmans who ran around with their saffron robes and a dirty string across the shoulder. They controlled who could sit where and what job they could hold, and they thought that murder of the untouchables who violated their rules was justified. She was also sexually repressed; I once overheard her say that little boys were dirty because they had to hold their penises when they pee. Extremely evangelical and intolerant, she reveled at the shortcomings of other people and their beliefs. All this would impact the family after Father's death.

My other older siblings were Emily, Kamala, and Lily. Emily was of modest temperament. And then came Kamala, a beautiful girl with delicate and refined features and light brown skin color. Her personality was as beautiful as her looks. Lily was plain; she lacked the fine features of her older sister. Mentally she was unbalanced, which would cause much grief for the family in the post-war era. My three younger sisters—Merlyn, Katherine, and Olive—closely resembled my mother, with petite stature and slightly more rounded face. Brother Jason was slightly built.

My Uncle James died in 1937 at a young age, leaving behind a large family. Father helped to build a house near ours and moved the James family from Insein to Kamayut. He also took on the burden of caring for his brother's children. The expansion of the extended family was welcome to us kids.

On Sundays we went to the Baptist Church, a city landmark at Fitch Square (now called Bandoola Square) in the center of the city of Rangoon. This was one of the oldest churches in Burma, built on land that the East India Company had gifted to the church. It was founded by the American Baptist mission in Burma. The Reverend E. A. Stevens, a Baptist minister from America and the first preacher, was instrumental in building the school that we attended (more about that below). The original land was on Merchant Street, but that was sold and in July 1896 the Barr Street Church was built. It too was eventually sold and the new one anchored the northeast corner of Fitch Square. It still stands there, now called

Immanuel Baptist Church. Its prominence in the center of the city caused eternal dismay among the Burmese, who never cease agitating to tear it down. In 1962 the Burma Army tried to get rid of it, but it has survived and still stands there. It held multilingual services: English, Tamil, and Telugu. In the church the women and children sat on one side and the men sat on the other side. Going to church once a month was special because it meant a train ride.

Figure 3. Immanuel Baptist Church, Rangoon. Photo by author.

Sometimes an American missionary would deliver a talk in English, and for those who were challenged in English (we spoke both English and Telugu, sometimes Burmese), a translator would interpret his sermon. There was much that was lost in translation, but stories from the Bible were nonetheless explained, and that was how we were influenced to accept the Baptist version of religion. I remember one such speech about slavery. The speaker explained that "slaves were happily housed in small homes, with sanitation, and other amenities. The slaves were happy, they sang gospel songs and would laugh and dance. There were schools for them." When asked about discrimination he said "as long as they stayed on the plantation there was no violence. It was the outside agitators who stirred up trouble."

Schooling was segregated in early twentieth-century Burma. Those of lesser means went to the dismal state schools, which had a poor reputation; there were no local schools in the sense that we have in America. Buddhists went to the monastic school, whose medium of instruction was Burmese; they offered mostly religious instruction, with little education in math or science. Hindus went to Hindu schools, where English was taught as a second language. Muslim schools were attended only by Muslims. The educated upper classes went to special schools: girls to Catholic convent schools such as St. Philomena's or the Good Shepherd convent; boys to Catholic schools typically run by Jesuits or to the premier school for boys, St. Paul's Anglican school.[1] The medium of instruction was English at all of these schools. The Burmese elite also sent their children to the best Catholic schools, where they took on Christian names (which they dumped after Independence) and learned proper English. The British tended to send their young to boarding schools in England or to British schools in the colonies.

[1] Long before the British arrived, the Italians set up Catholic schools in Burma and English-language schools. In 1719 Pope Clement XI sent learned Barnabite emissaries to China, but the papal legate, Carlo Ambrosio Mezzabarba, was not successful there. In 1721, Father Sigismondo Calchi went to the Kingdom of Pegu (then a separate kingdom from the Burmese) and founded the first mission. He took the arduous journey from Syriam in Burma to Pegu, a journey of fifty days. He made a lasting impression on the king of Pegu, who allowed Calchi to set up schools and who decided to send a good will mission to the pope in Rome. Calchi was a full-fledged teacher; he had taught at St. Alexander's College of Milan (which, as of 1960, was still in existence). Through the efforts of this Barnabite father, Pegu became the first permanent Catholic mission in Burma. Calchi learned the local language, studying both Burmese and Mon, and taught European languages to the Burmese, thereby sowing the seeds of early Western education in Burma. Father Vittoni was sent as the king's personal envoy to the papal court, with presents of rubies and sapphires and a message of peace and good will. The Barnabites built schools similar to schools in Europe. The curriculum included writing in European style but also taught arithmetic, geography, and nautical sciences. Theology was a part of the curriculum, along with Italian and English. Another Barnabite, Father Carparni, supervised the first casting of Burmese type in Rome. The Burmese king Bodopaya (1762–1819) invited the Barnabites to set up more schools in Pegu and sent all of his children to be tutored by the Italians. Thus, when the British invaded Burma in 1824, there were Catholic schools teaching English. The British colonial authorities imposed and codified their own rules of the British educational system. See Vivian Ba, "The Beginnings of Western Education in Burma—The Catholic Effort," *The Burma Research Society* 92 (December 1964): 287–323.

Not fitting anywhere, our family was part of a small Christian minority belonging to the US Southern Baptist church (conservative, rigid, and sclerotic); we went to the school run by the American Baptist mission. It was housed in a large, nondescript building in the heart of the city. The fact that we belonged to the Baptist church was helpful to our admission to the school. I believe the school was subsidized by the Judson Baptist mission of the US, whose presence was strong in Burma. In fact, Mr. Judson created the written Burmese language and wrote the Karen Bible. The Baptists naturally imposed their repressive sexual beliefs and a rigid Christian morality on its church members. In spite of its name, the mission school was not just a religious school; it was a vernacular school. English was emphasized, and the curriculum was the same as at the high-end schools. The teachers were mostly Indian-Christian. My teacher was a happy, bespectacled, slightly plump woman with a square face. She was a good teacher and worried about her charges. She was particularly hard on me as my handwriting was terrible; she harangued me till I practiced to improve. As matter of fact, once I did write an essay that she could read, and she read and waved it in front of the class, which broke out in applause. I cannot recall the rest of the teachers, nor do I remember the headmaster, as he was rarely seen except on special occasions. Sometimes an American preacher would appear and give a speech, which would be interpreted by one of the Indian preachers. Americans also ran an all-girls school in another suburb, Kemmendine, where a number of Americans lived. My cousins, the James girls, went to the American Baptist girls' school there, and when the two families got together the girls giggled over the American women who stripped down to sunbathe on the roof of the girl's school.

Going to school was quite involved. We walked from our house to the nearby Kamayut train station (we had second-class passes). Second-class coaches were clean, the seats were polished teakwood, and the carriages were not crowded. Watching the train conductor was a favorite pastime of mine. At night he waved the green lantern, which to me was endlessly fascinating. Moreover, the main station was always busy with trains going in and out, and my special pleasure was

Figure 4. American Baptist Mission School, Rangoon. The building was converted into Kempeitai Headquarters during WWII. Photo by author.

watching the long-distance train that went to Mandalay and beyond. Built in Scotland where other great engines were made, like the flying Scotsman, the engine was green, a beautiful piece of machinery.

Of the six rail stations between the suburb of Kamayut and the city of Rangoon, the most interesting to me was Gymkhana station. It was in close proximity to the exclusive Whites-only Gymkhana Club, where the British played polo and British men and women rode their horses. It was the one place we saw English girls (unmarried young English girls who came looking for husbands) boarding the first-class carriages, which were also exclusive.

My sisters and brother and I traveled in a group from home to school. At the main station we got off the train, climbed the stairs, took the overhead bridge, whence a short walk took us to Phayre Street, which was a north–south street, then to Dalhousie Street (an east–west street), and finally a couple more blocks to Sparks Street where the school was located. In the second block of Phayre Street there were many distractions for me, especially the car show rooms, the Auto Union, Humber motor cars, and other new models. I would glance enviously at the cars and sometimes lingered to gawk at the cars, especially the roadsters. When I fell behind, my older sisters would constantly admonish me to hurry up. My older sister Emily would scold me, grab me by the arm, and tell me to fall in line.

The school building was a typical multi-storied colonial building. It had no green space, just a small courtyard all covered with asphalt, with little room for play. (For sports I practiced running in the meadow behind the house, but my lungs hurt so badly that I could run only a short distance. I practiced for the 100-yard dash once, and on one occasion I thought my lungs were going to explode. That was when I realized I would have difficulty with sports and discovered I had Asthma.) Sports were not much emphasized, but religion was. In addition to the regular curriculum we had Bible school. I enjoyed and did well at school (except for handwriting and spelling), passing each year.[2] I excelled in one subject, geography.

The top floor of the building housed administrative offices, and like so many buildings there was no lift. The classrooms were average size, and the desks and seats were small but comfortable. We had few Muslim or Hindu classmates, and no Burmese at all. During the war, the building would gain notoriety as headquarters of the notorious Japanese Kempeitai. If the walls could talk and we could hear the interrogations and tortures that took place there, it would expose the cruelty of the Japanese.

In our family there was a big age difference. My half-brother and sisters went to school earlier than the rest of us because they were older. My problem was Jason, my younger brother. He had a coping problem and never got used to school. He caused me endless problems, yet in a strange way the family protected him, and my sisters coddled him. I was frequently called to clean up when he would soil himself, and finally when he defecated on his seat, I took him to the bathroom, helped him clean up, then gave him a thrashing at home. My mother did not like my giving him a thrashing, a problem that would worsen with the passage of time.

---

[2] The system in colonial schools was that the state education department tested pupils, at the 5th, 7th, and 10th standards. At the end of each academic year, you took the state exam. If you passed you went on to the next standard.

I learned the facts of life from the street. Sitting at the desk next to me in school was a fourteen-year-old Hindu boy. We got to know each other, talking about magic, rope climbing, about some sadhus who would bury themselves for hours, and so on (later I would learn that it was skillful use of air pockets). And so it was that we got to talking about sex. He wanted to know how much I knew about where children came from, so he explained, and I was aghast. I told him my mother would never do a thing like that; after marriage, mothers and fathers hold hands and pray. He laughed uproariously and told me "your father did it to your mother." I chased him around the block till I ran out of breath.

The town of Kamayut where we lived was bisected by the railroad into east and west. The west was dominantly Tamil, Indian. Our east side was more diverse, having Buddhist pagodas, Hindu temples, Muslim mosques, and a Christian church. Within our neighborhood block there lived Burmese, some Eurasians, Muslims, and Hindus. We developed good relationships with our neighbors of all backgrounds and belief systems; aside from some occasional snide remarks, we got along and helped each other. I had the privilege of mixing with Hindus and Muslims and Eurasians and came into contact with their preachers, priests, monks, and imams—and with their rigid religious beliefs. We enjoyed each other's festivals, respecting religious differences. The Burmese celebrated their festivals with great gusto, especially the new year (in April). Their celebration was long, lasting four days, during which everybody threw water at each other. It was unpleasant to have buckets of water thrown at you, so most of the time we just stayed indoors to avoid getting doused.

The southwest monsoon, a huge weather system, influenced life and livelihoods in much of Asia, and Burma was no exception (except for people living in the mountainous far north, which had a subtropical climate). The monsoon started in mid-May with several days of lightening, thunder, storms, and increasing humidity. Along with this came insects and mosquitoes. The sky would light up, then open, and the rain would come down with great fury—sheet upon sheet of heavy rain, coming with such volume that it filled the gutters quickly. Small dry ponds filled rapidly, snakes came out of their holes, and little fish appeared almost spontaneously. Humans rarely ventured out; it would take hours before a storm let up.

People abandoned footwear and took to the street barefoot. In the downtown offices, the British frowned on such deviation from the norm, but there was little anyone could do. Aside from the metaled roads, streets became impassable to motorized traffic. The rains were most intense by July and August. There would be some rain-free days at new moon, and sunshine would appear for a few days, but it remained hot and humid and by full moon the rains would intensify again. By the end of September, the monsoon would sputter, and by mid-October it would end. The rains and heat would dissipate, bringing great joy for people.

For Burmese families, this meant "lent" celebrations. Thadingyut, the fall moon, is spectacular and unsparing in brilliance. Homes and buildings are lit with lanterns and candles. It is also a time of romance for young Burmese, who stay up all night to watch the open theater called the *pwe*. I rarely attended these events.

Shortly after the Burmese "lent," Hindu festivals would start. Diwali, the Hindu festivals of lights, is celebrated with nights full of parades, sometimes noisy. The Tamil Hindus of East Kamayut came out for their celebration to take their gods to the temple in West Kamayut, near our home. We were forbidden to go to the temple. I was warned by my sister Margaret that to do so would be tantamount to worshiping idols and would mean going to hell. Once I followed the procession to the temple, however, where the god image would be taken inside. That was my first look inside the temple.

Because school was far away and had no sports facilities whatsoever, it was at home that I engaged in outdoor life. There was a large, leafy, bucolic meadow behind the house, from which I could see the railway station. If I was running late, I would hear the toot of the engine and could run to the station in time to board the train. Sometimes youths gathered together to play outside. There was almost no money for sports. On tropical moonlit nights we gathered to play "Aundoo," a simple game whose origin is unknown. It required no equipment, no bats, no balls; just a bucket of water and sometimes lime water to draw the lines on the road. You started at the top line and ran till you reached the last line, then ran back, always trying to avoid being tagged. We did not have fancy toys. One of my playthings was the rim of a bicycle wheel, which was hit gently to make it move; whoever kept it rolling the longest won.

Father earned a good income and even received a medal from the crown for his service, so that we children had a good middle-class life. Life was simple until the summer of 1939, when everything began to change. Our idyllic life would end soon.

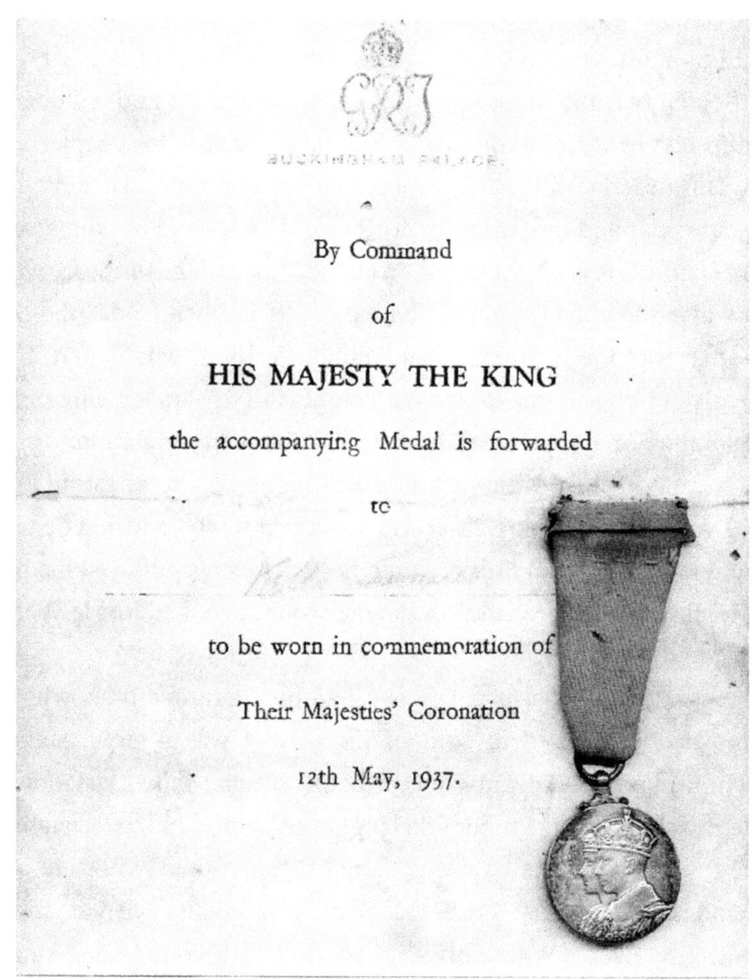

BUCKINGHAM PALACE.

By Command

of

**HIS MAJESTY THE KING**

the accompanying Medal is forwarded

to

to be worn in commemoration of

Their Majesties' Coronation

12th May, 1937.

Figure 5. Medal given to my father, with declaration. Photo by author.

# Chapter 4
# Political Unrest in Burma

Since 1920, political movements in Burma had been agitating for Independence. The older, seasoned politicians called for an orderly transition to Dominion status. In this they were in sync with independence movements in India, led by Gandhi and Nehru and the Congress Party, whose intellectuals—local as well British socialists like Annie Besant—advocated an orderly and peaceful transfer of power. In contrast, the youthful Burmese revolutionary leaders were headstrong and in unseemly and dangerous haste. They lacked intellectual depth, experience, or administrative skill, so they often resorted to violence and plotted to take power by violent overthrow.

Much of the agitation originated at the university. Prior to 1920, Burma had no university. That year the colonial authorities set up the University of Rangoon along the lines of the University of Calcutta. Some students came to learn, but others came to participate in political agitation. Outside agitators—fascists (Japanese) and communists—quickly exerted their influence on the naive students, claiming that the university offered only a colonial education. Their agitating was responsible for much of the turmoil of this period. The colonial office sent Mr. Chelmsford to institute reforms, but these negotiations failed. The young activists formed the Thakin Party and the DoBama Party,[1] both of which decried the so-called "colonial education," rejected gradualism, and started a disobedience campaign. The elders were open to teaching of science such as Newton's laws of motion or Einstein's $E=MC^2$ and were non-political, but the seditious young were not listening.

By 1937, the independence movement was divided into three groups. There was a party of senior administrators who were experienced in bureaucracy and worked for the peaceful, orderly transfer of power. The second group was led

[1] Thakin means "Master race" or "men of higher standing." The honorific term was usually reserved for the British. DoBama Asi-Ayon means "We Burmese."

by Thakin Nu (socialist), Thakin Than Tun, and Thakin Soe (communist), who took moderate positions. The last group, the DoBama, called themselves realists. This group, which included Aung San, Ne Win, and other college students (who were barely 30 and still wet behind the ears), advocated a violent overthrow of the British colonial government. Their motto was "now"; in their quest they would make a Faustian bargain with the devil if needed, to obtain arms from the Chinese and, if that failed, the Japanese imperialists. This violent group was aware of what terror Japanese fascism had wrought in China and Korea. They were aware of the cruelty of the Japanese at Mukden in 1931[2] and their using the incident as an excuse to seize Manchuria. The Marco Polo Bridge incident in 1937 was similar: When, during exercises,

> the Japanese discovered that one of their solders was missing, they demanded to join in the search, they then tried to force their way to Wanting. The Japanese infantry and armored divisions attacked the bridge, and that was the beginning of Japanese expansion. The Japanese advanced to China's interior, resulting in the Rape of Nanking. All this was known to the Thakins, but they argued that it did not matter whether the aid came from China or Japan or anyone who might care to help. Realistically, they could not start an armed struggle against the British and achieve Independence without sufficient aid of arms.[3]

To the DoBama, independence was the only thing that counted. And so Aung San gathered young men and held a blood-drinking ceremony, saying that morality did not matter, as long they received arms and money; and thus this group solicited arms and help from the Japanese Imperial Army. The Japanese helped them with money and training camps and surreptitiously armed them. This rag-tag

---

[2] Where the Japanese created an incident at the railway near the city of Mukden (carried out by the Japanese soldiers disguised as Chinese); it was the beginning of the conquest of Manchuria.

[3] See Ba Than, "The Roots of Revolution," *The Guardian* (Rangoon, 1962). A Japanese colonel named Suzuki came as a press correspondent for Domei Press; he established an office on Judah Ezekiel Street, Rangoon. Colonel Suzuki was actually a spymaster. He was of the regular Japanese Army Intelligence and headed the clandestine organization, the Minami Organ. Thakin Nu, to his credit, did not want to join the Fascist movement.

army[4] with a core of some 300 trained soldiers became the core of the rebel Burma Defense Army (BDA), which collaborated with the fascist Japanese Army. The numbers were swelled by thugs, robbers, and other subversive elements.

All this agitation brought about Burma's administrative separation from India in 1937 and started to change the country. The educated elite had better jobs, but it did little to improve the lot of the farmers and the less educated. Rangoon seemed like an alien city to the Burmese, full of foreigners who, for the most part, controlled the economy. In fact, the economy was controlled by the British and Indians and their capital. The tram service, for example, was funded by wealthy Sindhi families from what is now Pakistan. Much real estate was owned by outsiders. The best hotel, the Strand, was built by two Armenian brothers; it was the great watering hole for the colonial establishment, but it was Whites Only. There was no Burmese equivalent to the Tata or Birla families, who in India built steel companies.

The farmers in particular were chronically short of capital, as the Burmese Buddhists did not place value on earthly assets; their culture considered earthly assets to be ephemeral. Instead they spent money to earn merit for the benefit of their afterlife; for Buddhists, earning merit was all that mattered. So there were few Burmese lenders. The country's pre-war years stock of money was small, emblematic of a culture that placed more value on life after death than on the present economic reality. Even during the reign of the kings of Burma there had been no banks, and credit had been nonexistent. The rice farmer never saw the inside of a bank. It was the middle-men—Indians who borrowed from the British and foreign banks and lent to the Burmese farmers—who bore the brunt of the animosity. The ire of the Burmese was reserved for those *chettiars*, South Indian moneylenders. With new foreign capital supplied by the *chettiars*, the production of paddy increased. But the Burmese farmers could not pay back their loans, especially during the depression. Burmese rice farmers had this habit of, if they had a good year,

---

[4] Led by Kowdaw Hmaing, Thakin Ba Han, later Aung San. See Ba Than, "The Roots of Revolution."

spending all their income on their children's *Shinpyu*[5] and other ceremonies. They paid little attention to long-term financial planning. When they ended up with no money to buy seed the next year, they would mortgage their land to the moneylenders and ultimately would lose the land, then blame the foreign moneylender. Politicians took advantage of this misfortune to foment trouble.

The underlying racial tensions soon broke out into ethnic riots. There were reports of violence of an extreme nature in the back-country, sometimes even murder. There was section of Bamar people who were quick to anger, and, when so angered, they unleashed a reign of terror on their "enemies." In the back-country and in isolated places, they hacked people with broad-bladed *dah*s (knives), mutilated and then beheaded them while still walking. In villages where Indians were in the minority, they were subject to brutality and lived in fear. Riots ensued even in Rangoon. Streets were empty except for dacoits and robbers, who went around in gangs looking for the weak. These attacks by berserk drug-crazed thugs were lurid and rather gruesome. In the majority-Burmese suburb of Kemmendine, a group of Bamar set upon a lone Indian coolie as he was leaving his workplace and hacked him to death. For three days the streets were deserted. Indian homes were attacked, and Indians were assaulted and even murdered.

This increased tension between Indians and Burmese was a worry for us. Even at my young age I realized the danger. Father stayed home, we stayed home from school, and we "locked down" the house. Father arranged for some friendly Burmese to sit on the front patio, with closed gates, to shoo away the thugs and gangs. We stayed indoors, occasionally sneaking a peek out. It was a frightening time, exposing our vulnerability. The British authorities were slow to respond, but once they did, they moved quickly.[6] Taking harsh measures, the police brought relative peace until 1940. Yet this resentment and violence would simmer, and small riots between the Bamar and other ethnic groups continued to erupt. For example, Burmans were antagonistic toward caste Hindus, whom they did not accept.

---

[5] Coming of age ceremony.

[6] Saya San, who tattooed his entire body, promoted himself as impervious to bullets and able to defeat the British (it was an attitude of Burmese soothsayers who frequently engaged in this mad behavior). Soon the police arrested him and suppressed the rebellion.

This despite the fact that Brahman Hindu priests had been sought out to help explain scriptures during the First Burmese Dynasty (849–1297). Sometimes when they felt offended by high-caste Hindu Indians, Burmans went to the trouble to look for the "thread" that the Brahmans wore to signify their high birth. The Burmans took particular pleasure in attacking high-caste Brahmans, and for three years there was much blood shed.

Anglo-Indians constituted a special class of mixed-blood people who also attracted the ire of the Burmese.[7] Their origins: Before the Sepoy War of 1857–58, British men took Indian women as wives, especially in the north, where the genetic distance between European and ANI was small. How the progeny looked followed Mendel's rules of segregation: the R haplotype (F) 1 generation looked Eurasian, especially the women; the (F) 2 generation would look more Eurasian; finally, as this process continued, some progeny would have blue or green eyes and fair skin. If the women had (H) MtDNA rather than being of the (M) haplotype, the genetic distance was even smaller. This created all manner of problems. If children were very light skinned and were brought up in an English-speaking household, they could pass as British, but the British would not accept them as European so they created a whole new "caste" for them, calling them Eurasians, or a "bit of the tar brush." In Burma we called them "Anglo-Indian." The British set up special status for them and employed them as policemen, in the railways as locomotive drivers, and in motor transport. Such families could not live in British cantonments but lived in upper-middle-class areas. Their homes were British style, with many of the amenities of British homes—separate kitchen and servants' quarters, and run-

---

[7] People of India today are a mixture of two highly differentiated populations—"Ancestral North Indians" (ANI) and "Ancestral South Indians"—who were genetically different from each other. The ANI are more closely related to the peoples of the Ukrainian steppes than to other East Asians. Everyone in the subcontinent is a mix, albeit in different proportions. No group in India can claim genetic purity. See Reich, *Who we are and how we got here*, 135. My quest to find out who my ancestors were would lead me to genetic testing. I sent off my cheek swab to one of the testing companies. In India there is a great deal of hubris about origins, most of it mixed up with the religious caste system. My Y chromosome analysis showed the STR goes all the way back to Syria, the so-called the fertile crescent and the Levant. On my mother's side the MtDNA shows that her DNA is of the M haplotype, the most common of the female line on the subcontinent. The MtDNA of my half-brother and sisters, the H haplotype, is genetically closer to that of the Basques.

ning water. They sent their children to Jesuit or convent school and did not mix with the rest of the locals. Both in social standing and in the workplace, they did better than the Burmese. The Burmese called them "Kabya," half caste, a pejorative word (the Burmese had a pejorative term for everybody but themselves).

After the 1937 riots, tension lingered for a while, but superficially, life was relatively tranquil. School closed in late May and resumed in September. We had a relatively normal Christmas. But change was coming fast, not only in distant Europe but also closer to home in French Indo-China (now Vietnam). Father must have had grave concerns, but he was loyal to the company and held his thoughts to himself. All the riots and increasing talk of war must have weighed on him, however, because his plans to improve and expand the house continued to be held in abeyance.

# Chapter 5
# The Changing World, 1937–40

From 1937 to 1939, news from near and afar would impact Burma. The menfolk each evening would discuss what they had read in the English-language press and what they had heard on the English-language radio broadcasts. These discussions took place in our house. I listened avidly.

Late in the summer of 1937, Japan intensified the war in China. Its expeditionary force expanded the assault to the west, drawing the war closer to Burma. Now Japan was demanding that the British close the Burma Road (Rangoon to Lashio). On September 1, 1939, Germany invaded Poland. His Majesty's government (HMG) in England demanded that Germany cease the attack and that, unless it did so, "a state of war would exist." Germany did not cease the attack, so Britain and France declared war on Germany on September 3, 1939.

After Germany crushed Poland there was a quiet period, called the Phony War. In mid-1940, however, Germany's Wehrmacht made multiple invasions: of Denmark and Norway in April–June; Belgium, Luxemburg, and the Netherlands in May; and France in June.[1] The Germans not only violated declarations of neutrality by Belgium and the Netherlands but also had no compunction about causing massive civilian casualties. France was ill prepared for an invasion through Luxemburg so suffered heavy losses. The British sent an expeditionary force to assist the French, but they could not stop the juggernaut and withdrew to the coast at Dunkirk, barely and bravely evacuating before the Germans overran all of northern France. The peace treaty signed on June 22, 1940, between Germany and France, split France into two administrative areas: Germany occupied northern France and all of that country's western coastline; southern France remained unoccupied but cooperated with Germany as Vichy France, governed by Marshall Henri Petain.

---

[1] This line of attack was based on a modified "Schlieffen Plan," devised before World War II by Field Marshal Alfred von Schlieffen.

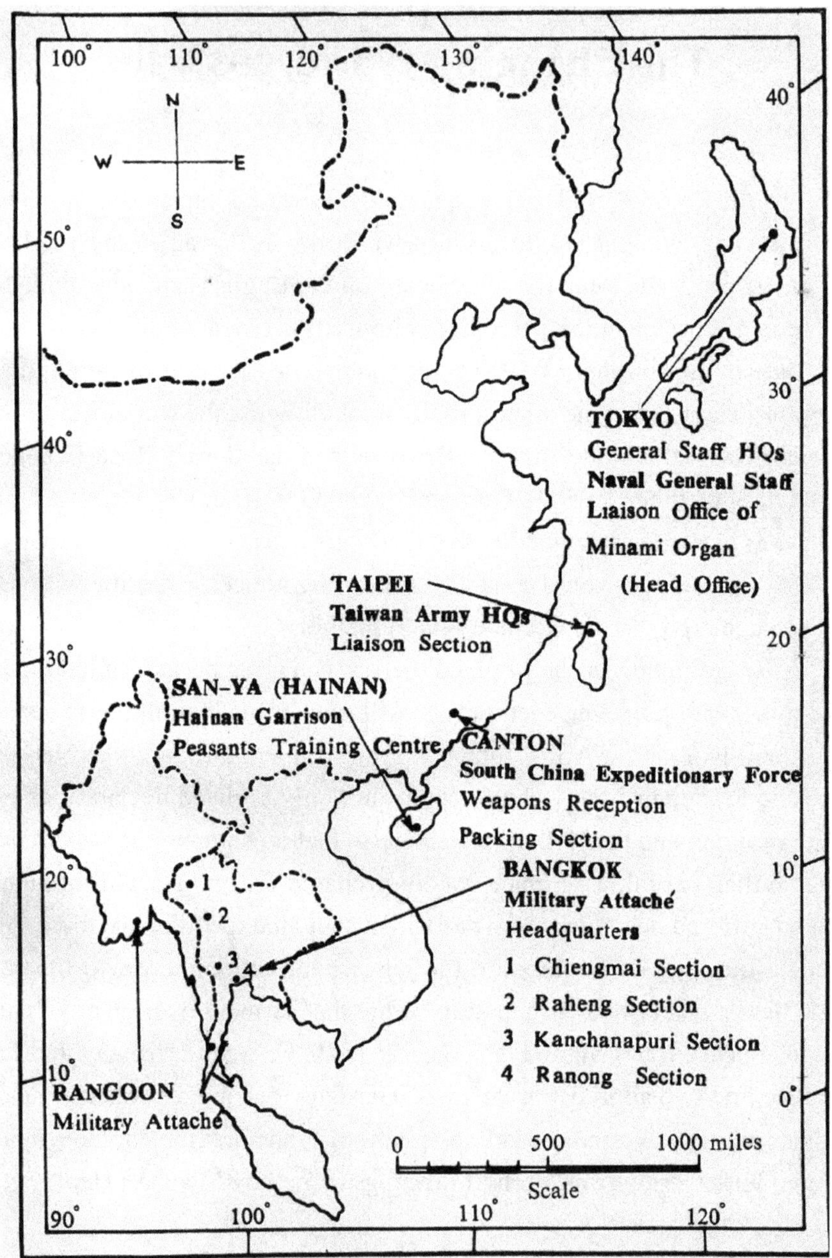


Figure 6. Map showing the development and related units of the Burmese Independence Army (Minami Organ) Feb.–Aug. 1941. From Izumiya Tatusuro, *The Minami Organ* (Tokyo: Tokuma Shoten, 1967), after p. 108.

The defeat of France and the installation of her Vichy government changed the situation for the worse for Burma and rest of Southeast Asia. Vichy retained control of French colonies in Indo-China. Because of his disagreements with Vichy, General Georges Catroux, Governor General of French Indo-China, was forced to transfer power to Vichy Admiral Jean Decoux in June 1940. Admiral Decoux was immediately pressured by the expansionist Japanese to allow movement of Japanese troops through the colony. He therefore allowed 3,500 Japanese troops into Haiphong (northern Indo-China). This allowed Japan to close all Chinese ports. In July, power changed in Japan: the Yonai cabinet was overthrown and a new, more aggressive war cabinet took over. Four days later, Japan signed the Tripartite Pact with Germany and Italy. On September 23, Japan demanded that it control Saigon and all of southern Indo-China, including the port in Camran Bay. Without permission, she moved another 130,000 troops into Saigon and asserted her right to control all airfields in Indo-China. Now that Japan controlled all of French Indo-China, she prepared for the invasion of Southeast Asia and the south Pacific. To that end, Japan created the Southern Army Command in Saigon and appointed Field Marshal Terauchi to command the invasion.[2]

The American president (Roosevelt) had warned the Japanese that any move by Japan into Southern Indo-China would invite American government sanctions. When the Japanese continued their moves, the president imposed sanctions on October 16: a ban on oil exports, scrap metal, all grades of iron, steel, and other material that was essential for war production.[3] The US also increased the amount

---

[2] Note passed on by teleprinter to O.K.W. and O.K.M. secret teleprinter. Tel. Ktr - 5 Jul 41. /60263. Telegram 10 July 1941 from German Ambassador to Japan, Eugen Ott: "All things point to immediate Japanese action against Indo-China. At least three divisions will be used to take the most important cities and positions, including Saigon. The day of invasion is said, according to a confidential announcement, to be 17 July."

[3] U.S. National Archives Doc. No. 4076 reads: "Failure of Japanese economic discussions with Netherlands Indies compels Japan to take the oil sources there by force, as her navy is otherwise incapable of action. In addition, Japanese occupation of Indo-China to obtain territory for deployment and as a springboard for winning Netherlands Indies is imminent. Occupation of Thailand not planned. Preparation and carrying out of operations through staff of South China front of General Ushiroku in Canton. Behavior of English force in Singapore is assumed to be purely defensive ... Entry of America into war against Japan and interruption of transport of Japanese troops and reinforcements by American sea forces expected." Duplicate to Tokyo Schol [*sic*]—Thomas.

of lend-lease supplies they sent to China through Burma. Japan demanded that the British close the Burma Road, (that linked Rangoon port with China), which did happen for a while, but it was soon opened again.[4]

Meanwhile, Britain was fighting for her life as the German Luftwaffe conducted air strikes in Britain. Germany's first goal was to destroy the Royal Air Force (RAF) so that a land invasion could follow. Fortunately, the RAF won the battle; the Luftwaffe suffered such losses that Hitler suspended his Operation Sea Lion in mid-September 1940.

We followed the air war over England closely. The local newspapers carried all this news with a delay of two days. The tea shops were filled with the ominous news. Reports of British losses dismayed us. As British subjects, we were keenly interested in the progress of the war in Europe, because Britain's fate would impact ours. But Japan's actions in the East also posed a threat to us as her forces moved ever westward toward us and as young Burmese Thakins hoped for the defeat of the British. The men of the family talked of the unfolding drama in hushed tones, assessing the impact it would have on Burma. For the family collectively, we felt safer in colonial Burma than in fascist Burma. Britain's survival was hope that we would not live under Japanese rule.

As the war clouds gathered, Father, Uncle Brown (related by marriage; he was Uncle James's brother-in-law), and Danam all seemed very anxious and talked of these developments. I was precocious and read avidly, even though I had difficulty with some words. Father read the English language newspapers daily. He appeared preoccupied and worried and became more distant. He discussed any fears he had only with the adult male members of the family. Mother understood English but did not speak it. We were a multilingual family; we spoke Burmese to our neighbors, Telugu at home, and English elsewhere. Urdu (with roots in Per-

---

[4] Tripartite Pact, Article 1: "Italy, Germany, and Japan henceforth conduct in common and jointly a war which has been imposed on them by the United States of America and England, by all means at their disposal and until the end of hostilities." After the signing of the Tripartite Pact (Japan/Germany/Italy) on September 27, 1940, Japan felt emboldened to pressure Britain to close the Burma Road.

sian) was the lingua franca of the British Indian Empire and the army, so we knew a smattering of that as well.

We were inspired to hear that the (colonial) British-Indian Army[5] was being mobilized and expanding. It was engaged in war against Italy, in Ethiopia, and in North Africa. Uncle Brown, who had some ties to members of the Indian Army, sat us children down to talk and warn us about what was coming. But in spite of all the bad news, it appeared distant to us kids; we were blissfully unaware of how profound would be the changes that war would bring.

Uncle Samuel (the doctor) was called back into the Royal Indian Air Force in India. I remember the farewell party we threw for him. My overall memory of my uncle was unpleasant, however; he terrified me. As a child, I suffered frequent bouts of constipation, and on one of his visits he gave me an enema. It was so traumatic that I did not make eye contact with him again.

In Burma, Japanese spies operated freely, with the help of their collaborators. Japanese could travel freely in Burma. Japan took advantage of this by recruiting young Burmese men for training in clandestine operations. The newspapers reported that saboteurs and agent provocateurs were operating in the countryside. After 1940 there was much gossip and nervousness. Japanese trading companies, such as the Yokohama spice trading company and others, were really nests of spies. British intelligence agencies were watching them, with little success; it was difficult, as the Japanese dressed as monks. One spy (confirmed later) wearing Burmese Buddhist garb was roaming the countryside, gathering information, taking photographs, and drawing maps. He focused on the Maymyo jungle (British) training school.

---

[5] The British-Indian Army was a separate organization from the British Army, with Indian soldiers and British officers. Indians joined in great numbers, which brought the strength to 2.5 million. They would be involved in operations from Iraq to Persia and the Dutch East Indies. The British-Indian Army would play a seminal role in liberating Burma from the Japanese.

# Chapter 6
# Respite

*There is much myth and misunderstanding about the "Burma Road." The road starts at Rangoon and heads to Pegu, thence to the rail junction at Thazi. Here the road forks: one branch goes toward Mandalay, and another goes to Lashio. This route to Lashio was the principal land route over which American lend-lease supplies were shipped to China. The Burma Road must not be confused with the so-called "Ledo Road," which connected Ledo in Assam, India to Kunming in China through Myitkyina in Burma. It was never very essential to the war: it was completed only on January 23, 1945; the first convoy to use it reached China on February 4, 1945; and the war ended just three months later, on May 7, 1945.*[1]

To ease the tension in summer of 1940, father decided to send us on a long train journey to the cool hill station of the northeast Shan State. He obtained two second-class coaches, first class being reserved for English (especially civil servants who sent their families to the cool hill stations of Maymyo and Kalaw). The coaches were comfortable, with fans, green leather seats, and bunk beds, which made the ride exiting. Our destination was Lashio, a border town with the main road connection to China. We started at the first platform of Rangoon's central railway station, where the English mingled with the locals. I walked to the front of the train. It was exhilarating to see the gleaming green and gold engine; it was called Y C class and had been made in Scotland. The engine driver tooted several times, and I returned to our coach. I hung out of the window to see the conductor wave his green flag. The wheels of the great engine chugged and turned freely at first, and then they caught the rails and the train started to move. The city rapidly disappeared as the train picked up speed. As darkness set in, in the lengthening shadows I imaged all manner of fantasies until the movement of the

[1] Many American writers erroneously conflate the two roads. The Burma Road was built during the Second Sino-Japanese War in 1937 by Burmese and Chinese laborers. The Americans began construction of the Ledo Road in December 1942 using US engineers and native labor.

train lulled me to sleep. The next morning, we arrived at the rail junction of Thazi for a change of trains (we kept our coaches). Our coaches were attached to a goods train that was on its way to Lashio. We branched off to the northeast, and by midday the terrain changed: the train started to climb, and the landscape ahead became hilly, even mountainous. I found the scenery quite beautiful. Then we came upon the most talked-about bridge in Southeast Asia, the Gotek Bridge. Constructed by an American company from Pennsylvania, it was built over a deep gorge, making it a star in its own right. As the train slowed, people hung out of their windows to view the magnificent sight. Stories abounded that there were tigers and other predators lurking in the valley below. Finally we reached Lashio, where the railroad terminated, a few miles from the Yunnan China border. We arrived late at night and were warned to stay in the coach, even at the rail station. Tigers and other wild animals came a-calling, right up to the platform, at night, the conductor warned. The dim lights of the station cast eerie shadows. I looked out and imagined I saw a tiger. It was more my imagination than real, although at night we could hear the roar of the big cats.

The sun rose the next morning in a cloud-free sky. Vendors quickly arrived on the platforms, selling everything from to coffee and tea (Burmese and Chinese) to bread and cake and from various kinds of savories—payajaw (a fried lentil savory), samosa—to Burmese tea-leaf salad. After morning ablutions, I went down the platform, which was populated mostly by Chinese and Shans. The climate was not hot but cool and pleasant, without the humidity of Rangoon. The jungle came right up to the rail tracks, and there were warning signs not to stray into the jungle. We, the young ones, took a short walk into town. It was different from anything we knew in the south. The main road, such as it was, was full of olive-green tarp-covered trucks—American-built Dodge and Chevy trucks. The local people said they were headed to China, with American lend-lease supplies for China. The Americans wanted to keep the Chinese in the war between Japan and China. *It is along this very road that the Japanese Army would advance from the south to Bhamo and, ultimately, to Myitkyina.*

We lived in the coaches for close to a week and walked about the city every day. We enjoyed the cool weather and the freedom from political tension.

The vacation ended all too soon. But before long, the Christmas season would be upon us and would provide another period of respite.

CHRISTMAS 1940

After Operation Sea Lion had been called off in September 1940, Father seemed somewhat relieved. Just before Christmas he went to town and came back late in the evening bearing gifts. Christmas traditionally was a time of gift-giving, not only to the children (boys) but also to his associates and supervisors (whether that included any Englishman we were not privy to). Each year Father would bring home ducks—big colorful ducks that we called "Manila duck," with a red comb, purple feathers, and a slow and lumbering walk that made them easy to catch. Manila duck was known as a delicacy. Too soon, however, Father gathered them all up and took them away, presumably to his superiors, friends, and coworkers. We rarely ate the ducks; they were too expensive for us.

I can still remember Christmas Eve of 1940. The girls had put up a Christmas tree, a shrub rather than pine, as Christmas trees were uncommon in Rangoon, and set about decorating the house with twisted colored paper. Before the family could enjoy the ambiance, however, Kamala lit a candle for effect and in her exuberance, unfortunately, had lit the tree with naked candles. The flickering candles touched off a fire, and the dried shrub quickly was engulfed in flames. Tears streamed down Kamala's face, and Grandmother muttered something, saying it was a bad omen. In superstitious Burma, this was not to be taken lightly.

On Christmas Day the family cooked a rice dish called biryani, a rich Persian rice dish with a variety of spices, cashews, almonds, raisins, and foil of silver which is baked in. It was very tasty, mostly reserved for special occasions. We invited friends and neighbors, with special attention to their various food idiosyncrasies: no beef for Hindus, no pork for our Muslim friends. Gift-giving was not much in vogue; instead there was much church-going and praying. Christmas was a time of reverence. We sang Christmas carols: "Silent Night, Holy Night" was always the favorite, along with other religious hymns such as "Blessed Assurance" and "Nearer My God to Thee." With Anglo-Indians and Karens we sang ballads, old country and western (Cowboy) tunes; we did not know the lyrics but created our own words and winged it.

In spite of the influence of the American Southern Baptists we did not observe the commercial practice of gift-giving, and I did not know much about Santa. But toys for the sons was acceptable, and opening gifts was exciting. I remember with huge excitement when Father that year pulled out a large box and gave it to me. It did not take long for me to rip the box open and discover a red fire engine inside. There were no batteries; it was spring loaded. So it took only a moment or two to find the key and wind the spring, and soon the red fire engine took off. It started to run with flashing lights and a siren and soon began running into the furniture. I stayed awake playing with it till midnight. My mother finally took it away and put me to sleep. But I got up early the next day to play with the engine again.

# Chapter 7
# Preparations for War in Burma

Britain's pre-World War II policies for the colonies were a mess. There was administrative confusion and lack of foresight, miscalculations, and an underestimation of Japan's military powers. This would lead to failed policies and mistakes that would result in disaster and tremendous loss of life. There was much confusion over plans to defend Burma and other British colonies.

Burma was administratively separated from India in 1937. The new power structure in Burma and the lack of experienced politicians caught the country wholly unprepared for rapid and uncertain changes. The British Governor, Sir Archibald Douglas Cochrane,[1] had no colonial experience and had not risen through the ranks of the Indian Civil Service. He was a political appointee. After the separation, he had little time to come up with a plan or policy to meet Burma's needs, and war preparations in Rangoon were moving in fits and starts. Unfamiliar with Burma, Cochrane appointed an executive committee comprised of Burmese to advise him, but he retained control of currency, defense, and foreign policy. His appointees were politicians and included communists, fascists, and a few civil servants who ultimately were outnumbered and ignored by the others. The new executive committee was charged with passing laws and appointing judges. This made all non-Burman residents of the country nervous, as there was hostility toward them. While the new bureaucrats were learning their trade, plans for the defense of Burma languished.

Governor Cochrane was aware of the inadequacy of Burma's defense. Rangoon had two half-strength battalions—the Yorkshires and the Gloucestershires—and a few half-strength Burma Rifles.[2] The British battalions were on garrison duty: one at the jungle training school at Maymyo in northern Burma; the

---

[1] Sir Archibald Douglas Cochrane was Governor of British Burma from 8 May 1936 to 6 May 1941, when he was succeeded by Sir Reginald Dorman-Smith.

[2] The first battalion of Burma Rifles was founded in 1917 as a regiment of the British-Indian Army.

other at the Rangoon airport north of the city. These forces would be inadequate if an attack came, and there were rumors that the Far East Command would ask the British-Indian Army to send a division. Of course the British-Indian Army did not have divisions to spare. It was spread thin, from the Middle East to Hong Kong. Moreover, there were no roads connecting India and Burma, so no way to move troops quickly. The colonial authorities from Lord Curzon in the late nineteenth century through succeeding Governors had dragged their feet on building a road from India to Burma.[3]

Worse, there was no certainty about who was responsible for the defense of Burma. Without a Burma Army to defend the country and now separated administratively from India, the British War Office transferred the defense of Burma to Singapore Command. This shift would prove disastrous. Singapore was struggling with its own defense, and the authorities there had little understanding of Burma. The Command was in the hands of an old, retired Air Chief Marshal, the doddering Sir Henry Robert Moore Brooke-Popham. Other old, sick generals, near retirement, held high positions in the Command. Moreover, this Singapore Command prioritized the defense of Malaya and Singapore over Burma. The 11th Indian Corps was defending northern Malaya, and Australian and British units were in the south along with ill-trained Malay territorial units.

By 1940, the army staff in Burma began to realize the true state of affairs, and they made plans to increase military preparedness. The Governor announced a plan to expand the army, counting on the Australian Prime Minister to divert one division to Burma. Too little too late, the British also expanded the number of Burma Rifle battalions to twelve and made plans to create motorized and mechanized units. To attract recruits, it offered a pay increase to 25 Rupees. But the qualifications (certain physical attributes and literacy) reduced the number of potential recruits. The Governor's plan gave preference to ethnic minorities, who received the news well. Karens and Kachins readily joined the ranks of the Burma Rifles, but the Bamar, who were the majority, refused to enlist. The Bamar did not like

[3] Lord Curzon was Viceroy of India from 1899 to 1905. On August 12, 2018, the India–Myanmar Friendship Highway was completed from the border with India to Mandalay.

the British, and the British did not trust the Bamar; they felt that the Bamar had no interest in the rigors and discipline of army life. With the exception of the Fourth Burma Rifles (comprised of local Gurkhas), the other units were comprised mostly of ethnic minorities, who made worthy soldiers but were ill trained and ill equipped. The Bamar people in general were ambivalent, pro-Japanese, or neutral. In contrast, the Karens, Kachin, Chins, and Shans remained anti-Japanese and pro-British or wanted a peaceful transfer of power with protection for the "hill" people such as themselves. They did not trust the Bamar.[4]

The Bamar were more likely to join the "Forward Block" (a coalition of political parties such as the DoBama Asiyone, Thakins, and others, which was to fight the British). The Governor was not aware that members of the "Forward Block" were slipping away to Japan to receive military training and then return to join the revolution. They also were providing intelligence to the Japanese, whose intelligence had thoroughly infiltrated Burma's government, recruiting spies and saboteurs, mostly from the Thakin ranks.

The "Thirty Comrades"—the young Burmese radicals, communists (Marxists and Trotskyites)—were getting ready to launch the revolution. They were young men less than thirty years old. They had no administrative skills or experience yet wanted to take over the reins of power immediately and rule. They had little understanding of economic systems and had no economic plan; they embraced communism and fascism, not knowing one from the other. To carry out their plan, they surreptitiously escaped Rangoon on the steamer *Hai Lee Drammen* to Japanese-held Formosa. There they received some military training, established connections, and with the help of Japanese intelligence units began to liaise with the Japanese leaders. They traveled to Tokyo to meet with Japanese leaders, formulated plans, and then stayed over to undergo advanced training from the Japanese Army in Formosa.[5] They were promised that they would then be attached to

---

[4] This would result in continuous warfare to this day.

[5] In 1937 the Japanese established the "Rear Staff Training School" (later known as the Nakano School), headed by Fukumoto, Iwakumo, and Akikusa. This school later became the locus for training saboteurs and assassins and is where Aung San and Ne Win got their first training. See Ken Kotani, *Japanese Intelligence in World War II* (Oxford, UK: Osprey Publishing, 2009), 30.

Japanese units and fight for Burmese Independence. These young rebels were easily deluded by the promises that the Japanese made.

To make matters worse, many British did not think much of the Japanese fighting ability. The theory was that their soldiers were poor material—myopic, poorly trained—and that the Japanese soldiers collectively could not hit the side of the barn, they were no equal to the British soldiers. This delusional thinking pervaded all levels of government. A high-ranking official, Mr. Duff-Cooper, came to Burma as the representative of the British P.M. to assess the situation. After his studies he told a military audience in Maymyo (a hill station and summer refuge for the British government and civil service) that they would not see active service. He was focused on the defense of Singapore and had few resources to spare for Burma. His assessment would be proven wrong.

Figure 7. The ship *Hai Lee Drammen*, upon which the Thirty Comrades surreptitiously left Rangoon for training by the Japanese Army on Formosa (Taiwan). Photo from old Burmese publication.

Figure 8. Aung San in Japanese uniform, 1942. Unknown author, Public Domain, via Wikimedia Commons.

Figure 9. Ne Win in Japanese uniform. Photo from old Burmese publication.

Figure 10. Aung San in Japanese uniform, 1943. Unknown author, Public Domain, via Wikimedia Commons.

Father and the elders watched silently and with increasing concern. India passed the Defense of India Act in 1939, which rapidly expanded its army.[6] It was being spread thin, from Iraq, Ethiopia, to almost all of Southeast Asia and beyond to Hong Kong and China. I wished I was older so that I could join the army. I was too young, but family friends talked about joining the Army and many did so. With stretched resources, the defense of Burma was neglected. Only at the 11th hour would London shift responsibility for the defense of Burma back to India Command. The duplicitous Bamar supported the Japanese fascists and the communists. After all the Chinese seaports were occupied by Japan, the Burma Road was the only route left to ferry American lend-lease supplies from the port of Rangoon to China. The Burma Road became a target.

## JAPAN DRAWS CLOSER

By summer of 1941, Britain was fighting for its life. I was fascinated by the war at sea, especially the sinking of the British battle cruiser *HMS Hood* and the German battleship *Bismarck* in May 1941.[7] I heard the news when the family went to the Minerva Cinema, where British Movietone news reported the events. The English press reported the progress of the war in Europe in the morning and evening papers. Britain had few resources to spare, so her colonies in the East had to stave off the Japanese with what meager resources they had. The defense of the colonies was a muddle, due to the frequent changes in command structure and frequent changes in responsibility, chief among them the change of responsibility for the defense of Burma from India to the Far East Command in Singapore.

---

[6] India and Burma (Emergency Provisions) Bill, HC Deb 26 June 1940: "The Government of India have come to the conclusion that, for the purposes of the urgent expansion of India's war effort, it has now become necessary, and, indeed, urgent, ... to introduce compulsory service for military, and in certain cases for civil industrial, purposes. To do so in regard to Indian British subjects is within the competence and authority of the Government of India...." There were 2.5 million Indians in the British-Indian Army.

[7] The sinking of the *HMS Hood* on May 24, 1941, was a sad blow. The subsequent sinking of the *Bismarck* on May 27, 1941, gave us hope. The local papers reported the blow-by-blow account of the chase, its final location off Brest in France, and the final demise. It was exiting to read about it and to see the movie many years later.

Singapore, an island at the southern end of the Malay peninsula, had been ceded to Stamford Raffles by the Sultan of Johore in 1824. It was mostly swampland. It was small in size—27 miles at its widest and 11 miles at its narrowest—and was sparsely populated in the nineteenth century. As trade increased, the British realized its strategic importance. Malaya was rich in resources that were important to Great Britain (e.g., tin, tungsten, rubber) and was a large earner of US currency from its rubber industry. Trade with China grew, and the city of Singapore at the southern tip of the peninsula grew along with it. After the Russo-Japanese War of 1904, Japan's ambitions grew and were alarming to the Western powers. Because Singapore had few defenses, in 1919 the Royal Navy's Admiral John Jellicoe (of the Battle of Jutland fame) recommended construction of a naval base at Singapore to protect British interests. By the 1920s trade was booming, the value of land had increased, warehouses were built for storing and receiving merchandise, and the city attracted traders and workers from coastal India, Arabia, and China. Only in 1934, however, did the British start to build the naval base that Admiral Jellicoe had recommended fifteen years earlier. With huge 15-inch guns pointing to sea, it would deter any invader. Fully developed by 1939, the naval base housed eight battleships (dreadnaughts). No foreign power would challenge this mighty defense; Japan could not threaten Southeast Asia without defeating the Royal Navy first. But this British plan had a fatal flaw, in that the defense was based on the expectation that any attack would come from the sea. The population and commercial center of the city was on the south end of the island, near the Kappel Harbor. It was a good deep-water port. The jungle in Malaya to the north was impenetrable, so the big naval guns pointed to the sea. A couple of papers[8] were published about the weakness of this plan, but they were ignored and not taken seriously.

The Japanese concluded that they would avoid a futile frontal attack from the sea and instead hatched a plan that would use the back door (from the north) and the jungle, and they trained for it. When the Axis powers—Japan, Germany, and Italy—signed the Tripartite Pact in 1940, "Germany and Italy had conveyed

[8] The future Lord Ismay, then based in Quetta in present-day Pakistan, authored one of them.

to Japan that Germany and Italy had no interest in fomenting war in Arabia and India."[9] In many conferences, Hitler had proclaimed that he had no intention of invading Arabia or India. His position on their ancient civilizations was that they would fight for their own independence. This point should not be forgotten, that neither Gandhi nor Nehru expressed any interest in violent overthrow of colonial rule. Aung San and his thirty comrades, in contrast, were committed to violent overthrow of British rule. To this end they would accept aid from the devil himself.

By now the Japanese occupied all of French Indo-China and had closed all Chinese ports. They planned to use Saigon as a base for military operations in Southeast Asia and the southwest Pacific. Japanese Field Marshall Terauchi built—in great secrecy—military and naval bases for Japan's invasion and conquest of Singapore. Saigon had many advantages: it was a warm-weather port with a vast hinterland, and it would serve well as the port from which both the army and the navy could launch war.

The *Rangoon Gazette* reported that an existing railroad from Indo-China was to be expanded. It hinted that Burma was not high on the agenda for the Japanese, though, which was, of course, a ruse. Field Marshall Terauchi's Southeast Asia Command in Saigon laid plans to attack Southeast Asia, Burma, and American possessions in the South Pacific.

By midsummer, Rangoon was being prepared for war. Mr. De Graaf Hunter, a British civil-defense expert, visited Rangoon to advise local officials and devise a plan to build a civil defense for Rangoon. One day when I was downtown with family, I saw that the windows of Grindlay's Bank were bricked over and layers of sandbags were stacked higher than a man. I remember asking where all the sand came from. In preparation for air-raids, all major downtown buildings took such protective action. Shelters were difficult to build, as the water table was high, but some were built. There was increased police presence, and armed guards stood watch behind the sandbags at the important buildings. Military vehicles were seen more frequently. Going to the city became fraught for us, as there were many checkpoints.

---

[9] Louis Allen, *Singapore 1941–1942* (London: Frank Cass, 1993), 30.

At first these preparations, including air-raid shelters, were conducted only in the downtown area, leaving the countryside under-protected. But soon, air-raid wardens (ARP)—retired policemen and mostly older Anglo-Indian or Burmese volunteers—visited the neighborhoods beyond downtown. They assessed our home and instructed us to prepare for future events. Dressed in khaki and pith helmets and holding flashlights, they walked around the house with a critical eye. They talked to Uncle Brown and instructed us to remove the regular lampshades and replace them with long green cones, to minimize the risk of providing beacons of light to the enemy. They advised us to dig trenches (shelters) and follow the warnings such as air-raid sirens. The very next weekend, Father supervised all the work and took all the recommended precautions. That night when we turned on the lights, it was surprising how dark the house was.

# Chapter 8
# War Preparations Strike Home

My Uncle Rao had a large family medicine practice in Lamadaw (the Chinese quarter of Rangoon), about three miles from the city center. He worked five days a week at the office, which was attached to the biggest pharmacy on Mogul Street, and on weekends he made house calls to see patients who were too ill to travel to his office. He often took me on his weekend rounds. I looked forward to this weekly ritual and would carry his medical bag. Uncle Rao had purchased a new two-toned blue and grey Wolseley, built by the Wolseley Car Company. It was a unique car. Uncle's car was new; it smelled of fresh leather. In its heyday, it was a luxurious little car, something that few in Burma could afford.

Figure 11. Two-tone Wolseley. Photo from classic car magazine.

On this particular day in 1941 we were driving towards the governor's mansion, the most heavily guarded place in the city. As we neared Ahlone Road, I saw a big crowd ahead, and presently we approached a sprawling peepul tree, in whose shade there swarmed a large crowd of civilians and police. The people and police clustered around tables that had piles of papers on them. As we got closer, we slowed and then were flagged down by a burly Anglo-Indian policeman. He demanded our papers, rather rudely, and took them away to a table. The papers passed through a number of hands, then the policeman came back and ordered us, "Get out of the car." We were both scared. He announced, "Your car is being commandeered by the order of the governor. We need the car for the war effort." Shocked, Uncle tried to protest, but he was brushed aside. It was an egregious and arrogant action. The policeman's assertion that "you can reclaim your car after the war" was a joke, of course. Uncle was so stunned that he could not speak. The police then shooed us away. Taking Uncle's medical bag and some papers, we started to walk home. I asked Uncle, "Why did they do that to us?" Uncle angrily said, "Because we are Indian. We do not matter. The British always took from us, the weaker people." "What will they do with our car?" I asked. He said, "Some white, or Anglo-Indian officer will use it." I asked Uncle if war was near. He just nodded his head, so angry that he had a hard time talking. We walked to the train station in silence.

Occurrences such as this and all this attendant tension worried Mother and the women of the family, but to talk to Father was next to impossible; he was distant. It is likely that he did not want to frighten us. For many Asian men, display of emotion to women was not accepted. The men talked among themselves as they gathered in the evening. They went over the day's events but never discussed any issues with us children, so we had to be satisfied with snippets of information. We had to keep quiet and listen, be seen but not heard.

On most long summer evenings, Uncle Brown came over. Uncle Brown was the intermediary between us children and our distant father. He was Uncle James's brother-in-law, about 50 years old, disabled with a foot injury (I never quite knew what he did; did he go to World War I?). He was a handsome, brown-skinned man with a wide handle-bar moustache, which added to his character and mystery. He had a full head of hair with streaks of grey and kind pale-green eyes (a recessive gene seen in parts of India); he was a mild-mannered and approachable man and also had a sense humor. Like many Indians who joined the (colonial) Indian Army, he must have had some experience. He knew a lot about war. Did he fight? Did he sustain the injury in the war? He would not say. The foot would not heal; it festered for a long time, then bone infection set in (in medical school I would learn that this was Osteomyelitis). He lost his job and lived with the James family, helping with housework. He was a good storyteller.

The cousins and the younger set would gather around Uncle Brown, sitting on the floor at his feet. The subject always turned to the coming war. He would talk to us about the possibility of war and how we should prepare for it. All around us preparations were afoot. I asked him about the green cone-shaped lightshades, why we had to dim the lights. "During air raids, enemy aircraft are attracted by bright lights that help with navigation. By dimming lights, the enemy planes will have a hard time locating their targets. If the lights are on, you could get hit," he explained, then warned: "If a siren goes off, go to the trenches. Do not go out of the house at night, especially to look at the planes, but instead go to the shelter." He must have felt that it was important to instruct us about war.

He finally talked about the first world war, telling of how the Indian Army fought in the Middle East and Mesopotamia. Knowing little, I asked him what war meant. "In the past," he said, "armies would gather in a strategic valley or city (he was talking of the Napoleonic wars), the two armies would clash and fight it out, big guns would boom and shake the ground, small-arms fire was common as was the clash of long knives; all this was accompanied by the thunder of horses, and some horses would die." This caused consternation amongst us. Innocently I asked, "so we can watch the battle from afar and not be hurt?" He laughed heartily. "Unfortunately," he said, "the way wars are fought now is changing. In far-off Europe the Germans bomb cities, hitting civilian homes and killing many people." He talked specifically of Poland, where public buildings and many homes had been destroyed and where many civilians had died. He equivocated: "We don't know how it will happen here, however." We all fell silent. I was sure I would dream about it.

Given Uncle Brown's knowledge and eagerness to talk, however, I picked his brain, asking more about war.

Me: "Will they drops the bombs on us?"

Brown: "Not directly, but sometimes bombs go astray. If we get in their way, we could get bombed, and if bombs go astray, we could be hit."

Me: "Why go to war?"

Brown: "Like people, countries get into fights; when they cannot settle their differences peacefully, countries go to war."

Me: "Did we do anything wrong?"

He shook his head.

Me: "Don't they go far away to fight?"

Brown: "Some people live far from cities, but civilians are also part of the city."

Me: "But won't they just shoot at one another and leave us alone?"

Brown: "Yes, but you may be caught in cross fire."

Me: "Here in the city, are we at greater risk for bombing or being caught in cross fire? Will we get killed?"

There was silence. The girls cringed and some cried. They clung together.

"But we could go away to the jungle!" one of them cried. "I want to run away to the forest and hide in a fig tree."

Me: "Can we leave the place of fighting?"

Brown: "It is not easy. Because he works for the government, your father cannot leave without the governor's permission."

Me: "The war in Europe is far away, yes?"

Brown: "We do not have to worry about that so much; we have to be afraid of the Japanese. They are waging a war now in China, and they could attack Burma."

Me: "Why?"

Brown: "The Japanese want to expand their empire. Japan needs the land, its oil and its resources. And the Burmese extremists want war." He paused and continued: "We as Indians have an additional concern, about the young hot-headed Burmans who have no compunction about committing violence or getting involved with fascists."

He had said enough. We kids went our ways, more than a little scared about the Japanese Imperial Army.

## THE WAR IN CHINA INTENSIFIES

Japan had established her "interest" in other East Asian countries as early as 1910 when, in the wake of the Russo-Japanese War, she annexed Korea and went on to mercilessly exploit that country. In 1931, in a brutal war, Japan had seized Manchuria, a province that historically had belonged to China. They provoked the war by means of the Mukden Incident on September 18, in which the Japanese set off a bomb blast that destroyed the railway but blamed the blast on the Chinese. In 1937 they mounted a full invasion of China, provoked by the Marco Polo Bridge Incident. In this fabricated incident, the Japanese ostensibly went searching for a missing soldier and accused China of killing him. The Chinese and Japanese forces met at the Marco Polo Bridge. The Chinese were defeated. This gave the Japanese the excuse to expand their war into central China. In Nanking between December 1937 and January 1938, the Japanese staged a brutal campaign, killing infants, raping women and young girls, and beheading or shooting scores men in the back of the head. Estimates of the raped reached 800,000 and of the dead 300,000. Having occupied all of French Indo-China and now most of China, the Japanese had cut off China from the rest of the world.

These developments in China brought war closer to us. Burma was indirectly involved because the US asked the British colonial authorities to allow them to land military supplies in Rangoon and then ship them to Yunnan and China via the Burma Road. This brought a sharp (second) response from the Imperial Japanese government and a warning to colonial authorities to close the road or suffer the consequences.

Stories quickly spread through the neighborhood about Japanese atrocities, of beheadings by Samurai swordsmen, bayoneting men and children, and punishment by death for the lightest offence. Rumors circulated that under Japanese occupation, stealing was a codified policy: the Japanese would invade towns and stage mass killings, loot houses of all valuables and then burn the houses down to the ground—for days on end. Then Japanese planes would bomb the city again and again. The minority Chinese community in Rangoon reacted with fear to the news emanating from China and these rumors. They hated the Japanese. Chinatown was soon deserted, and most shops closed. Rangoon's tea shops were empty.

Then came the big news: in June of 1941, Germany invaded Russia! The invasion was called Operation Barbarossa, and the newspapers were once again full of war news. The news from the Russian front was followed closely and was uniformly grim and negative. Communists all over the country (Red and White), including Aung San, were depressed about the terrible losses that the Russians suffered. News from Eastern Europe was also troubling. We heard of strange place-names like the Pripyat marshes or the Carpathian Mountains where thousands were being killed and taken prisoner. It was rumored that the Germans would be in Moscow by winter. This added to the anxiety of the Burmese communists, but the fascists rejoiced.

The *Rangoon Times* (English language newspaper) provided coverage of the war with photos and reports of atrocities; they looked frightening. Father's concerns grew. He started to buy provisions, stocking up for the long term: 60-lb. bags of rice, cooking oil, cans of kerosene, pulses, and salt. A little nook behind the bags of rice became my hiding place. The adults must have worried about the future and weighed their options. Will the Japanese invade Burma? If they did, what will happen to the family? Uncle Brown and Danam tried to assure us that war was "still far away." We children may not have understood all the talk of war or the details of various war operations, but we were fearful nevertheless.

# Chapter 9
# My First Brush with Death

My family's manservant, Lingam, was close to me, and sometimes, late in the evening, I tagged along with him when he went visiting his friends in the neighborhood. It was one of those evenings: I had gone with Lingam on his outing to visit his friend who worked as the manservant at the nearby home of a well-to-do Anglo-Indian family. The house was big: a two-storied home, built on stilts. The family lived upstairs, away from the people on the streets. The kitchen was on the ground floor, and the servants' quarters were in the back of the house, as was usual.

We walked under the house to the servants' quarters. Lingam called for his friend, and while he waited, I took a few steps away from him. Suddenly I felt something crawl over my left foot, then I felt a sharp prick. I instantly knew it was a snake. It started to crawl away. I tugged at Lingam's dhoti and told him that I may have been bitten. He was quick; living here meant we had to be aware. He instantly took a stick and beat the snake till it was paralyzed and dead. He then touched my foot and felt some fluid; it was blood, coming out of two tiny holes. Obviously, the fangs of the viper had broken the skin. In a few minutes I felt intense burning and cried in pain. Lingam picked up the dead snake in his hand for identification, threw me over his shoulder, and ran all the way home. He laid me down on the bedroom floor and immediately called for my grandmother, to tell her the details. All the hospitals were in the center of the city, miles away, and they were busy handling the military. We did not have a car, which meant getting a taxi at this late hour.

Grandmother took charge. She summoned the Hindu preacher and herbal doctor, and she commanded Lingam to go get the snake charmer. "They know more about snakes than a doctor," Grandmother said.[1] She placed me on the mat

[1] Grandmother may have been a Christian, but she clung to many beliefs from many traditions. Her belief system was syncretic. She read the Bible and quoted from it, but I also heard her pray during the monsoon to Argun, the Hindu god of thunder. When my sister Kamala was pregnant with her

and, while mother and my sisters gathered around, started the massage. The snake charmer arrived in due course, and he then took over. He kept massaging and wiping the blood away. In spite of their ministrations, the foot started to hurt and then swell. I remember the tingling and pain, intense burning, and then swelling. I overheard my sisters whispering that the swelling had gone up to the knee. The Hindu priest sat down next to Grandmother and rubbed salve onto the open bite. He then went into a trance and continued his mantras. Candles were brought, then prayers were said. I was only half awake and went in and out of sleep, so I do not know how long this went on. After some hours the swelling did go up to the knee, and the pain continued. I eventually fell into a semi-coma. The family that was gathered around also fell asleep except for Grandmother, who stayed up with me through the night. Apparently, I frequently asked for water during the night. The next morning, Grandmother propped me up against the wall and again continued to care for me. Mother was distraught, cried, rubbed coconut oil on my hair, and reassured me I was going to be OK.

Father looked at the dead snake: it was about four feet long and had distinctive pits. It was the Pit Viper, no doubt one of the deadliest poisonous snakes in Burma (beneath those pits is an organ that is highly sensitive to temperature. It can sense warmth, by which it can search for prey). The venom is a mixture of toxins. It is an aggressive snake and attacks unprovoked. I got a first good look at my foot in the morning as well. Symptomatically, morning is the worst time. The pain persisted. Although I was only half awake, I saw the bite marks, and my leg looked elephantine; the forefoot was a mess. The ulcer looked ugly. I could see the skin peel back to expose the muscles, which looked like they were smashed. A bandage (with lots of Iodine) was applied. In about a week I was able to walk again, albeit with a limp. The leg would hurt when bearing weight. Years later I asked Mother her feelings, and she said, "I thought you would be dead by morning." Uncle Rao said: "Its venom is a deadly hemo-toxin, a mixture of nerve and blood toxins. People die from such bites, or lose limbs."

---

first child, Grandmother removed all knives, scissors, and metal needles, even knitting needles, from the house because ancient Hindu belief held that a pregnant woman cooking and cutting would cause deformity to her unborn child.

By the next evening I was awake but was still quite sick. Grandmother said that it was a good sign that I felt better, but it took about ten days for the swelling to subside. The dead skin around the fang wounds was debrided but still looked raw and ugly, like dead meat; for some time, I could see the white tendons move. The two bite marks would leave permanent scars that persist to this day. It would bother me all my life, especially at the end of a long and stressful day. My left leg would always be weak and would go numb when subjected to stress. Even to this day I remember that dreadful night, and the de-pigmented skin around the bite marks will always be a reminder.

Years later, in my fourth year of medical school, I learned why I survived. It had more to do with luck than the ministrations of the priest or my grandmother's native medical skills. In my course in Public Health I learned that many snakes spend a lot of their venom in killing their prey. I could speculate that the snake that bit me had eaten its prey and was resting for the night, so that when it struck me, its venom was depleted. The leg would never have recovered if the venom sacks had been full.

After this painful experience, I learned to defend myself and the family from snakes and learned a few more facts about them. When a snake is busy swallowing a frog, for instance, the frog emits a high-pitched bleat. So, looking for the snake is easy. When it is eating is the best time to kill a snake; it is immobile and vulnerable so presents an easy target. One blow to the head with a small bamboo pole would be enough to disgorge its prey; then I would impale the head with a sharp stick to finish the kill. Snakes would come out of their underground burrows after the heavy rains, when the gutters get filled with rain water. The prevalence of snakes increased when the rat population increased, which happened when municipal control declined as the war came closer. Occasionally, looking carefully and in good light, one could see their beady eyes hiding in the rat holes. The unkept Mughal garden opposite our home was ideal nesting ground for snakes. It also was home to a large nest of "Russell Spitting Vipers," one of the most aggressive snakes. It charges and spits its venom at prey. The venom can be deadly when it comes in contact with open wounds. Some other dangerous and also colorful snakes include the Banded Krait, with yellow and gleaming black bands. One of several members of the Krait family, it is one of the most dangerous snakes. It is aggressive and attacks unprovoked. Burmese Buddhists called it a "Pongyi snake" because its yellow and black bands resembled the color of monks' robes. Some considered it holy, therefore, and took offense at killing the snake.

Killing a dangerous snake often brought an angry response from Buddhist neighbors. On my way home one day, about fifteen feet from the house, I noticed a large Banded Krait heading towards me. It looked mean, fearsome, and malevolent. It had a shiny black face with large evil eyes. A crowd gathered around me and the snake, and they protested, but I was going to kill it. It felt a little odd. I would make note after that of excessive and unreasonable extremes of religion; real life and religion don't always mix.

If I thought I would be done with snakes when I left Burma, I was going to be wrong. Living in Arizona I would come to face to face with them again. Killing a rattler in the presence of Juleen was a new experience for her. Alternately whimpering and screaming, she kept asking when it was going to die. One of the tricks, I explained, was to hold the snake firmly to the ground with a long-handled implement and hold it till the snake stopped moving.[2] We keep such an implement outside each door to our house.

[2] Many myths about snakes abound in the old world. In India, for example, it is said that unless the snake's head is smashed, it will regenerate again. An anecdote tells about an Englishman who had killed a cobra while stationed in India during the colonial period; when he returned home later and opened his trunk, the cobra raised it head, struck him, and killed him. These myths were spread by snake worshipers in India, where snakes were among the pantheon of gods.

# Chapter 10
# War Starts

On a cool December day in 1941, somewhere in the South China Sea, the Japanese invasion fleet set sail from Camraunh Bay (old spelling) and was moving from Saigon to Malaya. This was the northwest monsoon season, so the Japanese had to be quick. Luck was on their side. On December 8, 1941, some two hours before the Pearl Harbor attack, past midnight Malay time, the Japanese landed troops at Kota Baru, a small coastal town on the Kra Isthmus on Malaya's east coast.[1] Soldiers of the 11th Indian Division in the pill boxes noticed shadows moving towards the beach and challenged them. But the assault by the Japanese 15th and 25th Imperial armies was overwhelming. After a brief firefight, the Japanese moved through the palm trees and dense underbrush toward the village of Kota Baru, overpowering the weak defenses there. Then the two armies headed in different directions. The *Rangoon Times* noted the night's events, sending shivers down our spines.

The 15th Army crossed over to the west coast, then north to Thailand and Burma. After a short skirmish they occupied Singora and Patani, Thailand,[2] giving the Imperial Army an edge. Britain's plans to stop the Japanese at the Malay–Thailand border were botched, resulting in disaster. The 15th Army continued their advance towards south Burma, planning to attack Victoria Point, the southernmost point in Burma. The 25th Army, with the burly General Yamashita in command, was assigned to take the rest of Malaya, including Singapore. It headed to Penang on the west coast, then moved southward, planning to attack Singapore from the jungles north of the causeway separating the city from mainland Malaya. All this was known to the public by midday.

---

[1] On the 50th anniversary of the event, my wife and I spent a week here. It is now called the Beach of Passionate Love and indeed is lovely. Some of the pillboxes still remain on the beaches.

[2] The Thais being Thais, quickly collapsed.

Figure 12. Pillbox, Kota Baru, Malaysia. Photo by author.

As the Japanese continued their advance toward Singapore, the news was uniformly bad. Rangoon newspapers were full of stories of war. "What next?" was on everybody's lips. Fear gripped the people of Rangoon. There was tension throughout the city, but the watering holes that colonials frequented were packed. At clubs like the Orient, Anderson's, and British-only private clubs, drinking and dancing continued way into the wee hours of the morning. Some American Volunteer Group (AVG)[3] pilots were invited to these British-only clubs, and some colonials hosted the American pilots to honor them for their help, but under all the celebration there was an underlying anxiety. Some in the British community were displeased by the pranks pulled by some of the AVG pilots, but fears of imminent war overshadowed those objections.

---

[3] The American Volunteer Group: civilian airmen recruited by General Claire Chennault to assist Nationalist China and protect the lend-lease supplies America was sending to China over the Burma Road. The Burma Road was built by the British (using Burmese and Chinese labor) after 1937. At that time the rail line existed only from Rangoon to Lashio, in northern Burma, and the Road extended that transport line from Lashio to Kunming in China. Rangoon was of paramount importance because supplies landed there before being transported northward to Lashio by rail; hence the presence of Americans in the streets of Rangoon.

In the early hours of December 10, 1941, the British Royal Navy's vaunted dreadnaughts, the invincible battleship the *Prince of Wales* and the heavy cruiser *Repulse*, sailed from Singapore towards the Gulf of Siam under the command of Captain Tom Phillips, in search of the Japanese fleet. They did not have air cover. Phillips was convinced that air power could not sink a capital ship, even though the American Billy Mitchell had proved that aircraft can indeed sink capital ships that have no air cover. As the British capital ships, the pride of the Royal Navy, sailed towards the east, one Japanese scout plane identified the telltale signs of the *Prince of Wales*. The Japanese 22nd Air Squadron assembled their torpedo planes, fighters, and heavy bombers and set out from Saigon. They had some trouble finding the big ships, but there was an element of luck in that one of their scout planes glimpsed the ships through the clouds. At 11:00 am the Japanese planes started their bombing run, with bombs hitting the deck of the battleship. The direct hits slowed the big ship, then torpedo planes moved in to take over the attack. At 1:30 pm the great ship rolled with 796 men including her captain. The *Repulse* also sank. That sent a chill through the British establishment. It was a terrible blow to the defense of the Far East, and the morale of the defenders of Malaya and Singapore took a hit. The event would lead Churchill to say "The Honor of the British Empire and the British is at stake. Senior officers should die with their troops."

The news about the fighting in Malaya was not encouraging, but the swift advance of the Japanese along the west coast of Malaya at least shocked the British out of their complacency. Singapore, now responsible for the defense of Burma, was under siege. London grew alarmed and once again changed the command structure to assign the defense of Burma back to India. The General Officer Commanding (GOC) of the Indian Army took over again. Delhi hurriedly transferred two Indian brigades of the 17th Indian Division to Rangoon, but, unfortunately, they had been trained for desert warfare in the Middle East, not jungle warfare. Entering the port of Rangoon piecemeal, these two brigades were disembarking and a third was still in India when, on the 14th of December, a combined force of Japanese and Burmese attacked Burma's southernmost city, Victoria Point, and captured it.

The attack on Victoria Point shocked the people of Rangoon. There was much hand-wringing and sadness. School was closed, but Father went to work.

The British Governor was aware that he could say nothing to reassure the population. But the arrival of fresh troops provided hope and uplift to the people.

To make matters worse, tragedy struck the family. My youngest sister Uku, a year and a half old, took sick. She was underweight and sickly and developed pneumonia. This was before the era of penicillin. Mother put camphor oil on her chest. I tried to keep her warm, holding her close, but one evening she took a turn for the worse. I covered her with a small blanket and let her sleep on my chest. Late that night she died. The family gathered around and sang religious hymns, and the next day we buried her. I thought about her later. It was probably for the better, for war came to Burma two months later. To drag her through the war would have meant she would never have survived and would have suffered needlessly.

Despite the bad news from Malaya and Victoria Point, we planned to celebrate Christmas, albeit in a tempered manner. I remember walking to our friends' homes to sing carols. Just before the holiday our plans were upended.

By December 22, 1941, rumors of war were on everybody's lips. Although fear was pervasive, preparations for the holidays were still afoot. Rangoon was quiet but tense. In the city center, evidence of preparations for war was all around: the big buildings—Grindlay's Bank, the Bombay Burma Trading Company, and the Irrawaddy Flotilla Company—were guarded by armed soldiers. Sandbags were piled high in front of buildings, and brick shields covered the windows. Each night, lights were dimmed. Already many residents, especially British women and children, were leaving.

The British Governor and military were well aware of the danger posed by the Japanese Army. In a Naval Cipher Telegram dated 22 December 1941, the US Consul Chungking detailed for the US government and the Governor of Burma why the Japanese desired to attack Burma:

- To cut military supplies to China by cutting the Burma Road.
- To establish bases in the Indian Ocean, for a future attack on India.

The assessment continued:

- The capture of Burma will have dire consequences for China. It will deprive China of all supplies, deprive China of contact with the outside world especially America, and disrupt American supplies to China. It would deprive America of part of Burma's mining output, especially tungsten from Mergui and other metals from the Mawchi Mines.
- Threat to India: it would deprive India of a third of its oil supplied through the loss of the oil fields at Yanangyaung and Chauk in central Burma. Capture of the oil fields of Burma will restore to the Japanese some oil supplies lost from Sumatra.

Finally the cipher described two possible avenues of attack:

- From north Siam, through Kengtung in the eastern Shan States, to Meiktila on the Irrawaddy river in the center of Burma, and cut lower Burma from northern Burma.
- From the Raheng/Tak province of Siam, across to Kawkareik in Burma, threatening Moulmein. First attack may come from Pattani in Siam, next to seized Victoria Point. Timing of the attack is uncertain–likely before Christmas–but will be part of the plan on Malaya and Singapore.

At the docks, British-Indian soldiers continued to disembark. From the airport, newly arrived American pilots of the AVG took to the streets; dressed in mufti, they caroused through the crowded city streets and did what the young do: crazy things, like putting the rickshaw man in the rickshaw and pulling him around themselves—much to the delight of the common people and the consternation of others, like the portly memsahibs and others of the British Raj. The memsahibs knew that the Americans were in the country to protect the Burma Road and keep China in the war,[4] not to defend the realm. In China the war was not going well. For Chiang Kai-Shek and the Kuomintang (Chinese Nationalist Party; KMT), the Burma Road was the only connection to the outside world. An American-supported enterprise, the Burma Road was kept open to keep American supplies going to China and thereby prevent the collapse of the beleaguered Chinese government. American lend-lease supplies were off-loaded at the Rangoon docks. Dodge, Ford, and Chevy trucks stored near the docks then transported the supplies northward.[5]

In these days before Christmas, in spite of rumors of war and an attack, sections of the city were in a celebratory mood. In colonial Burma, holiday celebrations traditionally started around the 20th of December and continued well into the new year. While the British nervously watched, revelers crowded the city, crisscrossing the city to visit friends and go to church. Small groups of young churchgoers sang Christmas carols. There was widespread disbelief that, on these holiest days, a war would be started.

Under the wide, semi-circular awning of the Excelsior Cinema at the corner of Dalhousie and Sule Pagoda roads, people were lining up to go to the cinema. The last picture show started at six o'clock and ended by eight o'clock. The Indian savory-makers and the Burmese *mohinga*[6] sellers were packing up for the night. I stood in front of the cinema to watch the antics of the AVG fighter pilots. By dusk, expats, mostly British and Europeans, packed the clubs, most of them exclusively for Whites only. Soon they were drinking and dancing the night away. Mixed clubs (where some locals were allowed) too were filling. Little did the party-goers know what awaited them in morning. Many partied late into the night, and some drank

---

[4] US Army Memo 356/db-52/41states: "Col. McEwan to be very interested in control of transport along the Burma–Yunnan Highway ... One hundred million U.S. dollars to China to effect that the United States will have the right to control and organize traffic on the Chungking-Burma Road."

[5] Naval Cypher, one-time table 2243/21. Feb: from Admiralty to B.A.D Washington, 556:

> 3. "Nevertheless, the holding of Rangoon is very important to us as long as our supplies get through to Burma and China. Even afterwards its denial to the Japanese as port will be vital to the achievement of the objective in para. 1, insofar as the defense of Northern route is concerned.
>
> 4. Therefore, seems to us the port should be held as long as possible...."

[6] *Mohinga* = a Burmese fish soup. Tea shops were small huts where tea was brewed and men sat on low stools around small, low, round tables. Here the Burmese men congregated and talked shop.

their concerns away. In the villages, life continued as always. Villagers were more concerned with their crops than what was happening in the big city.

On the morning of 23 December, the sun began its ascent in all its tropical glory. It promised to be a cloudless, sunny day. The tea shops and food stalls were rapidly filling in the city and serving breakfast: *dosa* (Indian crepes) for the Indians; *mohinga* for the Burmese; coffee and bread with marmalade for others who could afford it. I had sliced bread and butter at home. We were all excited about the holidays. We planned to go caroling that evening, a chance to visit old friends, sing, and enjoy banter.

The rising sun was still low on the horizon, and it was not yet hot. This peace was interrupted by the mournful sirens, which soon ceased. Suddenly, an unusual and faint noise came from the distant southeast: a low drone that soon became the ominous noise of heavily laden bombers. Spotters were calling in to warn of hostile aircraft, and soon small dots appeared high in the sky. Only then did the allied aircraft spring into action. At the Aerodrome, antiquated American-built Brewsters[7] of the Royal Air Force (RAF) Squadron 67 took off. They joined the American P-40 (Curtis) fighters and headed to meet the oncoming planes. The long-rumored war had started, and for those of us who lived in Burma, it changed everything.

Earlier in the morning, heavy Japanese bombers, the Mitsubishi KI-21, along with Nakajima 27 (fixed undercarriage) fighters, had taken off from Tak (Thailand) air base and set out to bomb Rangoon. The enemy planes were now close to the city, and before too long a furious air battle was in progress. With each passing minute, the intensity of the sound progressed from a low drone to an intense high-pitched whine. Later I was to learn that the unsynchronized engines made the sound more terrifying; the change in pitch added to the fear.

The dogfight was in progress to the south of the city. From high in the sky, RAF fighters and American (AVG P 40) fighters tore into the bombers while the Nakajima fighters tried to draw the allied fighters away from the bomber forma-

---

[7] The Brewster Buffalos were built for the Marines in 1937, were rejected by American military services, and were subsequently sold to the Royal Netherlands Air Force and to the RAF.

tion. The AVG planes dived into the bomber formation, taking on the Nakajima fighters. The noise was deafening. Screaming planes plummeted into the soft soil of the delta. Watching bombers catching fire and spiral to the ground was satisfying in a way. Despite efforts by the RAF and AVG, however, the Japanese bombers kept their tight formation and arrived over the city. They dropped altitude and started the bombing run. Despite all the announcements the government had issued, most people ignored the warnings and did the worst possible thing. Curiosity took over, and they went out of their houses to look anxiously skyward. Not me. In the shelter, I rolled into a ball, covered my ears, and buried my head into my chest. I took a peek from time to time and saw puffs of smoke around the bombers. The bombs whistled and, as they reached their terminal velocity, screamed, and then came thunderous explosions, the ground shook. There is no way to describe the noise, no words to describe the experience.

At Brooking Street Wharf (where my brother worked), the bombs hit the cranes and the dockside facilities. The tall cranes crashed in quick succession. Spouts of water rose skyward; fire and smoke also billowed skyward, obscuring the sun for days on end. Closer to home, the power plant at Ahlone, just north of the city, exploded, sending huge plumes of smoke into the air that could be seen from our home. After they hit their targets, the Japanese bombers turned north to the aerodrome, which was located to the northwest of our house. As the noise got louder, the dirt on top of the shelter flew into the entrance, partially obscuring it. Fearing it would collapse, we rushed out of the shelter to the large meadow behind the house, where we cowered in a gully behind the tall bamboo fence. We could hear machine-gun fire. Later I learned that some Japanese fighters were machine-gunning the hapless people in the streets of the city.

As the first wave of bombers moved away from the city to the aerodrome, antiaircraft guns began to fire. Puffs of smoke could be seen around the planes, but the bombers just continued on to the RAF air base. Obsolete antiaircraft guns fired at the bombers but were hopelessly inadequate. The bombers hit the landing strip and the Gloucestershire barracks across the road from the aerodrome. Fires broke out, and now we were surrounded on all sides by fire. The fires spread, and many shanties, huts, and even brick-and-mortar structures caught fire. Fires at the aerodrome spread in the north; smoke billowed from the airport's oil-storage tanks. Finally, in the late afternoon, the sirens sounded the all-clear, signaling the end of the raid.

Ghastly tales of horrific scenes from the city spread: the injured jumping into gutters; abdomens ripped open to expose the intestines; the wounded running while still holding their exposed guts; people's heads cut off. It was gory. Ordinary people were worst hit. Instead of taking shelter as they had been instructed to do, they stood outside gawking and got slaughtered. The Japanese fighters mercilessly machine-gunned the civilians, foreshadowing the cruelty of the Japanese. The dead piled up in the streets and the gutters. For hours afterward the poor laborers ran this way and that but ignored the shelters. It was a grotesque scene.

By late afternoon people came out of congested apartments to survey the damage. Fire brigades and St. John's Ambulance were trying to cope with taking the wounded to the hospitals. Firefighters were busy putting out fires. Rangoon General Hospital, with about 200 beds, was filled with the wounded and dying; people were lying in the wards and spilled into every available space. British, Indian, and a few Burmese doctors were working at full speed. News filtered out that it was not the physical damage that was so terrifying; it was the numbers of the dying and dead. Huge fires engulfed the city and, along with the smoke, shut out the sunlight. As dusk approached, more fear gripped the city. Mother made sure that all of us were there, and we crawled back to the house. We were not hurt but were scared out of our wits. Physically in shock, fearful and terror stricken.

This was my introduction to the war. I was barely eleven years old. That night the lights went out as we crawled into the darkened house, shaking with fear. In spite of all the warnings from air-raid wardens, many people died from not following rules. It was not till the next day that a rough estimate of damage and deaths was made: Three AVG planes had been lost, two US pilots were dead,[8] six British Buffalo fighters had been downed with their pilots. Civilian deaths numbered

[8] AVG pilots Hank Gilbert and Neil Martin went down with their planes. George B. MacMillan bailed out and miraculously returned to base.

2000, mostly labor and coolies. Sanitation was a mess; the removers of night soil stayed away. The Governor declared an emergency.

Stories of the wounded were heartbreaking. Rangoon General hospital was filled to capacity, the wounded lying next to the dying, who were slow to be removed to make room for the living. Some lost their legs; some had their abdomens cut open. The power station, the port, and the aerodrome were all badly damaged, as were the wharf, the warehouses, and the electric power stations. Danam survived. He had worked late at the Port Trust, and we had been worried about him when he had not returned. Finally, towards sunset, he came home; he looked frightened but had not suffered physical injury. Like us he showered and tried to suppress his fear. There was little conversation that night; we welcomed the night for the protection it offered from bombing. Nobody talked about dinner. I remember crawling under the bed and staying there all night. What followed would be talked about for years.

There was some respite on Christmas Eve, but the calm was deceptive. Extra police patrolled the street. We had hardly recovered from the air raid. Dead animals still lay in the streets, and the stench of death pervaded the air. The rubble that obstructed some city streets was still not cleared, and bodies remained under the debris. In spite of the air raids, some held on to the view that they could still celebrate Christmas. So, they went to church and prayed. Grandmother prayed to both Christian and Hindu gods. With lights out there was no usual feast. Glumly we ate the food and went to sleep.

Christmas morning, we got up early. As usual it was another clear and cloudless day. The mood was somber, but we were in for a surprise: the dreaded sirens came alive again, with their mournful and ominous sound! This time when the sirens went off, people ran for cover. In the distance to the south, bombers could be seen flying in V formation. The path of the bombers was different now, closer to our home. They were headed to the rail repair facilities, two miles from the house; hence the different flight pattern. The bombers flew overhead just to the north of our house, and because their target was closer to home, we felt the shock. The air-raid wardens had warned us not to seek shelter in rooms with windows, as the glass could shatter and cause serious harm, but to go to the shelter. But with the bombers so close, we were afraid to be outside in the shelter so stayed in the living room. It had one door to the outside and no windows. With the big door closed, it provided some comfort. For a while, the bombers flew directly over our house to the facility at Gyougone. This place was a large railway complex, with workshops, the marshaling yard filled with rail stock and engines, huge sheds, and multiple train tracks; it was the largest facility in the country. This is where the locomotive engines and rolling stock were repaired and maintained. Many middle-class families lived close to the rail yard, and the railway quarters were nearby: row upon row of dark but neat and tidy homes. A little further removed were the more substantial homes of the colonial heads of the various railway officials: large, two-storied structures whose lower floors were constructed of brick and whose upper floors were constructed of teakwood, with airy verandas. The bombers were now in position. First came the dreaded whistling sound, then the explosions. It was like an earthquake. With each round of bombs going off, the walls of the house shook. It seemed as though they were closing in around us. This went on for two hours, then the drone of the planes started to recede. The smell of the acrid, dark smoke was overpowering, and it seemed like the whole town was aflame.

The all-clear sounded, and we slowly glanced at the sky. One thing you learn very quickly is never to rush out of any shelter. It was wise to linger there for a while. We came out of the house more than a little rattled. News of the bomb damage trickled in that afternoon, and as it came in, I was stunned by the reports from Gyougone. My classmate and best friend Joe (I do not remember the family name) who lived there was dead. Like me he was Christian, we were of the same age, and we played together. Danam had come home with the bad news that "the rail yard suffered much damage; the workshops were leveled." Later he mentioned in passing that Joe's family had perished but that there were no external injuries. I was shocked beyond belief. Danam said, "the entire family was found dead, the roof of the shelter was blown off, and they were all sitting out in the trench with no obvious injuries." I started to cry and said that I wanted to go see for myself. My sister and brother grabbed me and sat me down. I cursed the Japanese. My family kept a close watch on me. It took me while to overcome the loss of my friend. Years later in medical school I would learn that sudden death (blast injury) can occur from shock.

For father it was a trying time. Even though Boxing Day (the day after Christmas, in British tradition) was a holiday, he went to check out the damage at work. When he came home, he looked grim and said little. He kept many facts from the family. On December 27 he went back to work. The railroad was on a war footing. Saboteurs, fifth columnists, and agent provocateurs had damaged the warehouse, and the entire crew was pressed to clear it. Father knew that under the rules he could not leave his job, and he worried about what he was going to tell the family.

Two days after the bombing, shops opened early and closed by 9:00 a.m. After a week, people wondered how long supplies would last. There was more shocking news to come. The Japanese changed tactics They had sustained heavy losses of aircraft in their raids, so they discontinued day raids. This brought some relief for us, but day raids were replaced by night raids. Night raids have their own special terror. In some ways they are more terrifying, for you could not see the plane, only knew by its deafening scream that it was coming. Some of these night raids were reconnaissance flights; sometimes they came to hit specific targets. The raid would commence at about 10:00 pm. First the drone of the aircraft could be heard, then the sky would light up with searchlights: one, two, three until all six lights lit up the sky. They waved and danced in the cool night air; they were trying to locate the enemy plane. One of the lights picked up the enemy aircraft, and soon all the lights focused on the plane. Were it not for the terror and the noise, it could have been exciting to watch. The ack-ack fire kept firing tracers and black puffs; the puffs could be seen but never reached the enemy plane. While one plane was preoccupied with the lights, others would dive to drop their bombs.

To add to the terror, one of the sisters, prone to having nightmares and breakdowns, had one of her moments as the drone of aircraft grew louder. She started screaming that she could see the devil on the ceiling, moving around. This added yet another level of terror for us. I took shelter behind the big bags of rice and dry goods, covering my ears and closing my eyes and crying myself to sleep. The bombing took a terrible psychological toll on all the people. The family kept its fingers crossed. We were waiting for the most ominous news of the land invasion. In the past, Rangoon had celebrated the New Year with gusto, with all the ethnic groups joining in. But this year people looked to the new year with fear and foreboding.

The next two weeks passed without incident, but tension was growing. The Japanese 25th Army had crossed the causeway between mainland Malaya and Singapore from the north, thereby rendering the naval base, whose armor pointed south to the sea, useless. Poor leadership and lack of coordination between the army and the air-force in Singapore had rendered the huge defense force of 85,000 Australians, Indian, and British troops helpless against 35,000 Japanese troops. Now the Japanese were preparing for a final assault on the command post. There was more bad news: the P-40s of the AVG were withdrawn from Rangoon's airport and sent to Magwe, in middle Burma, then soon left Burma altogether and flew to protect China. The RAF also retreated to the north and sent their Buffaloes away. There were rumors that some Chinese troops were to defend Toungoo, to the north of Pegu, but these were only rumors. This left Rangoon defenseless.

The news was not encouraging in the least, as the Allies suffered one defeat after another, and a sense of resignation set in. The Rangoon newspaper in big bold headlines said: "The Invasion is Imminent." Uncle Brown tried to reassure us. Father was beside himself. The situation in Rangoon was getting desperate. Food and water were becoming difficult to obtain. Nonetheless, Father managed to buy more supplies: rice, cooking oil, and kerosene to be stored in the living room. We had to move the large pieces of teak furniture to the edges of the room to make room for it all. The children all slept in the living room. The lights were turned off after sunset. Although by tradition in the tropics people ate late, now food had to be consumed by sunset. All the doors and windows were secured. Sometimes we sang hymns and other songs until it was time to sleep. But sleep was never deep; one ear was always tuned to listen for enemy aircraft. Although the men did not tell us children much, it was clear that something was afoot. Mother tore up some bed-sheets and gave each of us a half sheet for our toiletries, then told us to keep our bundles well hidden but accessible in a hurry. Father called the men together to talk over the ominous information from the front. It was just a matter of time before the Japanese would be in Rangoon, he opined. It was obvious we were waiting for instructions.

# Chapter 11
# Flight and Disease

*Cholera, a short curved, motile gram-negative bacillus, has a single flagellum. It is endemic to almost all of Asia, residing in ponds, small lakes, and in streams. The organism causes intense human suffering when access is denied to clean drinking water: it quickly causes diarrhea, vomiting, and dehydration. If left untreated it can lead to death, however it can be treated with fluids and salts and can be prevented by vaccines. In wartime, however, these systems break down. In addition to cholera and other such diseases, the other great scourge is bacillary dysentery. Caused by bacillus shigella, it is highly infectious and is said to have infected 2 to 3 percent of British troops during World War II. The Japanese had a higher rate than that towards the end of the war. The only medication was sulpha medication and rapid rehydration.*

Even before any military operations against Burma began, rumors had been enough to rattle the people of Burma. The terrified rich, the well-to-do British, Europeans, wealthy Anglo-Indians, and other foreigners all prepared to leave. The wealthy Indians carried their jewels and gold out of the country. Those who could leave early booked every ship, train, and plane. When they could not board ships, they took the trains to the border and hired poor coolies to carry suitcases of clothing and other valuables across the border. The poor, the laboring class, left behind what little they possessed, wrapped their meager possessions in a dhoti, and began a long trek on foot along the railroad tracks to Prome and Mandalay. It was pathetic to see little girls carrying

Figure 13. Barefooted, refugees flee Burma for India. I made this xerox in London, but London's Imperial War Museum cannot locate it in its archives.

their dhoti knapsacks, following their fathers down the road. They had no maps, no directions, and knew not what lay ahead.

The exodus changed from a trickle into a raging stream. Shipping companies were flooded with refugees. British families filled the first-class berths, better-off Anglo-Indians, Indians, and rich, land-owning *chettiars* filled the second-class berths. Bullock carts piled high with poorer refugees and the goods they could not bear to leave behind clogged the roads, while the poorest set out for India on foot. What faced them, they had not a clue. They knew nothing of cholera, plague, lack of food, and robbers who would prey on them. They had no idea what roads there were, how great was the distance they had to traverse, but they could not afford the fare to India so had no choice. When I went looking for our manservant Lingam, he was nowhere to be found. I went to the back room where he slept with his few

Figure 14. Poor citizens flee Rangoon as Japanese war planes approach December 1941 [https://commons.wikimedia.org/wiki/File:Rangoon,_poor_citizens_flee_as_Japanese_planes_approach_December_1941.jpg] from *Japan: Friend or Foe?* By Bipin Behari Kapur, Rangoon Gazette Limited. Public Domain.

Figure 15. Indians leaving Rangoon, 1941 [https://scroll.in/article/967459/the-indian-exodus-from-burma-in-1941-is-a-forgotten-piece-of-world-war-ii-history] by Bipin Bihari Kapur. Public Domain.

possessions, but he was not there, and his belongings that he had kept wrapped in a dhoti were gone. We never found out what happened to him. He must have joined the exodus of poor civilians: pitiful columns of men, women, and children who set out on a futile quest to walk to the safety of India.

There was no help from the authorities. In an unbelievable act of cruelty, the British administration and their Burmese supporters turned many of the trudging refugees back to Rangoon. Their theory was that to encourage such an exodus would deplete the city of vital labor, to unload the docks, empty the thunder boxes, and so on.[1] The returning refugees brought tales of the horrors of the road. Shortages of food and water drove people to drink from creeks and ponds. Cholera spread like wildfire.[2] There were few medical preparations and only a limited

[1] The British authorities were severely criticized for the lack of humanity and provision of services.

[2] Shigella dysentariae causes an acute diffuse inflammation of the mucosa of the colon with the formation of a false diphtheritic membrane, followed by necrosis and ulceration.

supply of cholera vaccine, which was soon exhausted. Refugees died in droves. Those who died rotted where they died. Lurid stories proliferated of gangs of Burmese collaborators, robbers, thugs, and dacoits who stalked the fearful, unarmed, defenseless refugees and attacked them without mercy. They would fall upon the hapless men, women, and children. There were stories of them dragging young women to be raped and then hacked to death. When these stories were told in hushed tones at night, it created great angst, fear, and sometimes terrible dreams. At eleven years of age, I was so fearful, that I would crawl between the stored bags of rice and stay there until dusk.

Any talk of fleeing the city was now out of question for the family, as Father could not leave his position and the authorities were turning back those who attempted to leave the city. Our family was told that we had to stay until the Governor released Father to leave.

# Chapter 12
# The Land Invasion

*"If Singapore falls, this will assuredly put more pressure on Burma. The defense of Moulmein and Rangoon is of utmost importance.... The Australian Prime Minister has refused to divert to Burma the Australian Division that was returning from the Middle East. You must depend on the Indian Division and the Tank Brigade that will arrive in February."*

*Most Secret Telegram, December 22, 1941*
*from the Prime Minister in London to the British Governor in Rangoon*

The land invasion of Burma began on January 17, 1942. It originated from the advance base in the Tak province of Thailand. From there the Imperial Japanese 33rd Division struck the small isolated post of Sukli Point, a tiny observation post perched on a hill overlooking the Thai-Burma border, near Myawaddy. It was manned by a small contingent of Indians, Gurkhas, and Karens. The enemy had good intelligence provided by Burmese collaborators and knew how to sneak up on the post. At first the defenders held, but after a short firefight, the platoon was overwhelmed. The defenders abandoned the post, leaving their dead, and retreated westward towards Kyondo. To their surprise they found that the Japanese, using jungle trails and with the help of collaborators, had outflanked them. At every stop they ran into Japanese. With the main road blocked, the soldiers took to the jungle, and the battered, frightened, and exhausted men finally joined the main body of troops near Moulmein. From the Thai-Burma border it took the Japanese fewer than ten days to run to Kyondo, due east of the city of Moulmein, whose pagoda and parapet Kipling had romanticized (although he never visited Mandalay):

By the old Moulmein Pagoda, looking eastward to the sea.
There's a Burma girl a - setting, and I know she thinks of me;
For the wind is in the palm-trees and the temple-bells they say:
"Come you back, you British, soldier; come you back to Mandalay."

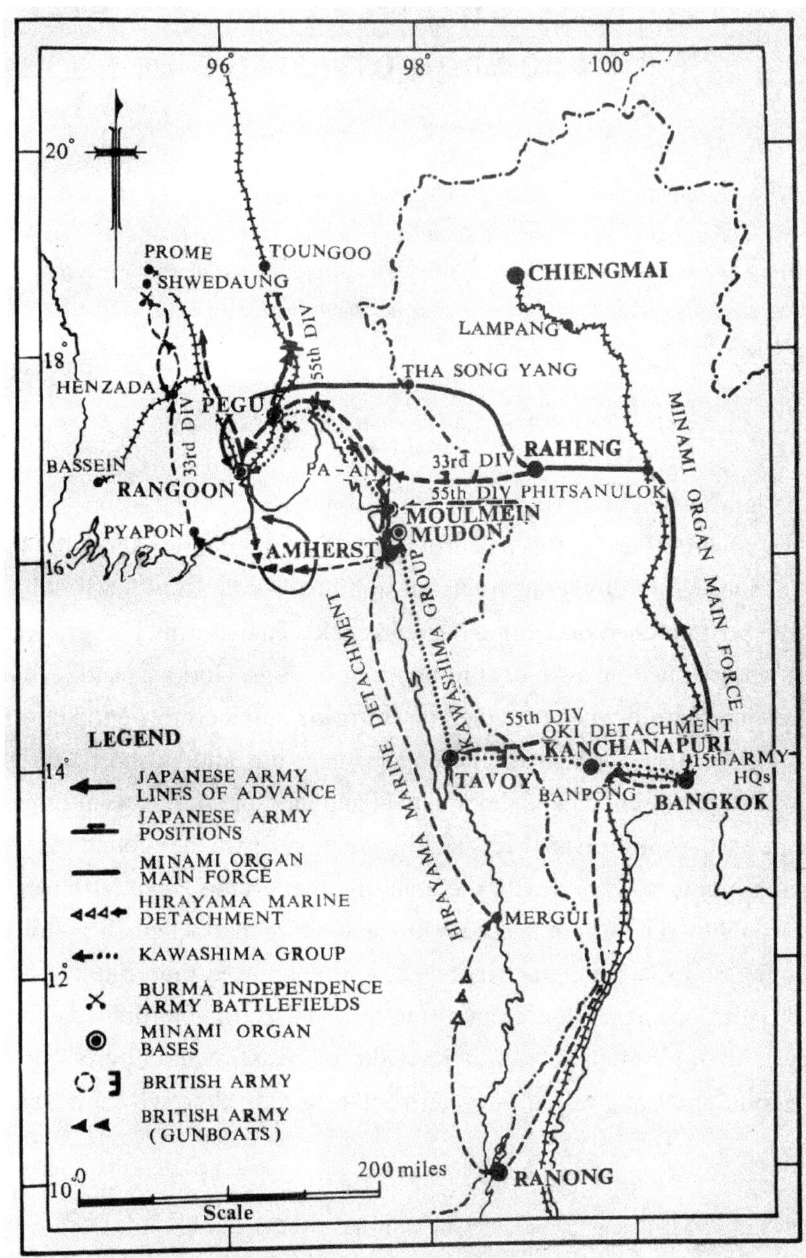


Figure 16. Map showing advance of the Burmese Independence Army (Minami Organ) and Japanese Army Dec. 1941–Apr. 1942. From Izumiya Tatusuro, *The Minami Organ* (Tokyo: Tokuma Shoten, 1967), after p. 93.

The enemy advanced rapidly from the south as well as the east. The second Japanese column advanced northward from Victoria Point to Tavoy toward Mudon, just south of Moulmein, supported by the Burma Defense Army (BDA) that was led by Aung San. On the way, the BDA committed many atrocities, just like the Japanese.

It is here that the first story emerged that Burmese army commander Aung San actually participated in the torture and killing of a Muslim headman of the village of Thotan.[1] Mudon—the last post south of Moulmein—fell in the face of the enemy advance, cutting Moulmein off on three sides. The Bamar came out of their homes, greeting the enemy as liberators and showering them with flowers, cooked rice, and fish. They embraced them and offered not only food but also any information that they had about British and Indian soldiers hiding in the countryside. The Japanese treated the Bamar well.

The only line of retreat from Moulmein was northward, across the wide estuary of the Salween River and to Martaban, the starting point of the railway that crosses the Sittang River and leads to Pegu. At Martaban, a train was waiting to take evacuees to safety in Pegu. Crossing of the wide estuary was fraught with danger, however. Many civilians followed the retreating troops as they took to flimsy boats. Enemy aircraft machine-gunned them in the water; it was a massacre from the air. Again the Japanese advanced quickly. They took to their bicycles and the jungle trails and outflanked the allied troops. They headed toward the Bogyagi

---

[1] The incident in question concerns the village headman named Abdul Rashid. Upon arrival at the village, Aung San put a rope around Rashid's neck and dragged him to the Thotan town football grounds and, in the presence of thousands of people, put him to death in the following manner. After crucifying him on the football goal post, Aung San speared Rashid with his bayonet. The spearing did not kill the man immediately. Aung San then fell to the ground and let his gang finish the job with their bayonets. George Appleton, a British official, recommended that Aung San "should have been arrested and executed" but Mountbatten stayed the order. In the post-war era, British authorities attempted to bring charges against Aung San, but it was not politically feasible, given the changed post-war circumstances.

A Yale graduate questioned me recently on Facebook about my comments about Aung San, asking if I had read his speeches. I replied that I don't listen to or read long-winded propaganda speeches. Why should we not examine Aung San critically? He is no god. After all, we have examined the lives of our presidents. Aung San suffered from a flaw present in some Bamar, namely, quickness to anger and violence, out of proportion to the reality. This flaw was shared with Ne Win and the rest of the gang and has been commented upon in the last chapter of this book.

rubber plantation near the Sittang River, where they planned to overtake the retreating troops.

Between Moulmein and the Sittang River is the small Belin River. This small river, traversing from east to west on its way to the Andaman Sea, was shallow at this time of year. It was the last line of defense before the Sittang River and its vital bridge. The beleaguered and battered battalions, including the Baluch (from what is now Pakistan) troops, retreated north and west to this next line of defense at the Belin River. They put up a stout defense but could not contain the Japanese. The Japanese 33rd Division troops routed the allied troops.

It was now mid-February 1942. At the British headquarters of the 17th Division (which comprised the 16th, 46th, and 48th brigades) at Waw, just west of the Sittang River, there was panic; panic spread among civilians as well. The sick old British general was unable to contain the situation. Weeks into the fight, the Japanese 33rd Division now was joined by 55th Division. It proceeded north to cut off the retreating 17th Indian Division heading on its last line of retreat to Mandalay. The 48th Brigade on the east side of the bridge was unable to slow the Japanese advance and suffered one defeat after another, one disaster after another. Some

Figure 17. Present-day town of Waw on the Sittang River. Photo by author.

troops reached the east bank of the Sittang Bridge at midnight but waited for their comrades before crossing. When the 48th Brigade reached Kyaikto, on the east side of the river, another disaster befell the retreating troops: they were fired upon by their own RAF and AVG planes and suffered heavy casualties, which further demoralized them. They were not aware of all that was happening, due to poor communications. When the retreating 16th and 48th brigades reached the assembly point at a place called Monkpalin, they found that advance units of Japanese and their Burmese collaborators had already reached the heights overlooking the bridge. For the 16th and 48th brigades, it was vital to hold the bridge till all the defenders crossed over to the west side of the river and safety. But this did not happen. The battle for the bridge would end in a crisis for the defenders.

Figure 18. Sittang Bridge from above, showing location of Sittang Village, Pagoda Hill, and Bungalow Hill. Photo from old British colonial publication.

The bridge was a dual-use bridge: rail and road. It was primarily a railway bridge but could be modified for motor traffic. The rail/road approached the bridge through a rubber plantation and then through a deep cutting made through the heart of Bungalow Hill.[2] Almost immediately, just south of Buddha Hill, the rail/road took a sharp turn to the west before crossing the river. On the west side of the river, from the Sittang railhead, the road led to Waw (division headquarters) and thence to Pegu. The dilemma for the British was that the 16th and 48th brigades were still some distance from the bridge, east of the river. The plan was to get both these units to safety across bridge to the fishing village. As those brigades were converging on the bridge, however, a small enemy advance unit arrived on the highest hill. Ne Win—one of the Thirty Comrades and the future tyrant—was one of the guides who led the advance Japanese unit. From the heights of Buddha Hill overlooking the bridge, the collaborators were pressed into service and set up a machine gun.

On the night of February 22, the threat to the bridge increased. The commander was relying on confused staff and contradictory intelligence. Knowing full well that half of his troops were on the east side of the river, the divisional commander nonetheless gave the orders to blow the bridge. This act of cowardice by the general caused an unmitigated disaster. It left the beleaguered brigades on the east side of the Sittang River to fend for themselves in any attempt to cross the river. The Indian troops, unable to swim, drowned in large numbers. This fatal error would determine the course of the war in Burma.

Survivors and stragglers of the 16th and 48th finally crossed the river and joined the 46th at Waw in a fighting retreat toward Rangoon. In the meanwhile, at Rangoon, the remaining garrison (Burma Brigade, 13th Indian Brigade, remnants of the 17th Division), commanded by General Hutton, was awaiting the arrival of the 7th Tank Brigade.

Rangoon was not a city that was built with war in mind. It was an inland port some twenty miles up the Rangoon River from the Andaman Sea. It was part of the Irrawaddy Delta and, during the rainy season, became an impassible

---

[2] There are three hills in the proximity of the Sittang Bridge: Pagoda Hill, Buddha Hill, and Bungalow Hill. Buddha Hill is the highest.

swamp.[3] From Rangoon, a fair-weather road goes north for sixteen miles and soon forks, one road going east to Pegu—via a small town called Hlegu. At Hlegu, another road runs northwest to the small town of Hmawbi, via Taukkyan. It then continues northwest to Tharrawaddy and thence Prome.[4] This complex road system was to play a part in helping the Rangoon Garrison to escape the Japanese trap.

The Rangoon Garrison was preparing to evacuate north to Prome and then Mandalay as soon as the 7th Tank Brigade arrived. The commander of the Japanese 15th Army, General Iada, planned to capture both Hlegu and Hmawbi at the same time, encircle the city of Rangoon, and thus cut off the escape of the Rangoon Garrison and destroy the British-Indian forces. The Japanese 33rd Division, under the command of General Sakurai, captured Pegu, infiltrated past the city, and then advanced to Hlegu, which cut off the Rangoon Garrison and prevented it from escaping to Mandalay. The Japanese set up a roadblock north of Taukkyan to encircle the Rangoon Garrison (details later). The road to Hmawbi was still open. The 48th Brigade was to guard this junction, but as the enemy advanced, the defense started to fall apart.

---

[3] The monsoon weather system develops in the Arabian Sea and Indian Ocean. As spring heats up the sea in May, a huge 500-mile low-pressure system develops and slowly moves eastward. By June it approaches land, and by July it covers most of Southwest, Southeast, and South Asia. Like all weather systems, it intensifies throughout the season.

[4] The road runs north to a rubber plantation at Wanetchaung, where we soon would seek shelter in our own quest for safety.

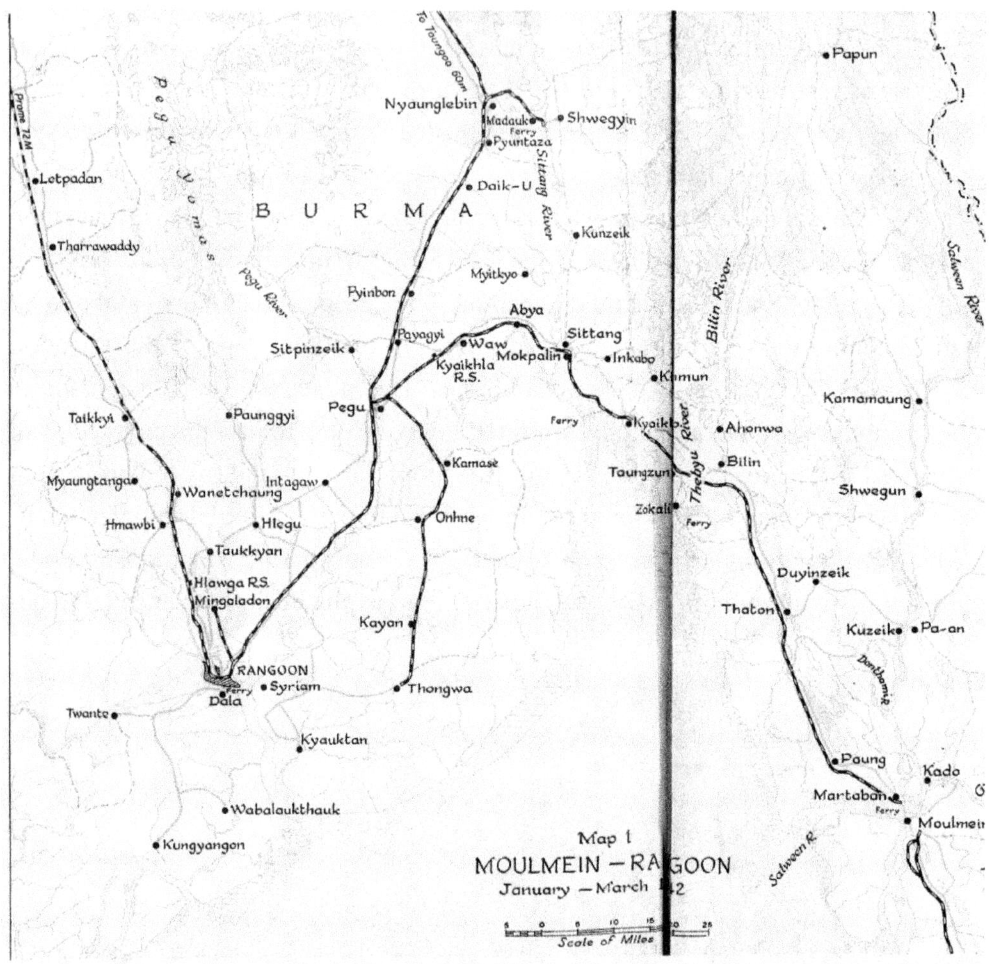


Figure 19. Map showing route from Moulmein to Rangoon. From Major-General S. Woodburn Kirby, *The War Against Japan*, vol. 2 (London: HMSO, 1958), after p. 22. Note position of Sittang, Waw, Pegu in center, and position of Mingaladon, Taukkyan, Hlegu, Hmawbi, and Wanetchaung at left, north of Rangoon. All will feature in the following pages

# Chapter 13
# To Stay or Flee?

We were not rich, but we had a comfortable middle-class family life. It was all going to change. Life would never ever return to the day before. We had already abandoned our beds and mosquito nets and slept on the floor for safety, covered from head to foot by a single sheet, to keep mosquitoes away. This practice lasted long after the war was over and would stay with me for a long time, even after I came to the US. My life changed with suddenness and so abruptly; to cope with it was hard to bear. Our daily routine changed in inexplicable ways; now it revolved around the air-raids and rumors. The routine was to go to the open-air market at dawn and buy vegetables and meat when it was available, then rush home; by 9:00 in the morning, everybody was home. We pretty much stayed indoors; if I went outside, it was only for a brief moment. My sister cooked rice and whatever else she could gather. Each day the food situation worsened. We would eat before dusk.

Living by rumors takes its toll on one's mind. We had been led to believe that the Japanese could not advance that rapidly, but now they were approaching Rangoon. Most of the police fled, adding to the insecurity and fear. Many of them were Anglo-Indian police, the most dependable. Rumors circulated that Burmese policemen joined the dacoits and thugs in looting the homes of rich people.[1] The early refugees who had walked to Prome were being turned back to Rangoon by the police to help with running the city. With them they brought horror stories of shortages of food and drinking water—as well as cholera. The health-care system provided paltry care to begin with, and now it was overwhelmed by the flood of refugees. This weighed heavily on Danam, a doctor, in advising Father that the risk of fleeing would be great: not only would we be in the midst of fighting but also there were epidemics of cholera and plague, and the vaccine supply was exhausted.

---

[1] Corrupt Burmese police were forced by other authorities to disgorge their stolen goods; some were hanged.

"Everything is in short supply and getting worse," he reported. If a siege by the Japanese lasted for more than a week, there would be mass starvation.

For the men in the family, the most frequently asked question was what should we do? Should we stay? Father's main concern was that there would be street fighting. In order to boost morale, the army said that there were enough forces to defend the country. But the army itself was slipping out of the city. Should we plan to take to the road or some other means of escape from the desperate city? Rumors told of British civilians being tortured after being captured by the Japanese. I read the newspaper avidly, even at that age, and while most of the details were beyond me and I had to ignore the big words, I could get the gist. The popular illustrated weekly magazine of Calcutta contained pictures of the war in Europe and Asia, which were both compelling and frightening. Most of our neighbors were leaving: the Burmese for the villages, others still attempting to leave for India. The lunatic asylum was emptied of its inmates. They roamed through the city, adding to the horror. Unable to feed the animals, the zoo-keepers took it upon themselves to let the animals free and then flee; reports spread of tigers, lions, and leopards roaming the streets.[2]

For Father it was a time of dismay, horror, and desperation. The Governor had ordered all essential personnel to remain at their posts. As a committed civil servant, Father could not leave the city until the Governor released civil servants from essential work, giving them what was known as the E pass. Father told the family that we could not join the exodus out of the city. Each evening the men talked of escape (that was all we talked about) from Rangoon. It would be a perilous and dangerous journey to flee war and gain the safety of India, but the men were now seriously talking about it. Father was aware of the danger of delaying but also was aware of the dangers of taking to the road. RAF reconnaissance planes detected, attacked, and sunk enemy boats loaded with Japanese troops and their Burmese allies; this seaborne invasion (by the Kawashima Detachment of the 55th Division) was much talked-about. Intelligence reports noted that the Japanese had crossed the Pegu River and were headed to Daik-U, north of Pegu, effectively cutting off the

---

[2] It is most likely that the terrified animals soon left the city and took to the jungle.

Rangoon–Mandalay Road in two places. Father finally decided, after talking with Danam, that we should plan to escape before all escape routes would be closed.

By the first week of March 1942, the only person left at Father's office was the *durwan* (night watchman); the rest of the staff had fled. He had received information that sappers were setting charges to the oil refinery and the equipment at the port. The *durwan* told Father that he should leave soon; men in military uniforms were going about laying wire—sappers preparing the place for demolition. "The whole place will be blown up," the *durwan* said, "and the Japs will find an empty, burning city." Father looked around for a *gharry* (a pony cart) but could find none; he walked to the front of the Strand Hotel but found no taxies there; he walked further up Phayre Street to look for a typically ubiquitous rickshaw and again found none. It was getting dark now, and he was getting hungry and thirsty, but he persevered. When he arrived home exhausted, he had finally gotten his E pass, which allowed him to leave his post. He probably also had cashed in his provident fund and used the funds to buy gold and sovereigns.

The quandary that father and older brother faced was how to escape before the last road closed. Escape to the west was the only option, and even this last escape route "would close soon," Danam said. Obviously, if Pegu were to be captured, escape from Rangoon would be nearly impossible. Danam, who worked at and had connections at the Port Trust where US vehicles were parked, promised that he would find drivers from the Karen community. Mother called the children and told us to gather up small items of clothing and tinned food. My sisters wailed, "Where will we go?" It was all terrifying; rumors and actions of saboteurs added to the psychological fear. Our last days in Rangoon were filled with a nerve-racking routine: eating a quick breakfast, watching for hostile aircraft, eating a hurried meal before dusk, and then staking out the most secure place to sleep for the night—under a table or next to the bags of stored food. Some evenings we, the young, would gather after supper on the front veranda, where, to boost morale, we would sing ballads popular at the time, even American country music like "The

Red River Valley."[3] What we sang most often was "Till the Lights of London" by Vera Lynn and "It's a Long Way to Tipperary."

On March 5 the Governor announced that he was turning the city over to the military and that only people with E passes would be allowed to leave. By the next morning, Rangoon was for the most part empty. An eerie silence descended on the empty streets. Rangoon radio went silent. There were only soldiers, mostly Indians with their British officers. For those who stayed behind there were no essential services. Dying cities have a feel and smell of their own.

One way or the other, we had to evacuate within forty-eight hours. Danam had two Karen friends from work who wanted to escape the city and go home to Karen State. They agreed to drive us north with them. Father asked, "Can you hold them till tomorrow evening?" and Danam's answer was "yes."

On the evening of March 7, the extended family gathered around on the living room floor, including the cousins from the James family and Uncle Brown.

---

[3] I recently heard this song on the radio and was reminded of why the lyrics were so poignant for us:

From this valley they say you are leaving
We shall miss your bright eyes and sweet smile
For you take with you all of the sunshine
That has brightened our pathway a while

Then come sit by my side if you love me
Do not hasten to bid me adieu
Just remember the Red River Valley
And the cowboy that's loved you so true

For a long time, my darlin', I've waited
For the sweet words you never would say
Now at last all my fond hopes have vanished
For they say that you're going away

Then come sit by my side if you love me
Do not hasten to bid me adieu
Just remember the Red River Valley
And the cowboy that's loved you so true.

Father, Uncle Brown, and Danam all sat on chairs; the women sat on the floor in a circle around them; and I held on to Mother's sari. We children were vaguely aware that danger and uncertainty lay ahead.

At any age, war is frightful and gory enough; for a boy my age it was impossible to comprehend. Words like "street-to-street" and "house-to-house" fighting were incomprehensible. I had visions or fantasies of the fighting: the bullets would fly in all directions; grenades would explode, and their flying shrapnel would not differentiate between foe and friend; a stray bomb would hit the house.... I also dreamt that our house would be spared. I trembled to think of the brutal methods that the Japanese used. We were told that they liked to round up suspects, tie them to a tree, and kill them with their bayonets and swords. In war, humans seem to go collectively mad. The Imperial Japanese Army was no exception: they showed no mercy towards the Chinese or, in Burma, toward the pro-British ethnic people, Indians, or Burmese. In one village north of Pegu, a grisly scene confronted the retreating British-Indian troops: the Burmese had tortured and killed men, women, and children in a mostly Indian village. When the British-Indian troops witnessed this, in spite of their British officers' best efforts, they went on a rampage, killing any Burmese they came across and torching homes in the Burmese village. There were war crimes committed on all sides.

# Chapter 14
# The Odyssey

In a bitter irony, on the morning of March 7, the new British commander, General Alexander, arrived in Rangoon just in time to take over an ugly retreat the next day. The prepared scorched-earth policy was instituted: the sappers and miners blew up stores, ammo dumps, and power plants. The Syriam oil refinery was set on fire; water pumps and electric power plants were blown up, to deny to the Japanese any assets that could benefit them. Fires burned all around us, smoke billowed skyward. The morning looked like dusk, and deafening sounds of explosions continued around us. We didn't need to be told twice to stay indoors. On that same morning, the city garrison was ordered out and started their long retreat as the city burned. The 7th Tank Brigade was hardly disembarked; they had been in the city for less than a week but nonetheless led the retreat. The long line of vehicles took to Prome Road.

That morning Danam had gone to get the American lorries. He told us to stay close to the house, as the military had warned people that they would be shot if orders were not obeyed. Danam was able to get the trucks because the lend-lease supplies—Dodge trucks, Jeeps, and 1500-wt Chevy trucks—were piling up at the port. The American colonel in charge of the trucks was talking about blowing all the equipment, so that it would not fall into enemy hands. He commented, "the British will hurry to protect their assets but will provide no protection for American assets. The British will withdraw, and support staff will be left to fend for themselves against the Japanese and the violent Burmans." The British would also the abandon Karens, who fought on their side, and for their loyalty the Karen would pay a bitter price.

Father gathered the entire extended family on the floor around him and instructed us each to carry some personal items only, in our little bag. There was no room for niceties such as toothbrush or toothpaste. We were terrified; some were crying. He tried to calm us down but told us honestly that the British had lost the war in defending Rangoon and that the Japanese would soon be here; we were going to leave. As soon as the trucks arrive, he said, we were to jump on the lorries, carrying only our essentials, and move to the front of the cab. Once we got on and moved to the front of the truck bed, others could board and find a place. "Keep your head down," he admonished.

Around 10:00 am, two regulation olive-green Dodge trucks driven by Danam's Karen friends pulled up in front of the house. Mother opened the main door to the house. Brother jumped off the truck and shouted at us to run and board the trucks quickly. They did not have a canvas top, and the cargo bay was bare, with no straps, nothing to hang on to. Grabbing my rag-tag bag, I was the first to board and rushed to front of the truck bed, looked through the window, and waved to the driver. I ducked my head below the side wall. The rest of the family, grabbing anything they could, followed suit, rushed to the front and huddled in the truck bed. How others got to the trucks I did not know. Father took a head count. "Quickly, quickly," he urged tensely, and kept repeating "hurry, hurry." Danam kept a wary eye on refugees trying to clamber on board. He closed the back door and signaled the drivers to leave. Many refugees cried for help, but the cabs were already full; we just looked at them in pity, for we knew the gruesome fate that would befall them on a trek to India. After everybody was on board, the trucks started up and we were on our way.

Figure 20. Dodge truck similar to those the family used to flee Rangoon. From old car magazine.

The Rangoon Garrison had been given orders to leave the city and had started early; there were long lines ahead. The winding, sinuous road took us to the traffic circle at Hledan Junction, and from there we headed northwest. I could see the crowded Rangoon–Prome road junction: traffic was piled up as far as the eye could see, the road filled with trucks, tanks, and vehicles of every description. Movement was reduced to a crawl. As each moment passed, the fear grew. I constantly looked skyward for enemy aircraft. At some point in the process, the fear grows ever greater, the heart pounds in the chest, you can feel the arteries in the head throb, the sweat collects on your scalp, and rivulets of sweat stream down from the head to the waist. After an interminable wait, the military traffic thinned out, our drivers moved the trucks into the traffic circle, and we headed to the north and west. We passed the storied Inya Lake, with its impressive colonial bungalows with still well-kept lawns, then headed to the airfield. On each side of the narrow road lay bombed-out trucks and cars. One car caught my attention: a green rag-top MG that I had seen in peace-time and had so loved; I had dreamt of owning one someday. Now it looked broken. After we passed the MG, we entered nightmare territory. The grounds around the airfield had received the most attention from the enemy, and the vast destruction stoked our fear. The runways were damaged, although the control tower was still operating and planes were still taking off. To the south was the view of the river. The road turned away to the north, however, and now we were headed into the unknown. The refugees on foot looked pitiful and hapless; some did not even to bother to look up at the passing vehicles; they kept their heads down and kept moving. Every now and then we passed abandoned cars, some burnt-out trucks, and all sort of native carts, broken and pushed into the ravines to the side of the road. By afternoon we had been traveling for more than three hours. Traffic crawled and at times was stopped by refugees clogging the road. They talked and spread more ominous rumors: "the road is blocked ahead," they said. Traffic slowly crept up the road for few miles, and then suddenly the long column of military vehicles came to a complete stop. We were at the very end. We could hear gunfire in front of us: machine-gun and small-arms fire. It was obvious that there was a roadblock ahead. We were tired, hungry, desperate, and fearful—scared out of our wits and wondering what was next. The "boom-boom" of artillery shells could be heard, accompanied by small-arms fire, which indicated a full-scale battle was going on. Exploding shells ahead shook the ground, and the rat-a-tat-tat of machine-gun fire intensified until the din became unbearable. As dusk approached, the trucks moved off the main road. The men of the family held a conference and talked in whispers, the gist of which was that we could not stay on the road the rest of the night. It seemed a disaster was unfolding.

A few yards ahead there was small Burmese village. It was obvious that we were not going any further. Danam approached the village and talked to the advance unit, who said that the Japanese had blocked the road ahead and advised that we get off the road. He said, "Get off the road and go to the jungle. There is a rubber plantation there where you can rest." Seeing the women and children in the trucks, the villagers offered to provide bullock carts for a price, and promised that they would take us there as the sun set. After a long discussion between the headman, Danam, and Father, money exchanged hands, and finally two bullock carts arrived. In near darkness, Father hurried us off the Dodge trucks and walked us across the road. Danam's Karen driver friends would return to Rangoon and take their chances there. We boarded the carts, quickly and fearfully. When all were accounted for, we took off into the darkness.

The "boom, boom, boom" continued, with intermittent machine gun fire. As we moved away from the road, the noise rose and fell but lessened overall. It did sound like thunder. The rhythmic rocking and swaying of the bullock cart lulled me toward sleep as the sound of the fighting grew distant, but the driver's bell kept waking me. As the night progressed, the darkness increased and totally enveloped us. Stinging insects took over. It was silent except for the buzz of mosquitoes. We were traveling by bullock carts through thick jungle but knew not where we were; all we knew was that we were headed somewhere. From time to time the cart would slow, but we continued moving. Once I opened my eyes to note water flowing; we were crossing a creek, shallow enough to ford, and then resumed the previous speed. It seemed the longest night of my life. By sunrise, a large growth of trees came into view, tall trees growing in rows, with all underbrush removed. Then I saw the cuttings and tin cans overflowing with latex. This was the rubber plantation mentioned above. In typical fashion, the undergrowth

Figure 21. Burmese bullock cart circa 2003. Photo by author.

had been removed to allow the workers to cut a track and collect the raw white rubber resin. We were in the rubber plantation named Wanetchaung.

Rubber plants were not native to Burma. They were native to Brazil. While working in Brazil in the nineteenth century, an Englishman, Henry Wickham, collected many seeds from there and shipped them to England. In turn they were shipped to Henry Ridley, head of the Singapore Botanical Gardens. The seeds took to the climate and grew so well that rubber flourished throughout Southeast Asia, not only in Malaya but also in Burma. Burma was a natural place for rubber. As in Brazil, the plants were planted in rows over many acres. After twelve years they grew tall, and the latex could be collected. Wanetchaung looked to me like a nice place to hide, as the trees provided cover and the absence of undergrowth made movement easy. We were going there to rest and hide. But we were in for a shock. Once again, events forced us to rapidly change plans.

Figure 22. Wanetchaung rubber plantation, circa 2003. Photo by author.

Figure 23. Rubber tree being tapped for latex. David Stanley from Nanaimo, Canada, CC BY 2.0, via Wikimedia Commons.

In a daring move, General Sakurai, who commanded the Japanese 33rd Division, had sent a regiment (the 214th) of the 33rd Division to isolate Rangoon from the west, but in the fog of war the move failed. General Sakurai, having reached north of Pegu, had felt confident that the 214th Regiment, commanded by Major Okanabu, would trap the Rangoon Garrison by blocking both roads and the towns of Hlegu and Hmawbi. The General's order was to take the rubber plantation and later hook up with the seaborne attack units, thereby completing the encirclement of Rangoon. However, the General lost contact with the regiment. Okanabu knew his orders were to block the Rangoon–Hmawbi–Taukkyan road and all roads leading out of the city, but he was confused. He summoned his radio operator to signal General Sakurai and ask for clarification. But multiple attempts at contact failed, and Okanabu now faced a dilemma. Having stopped the British column at Taukkyan (where we had heard the fighting and had left the road), he took it upon himself to lift the roadblock and move west to encircle the city. This move saved the British Garrison.

Every so often, war plans do not go as smoothly as planned. The lifting of the blockade allowed the Rangoon Garrison to escape the Japanese noose. On the morning of March 8, the retreating British tank regiment, part of the Rangoon Garrison, had been beginning to make progress but had encountered intense fighting. The British-Indian and Gurkha troops tried to dislodge the enemy. To the delight of the British, they cleared the remaining enemy snipers by morning. With much relief and haste, the Rangoon Garrison escaped to Tharrawaddy, a town to the northwest of Prome. I would learn about these events many years later, while I was in Australia.[1] That event was a perfect example of the vagaries of war. In war, whether you survive or not depends more on luck and serendipity than brilliant planning. Some call it fate, some call it the fog of war, which changes history.[2]

---

[1] I purchased several books in Canberra that were unavailable in the U.S. The most valuable was Louis Allen, *Burma: The Longest War 1951–1945* (London: Dent, 1954).

[2] The fog of war worked for the allies, and for a time seemed to work for us.

Figure 24. Author at Taukkyan intersection. Left to Prome; right to Pegu. Photo by Juleen Eichinger.

Oblivious to these military actions, we proceeded through the rubber plantation to the north side, where the bullock-cart driver told us that the offices were located. After a while a clearing appeared: plantation headquarters. We found tables full of sheets of white rubber (adding acetic acid into raw rubber turns the rubber into white sheets, which are then left to dry).

The carts advanced up to the small sheds, rubber plantation labs. In normal times these are pristine, clean places; but now there was the detritus of war. Something bad had happened here the night before. It seems that the workers had left hurriedly. The place was deserted. It appeared that there had been fighting, evidence that British-Indian troops had been here recently, but there was evidence that the Japanese had been here as well. At the clearing were the administrative offices. Danam nervously looked around the huts and carefully walked over to a small shed. He knocked on the flimsy door, and soon a bent-over old Indian man appeared, the caretaker or *durwan*. Danam exchanged greetings and talked to the old man, who appeared anxious, turning his head to look one way and then the other. Danam later explained what it was that they talked about. The old man had

Figure 25. Sheets of rubber hung to dry. Photo by author.

said, "The British army was here a little while ago, they left in hurry. ... Then the Japanese were here too; they came last evening. After ransacking the place for food, they left and went to the west to the railroad and the river." This would be the first time we would cross paths with the advancing invading enemy. "You should leave, as the enemy could be back," the old man said nervously.

The bullock-cart driver hurried us on, saying, "it would be dangerous to linger here." Perhaps he simply wanted to get back to the safety of his village. He was right, though: if the planes came back, they would shoot at us in this exposed clearing. "So, what can we do?" Danam asked. The old man responded, "about a mile from here is the river. You go there and rent a boat." Danam gave the *durwan* four annas, then came back and told the family that we could not stay here. "There is not much time to escape from the rubber plantation," older brother said. We had not had any food since we had left home, and we were all hungry. One of the older sisters opened a can of Norwegian sardines. Given the number of mouths, it was a small amount of food, but it would do.

Danam led us out. I remember leaving the cover of the woodland and going out into the open paddy field. At this time of the year, the fields were mostly dry, as the seeds had not yet been planted. In a few weeks the fields would be water-logged and green with paddy. Crossing the open paddy field was risky and scary. I kept looking up at the sky, as this is where the hostile aircraft would appear. Mother could attend to only one child at a time, but her older daughters helped. As we crossed the railroad tracks, we saw the wrecks of a locomotive engine and carriages, but we kept going to the river bank. The hope was that we could hire a country boat and head north and west. This was the only avenue of escape from Burma; the other routes, far to the north, had been cut off a long time ago. Finally, we arrived at the shore.

Figure 26. Railroad tracks and station at Wanetchaung circa 2003. Photo by author.

After a while we found a large country boat that transported rice and produce from the hinterland to the urban areas. It was a big, tall boat, about 50 feet long and built entirely of teakwood. The bow was curved high, the stern even higher. One man was seated, smoking his cheroot and holding the rudder while other men handled the oars. After money was exchanged, we started to board. Mother was terrified by the narrow plank. The Burmese captain urged us to hurry and then shooed us down to the bottom of the boat. I walked down the plank carrying my little bag. After a hurried move down the narrow stairway to the depths of the boat, we settled in. Deep in the hold it was damp, and it took me a while to find a dry spot. I eventually found one, but it still was dark, damp, and musty. On the main deck there was a small kitchen, but Father and Danam had been warned that we should stay down during the daylight hours because there were hostile villages along the way. These boats were not electrified; the only source of light

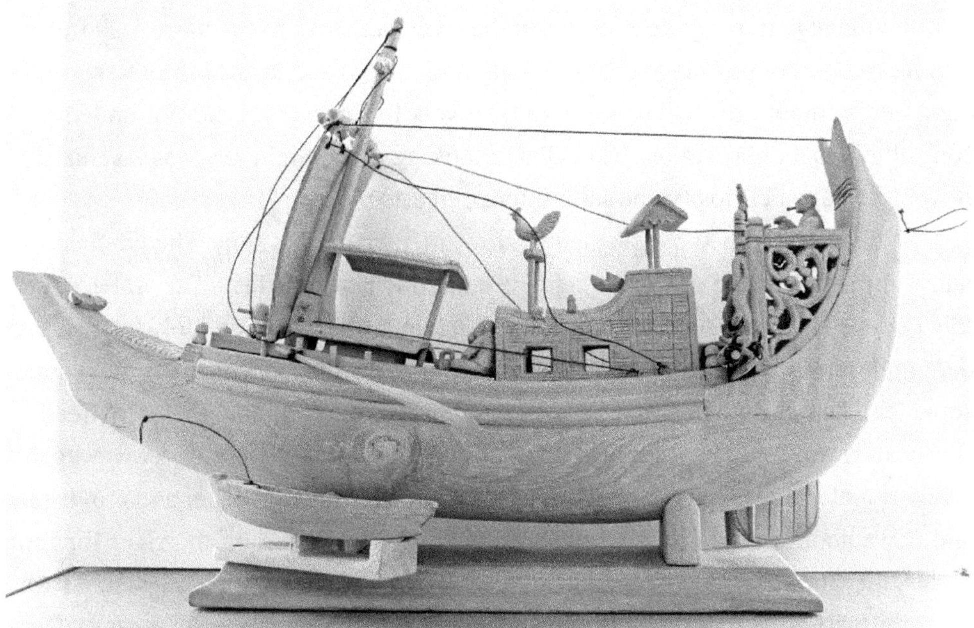

Figure 27. Model of a Burmese country boat, carved from Burmese teakwood. Personal collection. Photo by author.

was the small windows at the wheel house and a hurricane lamp that shed a dull orange light. The tide was rising, which meant that we had to wait a while before we could take off.

We could feel the tide raise the boat; it is surprising how fast the tide rose. When the boat got underway, it rocked and swayed. As the men pushed the boat with long poles into mid-stream, the tide was with us, so that after we got under way it speeded up. There were few boats on the river. The long stay in damp conditions would set off sneezes and colds. Despite warnings to stay below, I went up the ladder to take a peep. We now entered the larger river; this is the junction with the Irrawaddy River. We ate some cold sweet rice packed in banana leaf, then darkness set in. I could hear the drone of planes overhead, and an occasional motorized boat passed by, but it was mostly smaller wooden boats plying the river. But for the lapping of the water against the boat, it was quiet; there was no other sound. The captain warned us not to put in an appearance when we were near a hostile village and to say nothing when the river ran close to the narrow shore. He was more open to us being up on the deck in isolated sections of the river. It was dark, and without city lights, the night sky was full of stars. I did not understand constellations, but laying on the deck and looking at the night sky was fascinating. It would create a curiosity and later interest in astronomy.

Eventually the boat seemed to slow, then came to a stop. The tide had run out. Tidal changes are powerful, and here the tide runs out fast. The water got so low that we could not see the river bank. I got up later to sneak a look, but it was a dark night. We had to wait again till the tide turned. In the morning the crew made some tea, then got the boat ready. It strained at its mooring, then the crew freed it. It rose and swayed due to the rapid inflow of the tide, and we were under way again. As we traveled, the captain stopped at friendly villages to fetch water and provisions and news about the progress of the war. After we had been on the river for four nights, the Burmese captain and his three crewmen grew concerned. The news was not good. Ahead, armed Burmese rebels would make our progress dangerous, and there were Japanese gunboats on the river. Japanese aircraft flew low over the river looking for hostile or British gunboats. As the day passed our chances at survival seemed to decline. Friendly villages were getting difficult to find, and our reserves of food were getting low. At the bottom of the boat it was always damp and smelly, but we had no choice but to stay down. As the tide rose again, Danam negotiated with the captain, who told us that there was a friendly village ahead where he would drop us off. We heard the Burmese crew say that there were Japanese boats behind (this would be the Japanese advance river detachment). Small fast boats passed us from time to time, and we held our breath for fear we would be boarded, but it was the drone of a fast gunboat that would bother us the most. At all stops there were rumors that the Japanese were not far away, but equally concerning were some unfriendly villages where men were armed with burp guns and ancient firearms. Danam had used to go duck and teal hunting here. Although the villagers had only old vintage guns, we had no defense against them whatsoever. Father held a conference and told the family that for our safety we would have to get out of the boat and go to this friendly village. "So, get ready," he told us.

Behind us, a new high-pitched noise of gunboats could be heard. The noise steadily increased, and it became imperative that we find a friendly village to get off the river. At last the boat slowed and the crew, using their long poles, pushed the boat to the small dock. This was Katiya, a small mixed village. Talks with the village headman ensued and, as always, money exchanged hands. We followed Father up a dirt road to a large *basha* (hut), long but not wide. One corner had split bamboo sides, and the split bamboo floor creaked with every step. Mother and Father settled us in, then, speaking in hushed tones, went to one end of the *basha* to hide their money and gold.

Early the next morning I got up to get fresh air, and a shocking scene greeted me. Three Japanese gunboats had weighed anchor at night! Our first brush with the Japanese was surprising and crude: some of the men were naked; the others took off their clothes and jumped into the river to bathe. Even though the villagers were friendly, they were all frightened when the Japanese then came ashore. Our first direct encounter with the barbarian enemy was not pleasant. They were rough and hostile, yelling "Kura, Kura," but we could not understand them. They searched houses, questioned the headman whether there were British or Indian troops, they leered at the young girls, and they roughed up the young boys and men. It was all very scary. The next day the gunboats weighed anchor and, in a deafening roar and spewing water from the exhausts, headed north. The fear subsided, but the village remained uneasy. Katiya was effectively under Japanese control. After a week or so, the headman approached and greeted the men of the household. After the conversation, the men looked downcast; the news was not good. The gunboats were only the advance units; the main body of the Japanese Army would soon take over and occupy the village.

### RETURN TO RANGOON

It was the end. The Japanese were now in full control the country. We could not stay here in this unstable place; it was too primitive, and there was not enough food or medicine. Yet going upriver was not possible because of dacoits, Japanese sympathizers, and the approaching Japanese gunboats. Another family council was held, which led Father to make the decision that we had to take our chances and go home. The thought of returning back and living under Japanese rule was a horrifying prospect. We were uncertain about how we would be treated, as we were both Indian and Christian.

In due course, Danam hired a Burmese boat to go back home to Kamayut, this time a smaller boat. The girls were despondent; they cried all the time and looked at Mother, but she too was crying. We clambered aboard the boat and awaited the morning high tide, when the river would reverse course and go south. In this littoral region, the tidal effect is extreme; the rise and fall can be more than fifteen feet. As the tide rose, the boat swayed and the water lapped at the deck. We clung to the boat as it started to rise and move. As darkness set in, the traffic declined, then all became quiet. At midnight the tide went out, and the boat slowed and stopped altogether. Again we would have to await the next morning's high tide.

Returning to Kamayut was uncertain and depressing. We had been on the run for many weeks. It had taken a toll on all of us. Father looked despondent, shocked, and terrified about what was happening. Things were spinning out of control. He no longer was able to protect his family. In the past he had protected the family's fortune, which meant keeping the savings away from dacoits and the Japanese. From time to time we found him in the rear of the boat looking away, looking westward, dreaming perhaps, wondering what would have been if we had succeeded. He said little, did not want to talk. In addition to fear there was boredom.

As we came closer to Rangoon, we looked for familiar landmarks. The river traffic increased, the noise of aircraft could be heard, and every now and then a patrol boat or gunboat came by. In its powerful wake, our boat swayed from side to side. Finally the smoke stack of the rice mill came into view. The captain left the main channel and moved the boat to the Hlaing River. The crew brought out long poles and slowly guided the boat to the small wooden platform, then tied up the boat. The small wharf had been partially destroyed and was deserted. Our home was about a mile and a half away. We disembarked and huddled on the jetty while Big brother went around trying to glean information about the safety of going home. We had been away from Rangoon on our odyssey for nearly six weeks, traveling by truck and bullock cart, traveling upriver and down again, walking and running and walking still further. We did not know what was happening near our house. The mill was not in operation; there was no power. We found a place by a wall where we settled down and spent several uneasy nights. Finally, Danam returned with enough confidence that it would be safe for us to return home.

Our neighborhood looked ghastly. As we approached, we found our front yard strewn with debris; the house had been broken into and been ransacked. With the exception of items that had been attached to the walls, all the furniture and personal effects were missing, probably stolen. The house was empty. We found a sign on the door written in red Japanese characters, but we did not know what it meant. Japanese were famous for stealing from the people of the lands they conquered. They called captured booty "Churchill supplies" but also stole private property. Weeks later we found out that the sign at our door was ominous: it said that the house was Japanese property and now belonged to the Imperial Japanese Army. Still we settled in. I found my corner and stayed there.

# Chapter 15
# Father Dies

The shock of the last few months took its toll on all of us. It was devastating for Father. Danam knew something was amiss when Father withdrew from the family, looked grim, and became more distant. It was depressing to see his decline and his looking away from the family. He had worked with dedication for almost forty years. His labors had been rewarded with a coronation medal for his faithful work. Now, without work, he was dejected. He feared that his records might fall into the hands of the Japanese administration (GG) and that our house would be declared enemy property and would be seized. That is what happened. Father had paid off the house loan before the war, but we could not argue with the Japanese. All we could do was watch in dread. To compound matters, each day brought more awful weather, which would have a deleterious effect on Father's health. The first physical sign of illness soon appeared: he looked ill, his feet swelled, and his weakness increased by the day.

Danam, the doctor, knew many pharmacists but could not find any of them. The pharmacies had all been located on Mogul Street, which ran the breadth of the city, but the doctors were now all in hiding. His desperate search for digitalis (the heart medicine) in all the places he knew would prove fruitless. Father's face now looked increasingly puffy, and his ankles were swollen. He did not eat much but slept most of the time. Mother tried to cook special meals, mostly soup, but he could not eat. He was fifty-eight years old but looked much older. We moved him from his bedroom to the large living room. He looked lonely, confused, and frightened. While his son constantly looked for medications, Mother turned to traditional herbal medicine. She and Grandmother brought in every type of native healer, faith healer, and medicine man. The healers rubbed herbs and prayed endlessly. Pentecostal preachers rubbed coffee grounds on his chest and prayed endlessly. But he seemed to get worse each day, and the heat and humidity made breathing difficult. Every now and again I caught Mother crying, and at my approach to her she gently shooed me away. Finally she broke down and cried constantly but otherwise she showed little emotion to us.

Daughter Emily sat by the bed and waved a fan to cool Father, but it did not help much. The weather was unbearable. His breathing became labored. One morning Danam sat next to Father and tried to talk to him, to ask if there was something he could do, but father's increasing confusion and disorientation did not yield results. He would cough often and make gurgling sounds; his swelling increased; he hardly moved, and slowly he lapsed into a coma. Now it was the end of May, one of the worst months of the monsoon, when mosquitoes came alive. His breathing slowed and became shallow; later he developed Kussmaul breathing. He was in a terminal state.

In the evening we prayed continuously, and preachers joined us in prayer. We softly sang Baptist hymns:

> Nearer my God to thee,
> Nearer to thee!
> E'en though it be a cross
> That raiseth me.
> Still all my song shall be
> Nearer my God to thee,
> Nearer my God to thee, nearer to thee!

It brought comfort and brought the family together. I cried till I was overcome by sleep. Mother stayed with him all night. Early the next morning he slipped away.

Each of the children was given a task. Mine was to inform the relatives, and my first stop was my Aunt Ava's house across the railroad track, near the river's edge, to inform her and all the extended family. I ran as fast as I could, barefoot (the shoes had worn out months ago, and there were no replacements available).[1] When I came home, I sat by Father's bedside. It was eerily quiet, then I heard gurgling. I jumped up and rushed over to Mother to say he was making noises; is there hope that life would come back? She brushed my hair and told me that this was the death

---

[1] I soon adapted to running barefoot and learned how to make slippers out of old tires.

rattle. She turned away with tears in her eyes. I sat by Father's bedside. Slowly the relatives and friends trickled in. They all sat around the bed, then someone opened a hymnal and softly sang "Rock of Ages" and we prayed again and again. Midday passed, and around 2:00 the hearse arrived. Instead of the somber black hearse of the past, this one was garishly painted saffron and orange, used by Hindus as well as others. The hearse-men wore bright saffron. Their arrival brought wails and loud crying. I cursed the men, but they were only doing their work. Although we knew that he was going to be taken, some of the siblings had the crazy notion that as long as he was in the house he could come back to life.

The journey to the burial grounds was dangerous. The hearse had to go past the railroad tracks and their fortifications. Fear pervaded us, as the railroad was a frequent target for air-raids by RAF fighter bombers. The cemetery also was fraught with danger from air-raids. There were no cars or taxis, so the hearse drove slowly while family and friends walked slowly behind it. Moving through the gauntlet was scary, and we soon quickened the pace to reach the corner of the burial grounds. The preacher arrived and led the mourners in singing "Abide With Me" while the men carried Father's body to the graveside and lowered it into the grave. I ran out crying and tried to grab the leg of one of the bearers; he pushed me away and then the prayer service began. At its end the preacher said "dust to dust" and threw the first handful of dirt; then mother picked up a handful of dirt and threw it on the coffin. I clutched at her sari as she nudged me to do the same. The men took their shovels and threw dirt to cover the wooden coffin while offering prayers. Then they built a mound. There was no headstone; the gravesite was never completed. Finally the family walked away with heads bowed. We sang again:

> Abide with me; fast falls the eventide;
> The darkness deepens; Lord with me abide.
> When other helpless, O abide with me.

But what I remember most was.

> Change and decay in all around I see....

By evening all the mourners had left the house, except for a few of the closest relatives still consoling the family. Even they left eventually, then a mournful silence fell upon us.

The death of my father left a profound impression on me that would persist throughout my life as I struggled with life and had to manage its many challenges.[2] The hymns we sang move me still today, even though my reaction is less religious and more one of remembrance. I also began to become a skeptic. I sometimes wondered about this, and other songs from my childhood (for example, the theme from Red River Valley). I would have dreams that Father was not really dead but was living in another place, another town. He would occasionally appear in my dream, promising to return in due course, but the dream would end. I would wake up sweating, soon saddened to realize that it had only been a dream, and then I would struggle to go back to sleep. This would happen all through my life. I learned that this is a non-psychiatric auditory hallucination.

More sad news was to come. Danam left to live with my cousins, the James family, who had lost both their parents before the war. In a couple of months, I would turn twelve. To be twelve without a father, during a brutal war and a hostile occupation, life would be difficult, but it was not the end. Mother was overcome with grief and had difficulty caring for the brood, but Grandmother was a tower of strength. I was now the eldest son in the house, but I was too young for anyone to say that there was a man in the house. In Asia, not having male friends or relatives in the family was dangerous. Two young men from our church group attached themselves to the family. Mother wanted some male presence, so she accepted the two of them to live with us. They would pose a problem later in the war by taking advantage of my sisters.

---

[2] I often wish I could have talked with my father as an adult. I have pages of questions I wish I could ask him. But I would tell him that his attempt to escape from Rangoon and its failure saved us in the end. Of the thousands of Indians, Burmese, and Anglos who attempted to escape from Burma, few would reach India. Those who arrived there walked into a famine in India. The fact that we had to turn back ultimately allowed us to survive.

# Chapter 16
# Japanese Rule

Now in firm control of Rangoon, the Japanese set up rules and a radio station. The so-called Co-Prosperity Sphere touted by the Japanese was officially called "Senryochi gunsei Jisshi ni kansuru Riku-Kaigun Chūō Kyōtei," but we called it "Gunshi Gumbo." Each day started with the broadcast and required singing of the Japanese national anthem and bowing to the east, to the emperor. Most able-bodied young men were forced to participate; failure meant a visit by the Japanese spy agency, which had spies watching us. After the national anthem came a language course: recitation of the numbers, then a review of the news. The news always began with propaganda, that the British were completely routed and will never come back. Japanese radio controlled our daily lives. Some people had their doubts, however, and some sought to duck the morning regimen. We closed all the doors and peeped through the windows. Japanese patrols passed by every now and then: small, short men with long Arisaka rifles, wearing field caps with gaiters to protect the back of the head and neck (the British called it a neck brace) from the sun. They rarely wore helmets. Anybody who looked suspicious was accosted with cries of "Kura Kura" and beaten, sometimes with bayonets and sometimes with rifles. I tried to get a translation of this phrase, but this generation of Japanese does not know what it stands for or would not tell me. What those words meant, I do not know to this day.

Slowly, people returned to their neighborhoods, but it was still unsafe to go beyond the railroad. A few vendors returned to the market with produce. We got by with scraps of food. Stories circulated about front-line troops being replaced by garrison troops who were a mixture of Japanese and Korean men. Regardless of who they were, they were crude, brutal, and frightening. Sometimes they gathered civilians to watch the bayoneting of suspects, cutting the abdominal wall open and pulling out the intestines, skinning men alive. Aung San's BDA did little to stop the atrocities. In fact, they clapped their hands with delight. The victims were so weak that their cries were muffled, although some wailed and screamed. The pain on their faces would influence my life forever.

The southwest monsoon gathered strength and slowly moved east, in one way bringing relief: no air-raids. But it also brought a mess: increased humidity day by day; swarms of mosquitoes. Because all our mosquito netting had been stolen when our house had been ransacked, we had to get by covered from head to toe. Still they would buzz around and would sound so loud that sometimes at night they would sound like the drone of a plane. The heavy rains brought life to nearly a standstill. Tea-shop gossip declined, and we simply got on with life. Each evening we gathered on the front veranda to hear stories, jokes, and memories of good times. Sometimes we sang—not Indian or Burmese songs but English and American ballads, cowboy songs. This brought us comfort and encouraged us to linger longer into the early moonlit night. When darkness set in, we retreated into the darkness of the house, ate whatever was available, and soon lay down for a few moments of peace. Sleep was never complete but always half awake and half asleep, always alert to the drone of the aircraft.

By mid-September the fierce monsoon petered out, and within the next two weeks the skies cleared. By this time we received information that the British were now out of Burma, completely. In October, air-raids returned and were in full force. It was a strange turn of events. By 1943, the Japanese Zero fighters disappeared from the skies over Rangoon and were replaced with British and American bombers. Previous RAF air-raids had been carried out by twin-engine Blenheim bombers and Hurricane fighters. By late 1943, the bombers were getting bigger and the fighters faster. The US Air Force (USAF) B17 was a huge bomber, powered by four big Curtis horizontally opposed, turbo-charged radial engines. It was a high-altitude bomber, meaning that it could fly as high as 35,000 feet. They belonged to the 10th USAF, and even at 14,000 feet looked huge. Each had a ten-man crew and bristled with machine-gun turrets fore and aft, on top and below. The B29 was an even bigger plane. Both were terror bombers. They came in waves, in formations of nine, in a tight box. Silvery, they were very scary, with a distinctive and ominous noise. These heavy American bombers carried huge bombs, around 8,000 pounds. They came out of the west, from advanced bases in India.

One day I was out late. On my way home, I could hear the bombers. Then I saw them about 35 degrees south, the point of greatest danger, flying to targets beyond the railroad. I dove into a creek of brackish, smelly water and waited till they passed overhead, at which position I would be safe. I got out of the ugly creek and ran home as fast as I could, but no amount of showering could get rid of the smell.

In this bombing season, each day started with reconnaissance flights, and then around 10:00 a.m. (on clear days) the main air-raids would start. To cope with the raids, we ate in early in the morning, cleaned up early, then waited. When heavy bombs fell, they shook the ground like an earthquake. The question was always what targets they wanted to hit. Some raids could last till 3:00 pm. Wave after wave of bombers would come in. The US heavy bombers were most terrifying. The heaviest bombing took place from February to April. Once again people fled the city, not to India but to remote villages away from big city. So, once again, we started the desultory task of leaving the home to seek safety in the jungle, usually in a small friendly village where there were no military targets. It always meant walking or, if we were lucky, hiring a bullock cart.

Together with our James cousins and Danam, we fled to a place called Singu, north of Insein. The village was in the forest; it was tree-covered land, tall teak trees growing towards the sky with some rubber trees and huge peepul trees that spread like an umbrella with purple flowers. Such trees provided cover, from both the sun and the bombers. Singu was a predominantly Burmese Christian village. It appeared peaceful and welcomed us. The village huts were built in a haphazard manner; there was no order. There was a community well in the middle of the village from which people could draw water. The village headman pointed us to a wooden house on the periphery of the village. It had a thatch roof that stretched almost to the ground on two sides; the rest was open. We had brought only what we could carry, unloaded our possessions, and settled in. Each of us rushed to our favorite spot, put down a blanket and a change of clothes, and staked out the place where we would sleep. I left my much-used blanket to mark my spot; the blanket was essential for covering oneself from head to foot to keep the mosquitoes at bay. It felt safe here. My sisters stayed close to the house, rarely venturing outdoors. All outdoor work was done by the boys: gathering wood and finding water. My younger brother was not dependable, so the burden was all mine. There were no servants. Drawing water from the well was a skill I soon acquired. Burmese wells were shallow, around about 8 to 10 feet in diameter, with a mud wall about two feet high providing some protection. Drawing water was a simple matter there; it meant dropping a pail with a rope attached at one end and pulling the water up. Two 20-gallon kerosene cans balanced on a bamboo pole across the shoulders was the means of carrying the water. I could not fill the cans to the fullest, so experimented with how much I could carry and did it twice a day, morning and evening. It took two or three buckets to fill one kerosene can. Old habits die hard: before noon each day, all eyes turned skyward at the slightest noise. At noon there was a break, and we would fill our plates with rice and whatever was available, like dried fish, dried prawns, or lentils. On Sundays, a single small piece of meat and sauce was added.

Figure 28. B29s attacking Rangoon, 22 March 1945 [https://commons.wikimedia.org/wiki/File:468th_Bombardment_Group_Boeing_B-29s_attacking_Rangoon_Burma.jpg]. United States Army Air Forces, Public Domain, via Wikimedia Commons. For a photo of the B29s attacking Rangoon in 1944, see https://commons.wikimedia.org/wiki/File:India-b29s-rangoon-raid.jpg.

Early one night we heard planes, first one, then more. I had fallen into an open sewer a day or so earlier, and was not feeling well; my lungs were tight and breathing was strained. Unknown to me, there were weeds I was allergic to, possibly ragweed. My sister later related the events of the evening: by nightfall I was sicker; I shivered and developed a high fever; by night I was delirious; my breathing was difficult; soon I "lapsed into deep sleep, into a coma." Mother summoned Danam, who examined me and explained that I was suffering from pneumonia. He injected me with the last vial of camphor in oil and said "if this does not do, it will be over." The sky lit up with search lights. Soon ground-fire started. Much to our surprise and chagrin, the bombs were falling close to the village. The airport, the bombing target, was just three miles away. Due to the intensity of the bombing, the family all fled to the community shelter, but my sister Kamala braved the air-raid and stayed with me all night, held my hand, and rubbed mustard oil (it had a peculiar odor) on my chest. The air-raid intensified, with more planes diving to the target. The noise increased, the falling bombs shook the ground, and I woke up briefly. Kamala held my hand and later told me that, before I passed out again, I had murmured for her to go to the shelter in spite of the bombers' screeches. Not till the planes left did she take shelter.

The next morning, I started to improve: my breathing was better. But it would be an exhausting recovery. It would be a week before I recovered fully. In retrospect, I do not think that the "camphor in oil" did anything; my sister's caring for me through the night helped more than the injection. It was strange what passed for good medicine in those days. Later in life I received injections of dilute Arsenic as a treatment for my asthma.[1]

In the village, food was always in short supply. Even in the good days, the supply chain had been poor and erratic; now it was downright sporadic. Medicine, soap, and other sundries vital to everyday life were limited and dwindling. Weeks passed before the bombing abated and it would be safe for us to return home.

---

[1] Looking back, I do not believe arsenic was medicinal. My later medical training showed that a number of medicines were used that probably did not do much.

To worsen matters, the Japanese launched a plan to remove whatever wealth was left in Burma. They withdrew all old colonial authority currency (issued by the Reserve Bank of India) and issued worthless Japanese notes. It was a financial blow to many families who had scrimped and saved to survive hard times. Moreover, the new currency notes were not accepted by all merchants, which exacerbated acute shortages and caused hyperinflation. People had little confidence in the Japanese currency. It was printed on crude paper and did not buy much. As rampant inflation took hold, money had to be carried in gunny sacks to buy the bare essentials. Sometimes prices doubled from one week to next. High-grade fine rice was no longer available, only third-grade rice with 50 percent broken rice. It was not appetizing; when cooked it became like gruel. People hoarded gold, but the punishment for owning old rupees or gold was draconian: death. Being charged with spying also could bring jail or death.

By 1943, the war had gone on for two years, and living was a challenge every day. Toward the end of the year the bombing slowed down, but the country had changed and continued to change. The long occupation and shortages of food and medicines made people desperate. If you got sick, more than likely you would succumb to disease with no expectation of recovery. This also was a very dangerous time for young men, as the Japanese needed labor. Even at my young age I had to find work, not just to earn money but to avoid being conscripted into slave labor. If I had a work pass, I could escape that fate.

Figure 29. Currency notes issued by the Japanese Occupation Government. Personal collection.

# Chapter 17
# The Rat Catcher, the Plague

*Ring around the rosies*
*A pocket full of posies*
*Ashes, Ashes*
*We all fall down.*

*So Nature killed many through corruption*
*Death came driving after her and dashed all to dust*
*Kings and knights, emperors and popes:*
*He left no man standing, whether learned or ignorant;*
*Whatever he hit stirred never afterwards,*
*Many a lovely lady and their lover-knights*
*Swooned and died in sorrow of death's blow.*
*For god is deaf nowadays and will not hear us,*
*And for our guilt men to dust he grinds good.*

The Plague ("pestilence") between 1347 and 1351 destroyed approximately twenty million people (30–50% of the population) in Europe (no records are available). They died from the Black Death—so named in the year 1800. It devastated cities and kingdoms. Now plague had broken out in Rangoon, about a mile and a half from home.

Not much was known about this deadly disease until A.E.J. Yersin, a Swiss bacteriologist, and Kitasato, his Japanese counterpart, described the organism thus: it is a gram-negative, (red) aerobic (can function in a low oxygen environment), and facultatively anaerobic, rod-shaped, non-spore-forming bacteria belonging to a class of bacteria called Enterobacteriales. These organisms foment glucose, are oxidase-negative, and reduce nitrates to nitrites. The gut of the rat is the primary reservoir of the infection, and the flea Xenopsylla Cheopis picks it up when it feeds on an infected rat; the inflected flea then bites a human, transferring the sickness to humans. Fortunately, the maximum altitude a flea can jump is 6 inches.

In late 1943, Danam called an emergency meeting of the men to report that "the Japanese and their contractors are seizing young men and boys off the street to work on the infamous death railway." He looked at me and said, "You better get a pass from the Japs; to do that you have to work for the Japanese." He himself, in spite of his fear and loathing of the Japanese, had taken a position with the Japanese occupation health service. He did it because it would keep him from being conscripted. It also facilitated removal of the placard on our house declaring it Japanese property. That is how I became a rat catcher.

In late 1942–43, the occupation of Burma was not going well for the Japanese. The vaunted "Churchill supplies" on which the Japanese had first depended after they occupied Rangoon were now exhausted; the good days were over for them. Their long lines of communication from Saigon often proved tenuous. Allied submarines were sinking Japanese freighters at an alarming rate, the war in Burma was at a stalemate, the need for supplies desperate. In order to assure a risk-free supply line, the Japanese would embark on a most treacherous, murderous venture: the building of the notorious Death Railway, also known by the British as the Thai-Burma railroad.

The idea of building a railway to connect Thailand and Burma, to enhance trade, was first proposed at the turn of the twentieth century by the British but was abandoned in light of the cost. The proposed railroad would start in Kanchanaburi in Thailand and end at Thambyuzayat in south Burma. The Japanese engineers knew it would be a daunting task, for they had no experience in road-building in the tropical jungle. Like the Germans, they went looking for slave labor to cut through the forbidding malaria-infested jungle. The Japanese would resort to the most brutal methods to obtain labor, second only to the Nazi death camps; the building of the railroad would go down in history as one of the evilest episodes in human history, and a war crime of gargantuan proportions.

The Japanese started with British, Australian, and other allied POWs who had been captured in Malaya and Singapore, but that was not enough, so they looked to recruit local labor, often by false pretenses. Asian labor contractors grabbed young men off the streets of Rangoon. Men sought to avoid being captured, always looking for a way to avoid the Japanese, and one way was to work for some agency of the occupation authority. The British colonial administration would later conclude that the "independent" Burmese government (headed by puppet President Ba Maw, who called himself the Head of State [Adipadi] and was supported by Aung San) was complicit in effecting this ghastly and horrible deed. They helped the Kempeitai (the Japanese Gestapo) by grabbing young boys and men off the street, promising to feed and pay them well; and then the boys and men were sent away, most never to be seen again. Some young men fell for the story put out by the Burmese collaborators; others tried to escape by hiding in the jungle. It was only after the war that the truth would be revealed, that thousands had died of starvation and disease. Many young men simply disappeared. In the post-war era, when the numbers were tallied up, it was estimated that between 100,000 to 200,000 Asians died in building the railway. Thai authorities note that more than 100,000 Asian bodies are buried on in a separate cemetery, unkempt, across from the well-preserved memorial for allied prisoners.

Poor sanitation, lack of medicine, and abysmal medical care would bring horrible tropical diseases to the fore. Cholera was ever-present, killing people all through the war; there were always one or two deaths each day in town. More deadly was the plague. The population of rats outgrew people and multiplied in enormous numbers. The houses being built so close together facilitated this. Plague followed the Japanese Army. Some of it was the fault of the Japanese themselves, who had experimented with the bacteria and used it against the Chinese as a weapon of war. Now, from their experimentation and the lack of medical care, plague followed war as night followed day. It took hold in congested villages, raged through whole towns, and soon would affect the army. Whatever the source of plague, the Japanese were now desperate, and they dealt with it in a unique way. They did not have the medical supplies or medical personnel to contain the epidemic. Instead, when a suspicious death occurred, Japanese teams moved in aggressively to the house, surrounded the property, and summarily removed all the inhabitants by force (these people were never seen again). Japanese epidemic-control teams arrived, the men suited up with jumpsuits, jack-boots, gloves, caps, and masks to fumigate the entire area. Coolies were conscripted to dig shallow trenches 4 feet long and three feet deep, then sheets of steel were placed in the trench to create a barrier extending above the surface of the earth, completely isolating the house (this supposedly was to keep the infected fleas from escaping, as they could only fly six inches high). What effect this had in containing the spread was not known.

Danam found me a job with the same unit. Plague was raging at a place called Thaming,[1] a mile and a half from our house. I walked the distance, either by road or up the railroad. To the west of the railroad was open grassland, and neither route was entirely safe, for running along the railroad tracks was risky. The program was to remove infected rats, so each morning I went out to the tract assigned to me. I had to distribute wooden boxes containing bait, and each day bring back the traps from the previous night to the health center—just a thatched hut, open on all sides, containing 55-gallon drums half filled with boiling water. I was made to dump the rats into a 55-gallon drum, then pick up the dead rats, cut off the tail, and present it to the overseer. I have no memory of the pay, only that it was with the cheap inflated Japanese currency. It was disgusting work. What's more, I wonder why I did not get infected.

My encounter with plague. On one work day I walked to the far end of my route. I could not find the trap. Curious, I walked up the bamboo hut step and looked inside: there a young man was lying perfectly still, apparently quite ill. He had no clothes on and seemed to be in pain. I kept looking down at his groin, then noticed the lumps (buboes) there. I knew it was bad, that the man was dying. Not knowing what to do, but scared, I returned to the station, cleaned myself and went home.

Handling the dead rats filled me with revulsion. I would come home feeling sick. I could not get over the smell; even after showering I still felt unclean. I knew this much: the fleas when hungry left the rat and went looking for a blood meal. I was told at work that the flea could only fly six inches high, but nevertheless I constantly kept feeling my groin for lumps. For protection and without any medical evidence, I kept a candle at my bedside. If I felt an itch, I would pour hot wax over the red spot on the foot or ankle, even though there was no proof that this

---

[1] My half-brother took me by hand to work at the containment center; that got me a work permit that prevented me from being grabbed by a labor contractor.

would kill the bacteria (Yersenia Pestis). Many years later, in the fourth year of medical school, I found out how lucky I was to escape from the dreaded plague.

The plague comes in two forms: one, the less lethal bubonic plague; and the other, the more lethal pneumatic type, which was deadly and led to a painful death. The bubonic type may have been less lethal, but it was also painful and often, in the end, also resulted in death. The buboes (tennis ball sized) caused masses in the groin and armpits. They would grow rapidly and become excruciatingly painful. The patient would grow progressively ill with fever, fall semi-conscious, and finally, before death, the buboes would burst open, spreading the disease. The deadliest form of the disease, the pneumatic type (called septicemic plague), causes the lungs to fill with fluid and the patient to drown in his own body fluids. As part of the symptom complex, it causes inter-vascular clotting of the small arteries, causing systemic small blood clots in the small arteries, turning fingers and toes black (hence the name "black death").

I am thankful that I did not catch cholera or the plague, strange and fortunate. I still wrestle with notion that the Japanese may have brought the infection to Burma from China with Unit 731. As an adult I read a book called *Factories of Death* about the actions of the infamous Unit 731 of the Kwantung Army and the terrible things that the Japanese did to Chinese civilians.[2] Very similar to their German counterparts, they tortured the Chinese, infected them with deadly diseases; and Japanese doctors would record the results so that they could be informed in their future campaign in the tropics.

Not every day went smoothly at work; there were many hazards. At the height of the epidemic, a part of the job was checking incoming passenger buses for suspicious people with obvious illness. Doing this one day, I ordered a sick-looking Burmese officer of the Burma Defense Army out of the bus to check for evidence of infection; he became enraged at a little "Kala" boy ordering him around, so he took his gold-gilded sword and hit me on the top of my head. It would be a lesson

[2] Sheldon H. Harris, *Factories of Death: Japanese Biological Warfare, 1932–45, and the American Cover-up* (London: Routledge, 1994).

to be careful.[3] At work I also was witness to Japanese army discipline, which often was brutal. For example, occasionally an officer's car (which, as it turned out, were captured British Humber vehicles) would come to the station, and if soldiers and other ranks failed to salute, the officer would turn the car around, alight, call up the careless soldier, and bark at him. Soon the soldier would be trembling at attention, and the officer would slap him so hard that he fell; each time he got up the officer would slap him again, multiple times, until the shaking soldier begged for mercy. I knew I had to be careful to never look directly at officers.

Sometime later I developed swelling of the legs and the skin broke down, soon taking on the appearance of lizard skin. At times the skin exuded a gelatinous (protein) fluid and the legs became tingly and painful, ultimately leaving some permanent scars. I was terrified that I had some sort of plague. Thankfully I was diagnosed "just" with beri beri, a vitamin deficiency, which makes the skin break down and weep and leads to a potbelly so large that the extremities look like sticks. It looked ugly, but I was relieved that it was not some deadly disease.

Figure 30. American fliers at Fukuoka Prison suffered this fate just after the Emperor announced surrender. Time, Inc., Public Domain, via Wikimedia Commons.

Figure 31. Japanese soldiers "finishing off" Indian troops with the bayonet after they had been shot by firing squad before bodies were tipped into the pit on the right. Imperial War Museum, Public Domain, via Wikimedia Commons.

[3] The Burmese puppets were just as bad as or worse than their Japanese masters, and not to be messed with.

# Chapter 18
# Fourth Year of the War

By early 1944, the war was intensifying and getting ever closer to us. We heard about intense fighting at the India-Burma border, and the air war escalated. Allied air-raids were becoming more frequent, as the allies moved their air bases closer to their targets. Previously it took some four to six hours to get to their targets; now, as the front advanced, air bases got closer. At times the raids lasted almost all day, making our lives even harder. There were reports of deaths from starvation, and the quality of rice continued to deteriorate, although with an empty stomach you ate what was available. Cooking and eating had to be done before the long raids; life meant planning your day around the air-raids.

The war was not going well for the Japanese. There was evidence that the Rangoon Garrison (Japanese) was thinned out, and the absence of Japanese soldiers became noticeable. It was a relief that there were fewer Japanese soldiers roaming the countryside looking for food, women, and booty.[1] The hitherto marauding soldiers now were supporting the front line. But when the soldiers did come, they appeared more desperate and leaner and hungrier. Grandmother kept her broom at hand to protect her chickens. On all fronts, the Axis powers were in retreat: from Russia, Poland, the Caucasus, and the South Pacific Islands. The Japanese in the Pacific were in full retreat; the island-hopping war by the Americans met with great success.

The political winds were changing as well. The Burmese enthusiasm for the Japanese was wearing thin, and the Bamar soldiers' romance with their Japanese masters was coming to an end. Japan had promised Burma independence, in return for cooperation from the Thakins. However, the Japanese never intended keep their promise of full independence. In fact, it was a farce, a phony independence. The Burmese politician Ba Maw had been named "President and Supreme

---

[1] Japanese solders constantly would ask us for "jiggy jiggy askanay" (sex), leering at young girls and even young boys.

Commander of Independent Burma," and General Aung San became Defense Minister.[2] The Burmese were only hired puppets, though,[3] and the Ba Maw government had to get clearance from the Japanese Army for any dictates.[4] Eventually, the turncoat Burmese collaborators knew that the war was not going well for the Japanese, and so they betrayed their former masters, going into hiding and secretly plotting against them. Some members of the Burma Defense Army became armed robbers, looting and robbing farms. Japanese soldiers too were "living off the land," arbitrarily taking food supplies from farmers, seizing transportation, and forcing men into slave labor camps or forcing them to spy on neighbors. For ordinary people, this added a new dimension, a new worry, a new angst.

Lack of medical care heightened the misery of life. The things so many of us take for granted, like medicines and dental care, were unavailable to us. Ultimately, more people would die from lack of medical care than as a result of actual warfare. Dental care was even worse. I developed a tooth infection; the entire right side of my jaw was swollen. The pain was excruciating. Things people do in such circumstances were pretty gruesome: they tied a string around the tooth and attached it to a door, then slammed the door shut. It did not work. I passed out. Finally, someone suggested that I go to Lamadaw, to a Chinese "dentist." There, a couple of people held me down while the dentist took mechanic's pliers and pulled the tooth out. My mouth was full of pus, revolting. Today you would be given penicillin and such infection would be minimized or cured.

---

[2] The Supreme Defense Council was established in August of 1943. It consisted of Army leaders (Colonel Aung Than was Vice-Minister for National Defense; Colonel Shu Maung was Commander of the National Army; Colonel Hla Maung was Chief of General Staff; and Lt. Colonel Boh Yan Naing was Chief of Operations) and Cabinet Ministers. See Intelligence Bureau, Government of Burma, *Burma During the Japanese Occupation* (Simla, 1943).

[3] Aung San is said to have struck Ba Maw at a cabinet meeting but could not be disciplined because Aung San received his commission from the Emperor of Japan (*Burma During the Japanese Occupation*, 157).

[4] Data obtained from US National Archives: Interrogation of Ba Maw, 22 May 1946, Sugamo Prison, Tokyo. Japan. "The Japanese High command was authorized to nullify any act of the Burmese and to direct that affirmative measures be taken if necessitated by the military reasons. The Japanese could execute arbitrary control over the national communications, transportation, utilities and the instruments of the government."

War took its toll on everyone in the family. My brother Danam would break under the stress. What demons possessed him I will never know. He took to drink but somehow survived the war. Margaret, my oldest half-sister took ill. The lovely, warm woman had married just before the war and had moved to the city, where she lived in a majority Indian community. It was a congested and unsanitary place. She contracted Typhoid, an infection of Salmonella bacterium, found in contaminated drinking water. One day she no longer could work, then developed high fever and chills. Her husband brought her back from Kalabasti (Rangoon's Indian quarters), and Danam took over her management. He took her to the living room of the James family's house where she lay very quietly on the bed. She had high fever and shivers, and no interest in food or drink. Danam confided to one of my cousins that he suspected that she had Typhoid. He tried to get her to a hospital but was turned away; hospitals were for Japanese only. All he could do was continue to check her fever and her heartbeat, and keep watch on the size of her abdomen.[5] He feared the consequences. Today, treatment would involve a tube in the stomach and intravenous antibiotics to keep her hydrated, but that was not an option in these desperate times. Danam's worst fears were realized: her abdomen started to swell. With his full open palm, he tapped her abdomen; she turned ashen, winced, and cried out in pain. She fell deep into a coma and then her abdomen grew in size (due to peritonitis). Danam knew the symptoms well; he knew that the end was near. He walked away hiding his tears. By morning she became unresponsive, and she died late that evening. Her death in the midst of the war was devastating. She was a wonderful person who had cooked and cared for us. I had missed her when she had married left home. But luck was not with her. She left four young girls behind, who would further tax the families' resources. Like with Father two years before, we sang "Abide With Me" before burying her near Father in the family plot. This grief was getting all too familiar.

---

[5] The most feared complication of Typhoid is that the bacteria localize in the patches of lymphoid tissue in the small intestine and cause ulcers to develop there, which then perforate and pour the intestinal contents into the peritoneal cavity, resulting in the dreadful peritonitis. Without hospital care, chances of survival are nil.

In the summer of 1944, we stayed in the house even as bombing resumed. We were exhausted. It was getting expensive and stressful to flee to the villages, so that spring Mother said, "We will stay. We can go Aunt Ava's. Her house is near the river and more remote." Mother was now without the head of the household, with a house full of girls. Older half-brother Danam was living with the James cousins, to protect them. Older half-sister Margaret, who had been such a great protector who had cooked and cared for the younger ones, was dead. I was now a teenager, the oldest man in the house. The glue that had held the family together by force of character, that had kept the family together, had been Father. Now that he was gone, there was no breadwinner. All the gold and jewels that Father had given to Mother were sold, and now there was little left. The older sisters would normally take over to hold and protect the younger members.

One episode in December of 1944 sticks in my mind, providing a lesson to guide me for the rest of my life. Early on December 14, 1944, the weather was cool and crisp as usual. The drone of planes could be heard in the distance; it would be another day of air-raids, I thought, but then I realized the planes were flying a different route. I looked to the northwest, but the drone of the planes was coming from the northeast. I ran to the front of the house and could not only hear but also see the planes in the northeast, apparently heading east to west, a strange trajectory. I was puzzled. Instead of seeking shelter, I felt safe because the planes were so far to the north and beyond the target range; there were no Japanese fighters in the air; and there were no anti-aircraft guns, as the planes were out of range. Nothing much happened for a few minutes till suddenly the planes approached abeam of our house, and a strange thing happened: I counted eleven gleaming silver Super-fortresses, flying in a V formation. The heavily laden big super-bombers flew majestically to the west and north, unimpeded by anti-aircraft fire or Japanese fighters. Fascinated, I kept watching, and then, just after they passed abeam, the starboard engine of one of the bombers at the tail end of the "V" formation caught fire. The plane belched black smoke and lost altitude, then a second engine caught fire. The plane soon fell out of formation and started to dive. I spotted a small white parachute. No sooner had this plane exploded than a second and third and fourth plane all belched smoke, turned to the left, and fell out of formation. In quick succession, four of the eleven B29s had lost altitude, with smoke streaming from their engines, had started to spiral, and then, screaming, had disappeared. It was the most planes I saw crash in a single raid. We eagerly waited for the news from both sides.

The Japanese gloated about the glorious success. That evening the Japanese radio—with much fan-fare, announced that "our gallant and brave air men and defenders had great success in shooting down the big bombers, a great achievement and victory." A Japanese news release at the time crowed:

> In broad daylight at about 1-20 o-clock (Nippon Time) in the afternoon of December 14, a formation of 11 B-29s flying at an altitude of about 6,000 meters audaciously conducted an assault over Rangoon area, but our crack ground batteries, which intercepted the enemy raiders, giving full play to their skillful and effective firing tactics, instantaneously hit and shot down five of them in rapid succession. The citizens of Rangoon, who were fortunate enough to witness the enemy planes enveloped in fire and crash down to the ground to meet their doom, were astounded at our impregnable air-raid defence structure and at the same time clapped their hands with thundering shouts of joy upon seeing the end of the enemy raiders. It is revealed that just twenty rounds of anti-aircraft shell were fired by our units, shooting down five out of eleven gigantic four-engined enemy bombers. This is indeed a marvelous feat accomplished by our ground battery and it will not be an exaggeration to say that it is a world record in percentage in the history of shooting down planed by ground fire in a single raid. ("6 Out Of 11 B-29s Downed Over Rangoon. Marvellous Achievement of Our Crack Ground Battery")

Of course they were lying. There were no Japanese fighters in the air, for the air defense was non-existent at this location. That night, curious, we crowded around the radio awaiting news from the other side. South East Asia Radio based in Ceylon (Sri Lanka) made no mention of any planes lost. Danam stayed up late for any news, listening surreptitiously to the Allied radio, and there never was any report of the great loss of allied planes. I thought it strange that neither side was telling the truth. This was first time I had my doubts about friend and foe alike.

What happened that night remained a mystery to me, all but forgotten until, many decades later, while working at the Veterans Hospital in Michigan, the story came alive again. Serendipity brought me in contact with an American veteran who had served in the China-Burma-India (CBI) theater of war operations. He talked about the war and recommended that I subscribe to the CBI veteran's newsletter. I did, and in one of those issues, an American airman—one of the men who had parachuted and survived—wrote about his capture and imprisonment in Rangoon jail. I then wrote an article about what I had witnessed. Through subsequent correspondence[6] I learned from him firsthand of the long story. Briefly: the 12th squadron of the 10th Air Force had set out on a flight, scheduled to bomb targets in Bangkok. But the weather in Bangkok was overcast, and their secondary targets were in Rangoon. What caused the planes to crash was a technical issue: the veteran told me that the bomb fuses were wrongly set, and additionally the bomb release mechanism malfunctioned, causing the bombs to become trapped in the bomb bay and explode prematurely under the plane. This caused five of planes to explode, and only one of the eleven B29s returned to base. That I would witness the event and would find the facts almost forty-five years later was astonishing. The man I spoke with was one of the men whom I had seen parachute that day so long ago. The moral to the story is that governments don't always tell all, especially if the news is unfavorable. I learned to believe in what you see, not what you hear or read. I learned to read between the lines. It would stand me in good stead in life.

[6] Some years ago, his wife wrote to me, and I still have her letter.

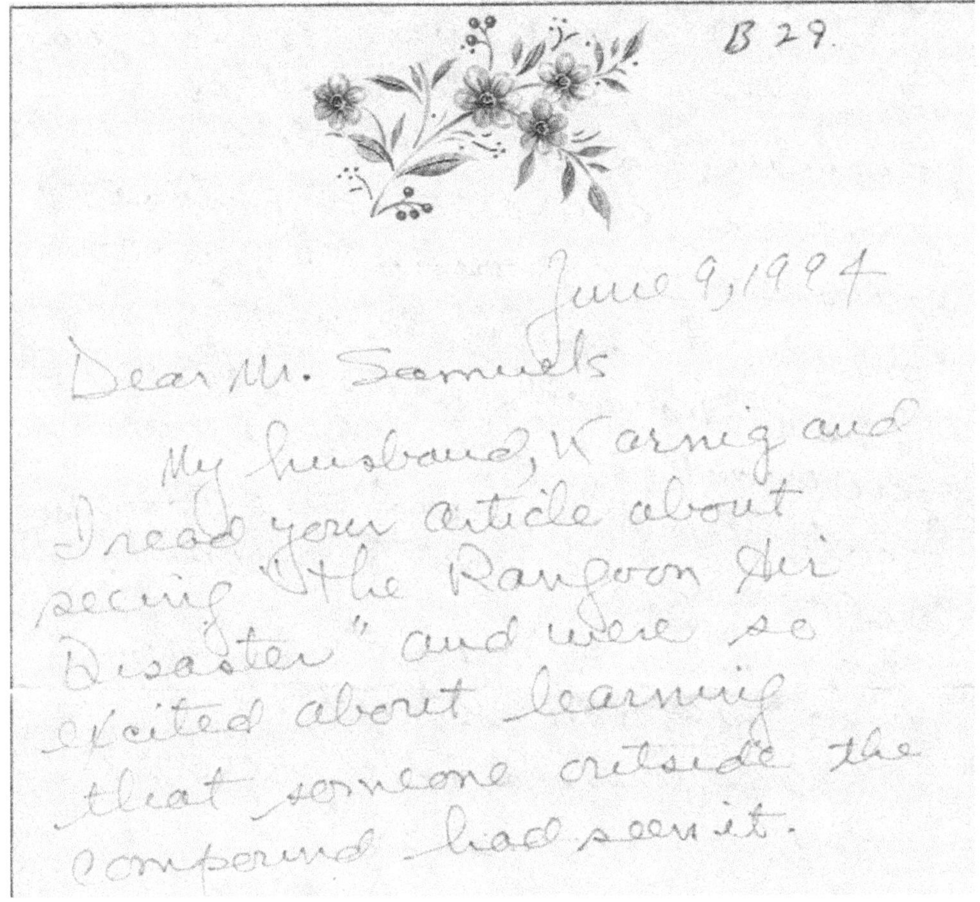

B29.

June 9, 1994

Dear Mr. Samuels

My husband, Warnig and I read your article about seeing "the Rangoon Air Disaster" and were so excited about learning that someone outside the compound had seen it.

Figure 32. Letter from wife of downed B29 pilot. Personal collection.

# Chapter 19
# The Tide of War Reverses

*The battles for Kohima and Imphal turned the tide of war.*
*They took place in one of the remotest parts of India, along the Burma border.*

War had raged since 1941, and by 1944 the war in Burma was at a stalemate. General Renya Mutaguchi, of the Northern Command at Maymyo, despite an endless supply of sake and geisha girls, was getting restless. He possessed intelligence reports suggesting that he could easily achieve victory against the British in northeast India, specifically at Imphal and Kohima. He tried to prevail on General Kawabe in Rangoon to allow him to wage this battle and thereby gain "Churchill supplies" for the troops. But Kawabe (and later Kimura) believed that this was too risky and so informed Southern Command in Saigon. The persistent Mutaguchi bypassed Saigon and contacted Army Headquarters in Tokyo, receiving their permission to attack northeast India.[1]

Mutaguchi entered into a collaboration with the INA (Indian National Army) leader Subhas Chandra Bose. He induced the INA (former allied soldiers from Malaya and Singapore, now allied with the Japanese) to participate in an attack on northeast India. Support for the INA was mixed in Burma, mostly confined to the Indian and especially Bengali people. Our family was deeply suspicious of the group, as they acted like the Japanese toward the civil population. Moreover, Chandra Bose was sympathetic to Nazism; he lived in Germany. Intense debate revolved around whether the civil population supported their goals, and they did

---

[1] Just before the operation against Imphal in March, 1944, Major General Seizo Arisue, chief of the 2nd Department of the Japanese Army General staff, opposed the operation. According to Ex-Lieutenant General Masatane Kanda, chief of the Military Affairs Department of the Army General Staff, the Operations Department tended to disregard the opinions of the Intelligence Department. "They planned operations based on their own views, sometimes collecting information they needed by themselves. ... [they] claimed that the work of the Intelligence Department was focused on political information, did not supply the materials required for operations. ... But ... the Operations Department ... did not make it clear what information they needed" and therefore "gathered information based on guesswork." Kotani, *Japanese Intelligence in World War II*, 101–02.

have their supporters. A women's unit of the INA (the Rani-ki-Jansi) had appropriated and was quartered in the same place that I had sustained the snake bite. Margaret shut all the doors and windows and swore under her breath about the duplicity of Indian collaborators. This terrified us. We feared the wrath of the Japanese if we overtly opposed the INA.

In great secrecy, General Mutaguchi planned his attack. It was a risky adventure to approach the Indian border, as it was some distance from Rangoon and Maymyo. There were no roads allowing access to the area; the border area was dense jungle, rife with wild animals and typhus, malaria, dengue, and other tropical diseases. The logistics were daunting: like in Roman times, all supplies had to be carried by mule and man, then the formidable Chindwin River had to be crossed. It was a desperate gamble. Mutaguchi mustered three of his most seasoned divisions that had conquered Burma (the 31st, 33rd, and 15th), accompanied by one INA division, for the attack on Nagaland, Manipur, and Assam in northeast India. He believed, based on the earlier rout of the British in Burma, that he could gain another victory, could gather booty, and, by threatening India, could force Britain to withdraw from Asia. If northeastern India could be brought under Japanese control, the British supply line linking Burma to India could be cut, and the effective American effort to supply the pro-American Chinese government would be in peril. Japan's Imperial headquarters in Tokyo was not keen on the invasion, but the general's influence with the imperial Japanese court persuaded the Burma command to go along with the poorly conceived plan.

The Japanese 15th Army opened the new front in East India in March 1944. The main thrust was against Imphal and its plain; capturing Kohima, the capital of Nagaland, would sever the essential road connection from Burma to northeast India. When news of the campaign reached Rangoon, we were horrified, for if the British-Indian Army lost this last outpost, we would lose all hope of the return of democracy and would live under the Japanese for the foreseeable future.

British-Indian defenses were weak, but the Eastern Command began to rapidly built up the area. We prayed and hoped.[2]

## THE BATTLE

The border between India and Burma was never fully developed. There were no all-weather roads in this region. On the Burmese side, the fair-weather road stopped at Tiddim, in the Chin State. On the Indian side, the major city was Imphal and its plain, and from there a fair-weather road went north to Nagaland. The Nagas were a fierce tribe living in the remote area of the northeast. They had converted to Christianity but were still head-hunters. They had developed a bond with the British but did not like the Indians or the Burmese.

The overall commander of the British 14th Army was General William Slim, an able officer who would turn out to be one of the best generals of WWII. Lieutenant-General Geoffrey Scoones commanded the 17th, 20th, and 23rd Indian Divisions at Imphal, later joined by the 5th Indian Division. The British colonel in charge of the Kohima garrison (Hugh Richards) was surprised by the presence of enemy troops and hurriedly gathered a scratch force consisting of half-strength units. These included British troops (West Kent, numbering 400) and Punjabis, Assamese, a company from Maharashtra, and the Karen V force. In total, allied combat forces numbered fewer than 2,500. The various divisions had not trained together as a unit. Kohima consisted of seven hills. It was densely forested, with tall trees and thick ground cover. It was a beautiful but remote country with poisonous snakes and insects and disease, including malaria, the dreaded black water fever[3] (caused by Plasmodium Falciparum), typhus, and dengue. It was also home to the great hornbill.

---

[2] Codebreakers at Bletchley Park warned in advance that the Japanese had reinforced their troops in the region with four additional divisions and seemed poised for an attack on Kohima and Imphal in Assam. Michael Smith, *The Emperor's Codes: The Breaking of Japan's Secret Ciphers* (NY: Arcade Publishing, 2000), 243.

[3] Of the four species causing malaria, it was the deadliest.

The Japanese assembled their three divisions, 30,000 men, coolies to carry supplies, and hundreds of cattle (to provide meat for the troops) and mules. Using stealth and surprise, they waged a savage battle, quickly laying siege to Imphal and then isolating Imphal from Kohima. Accompanied by clashing cymbals and shouting "Banzai, Banzai," the Japanese attacked.

The siege nearly crippled the British-Indian forces. The defenders beat back the attacks night and day, for two weeks. Casualties mounted, especially on the Japanese side.[4] Even then it was hair-raising: when the Japanese were low on ammo, they took to bayonet, sword, and even sticks. In an epic defense, the allies, out-gunned and surrounded, persisted. They gave ground day by day, every day their perimeter shrunk, but always they beat back the attack. In spite of losses, the spirit of the defenders grew; they lost whole companies but hung on. Japanese radio declared victories and crowed that soon they would defeat the enemy and take control of Bengal. This news was devastating to us.

The defenders—short on food, ammunition, and medical supplies—kept the fight going. Now the allies had a new weapon: both RAF and USAF air power. The Allied air force kept supplies flowing to support the defenders, and they were finally able to break siege of Garrison Hill. This resulted in a total rout for the Japanese. For the Japanese, there was no prospect of reinforcements or resupply of ammunition or medical supplies. More Japanese soldiers died of disease than from gunfire. But General Mutaguchi stubbornly refused to admit defeat. Then the Japanese chain of command crumbled: in a remarkable break with protocol, the divisional commander of the Japanese 31st Division, Lieutenant-General Kotoku Sato, broke with his senior commander in faraway Maymyo, disobeying the general and shouting that he was going to stop the carnage. Sensing how hopeless it was, he halted the attack and started the long retreat, which brought the war to an end in upper Burma and would constitute one of Japan's worse defeats in the entire war.

---

[4] Many books were written of this battle. I collected five books describing the battle long after the war, and there are still pamphlets and books being published.

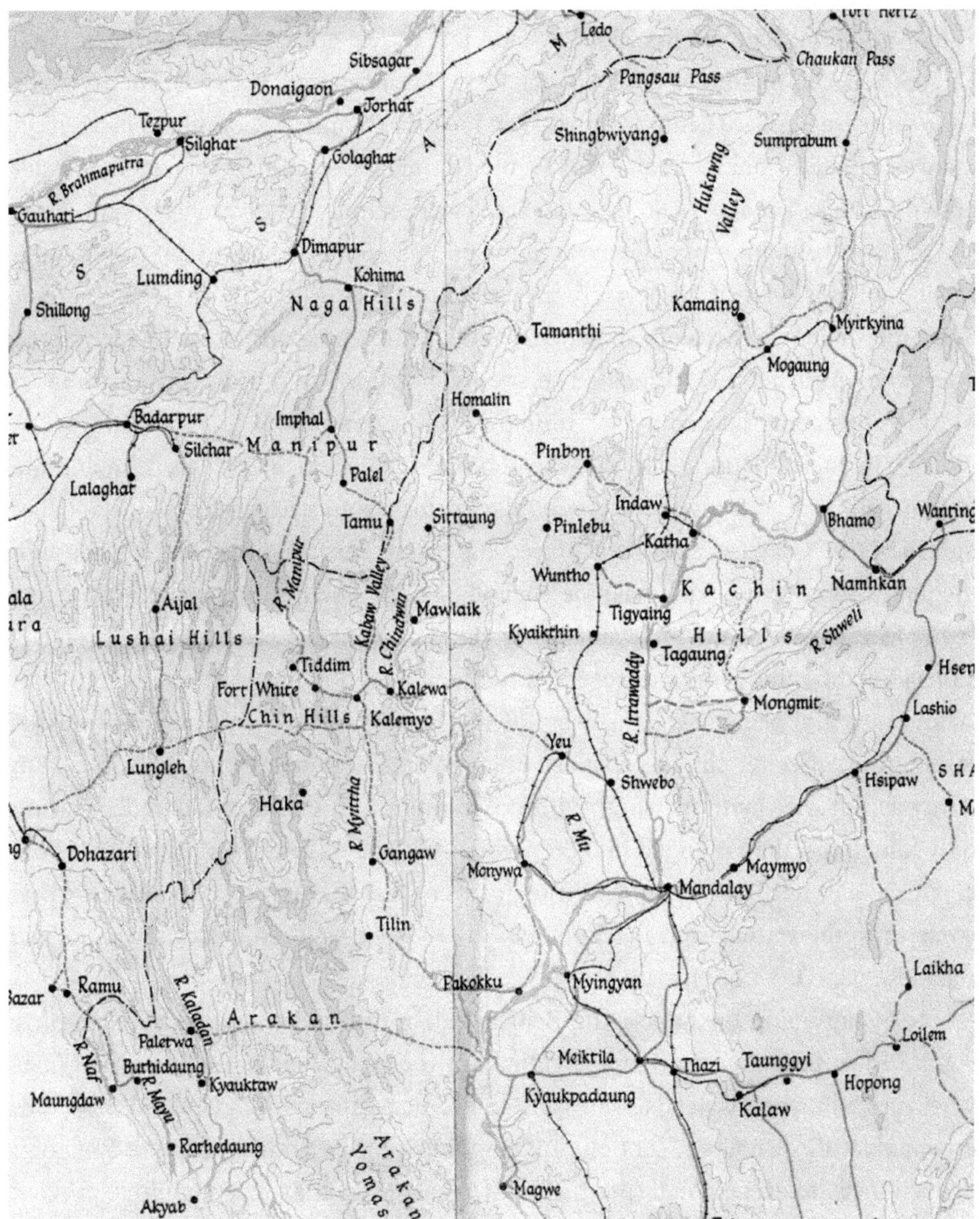


Figure 33. Map showing the Burma-India border relevant to the Battle of Imphal. From Major-General S. Woodburn Kirby, *The War Against Japan*, vol. 2 (London: HMSO, 1958), after p. 434.

General Sato led his 31st Division in a retreat southward toward Mt. Popa and the Shwebo plain (see book cover). Here the Japanese 33rd and 15th divisions were retreating toward central Burma. The Japanese Northern Command in Myitkyina was isolated from the main body of the Burma area command. Two other Japanese divisions (Tanaka's 18th and the 56th) were retreating toward Thailand.

In a brilliant move, General Slim sent his 36th Division to cut off the 18th Japanese Division as it desperately tried to retreat toward the Burma–Thai border. The 36th made contact with the enemy units somewhere around the Mogok area (well known for its ruby mines). The enemy was thrown into disarray, with most of the troops being herded by the 36th toward Moulmein.

In central Burma and the Shwebo plain, the British 2nd Division and the Indian 19th and 20th divisions chased the enemy as it retreated toward Mandalay and Meiktila. General Slim next played his trump card: in great secrecy through the jungle terrain, sneaking past the enemy, he deployed his armor and, with tanks in the lead, captured the vital railroad junction of Meiktila. The Indian 17th Division (joined by the 19th) was reserved to block its old nemesis, the Japanese 28th Army, now trapped in Arakan, west of the Pegu Yomas (hills) and desirous of joining the other retreating Japanese units. What happened to the Japanese 28th Army is not pleasant: starving, with no ammunition, clothing tattered, wearing only loincloths, they plunged into the swollen Sittang River. I could spend a whole chapter detailing their travails; suffice it to say that the unit lost about half of its strength in the retreat, and the Indian 17th Division savored sweet revenge. The Japanese were now on the run.

Continuing the attack, the British-Indian divisions rapidly moved further south to just past the junction at Pyinmana, where the road splits: one road goes westward, and another leads southward to Prome and Rangoon. General Stopford, commander the 4th Corp, sent one Indian Division (the 26th) to capture Rangoon and another Indian Division (the 17th) down past Mandalay to Toungoo to prevent the retreat of the Japanese 28th Army, now to the west in the Pegu Yomas. The 17th Indian Division was to avenge its loss to the Japanese 28th Army at the Sittang Bridge three and half years earlier. The retreat of the Japanese 28th Army and the success of the 17th Indian Division would be a terrible tragedy for the Japanese.

The speed of the British-Indian advance surprised Rangoon. It was rumored that the war was nearing the end, but there was still a lot of fighting ahead.

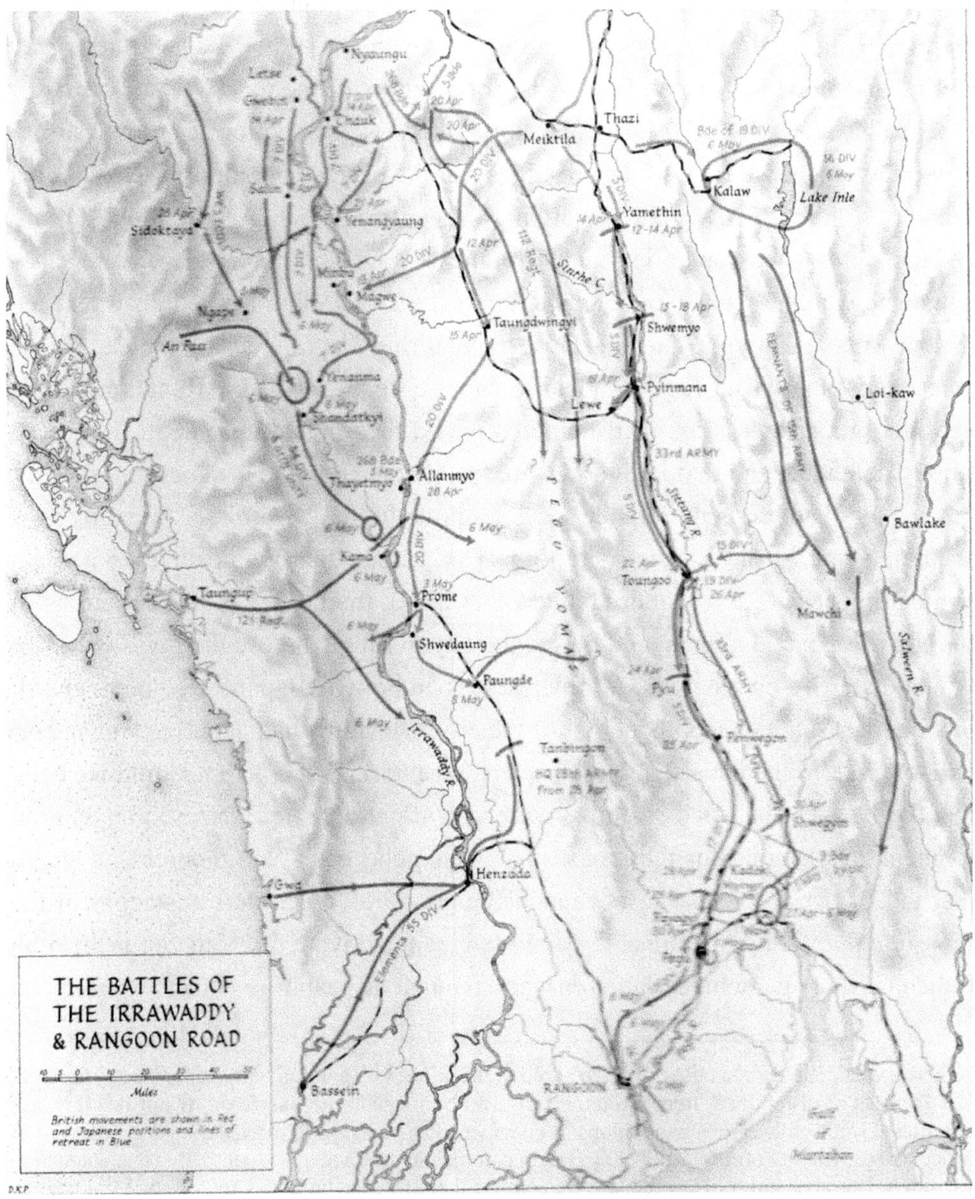


Figure 34. Map showing British advance and Japanese retreat, 1945. From Major-General S. Woodburn Kirby, *The War Against Japan*, vol. 4 (London: HMSO, 1965), after page 400.

By late summer, change was in the air in Rangoon. Not only were there fewer Japanese soldiers on the streets but also, strangely, the BDA was missing in action. Actually, it was hiding from its former ally, the Japanese, and negotiating with the British to fight with them against the Japanese.[5] When we heard that British-Indian troops had secured Meiktila, followed by Mandalay, we knew the war was inching closer. Danam (from his vantage point) kept us informed of news from Radio Ceylon (allied radio). The pro-allies Karen Special Operations Exchange (the Jedburghs, Force 136) started operations. The British parachuted in supplies, trainers, and commandos operating under Southeast Asia Command; these were saboteurs who were blowing Japanese positions. The 26th Indian Division had reached the outskirts of Toungoo and was close to capturing that city, which meant that the allies were closer. But first they had to capture Pegu. Japanese (Rangoon) Radio kept the propaganda alive that the allies would face defeat, that Pegu was being stoutly defended, and that Rangoon would be defended to the last man.

When there is no reliable news, rumors thrive. It is quite astounding how accurate some of these were. One told of an assault that would involve a naval bombardment before a seaborne attack. As usual, there were many variations of the story: big naval guns would pound the city to rubble before the invasion, there would be terrifying air-raids. Another described how the Japanese soldiers guarding allied prisoners had slipped out of the city; when this had occurred was uncertain, but indeed the usual Japanese patrols were not out and about. Could we hope that the Japanese had fled? Rumors were also afloat that the Burmese puppet government was leaving for the jungle. This was good news, but there was concern that the British troops could not reach Rangoon before the full onslaught of the monsoon. Realizing this himself, Slim planned to activate the 15th Corp (the 50th Indian/Gurkha parachute battalion) and launch a seaborne attack directly on

---

[5] There was a great debate about the BDA among the allies. General Oliver Leese of the 14th Army saw them as ill-disciplined, treacherous terrorists to be treated with suspicion, if not hostility. He questioned whether these renegade troops, if given weapons, would submit to the supervision of SOE officers of the Karen Force 136 and obey British commanders. However, Mountbatten overruled him. Governor Dorman-Smith also opposed welcoming the BDA to the allied force, but Mountbatten overruled him as well and foolishly embraced the young general Aung San as a force he could work with. History was to prove Mountbatten wrong.

Rangoon. This would give a foothold to the Allies in Rangoon and allow the land-based divisions to reach the city.

As the forward air bases moved closer to Rangoon, the nature of allied air-raids changed: they were more frequent and used a new fighter. This new de Haviland Mosquito, the fastest fighter known in 1945, was built entirely out of wood and canvas and now was roaming the skies freely. It was extremely light and had two Merlin engines, which gave it an advantage over other fighters. While conventional planes were flying at 400mph, this lightweight fighter could travel in excess of that speed. There were no Japanese fighters or anti-aircraft fire. The Mosquitoes were attacking targets of opportunity, which meant more danger to civilians. My encounter with this marvelous fighter bomber nearly cost me my life.

As the Japanese troops were withdrawing from the city, many residents broke into and looted Japanese supply depots. People ran through the streets carrying 20-gallon cans of quinine, aspirin, and assorted food and medical supplies; also ammunition and other military supplies. Some people known to us were killed in air-raids on these underground supply depots. One was located near our house around 8th mile and the airport. I decided to go look at this. I thought it was my lucky day; I did not see any aircraft. I set out gingerly and, as I neared the depot, heard the sound of aircraft, Mosquitoes.[6] Mosquitoes were not only fast but also could fly low over the treetops. Flying close to the ground, they targeted Japanese positions and blasted away at anything that moved. And so it happened this day. The shock waves were like an earthquake, knocking me to the ground. I got up, checked for any injuries, dusted off the dirt, and then, petrified and keeping an eye on the air above me, ran as fast as I could to get back home and hide in the darkened room, promising Mother that I would never do this again.

For almost four years we had endured war and privation, tragedy and death, and constant movement from one safe village to another. Our only solace was to gather on the veranda with our neighbors, especially the Karenni men who would bring their guitars and, with the full moon directly overhead, would play

---

[6] The Axis powers were so chagrined with this fighter that the Germans paid a spy named agent Zig Zag to blow up the factory making the planes, but Zig Zag was a double agent, and he just faked it.

their guitars while we sang. The full moon in the tropics can be brilliant and magical, the light so bright that some said that you could read a newspaper by it. The music brought some relief from the uniformly bad news, and we often stayed late. On the night of December 31, 1944, in spite of the tension, we gathered with our cousins and a few friends on the side road where my cousins lived, to celebrate the new year. The townsfolk were asleep. We formed a circle, wary of enemy soldiers. One of us had brought a battered old watch. As midnight approached, we started to sing: Christmas carols, pop tunes, ballads; and at midnight we sang "Auld Lang Syne." We were not sure of all the words but kept singing. We finally retired, went home, and slept, hoping that the new year would see the war end.

# Chapter 20
# War's End

As a British colony, Burma's fate was dependent not only on defeating the Japanese but also on preserving the independence of Britain by defeating Nazi Germany. It brought comfort to gather with relatives. At such gatherings they shared snippets of information and talked about myriad rumors. The Wehrmacht was being pushed back to the German border, which brought hope. Some were optimistic that the British would come soon or would drop supplies to prevent famine. In all this despair there was faint hope, that the war would end soon.

Southeast Asia Command broadcast radio news on a regular basis. Radio reception was excellent late at night; due to "skip effect," it sounded clearer than nearby stations. Quirky and unpredictable radio transmissions meant that some days, reception was better from afar than from London—sometimes from faraway places such as Moscow. Listening was thrilling. These broadcasts kept us informed about what was happening in the European theater of war. They were both encouraging and frightening. We heard reports of fighting on the Eastern front; heard strange names such as Pripyat Marshes, Kursk, and Warsaw (all occupied by the Russians); followed with great interest the uprising in Warsaw and the agonizing suffering of the people of Poland; but also watched the advancing Russian armies in the east and the allies in Western Europe. Since Stalingrad, the Russian army had gained strength, and the German army had endured defeats. Reports predicted that the war on the eastern front was coming to a climactic conclusion. On April 20, 1945, we heard that the Russian armies had reached the Oder River, just sixty miles from Berlin.[1] The Americans were capturing islands with strange names like Saipan and were closing in on the home island of Japan. These allied gains and fascist setbacks gave us hope that soon there would be liberation. We were less sure about what was happening closer to home. In fact, the British-Indian Army was now about

[1] Later in life I would visit the Russian Museum of the Great Patriotic War and would study the campaign in detail.

sixty miles away. If an Allied attack on Rangoon was to be successful, it had to come before the monsoon set in, which meant that it was coming soon.

Only after the war was over for us did we realize the truth, that the Japanese had been holding Pegu tenuously, this only to keep the corridor open for escape. The head of the Rangoon Garrison, General Kimura, made bold comments about defending Rangoon to the last man but had himself secretly fled the week before. Prime Minister Ba-Maw (of the puppet government) and his family were seen leaving by road. None of these stories was confirmed, but they were harbingers of good things to follow. Still, Japanese propaganda declared that they would hold Rangoon, and every night there would be gunfire. The nights were full of terror, as it was impossible to know who was shooting. Meanwhile, the Japanese in Rangoon were in panic mode, beheading and murdering suspected spies without benefit of trial.

Markets were closed. We still had some rice, but it was fast running out. We often exchanged rice for cooking oil and dried fish with friends. But there was fear; each morning we prayed to be alive till nightfall, and each evening we prayed that we would see sunrise. The Karen irregulars (who had been left behind by the British in 1942), now trained and armed with new reliable radios, were active against the Japanese, sometimes massacring Japanese stragglers. Inmates of the Rangoon jail, including American POWs, suspected that the Japanese were on the verge of defeat. The one bit of bright news was that a strong contingent of the Indian National Army would stay in Rangoon to prevent a massacre of civilians. The Burmese feared the allied soldiers, the Karens feared the Burmese, the Indians and other foreigners feared the dacoits, armed robbers, and stragglers from the collaborationist Burma Defense Army who were roaming the empty the streets. The INA would provide security for all.

## RANGOON LIBERATED

The heat and humidity in late April were making life unbearable. And yet we prayed for bad weather, because it would preclude enemy air attacks. Every day brought the war closer. Rumors of a coming naval bombardment were ever present. The 26th Indian Division was racing down past Prome to retake Rangoon.

Figure 35. Indian paratroops waiting to jump over Rangoon [http://www.awm.gov.au/collection/C326421]. Unknown author. Public Domain, via Wikimedia Commons.

Indeed, the attack would come from the air and sea. In the early hours on May 3, 1945, there was a steady monsoon drizzle. Nobody expected a raid at this time of the morning, but we clearly heard the drone of multiple planes. To the surprise of the people, instead of the rain of bombs, little parachutes were coming down! Word of mouth spread faster than a wild fire that there were paratroopers, and we all took to the streets, for the first time without fear, to watch the planes. I was at Aunt Ava's house, close by the river. Paratroopers of the 50th Gurkha Battalion captured Elephant Point, then a wave of more Dakota transports flew over Elephant Point dropping more parachutes. The troops then boarded pontoon boats and, after landing, advanced on the city center. There was some gunfire, but nothing like the street fighting we had experienced in previous years. For the first time

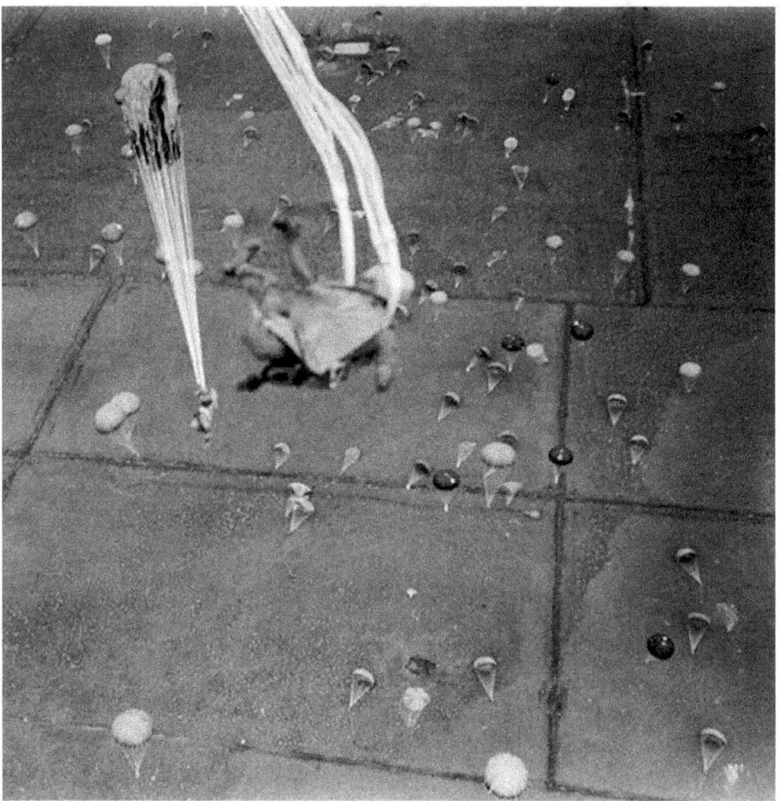

Figure 36. Indian paratroops jumping over Rangoon, Burma [http://www.awm.gov.au/collection/C326422]. Cropped. Unknown author. Public Domain, via Wikimedia Commons.

in years we felt comforted, but soon attention turned to the north, where there were indications that troops were also advancing down Prome Road. The Japanese were nowhere to be seen. As time passed, people slowly emerged from their homes. I remember running two miles to Prome Road, the main thoroughfare, where I could hear the rumbling of trucks. The joy of seeing allied soldiers cannot be described. Many watched with tears rolling down their faces, and our family joined in the joy of liberation. There would be no naval bombardment, no street fighting, no Japanese, and no Burmese collaborators to fear. Old and young fell down on their knees, whispering "Welcome back" and "God bless you." I recall vividly my first encounter with allied soldiers: a Gurkha NCO with his jungle hat, a white belt around his neck connected to his revolver, and then an Englishman in khakis. They looked like real soldiers.

Most of us civilians were hungry, malnourished, and yet happy to see the end of almost four years of brutal war. T.L. Hughes, in his "Report on the Civil Administration of Burma, October 1945," described Rangoon thus:

> Most people were wearing rags and … the city was the scene of extraordinary levels of destitution. No public transport existed. There was not a single train, tram or bus in existence, except on the outskirts of the city where "a few dilapidated pony carts, pulled by mangy scarecrows of ponies were plying for hire at exorbitant rates." The streets were two feet deep in filth and open drains had long since ceased to be anything other than a depository for garbage. The city suffered complete blackouts at night because there was no electricity or even kerosene. All heavy moorings in Rangoon harbour had been destroyed … and the signalling system on what remained of the railway had collapsed. Whole blocks at a time had been demolished by Allied bombing and the once pretty residential areas around the lakes were unbelievably dirty and unkempt.[2]

I was no longer a child. I was a now a teenager, in tattered clothes, with swollen legs, and for years I had cried more than I had laughed. I had endured many hardships and had escaped disease, danger, and death. During the war years, Mother had sent me to the market, as it was too dangerous for my sisters to be out on the street. I had been a rat collector for the Japanese occupiers. I had seen my father and two sisters buried. The memories were vivid, and my precociousness made me aware of the events. For me and for most of us who lived through the occupation, the physical scars of disease and bombs would heal, but the emotional scars would take time.

Events moved rapidly after this. British and Allied troops occupied Rangoon on May 3, and Britain agreed to eventual independence of Burma within the Commonwealth. On June 15 there was a victory parade in downtown Rangoon. I made a point to be there when it happened. It was poignant, and I felt comfortable

[2] Quoted in Christopher Bayly and Tim Harper, *Forgotten Wars: The End of Britain's Asian Empire* (London: Penguin Books, 2007), 437–38.

and fearless—a new experience. When I heard aircraft, I did not run to the shelter but just stood and watched. I was still hungry, however. Thankfully, food supplies were coming in, and the tea and *mohinga* shops were opening up.

Friendly allied soldiers (importantly) shared food with many of the city's residents: C rations, biscuits, butter, and precious chocolate, making us feel alive again. Indian army officers flocked to our house and the James's. We ate chicken, goat meat, and eggs for the first time in three years. I got my first Jeep ride, and one day I was told that I could drive one of those beauties. A few days later there was a moment of brightness: a shiny olive-green Jeep arrived and a spirited young man jumped out and haltingly approached and asked for Mother. We invited him in and offered a chair, and he began to talk to Mother in Telugu. "I am your relative," he said, "and I was asked to look in on you and enquire after your health. How are you?" Mother just nodded her head. The young man excused himself went out to the jeep, picked up a bag and brought it in; then he took packages out and handed them to those in the house. I opened my package; it was military rations. It smelled wonderful: chocolate, big chunks of American hard chocolate, hard as rock in spite of the tropical temperature, but tasty. It was the first chocolate I had tasted in four years. The young man spoke to Mother at length about relatives and friends, which brought joy to her, lifting her spirits for a while.

The euphoria would not last for long. Our relative soon left, and we never heard from him again. Indian troops were being withdrawn from overseas assignment by the government of India. Their stay was all too brief, and now they were being sent home to be demobilized. British troops were also being thinned out. The British government changed hands: Churchill had lost the election, and the new Prime Minister Clement Attlee, from the Labor Party, faced the daunting task of shortages at home and the repayment of lend-lease loans. Britain was intent on winding down her empire. Reconstruction had hardly started; there were many bombed-out buildings in the city.

The Asian custom of hoarding gold and jewelry had served us well, but Mother had exhausted her savings and was panicked about how she would care for her brood. There was no money, the savings were gone, and with Father's death there was no income. The home was almost empty of furniture, and Mother had only a few jewelry pieces left. The one fact that kept us from joining the homeless was that we owned our house. Many people who had lost their homes would become homeless and stateless. We were still worried, however, as we had no papers showing ownership; if Father had them, we did not know where they were. Long after any war, it is the winners who get to write the history, but there are those in the middle, like us, whose lives became tenuous.

## POST-WAR REFLECTIONS

Fear kept the extended family together. We were weary. The bombing was over, but the experience of the war left a lingering toll. I still jumped at loud noise and aircraft. We were not displaced people, but the day of reckoning would come soon. We would lose our status as British subjects. After the independence of Burma, as persons of ethnic Indian origin, we would not be granted Burmese citizenship. The Burmese had declared that in independent Burma there would be few chances of good jobs for Indians. We would join the millions of stateless refugees and displaced persons, without money or jobs. Some of our family joined the exodus to India, a country about which we children had no knowledge. What do we do? Instead of holding together and supporting one another, we started to splinter, allowing pettiness and selfishness to destroy our unity.

On long, magical, moonlit nights. I would sit on the steps of the veranda and reflect on what had transpired. I came to question the most fundamental beliefs. Father's early death would also affect my beliefs. At church I questioned my minister about the unfairness of it all; he listened quietly but had no explanation and actually brushed aside the question. "We are sinners," he said; "God works in mysterious ways," he counseled; "You must have faith," he admonished; "God had a reason for you being here and there is a purpose to all that has happened. You must pray, and pray every day." This did nothing to relieve me of my distress. It was not a satisfactory answer. I recalled the constant praying at Father's deathbed, and the fears would not go away. Mother put pressure on me to be baptized. I kept putting it off, due to my skepticism about religion, but pressure came from the

Telugu church minister as well as from Mother. I wrestled with this for a long time and finally consented, to please Mother.

On the issue of the basis for the war: the most egregious part of the war was the fascist Nazi philosophy based on racial superiority, purity, and the need to remove from the face of the earth people of lesser gods—Jews, gypsies, the weak and the infirm—in order to make room for the superior race. The Asian counterpart, the Japanese, followed a similar policy: they were the "master race" and hence had the inherent right to kill (in the most the barbaric fashion) the hapless Chinese, and the peoples of Vietnam, Cambodia, Malaya, Singapore, and Burma's Indians and Anglos and ethnic peoples. The people bore the brunt of the war. The post-war Germans acknowledged their sins and renounced Nazism, but the Japanese never fully acknowledged their war crimes and mistreatment of civilians (e.g., forcing women into prostitution to keep soldiers sexually satisfied). To this day, some in the Japanese community argue that some Asian colonies should have been given to the Japanese at the end of the war. Allies too had their failures, for example, General LeMay's fire-bombing cities in Japan and the British bombing of the German city of Dresden.

In spite of the end of hostilities in Burma, war continued to rage in the Pacific. The Americas were still island-hopping, whittling away at the Japanese empire. With the capture of Okinawa, the invasion of the mainland was fast approaching. Newspapers in Rangoon and radio broadcasts were full of news about the end; reports of secret negotiations to end the war were filling the news columns. On August 7, the *Rangoon Liberator* (a new newspaper) headlines screamed of a new kind of a bomb with enormous explosive power. They reported a giant flash, a mushroom cloud, a fireball; and they spared no gruesome details about how people died. It was horrifying, yet there were celebrations. In Burma, the defeated Japanese, having surrendered to the British forces, were now being held at the Thai–Burma border. The Burmese collaborators, stripped of their uniforms and wearing native clothing, became all but invisible. Yet they were armed to the teeth and waited.

The effect of nuclear weapons would be part of the curriculum in my fourth year of medical school, where I studied the medical history of the war. It could be said that those who died instantly were fortunate, because for those who survived with horrible injuries and burns it was a living hell. In spite of the passage of time, it was still terrifying to contemplate how people died in a flash, or the long lingering death from exposure at a distance, wherein people would lose their skin and hair. For those who survived, the effect on the gut—the sloughing of the endothelium cells of the gut and the ensuing diarrhea—would torture them for life. The nuclear bomb ended the war, and for that and the unconditional surrender of the empire of the Japan we gave thanks. The war would leave us derelict, malnourished, disease-ridden, bereft of money, and without a father, but we survived.

As battles go, Burma and Rangoon might be a footnote in the larger history of World War II. But for the family, my father and two sisters never lived to see the war's end. We were subject to the same weapons, bombs, bullets, and shell-fire, privation, hunger, and disease that ravaged Europe and are better known to the world. We were terrorized mercilessly, through no fault of our own, forced to endure hardship we did not deserve. Sixty million human lives were lost during the war, some obviously of fighting but countless others, civilians and non-combatants, died on long forced marches, endless treks through unfamiliar and hostile jungles, from lack of food or medical care, exposed to diseases they never heard of, from bitter cold, heat, humidity, rains, and mud.

There are no accurate statistics of the number of people who died in Burma. More than 500,000 who attempted to escape the Japanese died. At least 100,000 died in the construction of the Death Railway. The number of actual combat deaths is estimated at 200,000 on all sides. The population of Rangoon is said to have been reduced to two-fifths of its pre-war level.[3] The toll we paid in our small town was enormous. About one-third of the young would die of war injuries, hunger, and disease. To enumerate would be too long; suffice it to say it was too many. The country was in ruins. War had devastated the country's economy and brought into sharp relief the tensions among the country's ethnic groups. Over the next several years, strife between the ethnic people and the Bamar would increase

---

[3] Bayly and Harper, *Forgotten Wars*, 438.

and intensify. Soon it would erupt into open warfare. Militias were in full-scale revolt. This was the beginning of Burma's second war, which continues to this day.

Figure 37. Diorama of Japanese surrender, Fort Canning, Singapore, 12 Sept. 1945. Photo by author.

Figure 38. Diorama of Japanese surrender, Fort Canning, Singapore, 12 Sept. 1945. All Commonwealth parties were included—representatives from the British, Australian, and British-Indian (General Thimaya) armies. Neither Aung San nor Ne Win or any representative from the BDA was invited. Photo by author.

# Part Two
# Post-War Life in Burma

# Chapter 21
# Interim Rule, Political Unrest, and the Aung San Army

*In 1941, activists rioted against British rule. Soon the riots spread and the people rebelled, then we chased the British away to India. Then we captured Rangoon from the Japanese in May of 1945.*

*—Tea-shop historians of Burma*

*The transition from fascism to a liberal democracy in Burma would prove to be a failure, due to choices made by Aung San and his comrades.*

In September 1945, the Japanese formally surrendered to the British. In October, Sir Reginald Dorman-Smith returned to Burma from Simla, India, and resumed the helm of a British interim government. With half of the Indian troops withdrawn at the request of the government of India, an uneasy peace prevailed in Rangoon that soon gave way to a collapse of law and order.

The multi-hued communists (Red flag, White flag) fought amongst themselves. Aung San's Anti-Fascist People's Freedom League (AFPFL; established in August 1945) (what hypocrisy) became the largest of the warring groups, each of which had its own militia. The Aung San/Ne Win militia (the Patriotic Volunteer Organization or PVO) had acquired weapons from all over the place, especially from stores abandoned by the fleeing Japanese. All of these groups were unhappy with the progress toward independence, and the Thakins now set about to destabilize the weak interim government.[1] An article in *The Sun* in 1946 accused Aung San and his AFPFL of encouraging dacoity and threatening the government with

---

[1] U.S. President Franklin Roosevelt had long been frustrated by Burma and its warring tribes, nationalist leanings, and shifting loyalties. In 1942 he wrote Winston Churchill: "I wish you could put the whole bunch of them into a frying pan with a wall around it and let them stew in their own juice"; Ben Macintyre, *The Times*, April 10, 2012; cited online at http://factsanddetails.com/southeast-asia/Myanmar/sub5_5a/entry-3009.html.

Figure 39. Tea shops such as this are ubiquitous in Burma. At such shops, news, information, and rumors are shared all day long. Photo by author.

demands for independence.[2] Under Aung San's leadership, the Thakins chose a path of militarism, socialism, and single-party and single-man rule—a path that would lead the country to political oppression and economic ruin.

Burmese political parties agitating for independence created such lawlessness, through strikes, walkouts, and other acts, that return to normalcy was slow. The new government in Britain, with war debt, mostly owned to America in dollars, was facing its own troubles. Burma also owed much money (sterling balances) to India, including monies for the defense of Burma. Tired of the multiple problems, Britain's new Labor government and British Foreign Minister Ernest Bevin wanted to rid Britain of the millstone around their collective neck and finally announced in no uncertain terms that Burma would gain independence.

---

[2] U Maung Maung, *Burmese Nationalist Movements, 1940–1948* (Honolulu: University of Hawaii Press, 1990), 223.

Figure 40. Ne Win (left) and Aung San (right) in British uniform, after they abandoned support for the Japanese and vowed to fight on behalf of the British. From an old Burmese publication.

The British colonial government in exile had previously issued a "White Paper" in which Churchill called Aung San a "Quisling" who should be tried, but this was not received well.[3] Britain's new Attlee government withdrew the white paper and outlined new plans for the future of Burma. The new plans addressed reconstruction, restoration, and opening of schools but also contained ominous news: immediate independence for Burma and for Burma to leave the British Commonwealth (the previous plan from May 1945 expected Burma to gain indepen-

[3] Vidkun Quisling was Prime Minister of Norway during the Nazi occupation, a collaborator and traitor. He was executed by the Norwegian government. It was suspected that Aung San raised funds by armed robbery and maintained authority by terrorizing villagers. Maurice Collis, *Last and First in Burma (1941–1948)* (London: Faber and Faber, n.d.), 260.

dence but remain within the Commonwealth).[4] Hearing this, we feared that the new independent government would seize all property of non-Burmans. Our family saw a bleak future.

The Burmese independence movement, especially the Burma Defense Army, had always hewn to the notion of "blood and race."[5] In 1942, for example, when a Japanese had been killed inadvertently, Aung San had promptly ordered two Karen villages, Kanazogon and Tayagon, to be razed to the ground and the inhabitants exterminated. The villagers were surrounded at night and, as they rushed out in panic from what they thought was a safe exit, were shot. Those who did not fall to gunfire were cut down with swords. It was a race war.[6] During the occupation, Colonel Suzuki, wanting to strengthen the partnership between Japan and the Burmese Thakin Party, had fostered ethnic tension. He always took the side of the Burmans in any conflict that arose between, say, Burmans and Karens or Burmans and Indians.[7]

Figure 41. Colonel Suzuki Keiji, Japanese Army, founder of Aung San's Burma National Army. Photo from an old Burmese publication.

---

[4] Churchill was furious that the British government was even considering parleying with Aung San, whom he described as a quisling and fascist. But he was forced to acknowledge that independence for Burma was all but inevitable. "The British Empire seems to be running off almost as fast as the American loan," he is reputed to have said. See Bayly and Harper, *Forgotten Wars*, 268.

[5] The notion that Asians had close blood ties, as opposed to the white "race," which has no commonality with Asian "blood."

[6] See also the incident detailed above in Chapter 12 in which Aung San murdered the village headman Abdul Rashid. Clearly Aung San had violent tendencies.

[7] Allen, *Burma: The Longest War 1951–1945*, 559.

THE NIGHT OF TERROR

One night soon after the end of the war, the militias surrounded our town. They cut off the town's two roads (one went to the railway station, the other turned northwest and connected to the main Rangoon–Insein Road), our main connection to the outside world. They surrounded the police station, disarmed the police, and rendered us completely defenseless. After darkness we heard gunfire on both sides of town, people went into lock-down mode, and then the assault began. Gangs of militia went from home to home (they had done their research well; they knew which homes had wealth), broke down the flimsy doors with their rifle butts, and gathered the family, separating the men from the women. Pointing guns to the heads of the women, they ordered the men to go fetch money and jewels. If they were dissatisfied with the loot, they turned on the women who kept the money and jewels. They disrobed women at gunpoint and forced them to reveal the hiding place. The women wept and wailed but eventually broke down and pointed to the hiding places. The militia took whatever they liked and moved to the next house. We had turned off the lights so our house was dark, and we too went into a lock-down mode. Through broken window panes we could see the men in front of the house. I held my breath. It was a very tense moment. They hesitated in front of the house, and in the faint light I could see a voluptuous young woman whom I had seen before; she belonged to one of the militias controlled by Aung San. She carried a carbine and had a bandoleer thrown across her shoulder, crossing her breasts and accentuating them. She was well endowed, her breasts full and prominent. She paused and waved the young men away, and they now headed to the homes of other wealthy families. By 2:00 am, having stripped most of the homes of their assets, the militias faded into the shadows. The militias and their cronies funded their campaigns from the loot they gathered. [8]

The years 1945–47 were trying and turbulent. Strikes—which at times turned violent—and the shutting down of services as well as the threat of an armed

[8] Bo Po Kun, one of the thirty comrades who was deputy chief of the party, succeeded Aung San on his death, and he would pursue an even more aggressive policy.

uprising by the Thakins all pointed to more troubled times ahead. The politicians encouraged their political parties to call out their supporters to the street. Their plan was to create such disruption and disorder that the colonial government would break down and the British would be forced to end their rule. The interim government was ineffective in halting these actions, as Burmese members of the government were secretly involved in the agitation.

Internal strife raged between various Burmese revolutionaries; lawlessness was rampant. The detritus of war included many guns, rebels had easy enough access to them, and militias soon mushroomed, each attached to a particular political group and all fighting amongst themselves. They robbed and looted and sometimes killed. With so many weapons, the scale of disorder increased. Armed robbers got bolder and began attacking during the day; robberies, theft, and murder increased. It was a time of horror. Moreover, any honeymoon between the Bamar and the minorities was soon to end. Karens, Shans, Kachins, and substantial numbers of Christians, distrusting the Burmese, were nervous and feared for the future. Astrologers and the soothsayers, however, promised a great the future. (In fact, rebellion would start less than a year after independence, and economic decline would set in that lasted till the present.)

The drive to force the British out continued, the fight for independence escalated. The Colonial Office in London urged caution, warning that the war-ravaged country was not ready, but the same young rebels who had helped the Japanese Army were now turning violent in their desire to push the British out of Burma. On November 3, Governor Dorman-Smith swore in Burma's new Executive Council, headed by Aung San. There would be no orderly gradual withdrawal of the British, no Commonwealth status for Burma. The country's politicians were in an ugly haste and pushed for immediate and complete independence. But full independence had not yet been granted, and the country was still administered by the British. Negotiations between the British government and Burmese nationalists would continue into 1947.

## HOW WOULD BURMA FARE ECONOMICALLY AS AN INDEPENDENT COUNTRY?

Burma's new Executive Council was focused narrowly on political independence from Britain. It gave little thought to economic survival or trade. Especially in the post-war years, however, trade and economic development were key to success. Having conducted an in-depth analysis of Burma's economy in the 1940s, the British were keenly aware of the strengths and weaknesses of the world economy and Burma's place in it. Buried in the National Archives at Kew, outside of London, the appendix to a WWII assessment by British Intelligence (after the fall of Indo-China in 1940 and prior to the fall of Singapore in 1942) concluded the following:

> ECONOMIC IMPLICATIONS OF A JAPANESE OCCUPATION OF BURMA
>
> The economic advantages to Japan of overrunning Burma derive less from what she could obtain for herself, even assuming that she had a secure sea transport route, than from what she could deny to us and our Allies. The economic resources of Burma which would be of most value to the Japanese and the loss of which would be of most consequence to ourselves and to our Allies are:
>
> (a) Tungsten
>
> By seizing the tungsten (wolfram) mines of Burma, Japan would assure herself of a surplus over the requirements of her relatively small steel and engineering industries and would be able to utilise a greater proportion in armour piercing shell. Much more serious would be the blow she would deal at British and American armaments production by denying us both the production of Burma itself and the Chinese supplies which reach us via the Burma Road. These two sources are at present together supplying about one-third of British and American supplies of tungsten, the demand for which for high-speed cutting tools, used throughout the whole range of armament production as well as for armour piercing shell is rising rapidly.

British and American requirements, excluding requirements for armour piercing shell are:

| | |
|---|---|
| Britain | 13,500 tons |
| U.S.A. | 25,000 tons |
| Total | 38,500 tons |

Of this, from or through Burma:

| | |
|---|---|
| American supply down the Burma Road | 6-7,000 tons |
| British supply North Burma | 2,000 tons |
| Tavoy and Mergui district | 4,000 tons |
| Total | 12,000 tons |

An increase in Burmese production in planned in order to cover part of our apparent deficit. 50% of Burma's output comes from the mines at Tavoy, 37% from Mawchi (Karenni) and 13% from Mergui.

The possibility of Axis interference with our tungsten supplies from Portugal, whence a further 4,000 tons are derived, gives added importance to the Burmese supplies.

(b) Oil

About 900,000 tons of crude oil per annum are produced at the oilfields at Yanangyuang, Yanangyat and Singu on the west bank of the Irrawaddy river. The fields are connected by a 400 mile pipeline to three refineries near Rangoon. The crude produces aviation spirit and has an important by-production of wax.

Japan's present stocks are estimated to be sufficient for nine months' war consumption, whereafter her import requirements are likely to be 5½ to 6 million tons a year. The oil resources of Burma would therefore supply only a small part of her needs and they could not in any case be used for home consumption before Japan had command of the sea route to Rangoon. Though Burma's oil, provided the Rangoon refineries were undamaged, would conveniently supply any bases Japan might use in the Bay of Bengal, she is more likely to concentrate her efforts on developing for her own use the far richer and nearer oil resources of the Dutch East Indies.

On the other hand, the Burmese oilfields have assumed an added importance to ourselves since the loss of Borneo's oil supplies, and production is being urgently stepped up. India has been drawing about one-third of her supplies through Rangoon and will wish to take more in present conditions. If Burma were lost, India's oil deficiency could probably be made good through the Persian Gulf, but only by longer and more vulnerable tanker hauls.

Unoccupied China, deprived of supplies from Burma would be virtually entirely without oil, once her small stocks were exhausted.

(c) Lead

About 80,000 to 90,000 tons of lead are mined and treated near Namtu and there are large stocks. Though Japan has stocks of lead estimated at about nine months requirements, her own production is 80% deficient and there are no other substantial sources of supply in the South Pacific area except Australia. Burmese supplies are of importance to India, particularly because of their accessibility. India has no domestic production of lead.

(d) Tin

Burmese tin production at 5,000 tons per annum (mainly from the Mergui area) is not large and would not be necessary to Japan now that she has the Thai and Indo-Chinese supplies. The Allied stock position is good, but if Malaya supplies are lost Burmese production will assume a new importance.

(e) Nickel and Cobalt

There is a small production of nickel-cobalt speiss at Bawdwin near Namtu which would be of value to Japan, since there are at present no resources of either available to her. This source is not of much importance to the Allies.

(f) Zinc

> The Bawdwin (Namtu) mines produce about 80,000 tons of 50% zinc concentrates. Japan's stocks may be sufficient for about nine months requirements, but her own production is 75% deficient. Indo-China may reduce this deficiency to 65% but there are no other substantial sources of supply in the South Pacific area.
>
> Burma's zinc, like its lead, is of importance to India, both quantitatively and qualitatively because of its accessibility.
>
> (g) Rubber
>
> Some 10,000 to 14,000 tons of rubber are produced, mainly in the Tavoy and Mergui areas. Production could be considerably increased. Japan should now be liberally supplied. The Allies, however, if cut off from Malayan and N.E.I. [northeast Indian] rubber, will need to exploit even Burma's comparatively small output to the utmost.
>
> (h) Rice
>
> Seven million tons of poor quality rice are grown, mainly in the Irrawaddy delta; two million tons are exported to India to supplement her annual production of about 40 million tons. Burmese rice would not be required by Japan.

Burma's economic importance was inextricably tied to extractive industries such as oil, gas, and minerals as well as some agricultural produce such as rice and rubber. WWII disrupted development, production, and commerce in these industries, and poor management of the country would further exacerbate the problems.[9]

Since this report was made, some production increased. For example, the Australian company Ivanhoe discovered and began mining copper after World War II. But also, many mines were closed. The gems and mineral sector was nationalized in the 1960s and provided income, although not as much as is typically

[9] As described in Chapter 27 and following, which detail my experience working at the tungsten mines in Mawchi.

reported in the Western news media. Likewise the timber industry brought in substantial sums of money for several years, but deforestation and illegal exports undercut its contribution to the country's GDP. Later, in the 1980s and 1990s, tourism became an industry that also lifted the economy, but the number of tourists visiting Burma has paled in comparison to the number visiting neighboring Thailand or other Southeast Asian countries such as Singapore and Malaysia. Exports of rice to Asian countries continued even though shortages within the country were noted, but exports have declined as a result of COVID in 2020 and the coup of 2021. It is almost impossible to make financial sense of the Burmese economy because the value of the kyat keeps changing. The government manipulates the rate and has several exchange rates. It is all a mystery. Suffice it to say that Burma's economic performance has been dismal. GDP in 2008 was about $32 billion and has not changed much in subsequent years.[10] Thailand and Bangladesh have exceeded this by three times. The Asian Development Bank projects Burma's GDP will fall nearly 10% in 2021 while that of all eleven other Southeast Asian countries is projected to grow between 2.5% and 6.7%.

[10] Online research shows that Burma's GDP was about 81 billion in 2020. Thailand's GDP, in contrast, rose from about 291 billion in 2008 to close to 502 billion in 2020. Bangladesh GDP in 2019 is reported at 302.6 billion, up from 91.6 billion in 2008. Vietnam's rose from 91 billion in 2008 to 261 billion in 2019.

# Chapter 22
# Pursuing Education

By 1946 things began to fall apart. No capital was going to flow into the country unless there was political stability. But the Burmese leaders had their eye only on political independence, not on issues of security, sanitation, and the rebuilding of roads, rail, and other infrastructure. Margaret was adamant that "the Burmese are not smart enough to rule the country; they will make a mess of it." I may have agreed with her on that score, but she was also, wrongly, convinced that "the British will be back and will stay." I shot back: "Indian independence talks are going well, and on the heels of Indian independence, Burma's will follow. We must prepare ourselves to survive and thrive in a new world." But it seems some in the family were reluctant to face the future, and I did not have the capability to change their minds. I worried that, although we were domiciled in Burma, we would not be able to get Burmese citizenship after independence. This was worrying. I kept reading about the plight of displaced persons the world over. An inner voice kept telling me that things will return to normal, but I knew it was unrealistic. I kept telling myself that, to escape this nightmare, I had to pursue an education; my future would be better.

I kept up my education by reading tattered and well-thumbed old books and took some lessons in writing, but it would not make up for the lost years. Happily, with the return of the British, the dearth of reading matter was quickly replaced by a plethora of magazines, papers, and books. The famed bookstores like Higginbotham's (an old British-Indian bookstore) and Smart & Mookerdem reopened. The US embassy consulate opened a reading room, as did the British Council. I thrilled to go into those reading rooms. Reading became the bright spot in my life. To improve my spoken English, I listened to BBC, the Voice of America, and Radio Australia. I paid close attention to pronunciation, syntax, grammar; it was all phonetic. I would go for a walk and repeat the pronunciation, again and again, till I felt comfortable with the phonetics. Again I practiced the way the words were used, then mannerisms.

After what seemed to me an interminable delay, the interim government announced new education regulations. All students whose education had been disrupted by the war would be allowed to make up for lost time by going to a recognized cram school (intense tutoring) for one year; at the end of that year, students could take the school-leaving-certificate (SLC) exam.[1] This was the minimum requirement to obtain a clerical appointment in the civil bureaucracy. Those who passed the exam would then be allowed to take the Matriculation exam, without which it would not be possible to go to the university. I was excited by the opportunity. When I told Mother that I wanted to go back to school, tears welled up in her eyes. I held her hand, but she did not say much. I suspect that she wanted to say that she did not know how to pay for it but did not want to disappoint me either. She was confused by all these changes; they were too much for her. She said, "Your father had a good record, can't you get your father's job back?" I shook my head. "The world has changed. The old ways are no longer operative." She could not understand or cope with it all. She covered her head with her sari and would cry quietly.

I began my search for a school—on foot, because bus service had not yet been restored. To my dismay the American Baptist Mission schools did not return, and I was told that they would not do so. Friends advised me to go the Catholic school, and I tried, but Catholics, who considered themselves to be a cut above the average, would not admit non-Catholics or those who had not been to Catholic schools prior to the war. When I visited the school, the priest listened to me quietly then said, "If you had gone to Catholic school pre-war, we could you consider you. But you did not, so we cannot accept you." I somehow had to make up four years of missed school, especially in basic math, algebra, and geometry. I knew I had to find a private school, but the Jesuit mission schools were beyond our financial means. I had tried to earn money by selling newspapers and taking other odd jobs, but they required long hours with little to show for it.

I finally found a school, the Vishwa Bahrati Academy. It was housed in a small building, really an apartment house with two floors and in four small rooms.

---

[1] The equivalent of 9th grade in the US.

It was run by a brother and sister (surname Baradawajai), Hindu Kashmiri devotees of Subhas Chandra Bose, the Indian revolutionary and Nazi collaborator. The sister, light skinned and very attractive, took a liking to me and was kind to me. I had explained my dilemma to her, that the Mission school would never return and that I needed to find a new school at which I could complete my education in order to gain the school-leaving certificate. The brother was tall, soft-spoken, gaunt—almost cadaveric—in appearance. They both shared an equally intense devotion to independence for India. Each morning they opened the day with a brief report on the political movement, and a report on Bose's life.

Going to school under the circumstances was difficult. The school was seven miles from home, so I either had to take the train or walk. There was no such thing as student bank loans so I had no coins to spare. If I did not bring lunch, I had to go hungry. It was difficult when the well-to-do students had lunch delivered or went out to eat in the tuck shops. None of the other family members resumed school. They either mocked or criticized my efforts. Given the time constraint and so much knowledge to cover, the study was intense. I did well in geography, English, and biology, but I needed extra coaching for algebra, geometry, and math. Math would be very difficult indeed. I struggled mightily, and most of my effort was spent understanding the order of operations, rounding, and algebra. Thankfully I liked geometry. My handwriting was always a weakness. I was careful to write slowly so that the examiners could read my writing. I burnt the midnight oil most nights, trying to keep up. It was hard to cram now five years of schooling into ten months of intense study, but, bleary-eyed, the time came to take the exams. My Brahman tutors wished me well and finally said goodbye. I never saw them again; the school closed soon after my graduation. I was scheduled to take the school-leaving-certificate exam two weeks later.

Fear consumed me as I contemplated taking the exam. The day before the exam, Grandmother insisted that we go through the ritual to remove the evil eye. She burned chili peppers and wafted the smoke around me. I went to the leafy campus, which was still used by the army. Classes were held in military tents and huts. Burmese and algebra were going to be most difficult. After taking the exam came a long wait. There was no formal procedure yet, which meant waiting for rumors and reading the papers every day. Then it happened: reading the crumpled newspaper, I reached the "S" listing and then it was there, my name, I passed. I paused for a long time while I rubbed my eyes to have the facts sink in, then I went home to tell Mother and Kamala.

I was determined to go to university, not enter the civil service as a clerk. The next step in that journey was the Matriculation exam, which would allow entrance to the university. That summer was a hot one, and there were no fans. In spite of the obstacles, I plunged ahead. Sometimes I was driven to despair, but I knew that perseverance, persistence, and hard work were the only way. I would frequently have dreams of Father, that he was now living in another city, that I was going to meet him there. I would walk and walk and the dream would fade. I would get up in tears. It took great effort to ignore the hostility of my cousins. To add to my woes, one relative by marriage, a bean counter, would say "Why do you pursue an education that is inferior to the pre-war education (meaning "the education I had")?" I was happy for the support of my two older sisters, Emily and Kamala. From time to time, Kamala gave me some pocket money.

People in the old world were insufferable in the belief of mysticism, karma, and fate. "Your Karma is your destiny," they said; "your future is set, it is written in the stars, and other than appeasing the gods you will not succeed; everything is based on your past sins and past life." The degree of ignorance startled me. Case in point: I kept a small croton plant in the house, with vivid yellow, red, and green leaves. It was an attractive tropical plant, and the rainbow of its colors intrigued me. One relative, upon seeing me water the soil around the plant observed: "You are wasting time watering the dirt and roots; the water is absorbed by the leaves, so wash the leaves." I argued that science teaches that water enters the roots and goes up the trunk to the leaves, and so the argument went. We set up an experiment: he would water the leaves of his plant and I the roots of mine. When his plant died and mine thrived, he shook his head. "It's all wrong," he muttered. Another point of contention: germ theory had not reached the place where I lived, and we had lost two sisters to infectious disease. In my studies I had learned about the importance of sanitation in stemming such diseases, but I made no progress with my family. I went to great lengths to make sure our drinking water was safe, but Grandmother would just dump water that she did not use back into the drinking-water pot (to save water). The same relative who argued with me about how to water plants would laugh at my efforts to improve sanitation. He would spread his hand, bend his head toward his crotch, and say "it is only a short distance to your rectum, so it could do you no harm." The depth of backwardness was not surprising, given the place and times, but nonetheless I found all these negatives depressing. It was hard to contend with the dismissal of my scientific knowledge and the negativity toward my educational pursuits. In my bones I felt that the only hope for my future was to pursue my studies.

Overcoming prejudices and superstitions is the first step that one takes in one's study of science. At that time in the third world, with large numbers of illiterate people, to do so was a daunting task. Most people believed in myths that had been handed down for centuries. Superstition and "black magic" were the coin of the day. I knew these practices were nonsense, but still I kept my curiosity. Not finding much reassurance or support from people around me, I sought out the psychics to see what they offered. I knew they were illusionists, soothsayers and practitioners of black magic. Their practices are so pervasive in Asia, however, that one cannot go through life there without consulting one. So, one day I went to see a palm reader at the temple, whose entrance was lined with soothsayers. I took a deep breath and sat down on the bamboo mat. The reader grabbed my palm, looked at it, and drew lines, "you will have a short life, and two wives," he pronounced. "Is there any good news?" I queried. "Hmm," came the answer; "I will make offering to the gods, and your luck will change for the better." I reluctantly paid him his fee. All manner of charlatans such as this preyed on the weak and the fearful. A common way to earn merit was to buy a bird (from the cage) and release it. Of course the trained bird soon flew back to the cage, to be sold again, but the buyer felt satisfied that he had earned merit. General Ne Win himself, the mad dictator, was obsessed with the numbers. His favorite was nine, and his belief in numerology ended up ruining the Burmese economy. Seers, futurists, removers of obstacles, readers of Tarot cards—all these took advantage of the weak and gullible and separated men (and women) from their last rupee.

One member of the family was an avid fan of horse racing, and each Saturday he burnt the midnight oil poring over charts. First he obtained the date and time of birth, the locations of the stars, and the sign under which the horse had been born; then he consulted the numerology chart (what these numbers meant was utter gibberish); and finally, having spent the night doing research, he picked his horse, and off he went to the races. He would inevitably come home late Sunday evening drunk, having lost all his money and having drowned his sorrows at the bar. He told me I would never finish college, that my karma was that I would stay in my current station in life for the rest of my life.

I quit believing in that silliness, stuck to science, which changed my life. After much study I was finally ready to take the Matriculation exam. After 2:00 pm the Department of Education announced the results. To view them meant walking to the Chancellery building and peering over the heads of other eager students. I finally found my name and was overcome with joy to learn I had passed. Now I had to prepare to go to university, which had announced that it would open in the spring of 1947.

Getting admitted to the university was not going to be easy. In the first place, admission had its hurdles, especially for such highly sought-after disciplines as medicine, science, and engineering. I was anxious about admission to pre-med, my first choice. Fortunately, the interim government realized the need for more engineers and doctors because so many of the old hands had gone to India and China and had never returned. The university authorities instituted new expedited procedures and went through the paperwork swiftly; in a week I was notified that I would be admitted to pre-med. I had overcome so many obstacles to get to this point.

The university did reopen in the fall of 1947. Its leafy campus looked unkept. The buildings had been used by the Japanese civil administration; the main buildings had suffered bomb damage. Some of the buildings had been requisitioned by the British Army and the new administration and would not be returned to the university in time for the opening of classes, so the first classes were held in Quonset huts. It was still exciting to be in a real class and in college. All students had to declare their ethnicity, all had to know English and a vernacular language like Telugu or Burmese. Thankfully, for the non-Burmese, the level of proficiency in Burmese was modified. The first English text was Shakespeare's "As you like it." The paperback was new and had a fresh smell. I had to write a review and, given my poor handwriting, dreaded it. I stayed up until the wee hours of the morning laboring over the review, taking a lot of time to write it. The instructor noted my poor handwriting and spelling but gave me a passing grade—along with the suggestion that I improve my handwriting.

I had led an insular life during the war, but now I was forced to mix with classmates, and that was a new experience altogether. For someone who had few friends in life, it was exciting to meet young men and women from different backgrounds, the most notable being students from the new upper class; it would be the first time I would come in contact with them. Some of the rich kids and I became friends, and I would go to their homes, which were impressive. One that I frequented was that of the chief engineer of Rangoon. It was built along colonial lines, with fine teakwood, high ceilings, and open verandas, which kept the house cool in the summer months. The estate had enough room for a guest house and a carport. I was captivated by the estate and home to the point that I would strive to hopefully live in a house like that someday. University would also bring me in contact with young women. Living in the repressed environment of my family, it was an eye-opener.

Going to college was difficult financially, but despite these obstacles I boldly plunged into it. Early on my brother Danam had helped. Now he had married; his wife was an oddball who did not believe in education. I drew some comfort from the fact that Uncle Rao had returned from India and had set up his old practice, and for me this was a godsend. He did not offer financial help; he said I should talk to my brother. But he did hire me to do some odd jobs for him and others, and I eventually saved enough to buy a bicycle. It was a burgundy-colored Royal Enfield—a much-desired bicycle that elicited envy from others. I became quite attached to it and rode it everywhere until it was stolen. I spent many hours plying the streets of Rangoon, looking for textbooks and used books. All my pocket money (from odd jobs) was spent on books. I found a textbook of physics by Crowther and from there I tinkered with gadgets.

Our house was now getting crowded, as my married sister still lived at home. But I was able to create an environment in the little room that I shared with my brother so that I could study without being distracted. I repaired the rickety old teak desk that Uncle had given the family, using nails and screws to hold it together. It was not the most comfortable but sufficed. Without a bookcase I stacked the books on the floor and, with a small light, read till the family retired. Then I transferred to the family room where the chair was more comfortable. In Burma, teak was so cheap that almost all the furniture was teak, and used teak furniture was used for firewood. Electricity was still spotty, so reading took place by the light of a little kerosene lamp. It was made of tin, about three inches in diameter, with a cap and an opening for a wick. It burned an unsteady, yellow light. Even the slightest breeze would extinguish the flame; and it was also so sooty that in the morning when I blew my nose, the phlegm was streaked with soot. It would prove harmful to the lungs.

# Chapter 23
# Hopes and Dreams

Family cohesion fragmented in the wake of the war. One group wanted to shun modernity and go backward. They clung to old traditions—superstition, karma, negativity—and consulted dubious priests, soothsayers, palm readers, and such. The absence of Father's firm hand was sorely missed, and family strife increased. My younger brother, never very astute to start with, was unwilling to go to school. Instead he took to spending time with his Burmese friends, hanging around tea shops and, when they closed at night, gambling till the wee hours of the morning. There was no curfew; he came and went as he pleased, often staying out until 3:00 am or later. My aging mother would get up to let him in. Then he would sleep until 11:00 am. Arguing that there was no future in education, he—still wet behind the ears—announced that he was not going back to school and—with much fanfare—proclaimed that he was going to take up gambling. If Father had been around, he would have given Jason a good whipping.

During the rule of the Burmese kings (when there had been no standing army) there had been a tradition whereby every night the headman would select a young man to be watchman (*singe*) for a night. A hut would be built in the center of the village where the *singe* was to keep night watch, to keep marauding robbers from attacking innocent people. He would be armed with sticks and would beat the gong as a warning to alert the villagers. In these post-war days, the guard hut soon became the hot spot and an excuse for young men to gather and, to kill time, play cards. At first it was fun for Jason to join the young men, but it soon turned deadly. Over time the gambling degenerated into playing for big money, much beyond his means. His gambling debts grew, and when they were left unpaid, threats increased. The family did not have the money to pay off the debts, yet not to do so would mean that Jason would suffer bodily harm. Some members of the family supported him. In this they were confused between correction of bad behavior and love for a family member. Destructive shortcomings should be overlooked, they argued, because "correction of his behavior would deny him love." This would bring me into conflict with my mother and sisters. Jason was a drain on the already-stressed family. I emphasized that "if we stay united, pool all our resources, focus on education, and embrace modernity we can survive." We had to prepare for the uncertain future. Mother, without Father, had a hard time coping. She was in despair. She felt that admonishing her children would hurt them, confusing discipline with not loving them. She was no tiger Mom. In this situation the selfish siblings would seek their own disastrous course. The more sensible ones started to think of the future, and those who could not see beyond their noses went astray. I went out of my way to keep the siblings together but met with minimal success.

I was more determined than ever to speed up my education and get out of this quagmire. To raise some money, I took to selling some artifacts I had gathered during the war, but I needed more than that could bring. For Mother, the immediate future was simply coping with the losses she had suffered in the war. Being left without her husband and with little savings was exhausting. Some of my friends would take the easy way out: working as a peon or in a clerical capacity, hanging around tea shops, doing occasional menial work, and rarely going to school.

Young adults who had endured four years of war and occupation all had their own dreams and ideas. Some would come to fruition; others would remain unfulfilled; still others would lead to utter disaster. In my immediate circle, the lives of Tin Thein and Nancy, an Anglo-Karen girl (not their real names), are instructive.

Tin Thein lived four doors away from my family. His mother, a generous widow, wanted him to be educated, to be a doctor. He was of medium build, with a broad face that was pock-marked, possibly from smallpox. As the war dragged on, his mother supervised his coming-of-age ritual. For this elaborate *Shinbyu* ceremony, he had to go to the monastery for one year. There he would learn Pali, have his head shaved, learn and recite Buddhist phrases, and go through rigorous training. He would rise each morning before sunrise to pray, then would take his lacquer bowl and join a single line of monks as they walked through the community, stopping at each Buddhist home where the devout would fill the bowls with rice, curry, and other food. After returning to the monastery for his single meal for the day, he would devote the remainder of the day to prayers and learning the history of Buddhism and monastic life. On the day set for his initiation, Tin Thein wore the yellow robe of a novice, he kneeled, brought his palms together, and bowed. His mother, with tears in her eyes, brimmed with pride. But there was another side to his life. In the monastery he learned how unhappy the Bamar people were, and he became angry at the British, vowing to take corrective action. After he returned home, he joined the DoBama group to go to war against the British and all foreigners. This unleashed his wild side, namely aggressiveness. In one episode, he found an unexploded ordinance (a 50-mm machine-gun bullet). Wanting to know what was inside, he hit it hard with a hammer. It exploded, taking part of his left index and third fingers. That did not moderate his aggressiveness, however. Another time he broke the nose of a British soldier who happened to flirt with an Anglo-Burmese girl. Later in life he had a falling out with the rulers, which led to a bad end for him. His short temper and extremist policies would lead to his premature demise, as I learned many years later.

Nancy was a teen when the war started. She grew up at a time when Western music, dancing, and partying were the norm. In the war years, this partying was suppressed, but as the Japanese were busy with the war in the far north, music and dance revived in private home. As soon as the British liberated Rangoon, Nancy assumed that life would return to normal. It did not. The end of the British Empire was at hand, which would mean the end of her way of life. For Nancy this was trying; her many attempts to cope with it failed, and her only hope was to escape. But where would she go? She had no particular skills, so her only hope was to find a man, a white man perhaps, who would could take her away from all of this. It was not to be. Through her sister Maureen, whom I later briefly dated, I learned that Nancy had married a Burmese army officer, with fatal consequences.[1]

Then there were those who were older than me and who had participated in the independence movement and had achieved "success" or notoriety in the aftermath of the war. *Thakin Nu, Aung San, and New Win pursued and perhaps achieved their dreams and ideas. But their achievements led ultimately to disaster for themselves and their country.*

---

[1] I knew three women who married Burmese army officers. All were abused and died at the hands of their spouse.

Figure 42. U Nu, first prime minister of independent Burma. Unknown author. Public Domain, via Wikimedia Commons.

Thakin Nu—a middle-aged, bland, moon-faced man inexperienced in statecraft—became, by default, Burma's first prime minister at war's end. This was simply because he was the head of the AFPFL (Anti-Fascist People's Freedom League). The League's membership, ironically, was fascist and communist. Thakin Nu was chosen as prime minister not for his skills but as a stooge by the puppet masters. His extremist policies, lack of skills, neglect of the economy, and devotion to Buddhist causes were the beginning of the decline of the country. He built the Kaba Aye Pagoda in 1952 and invited scholars from all over the world to the Sixth Buddhist Council held there from 1954–56, but while he was thus engaged, civil affairs took a second or third place. His frequent assertions that Burma was for Bamar struck such fear in non-Burmans that most skilled non-Burman civil servants, doctors, and technicians made plans to flee Burma for the UK or Australia, taking their valuable skills with them. If Thakin Nu had possessed foresight, had managed the economy better, and had protected the minorities and non-Burmans, the country's history could have been far better for all inhabitants, and seventy-five years of civil war could have been prevented.[2]

Aung San, the founder of the Tatmadaw, became a student leader in 1933. The University of Rangoon had built a student union building, where the politically inclined would go. Instead of socializing, they would hatch conspiracies against British rule. Embracing fascist and communist views, they finally linked up with Japanese intelligence agents. Aung San was famous for his declaration: "We will seek help from wherever we can find it—China or Japan." He rose to become a

[2] Instead, U Nu's actions reflected his belief that "the real independence of Burma … would occur when the country reconnected itself to its glorious past and recognized Buddhist contemplation and self-control as the central discipline of the new state." Bayly and Harper, *Forgotten Wars*, 321.

Figure 43. Aung San in BIA uniform, 1942. Unknown author. Public Domain, via Wikimedia Commons.

Figure 44. General Ne Win [https://commons.wikimedia.org/wiki/File:General_Ne_Win.jpg]. Shephard 96, CC BY-SA 4.0, via Wikimedia Commons.

major general in the puppet Burma Defense Army. He would be assassinated in 1947 when he was just thirty-two years old.

Shu Maung (later changed his name to Ne Win) was born to a Chinese father and a Burmese mother in Henzada, a small town in western Burma. The town was in turmoil, and his early life experience was painful. Rice farmers were having a bad year. The rice mill had broken down. To revive it, the mill had to buy parts, but they not only were hard to get but also could be purchased only in hard currency, making repair impossible. The mill closed, throwing his father out of work. In desperation, his father sent him to Kemmendine (Kyi Ming Dine), a suburb of Rangoon, which turned out to be a breeding ground for revolutionaries. For Shu Maung, this was a dream come true. He had difficulty at school and failed his first attempt at Matriculation; only after memorizing all the answers was he able to (barely) pass the next year. He did not like to mix with non-Bamar and deeply disliked Kalas (Indians). His going to university changed him. At the student union he ran into other rebels and soon took up the cause of independence by any means. He changed his name to Ne Win and would become the most demonic, murderous, ruthless dictator. In 1962 he staged a coup that would plunge the country into military dictatorship, he would be responsible for the brutal murder of civilians by the thousands, he would massacre young students and monks who revolted against his military junta. His "Burmese Way to Socialism" would plunge the country into economic stagnation for many years.

The legacies of Thakin Nu, Aung San, and Ne Win persist to this day. The military government arranged a power-sharing agreement with the NLD (National League for Democracy, the party of Aung San Suu Kyi) in 2015, but in 2020 the NLD captured all but thirty-three seats in Parliament and was ready to form a new government. A disciple of Aung San, Ne Win, and Than Shwe, General Min Hlaing could not accept those results. Like the generals before him, he would stage a coup. To justify his action, he used the hackneyed excuse of "election fraud," and on February 1, 2021, he began a brutal military suppression—perhaps more brutal than anything that Ne Win had unleashed.[3] Again Burma is plunged into military dictatorship that could have been prevented if the generals had not been so short-sighted, power- and money-hungry, and xenophobic.

---

[3] See the last chapter of this book for my reflections on this coup of 2021.

# Chapter 24
# Independence and Rebellion

*"This is the most violent place in the British Empire."*

*—George Orwell*

*A single instance in which a country, motivated by high idealism and nobility of Purpose, has sacrificed its life for property solely for the liberation and welfare of the oppressed peoples, Nippon seems destined to that historic role for the first time in the Chronicles of mankind.*

*— Thakin Nu, the future Prime Minister of Burma*

On January 4, 1948, in the early hours of the morning (an hour determined by astrologers to be most auspicious), with great fanfare, banging of drums, and blowing of the conch shell, the British finally lowered their flag in Burma. The Burmese raised their Independence flag and celebrated with gusto. History would prove the astrologers wrong: less than one year later, war would break out between the Karens and the Burmans. Seventy years of misrule and ethnic war lay ahead and would lead to utter failure.

Thakin Nu, Burma's first post-independence Prime Minister, wanted Burma to bend to his dogma. He wanted all non-Buddhists out of the country and sought to return the country to the glory days of Bamar rule. Many non-Burmans had already left the country. During wartime, they fled on foot to India, although only a small number ultimately reached safety. Most were never heard from again; they just disappeared, forever. It was terribly sad. Even sadder was the fact that their plight was never chronicled, no books written, no stories told; they were dispensable. We do not know what happened to Uncle Brown or our manservant Lingam. Now, after the war and in light of Thakin Nu's rhetoric, more non-Burmans were eager to leave. Many friends—mostly Anglo-Indians and Christians—with close ties to relatives in England, Canada, and Australia made contact with those relatives and prepared to leave. Others left for India or China. In comparison to those who had left in the early days of the war, these later emigrants would receive preferential treatment by the government of India.

### SOCIALISM WILL CORRECT THE EVILS OF CAPITALISM

This was the mantra in states newly liberated from the British, Dutch, and Japanese. Huge changes were taking place around the world as the old world order was being replaced by a new one. Post-war changes were all about overthrowing capitalism, as it was considered tainted by its association with colonialism. It would be replaced by communism and socialism. In China, the Long March had ended gloriously, and now in 1949, Chinese Communists were advancing south. The corrupt Nationalist (KMT) government of China had been losing their struggle against the Chinese communists even before the war ended. The advance of the Communists was rapid, especially to the southwest and the Burma border. By late spring of 1949, the beaten KMT forces, consisting of two divisions, arrived at the Burma border. They crossed into Burma and did not pause in their flight. My memory is that they were entrenched in and around Kengtung in 1949. They advanced deep into Burma, into remote jungle, and set themselves up growing opium and refining it into heroin. They were to be an ill wind. In 1959 I would encounter them in Kengtung, where my medical responsibilities included caring for inmates of the opium hospital.

In Indo-China (Vietnam), Ho Chi Minh was attempting to overthrow the French colonists, and the enfeebled French were not doing well. Revolution was spreading. American Secretary of State John Foster Dulles (along with his brother, Chip Bohlen, and George Kennan), believing in the domino theory, prevailed on the countries of Asia to join in the fight to prevent the spread of communism. To this end the US helped to create the Southeast Asia Treaty Organization (SEATO).[1]

---

[1] A treaty signed in September 1954 in Manila and instituted in February 1955 in Bangkok with the goal of blocking communist gains in Southeast Asia. Despite its name, the Philippines and Thailand were the only two Southeast Asian countries party to the organization. Members included many colonial powers: Australia (Papua New Guinea), France (Indo-China), New Zealand, Pakistan, Philippines, Thailand, the UK (Hong Kong, North Borneo, Sarawak), and the US. Considered a failure, the organization disbanded in 1977.

Leaders of the newly liberated countries were unimpressed with Dulles, however, and more determined than ever to stay neutral.

Even before Burma's independence, many minorities felt betrayed by the British. Fearful about our fate under Burmese rule, we wondered how we would make it. The British may have contributed to some discord, but the bitterness of the ethnic conflict was longstanding. It would play out in all its ugliness. The Karens were deeply distrustful of the majority Bamar and revolted against the Bamar majority rule (later the Kachins and Shans would join them). There were more guns than people on the streets. Dacoits and thieves roamed the streets after dark. People did not venture out onto the street where we lived.

One night while studying for exams, at about 8 pm, I heard the familiar rat-a-tat-tat of gunfire. At first I thought it was the usual armed robbery, then realized that it was increasing in intensity and sounded like a high-caliber machine gun. It was not armed robbery but war. Along with others in the neighborhood, I dashed outside and looked north, to where the firing was taking place just a mile to the north of our house. I could see familiar tracers, which meant machine guns, used by the military. That meant something serious was going on. We were terrified but watched the firefight in fascination. When it continued way past midnight, most people began to run away to safety. Just a year and a half after the war ended, the long-expected rebellion of the Karen National Defense Organization (KNDO) against the Burma Army had started with this, the so-called "Insein Incident."

By morning, Burmese women and children were streaming out of Kamayut, towards the safety of Rangoon city. Fearing the spread of fighting, they gathered their valuables and fled. It was rumored that the Karens had overtaken the police and military outposts in Insein and Thaming (the same place the plague had ravaged during wartime). I persuaded the women and children of the family to go to live with my sister Emily, in her crowded home in the city. I stayed to guard the house. The gunfire was now less than a mile from our house. Tracers (one in ten machine-gun rounds have a tracer) approached closer to the house.

Rumor had it that the Karens had broken through the Burmese defenses and were slowly heading our way. The Burma Army was expected to lose the engagement. Ne Win was up north in Arakan, suppressing an Arakan rebellion.

Thakin Nu (U Nu, the Prime Minister) summoned Ne Win back to Rangoon and quickly turned over command to him. Ne Win called up reinforcements as fighting continued and intensified. Tea shops were full of talk that the Burmese Army was short of ammunition and had to get supplies soon from somewhere. U Nu appealed to Prime Minister Nehru of India, and the Indian government sent supplies in short order.[2] The KNDO appealed to their fellow Kachins up north to come down to help. A Kachin battalion indeed was coming down to support the Kachins, but the Burmese persuaded them to stop at Pegu and thus successfully averted a crisis. I tried to go up the Judson College tower from whence I could see the fighting, but it was closed. Fighting went on for days and then suddenly ceased. There was silence. The truth was that the Karens, faced with overwhelming force, withdrew across the Hlaing River, as the government proudly announced the next morning. Of course, nothing was resolved. The Karen retreat was a strategic withdrawal into the delta, and the rebellion continued.

---

[2] Ne Win never thanked the Indian government; his hatred was so great that he would not seek help from the Indians.

# Chapter 25
# My Medical Education

The University of Rangoon campus was set on the edge of Inya Lake. Part of it faced the lake directly. The campus had much green leafy space, a boat club, and an area for swimming. It was indeed a beautiful setting. The buildings were magnificent, in classic colonial style. The army had finally left the campus, and life there was returning to normal. However, many buildings had been damaged during the war. Four years of neglect had left intact buildings in need of paint and refurbishment. Chairs and desks were in short supply. The grounds had great areas where the grass was brown and riddled with puddles of water. The classrooms were not segregated by sex, but students who knew each other tended to stayed together. I sought a group that I could fit into. Social life was not all grim. I was now nearly twenty years old but had never dated or asked girl out, nor had I kissed a girl. Living in a repressed society and home, this was not surprising.

Social life continued, but it paled in comparison to pre-war life. The Anglo-Indians, Christians, and Anglo-Burmese continued to go parties, listen to pop music and jazz, and dance. There were dance halls, some above board and others that were dens of iniquity. Local bands played pop music and some danced the latest dances; the jitterbug and war-time music were all the rage. It was fun to watch them and dream. Jazz was very popular. One happy episode sticks in my mind as one of my most pleasant university experiences: In the 1950s there was intense competition between the US and the Soviets for the hearts and minds of the people of Burma. The Americans went over the top, bringing Louis Armstrong and Benny Goodman to the university campus. This brought many music aficionados to the University campus and greatly excited me, although the Burmese showed little excitement.

As soon as the foreign embassies opened offices in Rangoon, with attached reading rooms, I quickly became a member. The American embassy on Merchant Street was the biggest, with its reading room in a building adjacent to the embassy proper. It had the *New York Times*, books, and pamphlets. As a member I could borrow books such as Eisenhower's *Crusade in Europe*, *Darkness at Noon* by A. Kostler, and other timely tomes. From time to time they gave away booklets, pamphlets, and some technical books, which I avidly collected and allowed me to build a small library at home.

My life was mostly consumed by going to college and preparing for the never-ending exams, but not totally. One of us organized small groups that practiced dancing and socialized. At Christmas-time I hired an ex-army truck and with others called on families who shared the faith. We were welcomed and went caroling. It was a great time. But with each passing year, things started to change. The middle-class community started to shrink, as many with foreign connections left the country. The dwindling number of families who remained drew closer. My knowledge of boy–girl relationships was sadly lacking, and I was blithely naive. Some girls—twins and their older sister—would come over to our house all dressed up. They would be welcomed by my sisters, and I would join them for chit chat. It would take me years to realize that they had a romantic interest in me. I admired them at a distance but was terrified to ask them out, even for ice cream.

I could not afford to board at the university. I walked or rode my bike to the university (about two miles) and reading rooms until it was stolen. While learning was my priority, others were more focused on political action. Many students were involved in strikes and other behaviors that the government frowned on. Soon the police would move in, and they would go missing.

The Non-Aligned Movement was born in these years. Occupying the middle ground between the dominant US and Soviet Union, the newly independent countries comprising this movement were determined to remain neutral. They did not want to be pawns of post-war colonial powers. They were concerned with resolving conflicts peacefully and improving the lot of their desperately poor populations; they were not interested in new conflicts between the Soviet Union and allied powers. They hoped to be spared from the ravages of another war. The giants of the non-aligned movement were leaders such as Jawaharlal Nehru, Sukarno, and Chou En-lai (Zhou Enlai). They frequently would visit the newly liberated capitals to give speeches, and Rangoon was one of those cities. It was a festive affair. U Nu organized elaborate public rallies, putting up giant posters bearing slogans in key points of the city. Prome Road and other main roads leading to the city were covered with them. The day arrived. The unions, students, and government workers were given a day off and pressed to attend the rally. I had deep misgivings about getting involved but was a young student fearful that if I did not join in, I would lose my status at the university. The impression was given that I had to be there. I was told to be at a certain place at a certain time. From the university we marched to the center of town carrying placards and shouting slogans. We marched through the Sule Pagoda and shouted more slogans. As the group passed in front of my brother's place of practice, I felt embarrassed by it all. The groups snaked through the city and finally joined up to become one giant rally at the old race course, a green expanse of land in an otherwise crowded city. Sitting on high, I craned my neck to hear the speakers. They talked about the new world unfolding and about their desire to mobilize their populations to keep the great powers from meddling in their affairs. They talked about protecting their newly acquired independence and warned us that, unless we protected what we had gained, we risked losing it all. To a man they were all socialist. They talked about the evils of capitalism and unbridled exploitation and how we, the privileged, should protect the poor masses. Some speeches were inspiring, others boring. Shortly after the concluding speeches, the twenty-nine heads of state issued their Ten Principles.

Amongst the Ten Principles were some that would irritate the Western countries, namely the clauses shunning any collective defense agreements with great powers, preserving Asia as a nuclear-free zone, and upholding mutual non-aggression or non-interference in domestic affairs. Regarding the non-aligned movement as a subversive movement, the Americans John Foster Dulles, Kermit Roosevelt, George F. Kennan, and Dean Acheson were all working to undermine it. Many years later I would reflect on these times and their effect on me. Some of those speeches would greatly influence me later in life.

As all this went on, I completed two years in basic sciences (intermediate) but was saddened and in despair because I was running out of money. I had to drop out of school and tried to find work, but jobs were few and employment prospects were bleak. I visited India and stayed with my aunt in Bangalore. It was a nice city even then, a cantonment city with a military base. It was diverse and clean in the main part of the city. But I was disappointed in that I did not find any future there, so I came back home. Finally, luck was on my side.

During this time, the World Health Organization (WHO) funded public health programs and had set up a TB diagnostic laboratory in Rangoon. TB was rampant in Burma at the end of the war. The WHO took on the task to contain the epidemic. They were looking for employees with science and university background. Luckily, I think the head of Bacteriology, an Anglo-Burmese lady who took kindly to me, recommended me, and I got the job. The laboratory was located in one of the newer buildings in the downtown area. There were brand new shiny microscopes, centrifuges, test tubes, and slides—equipment rarely seen before in Burma. The head of the lab was an Anglo-Burmese bacteriologist. Her counterpart, a foreign liaison officer, was a seedy-looking Englishman with a personality to match; he had a wandering eye. Tuberculosis's acid-fast bacillus (AFB) was a difficult organism to grow. It required special ingredients to grow in the lab. Slides had to be made with infected sputum. My job required that I prepare the slides with special dyes, without gloves at times. I was paid well, according to the international pay scale rather than the local pay scale, which was a pittance. I enjoyed the work and learned much about laboratory procedures. Besides the work, I had access to the newest books and medical journals. But I wanted to go back to university, to medical college. I paid off a small debt that I owed and then went on to save money. It took eighteen months, but with enough money saved to pay for the first year of college, I re-took Burmese and English classes, passed the exams, and took the entrance exam for medical school. But my entry to the curriculum was delayed.

By 1951 I had completed the university curriculum in basic science, had saved money for medical school by working for the WHO, and had taken the exams allowing entry into the medical college. But the government had yet to announce a formal policy for admissions to the medical curriculum. Rumors were that Judson College would close and would be amalgamated with the university, with a joint board that would set the admissions policy. If this came to pass, Judson's Botany professor, Dr. Dickason (an American), would join the university. He had a reputation for holding very strict views about who should be admitted to medical school, believing that admission should be restricted to a small, elite, group from good family backgrounds—code for Bamar elite.[1] This caused much concern amongst non-Bamar students. Since the school term had already started, I entered the physics program while waiting for additional news about the medical college.

The wait was excruciating and disturbing. There was delay after delay. The newly constituted Board of the university finally recommended a restrictive admissions policy,[2] but the Ministry of Health apparently overruled that, saying that more doctors were going to be needed. The Ministry set new standards that allowed a broader and more diverse group of students to be admitted. I was delighted to finally be accepted by the Medical College of the University of Rangoon. A respected institution, it had been built in 1927, the first medical school in Burma. The then-Governor Sir Harcourt Butler had laid the foundation stone for the building in Lamadaw, three miles from downtown. It was an attractive, red-brick, colonial-style building. The only negative was its location: within walking distance of the central jail, an ominous, ugly, and forbidding building behind the college. Behind its walled façade the jail held some of the most notorious dacoits and murderers.

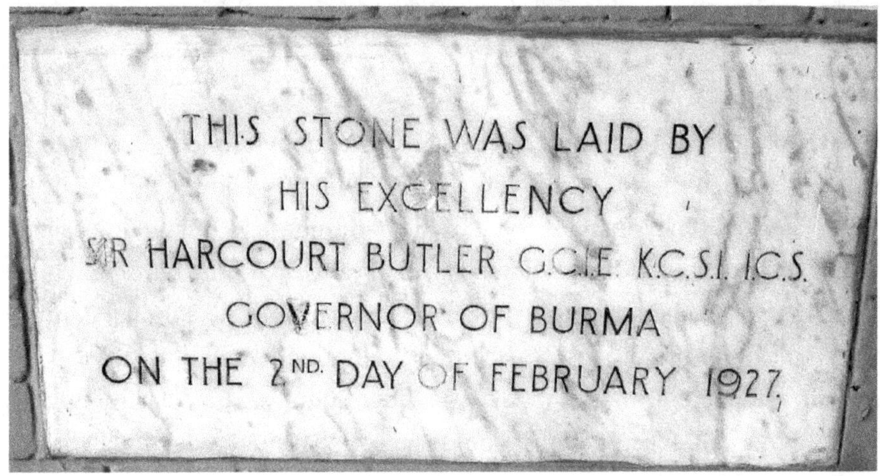


Figure 45. Foundation stone of University of Rangoon Medical College. Photo by author.

---

[1] At higher levels of education there was always a powerful body that wanted to advance the elite, and a particular ethnic group.

[2] Much like the debate taking place today at some universities.

Figure 46. University of Rangoon Medical College. From Institute of Medicine 1, Rangoon, Facebook page.

The interior of the medical college was equally attractive as its exterior, with marble and teak floors. One wing housed Anatomy and related sciences; the other wing housed Physiology. In front of the building was a quadrangle, a parking lot, and a well-manicured lawn. In the back end of the building was the wonderful medical library, which had stacks of fine teak bookcases. The colonial administration had made sure that it was a place that was attractive so that students would linger and read. Like at most schools, the classrooms were "theaters" with front doors and a rear entrance (students could sneak out when the lectures got boring, like Public Health). I learned much about medical care in advanced countries. I shuddered to think that I had received no vaccinations, not even for tetanus. I shuddered to think that I had gone through the war and rebellions not being aware that injury could expose me to serious risk. The same applied to dental care. It is hard to believe that it all turned out well.

While being focused on my studies, I did not ignore what was happening in the outside world, especially in post-colonial Asia. During my long nights of study, I took a break every fifty minutes on the hour. At 10:00 pm I listened to the foreign radio broadcasts with a battered war surplus radio, BBC and VOC (it was news delivered by announcer Mr. Conover as well as a good dose of pro-America propaganda). I was following the war in French Indo-China (Vietnam). On the night of May 7, 1954, the announcer in a ponderous voice (under stress) announced the sad news: General Christian de Castries reported that French resistance had collapsed. The French redoubt at Dien Bien Phu, being bombarded continuously for days on end by the communists, had fallen to the Viet Minh. From a young age, during the war, I knew that it was important to be aware of what is going outside the country, as it would have an impact on my life.

Back to medical school. My fellow students were a polyglot group. Less than half were Burmese; the rest were Indians, Chinese, and a few Anglos. Given the cultural differences, the students tended to cluster, and I had the good fortune to team up with a group of Christian and Anglo boys. The tuck (tea shop) was the center of social activities on campus and was where we gathered to talk and socialize, where we discussed happenings in the city and the outside world. We talked about the future, all of us worried about what jobs we would find after we graduated. Those of us who did not yet have citizenship were concerned and always talked about going abroad. There were no frat houses that we could go to.

Every medical student dreaded Organic Chemistry. At school, each step was a weeding-out process. Organic Chemistry class was where "the wheat was separated from the chaff"; in the first half of the year, its difficult math, diagrams, and formulas would end the dreams of many students. The Organic Chemistry exam was a method of weeding out low scorers; it "separated the boys from the men." About one-quarter of the students failed, which would terminate any further pursuit of medical studies. The lecturer was a man of Chinese descent. He did not always wear a jacket, and when he did, it was sometimes with a mismatched tie. He did not engage in unnecessary banter but instead said little. The students all wondered what he was thinking. For students he was a nightmare and greatly feared. He had the power to end your career with a failing grade. His was one class that I made sure to never miss. But it was said that, although he was a hard task master, he was a fair man and did not play favorites. He knew his subject well and was a good teacher. The course lasted six months. There were no new text books, only a limited number of old chemistry books in the library. I memorized all the complex formulas. I wrote and rewrote the formulas—the benzene ring, the many-sided ring, the Henderson-Hasselbach equation—which was a challenge. Then came the exam, the day of truth. With great anxiety I took the exam, knowing that if I failed, my quest for a medical degree would end then and there. Every day after the exam I would take the train to the medical college to look for the announcement of test results. Finally the day arrived. With immense trepidation I approached the board on which the results were posted. I passed! It was a great relief to see my name on the passing list, and I was overcome with joy.

The rich and the upper-class students were driven to school by liveried drivers in well-kept cars; the rest of us came to school by bus, train, and at times on foot. I looked for like-minded colleagues regardless of background. My closest friends came from different backgrounds. One was George, a light-skinned Anglo-Arakanese, a Muslim;[90] another was Godfrey Lewis, the gangly, irreverent, privileged, and happy-go-lucky son of the highly respected Professor of Anatomy at the medical college. He must have driven his father to despair.

Professor Lewis, an Asian, succeeded the last of the old guard British professors. He had gone to England to get an advanced surgical degree, and this would lead to his status as a highly valued Fellow of the Royal College of Surgeons. He was a Christian, a small and intense man who paid attention not only to a student's mastery of anatomy but also to the student's behavior, to assess whether the student would make a worthy physician. He was stern, professional, and distant. He had very high standards and expected much of his students. Stories abounded about his tough questions at the oral exams. He held to traditional rigorous standards. Yet he took kindly to me and would ultimately be one of my mentors who would influence me greatly. I was respectful and diligent in class and got an occasional smile from him. After the dreaded Organic Chemistry exam came the Anatomy exam. I took

[90] A much-maligned group in Burmese society even then.

the written exam and felt confident about it, but the oral exam caused anxiety. Professor Lewis took a model of the brain and pointed to a small dark spot of the brain for me to identify (the substantia Nigra). Next he pointed to another area of the brain for me to identify (the putamen, whose function was not well understood). He shook my hand and wished me well. I knew I passed.

There were many good educators and mentors at the medical college. In the third year of medical school I had to take the Bacteriology exam. I thought I had failed the written exam and also had broken out in a rash so was afraid to go to the oral exam. I did not keep my appointment for it. I thought I was finished, but one of the examiners, a noted outside examiner, was not going to let me off so easily. Ultimately, my professor would save me from myself. He was of the old school. Like the British he used the title of his military rank ("Lt. Colonel") rather than "Doctor." He had joined the exodus to India during the invasion in 1942, rose to the rank of Lt. Colonel in the Indian Army, returned in 1945, and became a professor of medicine. When I did not appear for the oral portion of the bacteriology exam, I was scared and dejected. Much to my surprise, the Colonel sent his own car to fetch me. It was a unique experience. His man came to the house and told me to get into the car. A short while later I was dropped off at the school. I entered the room a nervous bundle. The Colonel wanted me to proceed to the oral exam room immediately, where he motioned to me to sit down. Three examiners asked me a few questions, then smiled and shook my hand, a clear signal that I passed. I was astounded at my professor's concern and generosity. I would never have finished my professional education without his kindness and perseverance, and I would never be here.

After I passed my third year, I prevailed on Uncle Rao to help me financially. He reluctantly provided some assistance, but the relationship was tenuous. The family by now was bitterly divided and fought frequently over the younger siblings, who took advantage of the dysfunction and went their destructive ways. Money was always a problem. I was chronically short of bus or train fare and would go without lunch. My friends George and Godfrey ribbed me about my shortage of money. I had no social life, could not even offer my friends a cup of tea. I lived on the edge and didn't have enough money to buy tea myself. My last two years of medical school were probably the most stressful. I did not quite know where the money would come from; all I knew was that I was going to persist and hope for the best.

My friends were more sophisticated and worldly than I and had more money. A small group of them would hire a taxi together, jump in, and go out for a night on the town. When I demurred, they would tease me. But I was doing well in school: Surgery, Gynecology, and Medicine were my strong suites. My professors hinted that I was doing well, and each year my grades improved. But I knew that it would end soon. The final exams were in Medicine and Surgery. When the final results were announced, I learned that I had passed, obtaining good grades and placing second in class. (When I went back in 2013 to look at my grades, the registrar graciously allowed me to look at the results of the year of graduation, which confirmed this memory.) Graduation was a tense family moment. While my friends' families were all present at the ceremony, my family (except my sister Olive) was entirely absent. That was a real let-down, to not be celebrated. My friend Godfrey brought his motorcycle so we went for a ride all afternoon.

Figure 47. Author at graduation from University of Rangoon Medical College. Photo taken by a friend.

Figure 48. Author in front of his alma mater, now named Institute of Medicine 1, Rangoon, 2013. Photo by Juleen Eichinger.

# Chapter 26
# Economic Hardships after Independence

Burma was a troubled country in the post-war years and after independence, riven with ethnic conflict. The ethnic peoples had long felt aggrieved and discriminated against by the Buddhist Burmans. This was aggravated by poor Burmese leadership and overemphasis on the Buddhist religion while denigrating other religions. Prior to the Third Anglo-Burmese War, Burma's economy had been small and local. Their principal exports had been rice, and lumber. Burmese rice farmers lived hand to mouth. The British made some investments in the country but never made loans to Burmese farmers, leaving that to Indian moneylenders. The infusion of foreign investments, both British and Indian, helped enormously. Farming improved, agricultural output increased, and Burma became the biggest exporter of rice in the early twentieth century. Following independence, services slowly ground to a halt. Post-war reconstruction needed capital, but with the country in turmoil there was little inflow of capital.

The government collected a small amount of war reparations from Japan; otherwise, investments dried up. Mismanagement would lead to poor policies and economic ruin, taking Burma from a country with a relatively good economy to one of the poorest economies in the world. In just one decade, the U Nu government hurt rice production especially, with an overt policy of discouraging foreign investment. Thakin Nu retained a strange admiration for the Japanese. "Looking at it historically, no nation has done so much to liberate Asia from white domination, yet no nation has been so misunderstood by the very people whom it has helped either liberate or to set an example to in many things."[1] It was this type of muddled thinking that pervaded his rule. He does not mention the enormous damage that the war wrought upon his country, or the hundreds of thousands of people who died in building the Death Railroad, or the millions who died in China at the hands

[1] Quoted in Allen, *Burma: The Longest War*, 564. "Even now, as things actually are, nothing can obliterate the role Japan played in liberating countless people in Burma."

of the Japanese; his main concern was that his Japanese masters had "liberated Burma from European rule." This type of thinking was common to Ba Maw, Aung San, and the rest of the gang.

In contrast to their praise of the Japanese aggressors, the Bamar have long held an aggressive attitude toward non-Bamar people. Historically, they had some military successes against neighbors such as Thailand, although none permanently changed borders. "Our civilization was superior," the Burmese were taught; "We conquered Siam, we defeated the (tiny) Hindu state of Manipur."[2] The Bamar elite lived in this strange fantasy land, believing that they are a better race and country than most other people and countries. They used pejorative terms not just for foreigners but even for their ethnic brethren. This led them to believe that if only all foreigners and subpar ethnic groups would leave the country, Burma would rise again to her [supposed] former glory. Never mind the facts: that Burma borrowed religion and culture from her giant neighbors China and India, that the Burmese made no lasting contribution of great art or literature to the world. Its arrogance is not understandable. The early Burmese kings misjudged the strength of the British, and the post-independence leaders would misjudge the strength and ability of the Bamar people to forge a successful independent state.

My immediate older sister went to work at a dry goods store, bringing in some income, but she was having adjustment problems. My oldest sister Emily was married off to an odd fellow who was a loser; he had no job skills. He contributed little to the household income and instead consumed our resources. He hung around the house in the morning, leaving the house at 10 am and returned past dinner time. We did not really know what he did. My poor sister had a child every year and a half. Her husband was a drain on the family. Kamala's husband had some money from his job as a bookkeeper at the US embassy after the war, and Kamala helped Mother from time to time. But the financial condition of the entire family was still precarious.

---

[2] Manipur is now more advanced than Burma in human rights and has a more robust economy than Burma.

Figure 49. The Rickhawdar Manipur (right)-Zokhawthar Burma (left) border crossing [Indo-Burmese Border.jpg]. By Ericwinny - Own work, CC BY-SA 4.0, via Wikipedia.org.

For me, the long nights of study were now over. It was a relief, but now I had to complete an internship and find a job. I had hoped that I would get some stipends after graduating medical school, but in the previous year, the government had declared that stipends would be awarded only to Bamar citizens; non-Bamar interns would not be paid. Rangoon still suffered from war damage. There was no rebuilding, and there were precious few jobs to be had. Some medical college graduates took jobs with drug companies or as medical salesmen. The pay was just above government salary, but these were dead-end jobs. It was becoming abundantly clear that I needed to prepare for every eventuality. To that end I vowed to improve my non-medical education so that I could go to England or America.

In the meantime, I started my internship at Rangoon General Hospital, despite receiving no stipend. Each day I took the train from home to the hospital. I bought a monthly pass for seven kyats, but could not afford to renew it when it expired. I got to know some ticket collectors who looked the other way for a while. Eventually I had to borrow to buy a pass again; it was most embarrassing to be a physician without money, but lots of things in the post-war era were difficult. At the hospital there was a kitchen for house officers,[3] where I could often find some leftover food. Sometimes this was the main meal of the day. Working at night usually meant there was enough food because I could officially partake of the meals prepared for house officers. Constant worry about money is pernicious. Halfway through the year I was becoming desperate. It is difficult to care for others on an empty stomach. Even with a medical degree under my belt, the family and I were desperate. I could apply for citizenship, but that would take time and many bribes, and even then, the chances of getting a job were low because I was Indian. Even if I did land a job, it would be in some remote town. The future for me was limited here in this country.

My friend Godfrey, the son of my Anatomy professor, informed me that a recent graduate, a Karen, had information about a job with a mining company. The man had served there for a year, had returned, and did not wish to return. What he did not tell me was why he did not return. He put out feelers for a prospective applicant. I sought him out and talked to him. The company was mining Tungsten (W)[4] in a remote part of the Karrenni State. The mineral had been discovered there some time after the British annexed Burma. Fortunately for my prospects, the Bamar did not like going to the border areas, as the people there were both afraid of and loathed them. I actually liked the border states, as the hill climate was quite mild, the places were cleaner and less congested, and the people were friendly. They had none of the tensions of Rangoon.[5]

---

[3] When on call, house officers could not leave the hospital, so meals were provided. It was the only benefit to working long hours through the night.

[4] Also known as Wolfram or Scheelite; the mineral was discovered by Peter Woulfe, a Swede. Scheelite means "heavy stone" in Swedish.

[5] Its geography and geology were complex: 65 million years ago, the Southeast Asia plate slammed against the Asia plate, uplifted the shallow sea, and formed the boundary between Burma and Thailand and Malaya. The uplift created extensive low mountain chains, making this a beautiful place, as well as a rich source of mineral wealth. It had the largest of deposits of tungsten (in the British

Tungsten Carbide (WC) contains equal parts tungsten and carbide. When combined with steel, it increases the density of steel and makes it twice as hard. Alloyed with iron, it is resistant to a high melting point. Mixed with nickel binder, it takes a high polish and luster, making attractive jewelry that will not rust, tarnish, or oxidize. It has many uses in precision instruments such as surgical equipment and for various military uses. For these reasons, tungsten was in high demand. The company, Mawchi Mines Ltd., had once been owned by Consolidated Gold Mines and listed on the (pre-war) London Exchange. The mine was located in a remote part of Kayah (Karenni) State. In colonial times it had been worked by the Burma Corporation and had been one of the chief sources of dollar exchange for the British Empire. During the war it had ceased operations and gone into receivership. The Japanese occupiers had stripped the mines of all the equipment, pumps, generators, and separators and had shipped the ores in storage to Japan. After the war, the British resumed operations but left after U Nu invaded Karenni State in 1948–50 and took military control of the mines. The Burmese tried to run it but soon ran it aground, so they brought in an Australian miner to start it up again. In 1957 a new corporation was formed, called Mawchi Mines Ltd. It was still a dangerous place.

The history of Kayah State was difficult. It was an autonomous state until it would be seized in 1962 by the Burmese military junta. Even in peace time it presented challenges: it was beautiful, but the jungle was everywhere in the remote hilly terrain; it was sparsely populated, mostly by Red Karens and other hill tribes; it was poorly developed, without much infrastructure; there were no all-weather roads; and there was no hospital or doctor within fifty miles of the mine. The people were poorly educated and lacked skills, so a non-Karen labor force was recruited to work the mines, mostly Gurkhas from Nepal who, after World War II, decided to stay after their service in the British Army. Even as the mine was restarted, the Karenni people (mostly ethnic Karen, noted for their long-necked

---

empire), wolfram, tin, and other minerals. It is typical of the edges of plate sutures that they are rich in minerals and that gems are formed. It was the discovery of the mineral deposits that brought the British geologists and engineers here.

women[6]) rebelled against the Rangoon government. The rebellion was now nine years old. With each passing year the instability increased and had now fragmented the countryside, with the government holding control of the mine area and towns. This attracted other groups looking for loot. I was told that the British doctor had been disabled. The company said it needed a good doctor to take temporary charge as acting chief doctor, and soon.

Telling Mother was not going to be easy. I finally summoned up my courage and told her that I had to leave and get a paying job. It came with several advantages: free comfortable housing, 24-hour electricity, a refrigerator (still rare in Burma at that time), flush toilet, and three servants (a cook, a gardener, and a housekeeper). It sounded good. Moreover, the temperature was mild and the hills were beautiful country.

I salivated at the prospect of having a good life. The pay, three times the average government salary, was the greatest inducement. I was concerned about reports of instability and the presence of a rebellion. Then I told myself that if I could survive all the travails of the war, I could survive. The Rangoon office was located on Merchant Street, a busy street full of offices. Extremely nervous, I submitted my application with references to the office. I waited a long time until I was finally called to their office. The chief engineer, Mr. Crozier, a tall, gangly Australian, was in Rangoon for a few days. He was quite charming and kind and soon set me at ease. I worried about not making a good impression, especially that I might make mistakes in accent. He asked me a number of questions and the interview ended on a positive note. The job was mine. It was to change my life forever.

---

[6] There are many stories about why women wore these polished gold neck rings. One explains that the area was infested with tigers, which kill by seizing humans by the neck. The shiny rings prevented tigers from killing women, whose job was to collect firewood.

# Chapter 27
# Mawchi Mines

The area of the country I was going to (Kayah State) was populated predominantly by Karenni (sometimes also called Red Karens because of the color of their traditional clothing). I thought it would be a happy time. My relationship with the Karens goes way back, to the war years when Danam's Karen friends were so helpful to the family in our intended evacuation from Rangoon. We had fled to Karen villages several times during the war, and we came to know them well. We spent happy times with many Christian Karens. They loved Western music; with an ancient guitar and a wooden box they could put together a band. They played popular pop music, especially American country music, and during the Christmas and New Year seasons we sang carols as they played the guitar. It was comfort music that alleviated the fear of wartime. I thought that my experience and good relationship with the Karens would stand me in good stead. What I did not understand was the depth of the poor relationship between the Karenni and the Bamar.

The politics of the country were worsening. The false notion that all Burma had to do in order to prosper was to get rid of foreign influence was naive. Burmese notions of capital formation, banking, and credit were woefully inadequate. The Burmese Prime Minister U Nu, facing a falling economy and high unemployment, was failing politically. He turned his attention to religion. He refused to grant the minority Karenni limited autonomy, which they had enjoyed during colonial times. This increased tensions further and led to another revolt.[1] I was assured by the mining company that I would be safe and not be attacked while I was in the pay of the company. I would have all the benefits of British staff. My feeling was that if there were British workers on site, it would be relatively safe for me.

---

[1] The promises made to the ethnic peoples were mostly words on paper made by General Aung San and his cronies like Ne Win; they never were serious about giving autonomy, they were deceitful. The Panglong Agreement (signed February 12, 1947) between his Burmese government and the Shan, Kachin, and Chin peoples was penned by the Burmese but never kept.

In this primitive land with few roads, the British had built a mining complex on the remote mountainside; crushers, processing warehouses, and homes for British miners and their families. Burma's largest hydroelectric power station, which supplied Rangoon's needs, was located in the region. In addition to the tungsten and other minerals, the area was also rich in timber. It was heavily forested with teak, ironwood, and the famed redwood (Padauk), which the Chinese craved and carved. Infrastructure was woeful, however. The roads near the mine clung to the sides of the mountains and were difficult to maintain; none were all-weather roads. From Toungoo (the rail head), there was only one long, tortuous, fair-weather road about 70 miles long, which frequently had to be closed due to rebel attacks. A shorter all-weather road from Toungoo to the mine had existed in peace time but now was totally "rebel" controlled and out of service. Thus road travel from Rangoon, once possible, was now impossible. I would have to fly the newly created Union of Burma Airways in a war-surplus DC 3. The reliability of the airline was questionable. Maintaining these aircraft was a hit or miss affair, for trained mechanics were few. It was an irony that I would fly in a plane just a few years after the war. I was terrified by the noise of aircraft. The sound of aircraft had meant trouble in wartime, but now, after seven years, the fear was much reduced.

I boarded the aircraft nervously. Getting onto the plane was not easy, as the steps were not stable. Shivers rippled down my spine as I climbed them. The Dakota still had military seating: long, crude, metal benches, with no overhead bins. I put everything I had into a small luggage compartment, then took a seat on the hard metal bench. Thankfully it was a short flight. The Loikaw (capital of the Karenni State) airstrip was crude—just a dirt strip, not much changed since World War II. As this was the dry season, the landing was bumpy but otherwise uneventful. The ride to the town was a short one.

Loikaw was a quaint little town, built atop a flat hill. Its only metaled road ran just to the edge of town. It had no hotel but had a guest house where I could make a brief stop to freshen up and have a bite to eat. The young Muslim manager who owned the guest house was polite but not warm. The Indian hotel cook made me a lunch basket containing a sandwich and a salad. Soon two Land Rovers[2] arrived: "short wheel-base" vehicles that had only four wheels (the longer version, called the long wheel-base Rover, had three axles and six wheels). The Karen driver welcomed me, and shortly the convoy was underway. He explained that the drive to the mine was "less than a hundred miles but it would take all day, due to the condition of the road, which is terrible. We have to take supplies for the mine and the miners." We set out on the all-weather road, which gave way at the town's outskirts to a rough un-metaled road that was cut through jungle. The jungle soon gave way to dense grassland, where tall elephant grass grew skyward, in some places to 8 feet high, shutting out the sunlight even at noon. If there were underground rebels in the area, they could never be seen. I suddenly was keenly aware of how much danger there was in the jungles of Burma. After the area of elephant grass, we passed through thick jungle, and the road twisted and turned as we climbed through some of the most rugged country in the world. The terrain soon changed. It was now barren, punctuated with large boulders that made it ideal ambush country. It seemed reminiscent of many scenes from wartime movies. In fact, most of the road was rebel-controlled, and many had been killed in ambushes during the war, on both sides.[3] As the road climbed, the land fell off steeply to its side. It was so quiet without traffic. No clusters of people, although every now and then we passed rusted vehicles down in the steep ravine, relics of the war. Looking down at them there was no way of telling whether they were old or recent, the result of reckless driving or rebel activity. After about four hours the terrain

---

[2] This model was the precursor to the Range Rover. It had a rooftop bin.

[3] In 1945 a terrible slaughter happened here. The Japanese 28th, trapped during the monsoon on the western slopes of a low mountain range, the Pegu Yomas, had to reach the railway escarpment and run the gauntlet; the 17th Indian Division was well positioned to take their revenge for what had happened three and a half years earlier at the Sittang Bridge. The "breakout," as it was called, was brutal. Thousands of Japanese were slaughtered by the Karens of Force 136, the Jedburghs. The precise number will never be known. Once they crossed the rail and road, the Japanese came across a flooded Sittang delta, where many drowned and scores died of dysentery and malaria. One of the roads they took on their retreat was the Toungoo–Loikaw Road, then on to Moulmein. Looking at the boulders and the narrow passageways, I could well imagine the rebels sitting on top of the hill and shooting down on the convoy of Japanese or Burmese troops like fish in a barrel. It would have been a massacre, bloody and gruesome. In fact, less than half of the two divisions of the 28th Army survived the march.

changed again: green hills appeared in the distance. Here and there would be a lone hut, and then we arrived upon a high plateau. The road next passed through a narrow gorge with two tall boulders on the left and one on the right. The road twisted and turned between them. As we approached the pass, out of the corner of my eye, I could see the driver look to his left and right, then make signs at unseen objects before resuming speed. I wondered what he was signaling to; probably unseen Karenni rebels. His broad faced broke into a smile, he looked at me reassuringly, and kept going. There were strips of cloth affixed to the branches of small trees, some green and some red, again probably indicators to the driver from rebel groups.

The sun hung low in the sky and the shadows lengthened as evening approached. The late afternoon sunlight barely filtered through the dense growth. For a city boy it was beautiful, but in a mysterious way. After six hours of driving, we finally arrived at the base camp, a large concrete block building beside a creek. "It is the mill," the driver said, "the ore processor and separator." The effluent ran into the creek. We passed the camp and started to climb again. The narrow road hugged the mountainside, and there were frequent switch backs. In another ten minutes we came to a flat area surrounded by hills, the hospital spur. This was situated midway between the mining base camp where the mill was located and the top of the mountain where the company headquarters were located. We pulled up in front of my new home, built into the cliff-side with the front on stilts. The driver stopped at the front gate and helped me unload. My three servants—a cook, a bearer (a Karen woman), and a gardener—were waiting for me and gave me a warm reception. The bearer took me into the house and showed me around. Cook had prepared some hot food that I ate, and then I settled down for the night. What struck me was the inky darkness and the silence.

In spite of its remoteness and its being built into the cliff, my new home looked imposing and was spacious inside, with a living room and two bedrooms, both furnished; a kitchen with a fridge and running water; and a bathroom with flush toilets. It was luxury I could have only dreamt about. I wondered how the builders dragged all the equipment up the mountains on the primitive roads.

Figure 50. Mawchi Mines hospital spur. Photo by author.

Figure 51. Mawchi Mines Hospital close up. Photo by author.

Figure 52. Author in front of first Mawchi house. Photo taken by a friend.

## THE MINING CAMP AND HOSPITAL

The next morning, I was up early to survey my new environment. The morning air was cool, unlike the heat and humidity of Rangoon. I took a short walk and, after an English breakfast, was driven up to the mountaintop to report to the General Manager, then report to the hospital. I paused to look at the scene: the mountains and the green valleys were quite breathtaking; flowers grew in well-kept gardens. There were five hills and a mountain about 6,000 feet high, on which the company headquarters was built. The office was built on a flattened-out portion of the mountaintop about 150 feet wide, similar to the hospital spur. To the north was a deep ravine. On one side was the "British pub"; in the center was a tennis court; and scattered around was housing for the mining administration. The General Manager greeted me warmly and welcomed me to Mawchi. In addition to the usual office equipment there was a huge safe and a radio telephone—which he told me was the only means of communication when the roads became impassible. He was reassuring and gave me sound advice. "Don't worry about the stories of rebels, they are all around, but we do not have to worry." What he did not say was that there was a tacit agreement that the rebels would not harm us. The office personnel explained other details, for example that the mail came about once a week. I was relieved to learn that mail came regularly, because I looked forward to receiving not only letters but also my precious medical journals, the *British Journal of Medicine* and *The Lancet*, as well as books I had ordered from Smart & Mookerdem, the bookstore in Rangoon. I next went out to the hospital, looking forward to meeting the good doctor. To my surprise, I saw the hospital porters carrying the doctor on a stretcher. I was told that he was comatose and would not be coming back.

Both the hospital itself and also the houses for the staff were low-slung buildings. The main hospital was not imposing but, considering its location in the remote jungle, was impressive. It had two wings (a women's ward and a men's) connected with a doctor's office, a small operating theater, and a library. Unfortunately, the skeleton staff was inadequate to serve all the needs. The head nurse gave me a tour. The personnel were mostly young Karenni women. In the system left over from colonial times, recently registered nurses wore a red longyi; senior nurses wore blue; and the most senior nurse wore green. There were only a few patients, mostly pregnant women and some infants in the women's ward (the staff had midwifery experience), and in the men's ward were patients with the usual tropical diseases such as malaria and dengue fever and a few with minor wounds suffered while working in the mine. I was to learn later that the rebels often visited the hospital at night, when the Burmese soldiers were safely ensconced in their bunkers. The rebels would collect (confiscate) bandages, iodine, and pain-killers. The management knew about this but were powerless to stop it. The head nurse gave me a list of medications that were in short supply and implored me to present the list to the General Manager.

I immediately began my work day with morning rounds. I visited two women who had just delivered and saw that they were being well cared for by a nurse. The ill and injured men were also receiving good care. To familiarize myself with the mine, I took time to go inside the mine. The crusher, where they crushed

Figure 53. Bulabu, a Karen village near Mawchi Mines. Photo by author.

the ore before sending it down to the separator, was huge. I reflected on the past few days, wondering about what I had gotten into. I was to be responsible for about 7,500 people in the village, including the English, Welsh, and Irish mine workers. I had just finished medical school and eight months as house officer (similar to internship) at Rangoon General Hospital. The hospital was not staffed to handle major illness or surgery. I was wary and hoped that I would not be confronted with a major medical problem, because all I would be able to do would be to provide triage and send the patient on to Rangoon. My first day gave me the impression that I would encounter primarily tropical diseases and injuries. Soon, however, I would see two patients with unusual injuries: gunshots wounds. Both of these men were non-Karen. They were Gurkhas, the legendary soldiers from Nepal, veterans of the British-Indian Army of World War II who fought to defeat the Japanese and refused to be repatriated and instead chose to stay behind. My job would be more challenging than I had thought.

Figure 54. Author with Mawchi Hospital staff outside hospital. Photo taken by a friend.

A week later a reception was held to welcome me, which perked me up. At the club I was introduced to Welsh, English, and Irish men and some of the men's wives. The English were mostly friendly. I had a tankard of beer and, as darkness set in, took my leave. There was only one way to get from one place to the other, and that was by Land Rover. These were the only vehicles that could climb the steep and narrow switch backs, and after dusk it felt rather scary. I was dropped off at the hospital.

Sunrises were spectacular and breathtaking. Mists hang low over the green valleys, clouds embrace and envelop the tall peaks, then the sun breaks through the morning mists. As the sun slowly dissipates the mists and the clouds, the silvery river, the Salween, can be seen in the distance, snaking through the valley. The nights were lonely, no other person to talk to, no radio, not much reading material except for what I had brought with me, medical journals and text books. After I had been on the job for about one week, I settled into my room at night to read one of my journals. The Burmese soldiers were comfortably ensconced in their bunkers. All seemed well until the still of the night was broken by the familiar rat-a-tat-rat from below my living room, seemingly from just five feet below my feet. My first reaction was to crawl under a table, but considering where the gunfire was coming from, that was not the wisest choice. I crawled away from the living room to the kitchen at the mountainside end of the house, where there was more protection, and held my breath. I could see tracers originating from under the house, directed to the mountaintop—an attack directed at the Burmese camp. The machine-gun fire was all too familiar. It was *deja vu* all over again. Fortunately, there was no return fire from the army bunkers; being caught in cross-fire was the worst thing for a non-combatant. It was scary. Finally the gunfire ceased and silence fell on the hills except for the chirping insects. I wondered why, when there was so much terrain, the rebels took to firing from under my house. The next morning the nurses assured me that I was not the target.

In spite of nightly gunfire, the mining camp was outwardly calm. The situation on the surface remained unchanged, but under the surface there was fear that something bad was going to happen. The rebellion that was thought to be contained in fact had taken a turn for the worse, and the rebels were suffering mounting losses in their conflict with the Burma Army. The intrigue between the government in Rangoon and the Karenni State capital was explosive, and the company was caught in the middle. In time it would soon descend into chaos and the breakdown of all agreements between the mine owners and the state government. It would no longer be safe to be in the mine.

Tension was increasing by the day, fear heightened, the rebel attacks worsened. The rebels turned to the mining company for under-the-table payments to increase their funding. Then the unthinkable happened: a convoy with a British engineer was shot at. We went into emergency mode, put him on a stretcher, and disrobed him. His clothes from the waist down were stained with blood but not saturated. He was borne on the stretcher to the operation theater. After the dresser cut his pants, I took a quick look: his left buttock had a small bullet-hole entrance; the bullet had exited a short distance medially, and to his good fortune and my great relief it was a superficial wound. There was no neurological or orthopedic injury. This was the first time that I had to care for a white man, which caused me great worry and anxiety about whether I would be up to the task. The man's wife, a tall, gangly, blond girl, was of course full of angst. It took me great deal of confidence to talk to her, to assure her that he would be well, it was not a serious wound, that the blood loss was small, that he was not in shock. I assured her that I would stay in the hospital. The man's friends descended on the hospital, and after another conference it was decided that he could go home later that evening. The next morning, he smilingly thanked me.

Tension was in the air, and mounting concerns led to a call made by radio to the headquarters. The longstanding agreement between the company and rulers at Loikaw had broken down. As usual, money was the issue. New players in the deadly intrigue had entered the field and wanted money equivalent to the payments the older groups were receiving. Given the declining income of the mine, this was just not possible. Paying one group was bad enough, but two was too much. The General Manager refused to bribe the new players, asking the ruler of the Karenni State to control the rebels, A few days later rumors were spreading that the negotiations had stopped some weeks before, due to the shooting in and around the hospital. The agreement between the Burmese, the British, and the Karens had broken down. The company now waited for the next move.

I was summoned to the mountaintop to see the chief engineer, the man in charge of the camp. There were times when he appeared tense, but beneath this veneer he was all steely resolve. Yet this day he appeared worried. He greeted me warmly, then said, "You are aware of the turmoil? We have to adapt and make some changes. Given the deteriorating security conditions, especially in the lower levels, we are moving some employees to the more secure mountaintop. You will move into a solid two-storey brick house" (actually, it was a beautiful, large, mountaintop house built in the base of the mountain for a family of four). He continued, "You will be safer here, especially at night. The Burma Army company is directly overhead." Each day I would be transported to the hospital by the transport pool, and my house staff would be moved with me.

Figure 55. Author's second house in Mawchi, at hilltop. Photo by author.

The front door of my new home opened to a higher mountain range. Between the ridge and the house was a deep green valley that glistened in the sunlight at high noon. What lay in the valley was hard to imagine, probably wild animals. To the south was a smaller round-topped mountain, where the rebels had built their stronghold. Two hundred feet and on top of the peak was a company of Burmese troops; they lived in defensive positions and hid in bunkers all day, only coming out after dusk to fire occasionally to keep the rebels at bay.

# Chapter 28
# Ambush and Aftermath

Like most mornings, it was cool on the mountaintop. I finished breakfast early and walked to the vehicle that would drive me down to the hospital each morning. The sun had burnt off the mist covering the valleys, and the fog had lifted. We were winding down the mountainside and had just reached a patch of tall trees, close enough to the hospital that I could see it. To my surprise there was lorry ahead of us, loaded with Gurkha laborers and their families, including children. Our vehicles clung to the mountainside and moved slowly; ahead I could see that the roadside ravine was deep and steep. The road was no more than ten feet wide in places, with multiple switchbacks. The only sound was the purr of the engines. It was peaceful and so far a normal day. Just fifty feet shy of the hospital, at a hairpin turn in the road, the quiet of the morning was brutally shattered: automatic gunfire exploded from the high trees on the ravine side. Bullets struck the truck ahead of mine. My driver turned the wheel, slammed on the brakes, and gripped the steering wheel tight with white-knuckled hands. He looked pale and terrified as the truck shuddered and swayed and the tires screamed before coming to a screeching halt and going slightly off the edge of the road. With great effort the driver had brought the lorry under control, and it and the vehicle ahead of us came to a halt.[1] Tall trees obscured the valley below, but the hospital could be seen just beyond the hairpin turn. I turned my eyes towards the unfolding disaster and saw that the other truck was hanging precariously on the edge of the ravine. Reflexively (as a result of my training), I took over rescue. I knew instantly that people needed help. There were screams, shouts, cries of pain and anguish; the cries and wailing of the injured was heard to bear. Many people from the leading vehicle hung on the sides of the truck. I ran to the scene and saw immediately that many had been wounded. The non-wounded and slightly wounded jumped out of the truck and, dazed, just lay on the ground. I jumped on board the truck bed, where

[1] The attackers were skilled; the attack was quick and brutal, then they melted away.

there were two dead. After ascertaining that I could do nothing for them, I turned to an elderly Gurkha man writhing in pain, clutching his left elbow and crying. I could see blood spurting from the artery. I took a handkerchief out quickly and applied it above the elbow to stop the blood flow. Fortunately, the accident happened close to the hospital, and by this time the nurses had rushed out of the hospital and arrived with a first-aid kit. As soon as the spurting slowed, I rushed the man to the hospital and stabilized him. He looked pale and semiconscious. I started an intravenous drip and ordered a morphine injection. I next went looking for the head nurse and had her organize teams to care for the wounded. They quickly separated the dead from those who were still alive and took me to the most seriously injured, who numbered thirteen. I had the nurse who was in charge of the operation theater prepare it for an operation and quickly looked at the other wounded and the dead. The nurses had attended to the wounded, dressed the wounds. By now the small hospital was crowded with friends and relatives, making care of the wounded difficult. Talking to the families of the slightly wounded was easy enough; I reassured them that they could stay at the hospital overnight to care for their loved ones. Regarding the elderly man with the gunshot wound in his arm: I came to the reluctant conclusion there was no hope of saving the arm. It would be very difficult to tell the family. My heart sank, and the wailing and crying increased as the extended family gathered. I had assisted at amputations, mostly of the leg, but never done an amputation of an arm on my own. There was nobody to consult. I took Nurse Amy aside and asked her if there was a library; she took me to the Chief Medical Officer's private library, which had remained locked since I had arrived, and there in one corner was an old book shelf. I furiously looked for a textbook of surgery and found an issue that was old but adequate. I thumbed through the pages quickly. I was most concerned with the blood vessel: if I could not control it, it would mean death, I learned the course of the artery above the gunshot wound, memorizing the anatomy of the brachial artery. I had a queasy sensation and was fearful that it would not turn out well, as the patient had lost a lot of blood. I asked Nurse Amy if we had instruments such as a saw, and she said "I will sterilize the instruments within a half hour, but there is nobody to give anesthesia."

I had to depend on the local nurses, and Amy was the best, the only one I could rely on. In the operating theater, I placed my gloved finger on the brachial artery, then opened the bandage away from the injured area, allowing me to look at the anatomy. The bullet had entered the lateral side of the elbow. It was small entrance wound, but the exit wound was large. It was a mess, with skin, torn muscles, fragments of bone. The powerful projectile had shattered the distal humerus, torn through the neuro-vascular bundle, and severed the brachial artery, destroying a centimeter of it. The bleeding had been temporarily controlled by a heavy bandage, but when I removed it, the arm started to bleed, the fingers were cold, the hand had no pulse. I had to control the bleeding by keeping pressure on the proximal artery. The man was awake; there was no anesthesia, only some chloroform. I had to think of what I had to do. This is what high-speed bullets do. There was nothing to do but to amputate the arm above the elbow. I would need to do the amputation without anesthesia or an assistant other than the nurse at the head of the table to give him morphine. I gathered myself together and made the first incision. As soon as the knife cut into the skin, the man started to moan. "Another shot of morphine," I called. I had to isolate the brachial artery and keep my finger on it proximally. I put a forceps on the artery, lifted it up from the muscles and bone, and tied it. I breathed sigh of relief. Next it was sawing the bone, and then getting all the muscles to cover the bone. In the best of circumstances, it would have taken forty minutes, but it took longer. The man was transferred to a small recovery room, I dreaded facing the family.

The man's large family gathered outside the theater. I had deep misgivings. I spoke no Gurkha so through an interpreter explained the gravity of his condition. His wife and his children were already crying openly and noisily. I explained that he had lost a lot of blood due to the injury to the artery and the time it took to transport him to the hospital, and that we did not have blood to transfuse. I wish I had been able to supply a blood transfusion or more IV fluids, but there were none. I explained that his chances were fifty percent. I ordered the nurse to stay on. I stayed at the hospital, worried sick. This was my big challenge, and the outcome was not very promising. He died a short time later.

The death toll was seven. The Gurkha community was in despair over the fact that they were being targeted and harassed. About 2:00 am, I felt I needed some time to myself, so I slipped through the side door of the hospital and went to my old home, which was only one hundred feet away. The fridge was still working and still contained some beer. I sat down and took stock of the day's events. Something was amiss. Normally there would have been only one vehicle on the road. Were the rebels gunning for the workers to set an example? Were they gunning for me, to force the company to negotiate with them? It was an ominous sign that the rebels were hitting non-Karenni labor. I was overcome with fear and depression. I learned more in this one day than in all the years of study in college. It was one thing to take some risks, but is it worth it?

The dysfunctional government in Rangoon was unable to promise security, as it had little control over the state government. The General Manager called in the heads of departments and appraised the situation. In the ensuing discussion, the majority determined that, unless there was security, the British families should leave. An informal poll revealed that they all felt it was unsafe to stay. The General Manager promised a decision soon and later called another meeting of the heads of departments. At that meeting he announced that the company would close the mine. All British miners and their families would leave except for a small "care and maintenance team" that would remain to protect the equipment and the ore and finalize the shutdown. They would do so only if there was a doctor on site. So I had to stay, to protect the care and maintenance team.

There were many sad good-byes. The families piled onto the long wheelbase Land Rovers while the local people lined the street at the village, some crying in despair. It was a somber scene and evoked immense sadness. I said good-bye to all the people whom I had gotten to know.

The General Manager instructed me to close the main hospital and move part of it uphill, just below the tennis court, to a small facility with about ten beds. This meant that over the next week I had the unpleasant task of firing and reducing the staff, a very upsetting job, and setting up the new smaller unit. All the medicines, bandages, surgical instruments and operating theater, and all tools, beds, and bedpans were packaged and moved, as were the patients. I wondered how I would cope if more serious injuries were to occur.

Cutting the hospital staff to a skeleton status was a difficult and thankless task. I made the mistake of firing the politically connected but lazy and incompetent chief nurse, which would create all manner of future problems for me. Leading the care and maintenance team was Pete, who was a pleasant, easy-going young man my age, educated, and a miner. The team consisted of Pete, a middle-aged miner named Art, and the radio operator. This closeness to the new team staff filled me with angst. Pete lived in a large house up on the hill, on the other side of the club house, with Art. I lived on the other side of the hill. Pete and I worked out plans to run the hospital. As my work load diminished, my skills eroded. The long hours of not seeing patients was depressing, and I wondered where it was all going. I could not comprehend it all, and my whole future was now in question. My grand house was just below the mountain bunker of the Burmese military. I got to know the commanding (Bamar) officer, or he got to know me, but it soon became apparent that he was using me to get information about the mine operation. My job became impossible. Supplies to the mine from Loikaw—food, drink, and medical supplies—were becoming scarce, and in the midst of all this a whooping cough epidemic began. There were no vaccines or antibiotics. I went out with an army convoy to the state capital to gather supplies, but without success. Returning empty-handed was not very comforting. We set out late in the afternoon on our return trip, and soon ran into trouble. Arriving at a village beside the Salween River, we noticed that there were no people to be seen; the village was empty. It was creepy. I walked into a hut and saw that there was food on the hearth, still warm; the inhabitants obviously had fled. The commander immediately ordered the convoy to leave the village, and when we stopped about mile beyond the village, we ran into a half-hearted ambush. The commander ordered us out of the jeep and to lie down on the ground. Fortunately, the light gunfire stopped after midnight. We spent the night sleeping on the side of the road.

Communications with the outside world were never efficient at the mining camp; we were all but cut off from the outside world, except for communication by radio telephone and, about once a week, mail delivery. Now there was no mail.

There was no telephone land line; only at the administration building on the top of the mountain was there a radio telephone that communicated with the head office in Rangoon, to keep abreast of negotiations between the London office and the camp. I sat on the balcony in front of my house and gazed at the scenery. I felt grieved and depressed that all my hard work had once again been all for naught. That my first job and my dream would end so soon and in so dismal a way was disheartening and frightening.[2] I had a dream house on a hilltop, with flush toilets, refrigerator, and good pay, and it was crushing me that this would end. I knew that I would never see this life again for a long time. The whole of Burma was descending into chaos and despair. The civil government was making a mess of civil rule, foreshadowing the military coup that was inevitable in a few years and would lead to the long age of darkness.

Once again I packed my bags and made preparations to leave. The day finally arrived. I turned to look at the tall mountain for the last time. I climbed the few stairs leading up to the house, happy to see the flowers still in bloom (the gardeners kept the place beautiful). Then I went to see Pete. He was waiting there. We hugged and shook hands; he thanked me profusely for staying under difficult circumstances. I recalled the many evenings that we had sipped gin together and wondered about the future. Pete wished me luck and told me I had a good future. I had to get hold of my emotions. All the uncertainty returned, but at least this time I did have money saved, so that I could survive till I got a new job. Going back home would be difficult. While I had sent modest monies to my mother, the household situation had worsened, with only one person working. My first job ended, and so did the romance. I went down to the waiting Land Rover, took one last look at my home, and set out to the state capital city of Loikaw.

On my way out I came upon a scene that would add to my wretchedness. A week before, I had examined a man, slightly older than I, a Gurkha of medium build, strong with a rugged frame, and handsome despite some pockmarks from childhood smallpox, which did not mar his appearance. He probably had fought in World War II, on the allied side, with tenacity and courage. Now he drove a lorry

---

[2] Fortunately, the General Manager gave me letter of recommendation, which I still have.

for the company, bringing supplies from and taking the ore concentrates to the capital, Loikaw. As he sat down, he appeared to shiver. He must have had a premonition. "I am to drive the truck to Loikaw," he said, "but I feel feverish. Could I get a medical excuse not to drive?" The nurse's notes indicated that his temperature was normal; his history indicated that he did have malaria, that he would have fever and chills every second or third day; but now he did not look sick. I examined him but did not sense that he was that sick. I knew that malaria came and went, and since he was not in an acute stage, I felt that I could not issue a medical excuse. He looked sad and left. I heard through the grapevine that his truck was ambushed and he was killed. Now, a week later, I was taking the same road to Loikaw. We came across the truck in the ravine, and I craned my neck to see the aftermath. It sickened me. I had seen this man a few days earlier and felt guilty that I had not given him a pass; after all, he could have gone another day in an armed escort. Was I too harsh?

MAWCHI MINES (1957) LIMITED.
ALL COMMUNICATIONS TO BE ADDRESSED TO THE COMPANY.

~~THE MAWCHI MINES, LIMITED.~~

~~(INCORPORATED IN ENGLAND)~~

LE ADDRESS: MAWCHIMINES.

ES: BROOMHALL'S IMPERIAL COMBINATION CODE. BENTLEY'S.

MAWCHI MINES, S.S.S.

BURMA, 28th. February, 1958.

TO WHOM IT MAY CONCERN.

Doctor Solomon Samuels was first employed by this Company in June 1958, he relieved the Chief Medical Officer and for eight months acted in the capacity of C.M.O.

In December 1958, due to circumstances outside the Company's control the Mine closed down and went on to Care and Maintenance routine. During this period Dr. Samuels carried out many duties outside the usual sphere of a doctor's responsibilities.

During December 1958, with a considerable lack of proper hospital staff, Dr. Samuels was responsible for the moving of a complete and quite large hospital from one site to another and the putting in running order of the transferred hospital. Also due to the lack of staff he was responsible for his own compounding of medicines, hospital inventory and hospital office work.

Doctor Samuels finally resigned of his own accord in February 1959.

Mawchi Mines (1957) Limited,

P.J. Comer
P.J. Comer.
i/c. Care & Maintenance Party.

Figure 56. Letter of recommendation from P.J. Comer, head of the Care and Maintenance team as Mawchi Mines closed down. Personal Collection.

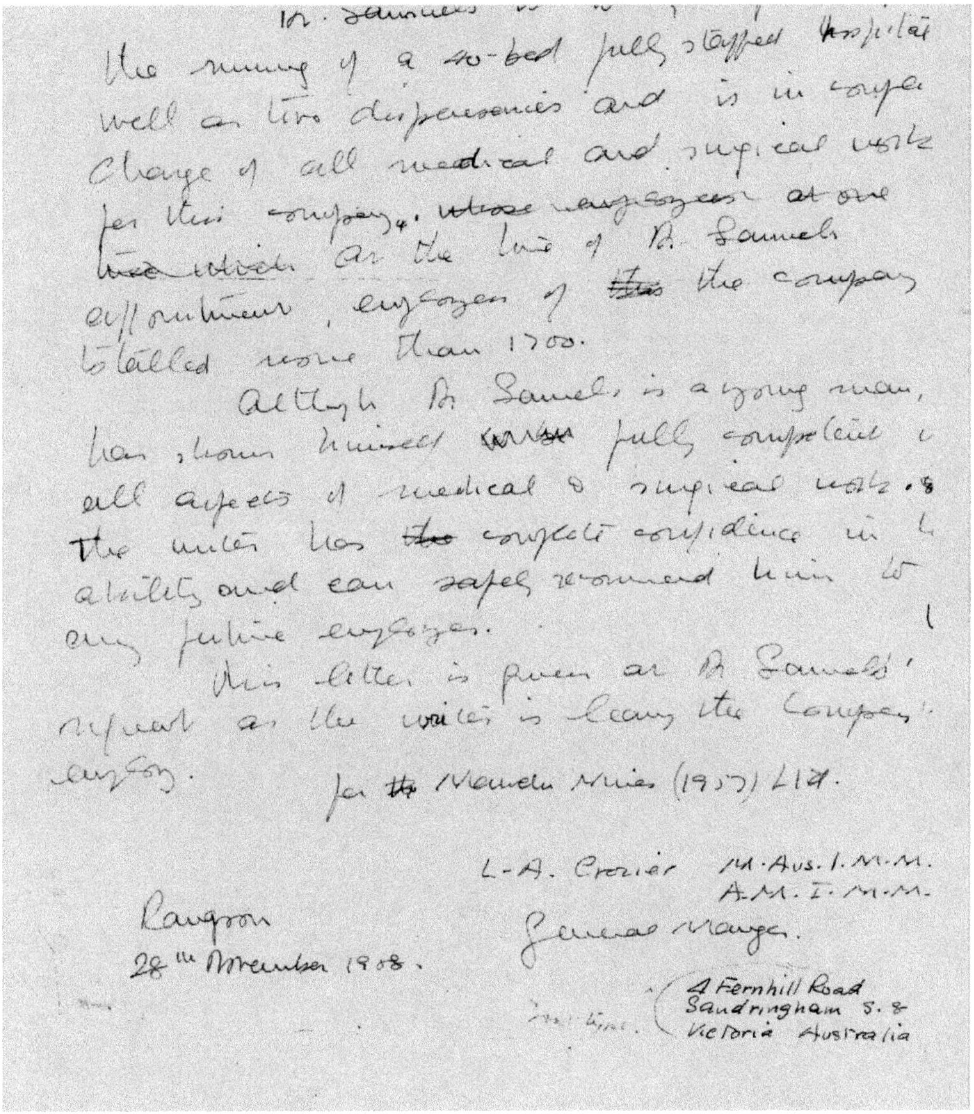

Dr. Samuels ...
the running of a 40-bed fully staffed hospital
as well as two dispensaries and is in complete
charge of all medical and surgical work
for this company, whose employees at one
time which as the time of Dr. Samuels
appointment, employees of the company
totalled more than 1700.

Although Dr. Samuels is a young man,
has shown himself fully competent in
all aspects of medical & surgical work, &
the writer has complete confidence in his
ability and can safely recommend him to
any future employer.

This letter is given at Dr. Samuels'
request as the writer is leaving the Company's
employ.

for the Mawchi Mines (1957) Ltd.

L.A. Crozier M.Aus.I.M.M.
A.M.I.M.M.
General Manager.

Rangoon
28th November 1958.

4 Fernhill Road
Sandringham S.8
Victoria Australia

Figure 57. Letter of recommendation by L.A. Crozier, General Manager of Mawchi Mines. Personal Collection. He wrote a wonderful book entitled *Mawchi: Mining, War and Insurgency in Burma* (Australia: Centre for the Study of Australia Asia Relations, 1994).

# Chapter 29
# A New Job

I went home for a short rest and to look for a new posting. Unless I got a new job, I would use up all my savings, so the search was urgent. I tagged along with my brother and his family on their vacation to Maymyo. There I met a man from Taunggyi who mentioned that a medical posting was open in the Shan (border) state. I learned that indeed the Shan State Government was looking for an Assistant Surgeon (a British colonial term) to fill a position in the far-off eastern city called Kengtung.[1] Medical care was spotty in the north country. Ethnic Bamar doctors would not go there because they were fearful of the mountains; they believed it was the abode of "Nats and Ogres."[2] The hill country had a particular attraction for me, and I had appreciated the cool climate, natural beauty, and friendly people in Mawchi. I submitted my application. The state government based at Taunggyi sent me an acceptance letter for the position of Civil Assistant Surgeon—a gazetted position. I was delighted.

I had some vague notion of the history and geography of the area: it was in the middle of the infamous Golden Triangle, in the remote and rugged area east of the Salween River. The Shan States had a checkered relationship with Burma and Thailand. For the most part of recent history, Kengtung was a backwater, more Thai than Burmese in language, culture, and ethnicity. During World War II it had been ceded to Thailand by the Imperial Japanese Army as a reward for help that Thailand had given to them. After the British Army liberated Burma, it was returned to the Shan *sawbwa* (chief) of Kengtung. The young ruler had spent the war in Australia and returned after the war to establish Khun family rule once again.

---

[1] Kengtung state was the largest of the many states that comprise the Shan States, and Kengtung city was its capital.

[2] The oft-told story: a Burmese man walking on a lonely road soon came upon a beautiful damsel. He was getting hungry, they came to a little hut, and she told him to go to the front of the hut while she cooked. Overcome with curiosity, he took a peek, and what he saw horrified him: out of her feet fire leapt, flames to cook the food. He realized that she was an ogre who would devour him, and without hesitation he took flight.

The British crown returned the state to the royal family but kept control of defense and finance portfolios.[3]

The tempestuous Salween River roars through this mountainous area in its race to reach the sea. For the most part it is not navigable. It forms the base of the triangle separating the eastern third of the Shan States from the rest of the Shan States and from Burma proper. To the south is the Karenni State (where Mawchi Mines were located). To the east lies the Mekong River and, beyond that, Laos; to the north is China. This border is the most dangerous part of the world, a topic that I will address later. This area is called the Golden Triangle, but that is a misnomer; there is no gold here. It has something even more valuable, however: the deadly poppy. Nobody knows how much money is generated from the poppy trade, but it is rumored that the underground drug economy supplies as much as one-third of Burma's GDP. Burmese generals, corrupt Thai ministers, Thai police generals, and even the Prime Minister and political establishment all make tons of money selling this product to the people of world.

I received my appointment papers with instructions. I flew into Kengtung on a war-surplus DC 3, and it was a wild and nerve-wracking ride: bumpy. I must admit that I was scared. Heavy rains had fallen the previous day, making the dirt air strip, which was left over from the war, wet, slippery, and treacherous. It was a fair-weather strip, built to handle light planes. The DC 3 landed with a thud, and while the pilot tried to control it, it ran off the runway and stopped in the open field beyond. Happily, there was not much damage, and no injuries were reported, although we were shaken up. The walk through the taxiway was also wet, but after some delay I passed the security check point. There were few amenities in the terminal. I was met by a driver who introduced himself and packed me and my belongings into a rickety old jeep. Like the plane journey, the ride to the city center was a bumpy one. Kengtung was bigger than Mawchi but, like Mawchi, was in one of the most dangerous areas in the world. I had heard that opium was common

---

[3] The British ruled this land as a "non-scheduled region": not direct rule but overseen by a British agent.

Figure 58. Kengtung house. Photo by Juleen Eichinger.

here, and indeed I would come face to face with it soon enough.[4] The city in general was poorly developed. The scenery was rugged but quite spectacular.

I arrived in the afternoon and, after the usual formalities, was shown to my quarters. I took a deep breath: it was a huge comedown. The house was small and crude, a three-room wood structure with a corrugated tin roof and minimal furniture. Aside from two tiny bedrooms it had a tiny sitting area and, in the front of the house behind this, was the bathroom and a kitchen, with a small stove and a table. It was a far cry from the house I had enjoyed in Mawchi. And I had no servants.

Late in the afternoon I went to the hospital, situated just on the east edge of the city. It was a low-slung building, a quadrangle around a courtyard. In front were the administrative and doctors' offices. The wings housed the various wards for men, women, and children. The hospital had been built not by the state but by

[4] Bhang (hashish) was frequently used throughout Burma, mostly by farmers but also common in Rangoon. The bhang leaves were mashed into a fine powder and snorted. In Burma proper there were no opium dens, no open facilities. Walking into a poppy field just a short distance from my home would be a new experience. As I walked the field, the air had a peculiar smell.

Catholic nuns. During World War II, the Japanese had looted and taken all the equipment they could carry before they left. The new (independent) Burma government provided no support. The nuns had mounted a valiant effort to keep the place going, but now they were aging and wanted to turn it over to the Shan State government to run. From the end of the war to the mid-1950s there had been no trained doctors; the nuns provided the only care. Now there were two doctors. The first was the man who would be my boss, the Civil Surgeon. The second was a Shan woman who worked part time and kept her own schedule; she was well connected and came and went as she pleased. I would be the third.

I met my future boss, the Civil Surgeon. He was a tall, balding man, about five years older than me. He was a Goan (part Portuguese, part Indian, Christian) who had graduated about four years ahead of me. The post of Civil Surgeon in colonial times would have been held by an Englishman. I introduced myself, he welcomed me, and, after a cup of tea, he showed me around the hospital, pointing out the inpatient wards and surgical wing. He introduced me to the Catholic nuns, who looked old and would soon leave. The hospital was larger and more active than the one I had left some months back in Mawchi. It was full of patients and had a laboratory and even a morgue. There were a number of nurses in blue and green longyis and a wound dresser. I saw a few old medical reference books but nothing recent. My boss briefly discussed the hospital problems and gave me my assignments. In addition to inpatient care, he said, I would be responsible for the outpatient clinic and opium hospital.

Next morning, I reported for work. Around 3:00 pm I was called to the operating theater, told that a woman was having severe vaginal bleeding (from a botched abortion) and that she would die without intervention. Committed to doing whatever was needed to save a woman's life, I scrubbed up and went to work, cleaned out the uterus and packed the vagina, and took a deep breath. Fortunately, the bleeding stopped shortly, she lived, and left the hospital in a few days. The next morning, I went to the busy and crowded outdoor clinic that catered to the general public. Everybody who came received some sort of treatment. I earned some kudos that first morning, attending to the needs of children, juveniles, mothers, and old men. Most of the complaints were of a routine nature: stomach aches, infectious diseases, malaria, dengue fever, pneumonia, tropical sores, boils, skin infections, and childhood infections. Lacerations were also common. With the help of Shan nurses who interpreted for me, I got to understand the nature of their complaints.

All the mothers wanted penicillin, no matter what the disease or injury. It would take a lot of explaining by the nursing staff that it may not be good for them. There were many cases of tuberculosis, which in the past had meant a death sentence. Now it could be treated with INH (Isoniazid) and the new antibiotic, Streptomycin. It saved many lives. It was good to see modern medicine helping age-old diseases. In contrast to Mawchi, medicines were readily available at the Kengtung hospital, and there were pharmacies in the city; the one right next door to the hospital was very affordable for those who could not afford high prices. Like in most countries in Asia even today, most antibiotics and pain medications could be purchased without a prescription.

What the textbooks described as rare was common here: advanced cases of cancer; patients with all manner of large bleeding breast tumors, some the size of a melon (most were infected because the women had gone to the local "doctor," delaying care and thereby making the tumors difficult to treat); huge gut tumors, muscle tumors, and sarcomas (now rarely seen, these were a weekly occurrence). I set up a team in the theater to attend to patients in the surgical clinic. We cleaned and debrided infected ulcers. It was wonderful medical experience for me that would stand me in good stead. The case load was manageable. Most surgery cases were referred to me. I was full of hope that I could help modernize the laboratory and the surgical theater. The job allowed me to put to good effect all that I had learned at medical college and in my internship. But I still felt the need for new information. There was very little reference material available, and in order to get the latest medical information I once again depended upon the *British Medical Journal* and *The Lancet*, eagerly awaiting their arrival. I felt the lack of interaction with other physicians quite acutely, however, as there were only three physicians, and one worked only half time.

After getting established at the hospital and in my small home, I took a walk to the town. Kengtung was once a walled kingdom with four gates located strategically, each wall about 20 feet high and 6–8 feet thick. The other walls of the city had long ago crumbled, but the eastern gate was still standing, near to the central business district. A short walk from my house took me to the eastern gate and the city center. The city was small, mostly rural. The streets were laid out parallel, but there were only four long streets that ran the length of the city; short cross streets connected the longer streets. The government buildings were centrally located. There were several small restaurants, serving frontier food, mostly Chinese or Shan-Chinese. Folks were shopping and dining outdoors, but to my surprise it was not teeming with people. One block down and three blocks over from my house was the city's only cinema. Once a week it showed C-grade Westerns. I walked to the edge of the city. About half a mile out of town the terrain changed: it was rugged but beautiful in the late afternoon sunlight. Purple jacaranda and flame trees, bougainvillea, yellow tiger claw, and red rhododendron grew in great abundance. It was pleasing to the eye. Toward the western end of the city was a small Christian community with a Christian church. My boss cautioned me against going too far beyond the city boundaries in any direction, for unsavory characters such as drug dealers lived there and might kidnap me. Few Bamar lived in Kengtung, maybe only 7 percent of the population. The Shan despised the Bamar, and the Bamar had no great love for the Shan either. Burmans in general, being extremely superstitious, avoided the mountains, the abode of the "ogres." I was glad of that fact. Nonetheless, I settled down and completed my paper work for citizenship, because the Shan State government took care of all the paperwork on my behalf and I realized it would be essential if I were to get on in the newly independent Burma.

There was little to do after hours. On my exploration of town, I had spotted a remarkable building: a Haw (palace) built in Mughal (Indian) style. It was the most prominent building in the city. The old ruler of Kengtung (the grandfather of the present ruler) at the turn of the nineteenth century had been invited to an Indian Durbar[5] at the coronation of the Prince of Wales, Edward VII. The ruler had been so impressed that he had built a small palace based on Mogul design. It seemed out of place here in the hill country. Now it was a club. Later in my stay I came to like it and was a frequent guest there.

[5] Durbar: Hindi term, derived from Persian, for a court held by an Indian prince or Governor.

The people were more Thai than Burmese; most spoke Thai and made frequent shopping trips to the border town of Mae Sai, the closest Thai town to Kengtung. I made friends with the ruling class, especially the younger brother of the Sawbwa, Saw Sai Noi (not to be confused with another Noi who was a senior politician) and his younger cousin George (that was not his real name; it had been bestowed upon him at one of the mission schools he had attended). Knowing the family eased my social life. George was a real character. He was tall and a little darker than most Shans. What his relationship to the ruling class was, I did not know and did not enquire about. It was obvious that he came from privilege. He was fluent in English, having gone to a Catholic school where he received a proper education. He was gregarious and fun-loving, a man about town. Foot-loose and fancy-free, he was a free spender although he did not have a steady job. The exact circumstances of how we met are hazy. He had a new Kawasaki motorcycle. One day he took me on a motorcycle tour of the city, took me to the palace, and showed me around the club. The club was owned by the royal family, the meeting place for the high and the mighty of the state. There was no formal application for membership; as long I was with George, I could go and drink beer. George introduced me to Saw Sai Noi, the ruler's younger brother, and his young wife Rosie. She was a young Shan of noble birth and privilege. Having gone to a convent school,[6] she spoke English well. The ruler himself had spent the war years in Australia. At the club, the privileged smoked a little opium or pot, but the main activity was Mahjong and gambling, which went on all night. Gamblers are peculiar people: indifferent to their surroundings, they sublimated their needs for sex and food; all was subsumed by gambling. Unlike in Burma proper, attitudes towards sex were far more relaxed here, and open, less repressive. Young women could engage in sex privately; it would be no hindrance to future marriage, and prostitution was accepted.

[6] Kentung [sic] Diocese, *Pontifical Institute for Foreign Missions*: Italian schools 33: 22 with 4,070 pupils; Middle schools 432 pupils; high schools 2, 59 pupils; technical schools 4, 109.

## MANHOOD

After a few beers at the club one night, feeling relaxed, I finally confided in George. My conversation turned to sex, or lack of it. I revealed to him that, coming from a very religious and sexually repressed home, I had no sexual experience, even though I was twenty-five years old. There was a long pause, he took a long look at me, then roared with laughter—enough to draw the attention of people around us. After his initial shock, he said, "We are going to change that." He asked me to pick a night, and on that agreed night the pretty young Shan girl knocks on my door. Typical of Shan girls, she was light-skinned, with rosy cheeks, cheerful and pretty. She was young: not quite twenty, about 5 feet tall, well endowed, with good strong legs. I opened the door, and before long she made plain why she was here: she went into the small bedroom and quickly got in bed; it was the first time I would see a naked woman (outside of a medical setting). It was a difficult night. I had a problem: I had taken some Sudafed earlier that day, and try and try as I might, I could not get an erection. She would burst into laughter at every try, much to my chagrin. I was angry as well as ashamed. She left in the morning without consummating the act. Two days later I met George. He shook his head and said "I went to all that trouble and you disappoint me." I sat him down and explained the effects of the medication. I pleaded with him to give me a second chance. This time I was careful to avoid any medication, and when she kept her appointment two days hence, it was different. She was patient, and it all worked out well. Before she left, I gave her a present. What arrangements she had made with George I never asked, but I had been initiated. I found the experience very satisfying and wondered why I had waited so long. I was now a man.

I felt safer in Kengtung than in Burma proper, but Kengtung also had a dark side to it. Some distance to the north was the main opium-growing area of Burma, and there was an active drug trade. Prior to the war, a small amount of poor-grade opium had been produced, poor man's opium. But Kengtung later would earn the dubious distinction of the opium capital of the world. What changed all this was the war in the north, in China.

# Chapter 30
# Opium

*It is not known where or when the opium-producing poppy plant originated or when its latex was discovered, but the ancients knew of its potency. It is said to have been in existence since at least 500 B.C. Some suggest that it was brought to India from the Middle East in 1806. The British kept tight control over its use in India. They refined the latex and extracted the potent morphine, studied its chemistry. It is said that a Swede discovered how to produce opium from the plant. After the annexation of Burma in 1885, the poppy plant was brought to Burma. And so started the opium trade. The British took to selling the opium to China through the back door: Bhamo to Yunnan and China.*

*The scientific name is Papavaer Somniferum, and the latex is called poppy tears. About 1% of the latex is alkaloid morphine. The alkaloids are Benzylisoquinline alkaloids. The latex contains 20% morphine and less than 5% each of thebaine, papverine, noscapine, and narcotine codeine (used as a cough suppressant). The plant grows in hilly terrain; it has a single stalk that grows about 4–5 feet tall. At the top of the plant stem is the ball, shaped like a tennis ball but some what flattened. Inside is where the raw latex is found. At the very top of the ball are thirteen precisely shaped fronds, following the Fibonacci sequence. In the shallow basin (of these fronds) are the plant's sex organs. When scored (scratched), the ball exudes a sticky yellowish latex, which is collected and set out to dry. The dried latex is then treated to form crude opium. Adding a analog of acetic acid produces crude morphine; further refinement produces good grade opium, which can be converted into heroin.*

The British brought the poppy plant to Burma in the nineteenth century. The British government of Burma signed the international opium convention of 1923, banning opium in Burma proper but allowing the Shan State to use 32 kilos per smoker per year. The trade burgeoned in the post-war years.[1] The

[1] Opium production in the Shan State in 1945 was 40 tons. In 1982 it had grown to 260 tons. Combined with production from Kachin State, production was close to 500 tons. See André and Louis Boucaud, *Burma's Golden Triangle: On the Trail of the Opium Warlords* (1985; rev. ed. Bangkok: Asia Books, 1992), 23, 24.

Figure 59. Three stages of an opium poppy [https://commons.wikimedia.org/wiki/File:Poster_papaver_5a.jpg]. Alvesgaspar, CC BY-SA 3.0, via Wikimedia Commons.

saga of opium in the Shan States begins in the late 1940s as the victorious Communist Red Army chased the KMT (Chinese Kuomintang under Chiang Kai-shek) to the Burma border. The Mao steamroller pushed the KMT Divisions 200, 96, and 36 (7,000 men) into Burma in a pell-mell rush.[2] The communists could easily have walked into Burma, but they stopped at the border. The weak Burmese government could not oust the KMT, so allowed them to settle in the remote, sparsely populated areas of Waa and Kokang. Here they were isolated, without any means to communicate with the outside world. They stayed in the hills, intermarried with local inhabitants, and tried to make a living. The place they retreated to was a crazy quilt of red- and white-flag communists, militias, gangs, and opium traders. At first they lived on the booty that they had brought with them, but soon those resources were exhausted. To support themselves, they then turned to robbery and mayhem and resorted to brigandage and trade in illegal drugs.

The US had supported the KMT throughout World War II and did not recognize the new communist regime in China. After the war, there was intense debate in the US about "who lost China." Many high-ranking officials went to mediate, including General Marshall, but all were unsuccessful. The policy makers finally decided that the KMT still had to be supported. So the CIA set up a long,

---

[2] It was the reversal of the Long March. The Communists defeated the KMT and were now at the doors of Burma.

tenuous supply line to the exiled KMT troops. This they did by setting up a clandestine airline called "Air America." With experienced pilots and easily available aircraft, they ferried arms, food, and medicines, all the requirements to help the beleaguered soldiers of the KMT now living in Burma. The Red Chinese were not happy. Only two decades later would the US give up on the corrupt KMT and recognize the People's Republic of China (PRC).

It was a huge task to keep the KMT supplied by air, so the CIA worked with smugglers. With the help of corrupt Thai authorities, the CIA set up other front companies, like the "Far East Film Enterprises" and other ventures, to support the KMT. However, given the scale of the operations, this support became an open secret. The news alerted the Burmese government, which took the case to the UN Security Council. The weapons supplied to the KMT would prove to be insufficient to ward off the Burma Army, and in time the KMT retreated further inland, into remote Burma. With typical Chinese zeal the KMT Chinese and their allies soon took over the poppy fields and, using new breeding techniques, made the opium more lethal. Now rich, they took over control of the Kokang and Waa States—places that in the best of times were wild and dangerous.[3] They were now producing grade-4 opium. Finding markets was easy: with the assistance of senior Thai politicians, police, generals, and even the Thai prime minister, they started shipping the opium and its byproducts to Asia and, more importantly, to France and the West.

Burmese officials soon joined forces with the CIA and Thais to aid and abet the drug trade. A protection racket grew. Convoys through the jungle trails were allowed to pass if they paid the fees, even at Burmese checkpoints. The primary method of transport was by mule train, with destinations including Chiang Mai and Chang Rai in Thailand. At the arrival point, the goods were taken over by international gangs and from there were transported out of Southeast Asia. American political groups made a secret deal with the defeated KMT. A strong lobby of pro-KMT groups, like the Luce family (*Time* magazine) and General Claire Chennault (of Flying Tigers fame), supported the KMT (the founder of the John Birch

---

[3] North Burma was primitive, with poor communications; the people were mostly wild Waa, who were, for the most part, illiterate.

Society, an anti-communist missionary living in China, was also an ardent supporter of the KMT). The Burmese involvement is another squalid story (too long and seamy to relate here), and later the DEA waded into the quagmire.

All this was done in great secrecy. Before long, underground crime syndicates and notorious mob bosses in America and in France took over the trade; Marseille became the French connection and the chief port of entry. Multiple news sources have reported that more than one-third of Burma's economy is related to the drug trade and that drug money funds the army's armament purchases. The new Burmese capital of Nay Pyi Taw was financed by drug money. Finally, when it appeared that the US was going to establish diplomatic relations with China, Nixon and Kissinger obtained the support of Taiwan and Thailand to evacuate the original KMT soldiers to Taiwan.

To my surprise, my assignment as Assistant Chief Surgeon in Kengtung included not only running the surgical ward and the outpatient clinic at the hospital but also overseeing medical care at the jail and opium hospitals. My visits to the jail typically turned up just a few problems, duly noted and treated. The opium hospitals were a more complex story.

## THE OPIUM HOSPITALS

In colonial times, opium was restricted in Burma proper, and a user could face arrest. This law did not apply in non-scheduled territory, however, like in Kengtung and the frontier areas. In the opium-growing areas, the rules were less rigid. As Assistant Chief Surgeon, I was to inspect the opium hospitals once a month, care for any medical problems originating there, and write a report. My boss let me look at the file of previous medical reports, which gave me a clue about what to look for. These opium addicts were not criminals. The families brought their addicted member to this hospital, rented a bed, and provided food and other daily necessities. The addicts could buy the opium in the hospital or in the street. The staff were all males who had some training in medical care. My first visit was an eye-opener.

Not owning a car, I drove myself to the opium hospital in the hospital ambulance, which had been donated by an international NGO. I was taken aback by

Figure 60. Opium weights. Personal Collection. Photo by Juleen Eichinger.

what I found. There was no fence around the facility and no guards; access was unrestricted. The hospital was, in essence, a large *basha*, that is, a long, open hut about 50 feet long, with a steep, sloping thatch roof that reached almost to the ground. The ward had no side walls. The nursing station had a lab with Burmese opium weights, a balance, and the paraphernalia of a medical aid station. I was greeted by a staff member. The first thing I noticed was how dimly lit it was: the sun rarely shined here, and it was dark like a cave. The smell was overpowering. Filled with smoke, the place reeked of the pungent, acrid smell of opium. There was row after row of bamboo beds, some with mattress and sheets while others had only threadbare blankets. The state provided the beds; the families provided the sheets and blankets. The type of bed built depended on the wealth of family, the staff member told me.[4] Next to each narrow bed was a bamboo side table on which there was a candle or kerosene lamp; a small container for the dark, sticky, doughy balls of opium; and a metal pipe (sometimes decorated ornately). The pipes were about

[4] I was told that some members of wealthy families had richly decorated beds, some even made of high-grade silver.

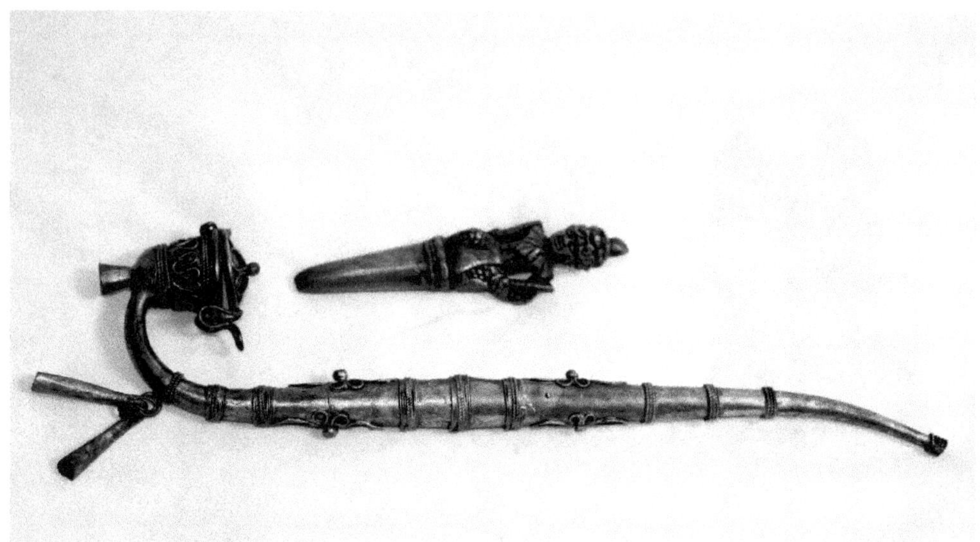

Figure 61. Opium pipe with tamp. Personal collection. Photo by Juleen Eichinger.

8 inches long, curved into an S-shape with a flared bell-shaped end into which the opium was packed, using a tiny spoon. I took out my medicine bag and randomly examined a patient. I checked his eyes: the pupils were constricted to almost pin-points, and I suspected he could not see me well. He lay flat for the most part, and his breathing was shallow. The other residents were silent, in various stages of stupor or wakefulness. I observed one man take a small portion of the ball and place it into the bell-shaped cup of the pipe; after he lit the ball and took a few puffs, he slowly fell into a recumbent position, lost to this world, in dream land.

I asked the male nurse if there were any acute medical problems; he shook his head. Occasionally a patient would cry when he ran out of opium, he explained, but the hospital always had a stock of opium under the control of the staff; such a patient would be provided with enough for the night, and the next morning the family would bring a fresh supply. I asked to see the bathrooms and the kitchen, noting the usual problems of poor sanitation in both places. I was surprised at how many people there were, and that some who had to go to the toilet had to be helped or carried there. I told the head of the staff that I would write a report stating that, at this time at least, there were no acute medical problems. This report would be submitted to the Chief Surgeon for review and then sent to the ruler's office. Then I took my leave.

I now wish that I had asked more questions, like how many actually go home or how long they lived after being committed to the hospital, but at the time it seemed unimportant. In retrospect I wish I had more curiosity, as I could have learned a few more facts. I thought about it many years after I left the place. I did note that, despite the easy availability and cheapness of opium, most people of the state functioned quite normally.

A few weeks later I was called to the hospital emergency room, where one of the inmates of the opium hospital had been brought with severe abdominal pain. The right side of the lower abdomen was swollen, red, and on examination very tender. It was obvious that he had acute appendicitis and was pretty sick. I called the Chief Surgeon for advice. It was late in the day. He told me go ahead with the surgery and to call him if I ran into problems. It took some time to read up for the operation. The operating theater had to be cleaned, and then, after an interminable wait, the surgery got underway. Fortunately, most opium smokers are underweight, so the patient had very little fat on the abdominal wall. Nervous but not showing it to the staff, I was able get the appendix out, insert a rubber drain, and stitch him up. I was gaining experience as I went along. I wondered what narcotic I would give him for pain. In the morning I consulted my Chief, and he advised me to go ahead and let him smoke his opium pipe. The day he was discharged the family brought me a little box (as this was a state-funded hospital, no bill was issued). I opened the box to discover a round ball of opium inside. It reeked of opium. I quickly closed the lid and handed the box back. I thanked them but said "I cannot accept." A few days later another, bigger, box arrived at the clinic, from the same family. I opened it to see that it contained a bottle of Johnny Walker—a much more acceptable gift.

I was also the medical examiner. Murders were routine out in the poppy fields beyond the city confines, and another part of my job was to go out to the fields to examine murdered bodies. I frequently had to examine gunshot wounds and gained quite a bit of knowledge on the subject. Forensic facilities were minimal: the police had a camera, but no other equipment; more often they made a few diagrams. I scribbled a few notes, made a record, and then issued a death certificate. That's all they needed. These deaths were not infrequent, and there was so much going on just to the north of the city that it could have been a drug deal gone wrong, a political murder, or a personal matter.

In spite of all this, life was pleasant in Kengtung, compared to Mawchi. I had a job, a monthly paycheck, and lots of patients and friendly people. Unlike in Rangoon, the people were not repressed, not noisy, there was no droning of monks on loudspeakers night and day. Since Father's death in 1942, this was the happiest time I felt. But bad times lay ahead.

# Chapter 31
# Thoughts of Emigration

By this time, politically the country was near chaos. If the interim pre-independence period had been violent, it was worse now. Political leaders were squabbling. In some cities there was a semblance of law and order, but in others there was instability. While I was paid well and life was good, I had a feeling it would end badly. The future looked bleak. I was eager to learn and wanted to continue my studies. Unless I did that, I would be stuck in a remote and dangerous place with little prospect for personal or professional growth. I looked forward to the mail, delivered two or three times a week, because it brought me not only letters but also my medical journals. I scanned the headlines and then set them aside for detailed study. They were great reading. I was three years out of school with no clear path to the future. I knew opportunities would decline with age. I had a burning desire to further develop my skills. I knew I needed to pursue additional training but realized that advanced training would be difficult to find in Burma and would take years to complete. I reluctantly turned to the idea of going overseas, to England or America.

I began to explore my chances and to that end went to Rangoon to gather information. Rangoon was getting grimy. The good restaurants were being replaced by Chinese bars: noisy, boisterous, and dangerous places with gambling and bar girls in the back. Once-comfortable second-class rail cars with polished teak seats were all gone, replaced with vermin-infested seats in dingy rail cars. The little refinement that had been evident in the post-colonial era was fading rapidly. Crime was increasing, and Rangoon was becoming a run-down, filthy, and boring city, with the monks blaring their religious mantras on loudspeakers, day and night, uninterrupted. Hostility of the government increased toward the non-Burman, non-Buddhist, Christian, Karen, Shan, Kachin, Indian, Anglo-Indian, and all foreign peoples. Law and order were breaking down, and non-Burmans were feeling the pressure. To cap off the bad news, the economy was in trouble, and in the midst of it all the Prime Minister, displaying his incompetence and lack of interest in human affairs, traveled overseas propagating Buddhist Sasana. He went to the Voice of America program, whose intent was to educate the Burmese people. But Prime Minister U Nu's goal was to spread Theravada Buddhist theology. His government paid scant attention to running the railways and other transportation sectors, took no action to stem the rising tide of crime, and evidenced no interest in providing services to the people, which led to the breakup of the AFPFL (Anti-Fascist People's Freedom League) party. It split into two factions with equally ridiculous names: The "Clean Anti-Fascist League" and the "Stable AFPFL." Calling themselves anti-fascists was hypocrisy, a monumental lie, and an oxymoron. It was comedic. They had been pro-fascist not so long ago and indeed still were. In the face of a declining economy and crumbling infrastructure, Prime Minister U Nu spent time and money to build Buddhist pagodas. He built a World Peace (Gaba Aye) pagoda and a cave and convened a Buddhist Synod to which adherents came from across the globe to pray and make peace offerings. To appease the Bamar he declared Buddhism a state religion, which, not unexpectedly, caused great consternation amongst the ethnic minorities, many of whom were majority Christian, soon joined by others. The minorities, Christians, and ethnic peoples were in full revolt.

Once the Pearl of the East, Burma was now a mess. It was fast losing its attractions. The streets were potholed, its aging restaurants and the old romantic colonial buildings were crumbling, most in need of paint and more. The streets were simply not safe; even during the day the various armed militia groups (Yebaw ["young warriors"], PVO, Union Military Police), all armed to the teeth, roamed the streets. They controlled various segments of the political establishment and operated openly, bullying, grabbing, and stealing. All the fears of old returned. My friends and their families were tense, filled with angst, and all the talk was about where we could go. During the Raj, the railways, motor transport, and other sectors had been mostly run by Anglo-Indians or Anglo-Burmese. Rampant nationalizing forced the retirement of many of these well-trained professionals, and their replacements were not qualified for the job; as long as you were ethnic Bamar, you got a job. Seasoned doctors, engineers, and other professionals were leaving Burma. Senior police officials, both Anglo-Indian and Anglo-Burmese, were leaving in droves.[1] Australia was indeed welcoming; it took in a huge number of emigrants and sent them to Perth to build the city. What was Burma's loss was Australia's gain. As skilled people left Burma, services declined to a point where life became difficult. The quest to emigrate was strong.

## THE MCCARRAN-WALTER ACT

Before 1955, going to the US for people like me was almost impossible. There were all manner of restrictions and restrictive laws. The Naturalization Act of 1790 had restricted citizenship to "free white persons" who had lived in the US two years, thus excluding Asians. The 1924 National Origins Act was still on the books. It labeled the vast majority of people from Asia as "not welcome"; they were ineligible to become full citizens. US Public Law 82-414, the McCarran-Walter Act of 1952, abolished these racial restrictions and established quotas for nationalities and regions.[2] The Act improved immigration somewhat but still only allowed limited Asian migration. Prior to the Act, immigrants of Asian descent were limited to 100 per country or 2,000 people overall annually. Not until 1960 would that number reach 12,000 people of South Asian descent living in the US.[3] My ability to come to the US was a direct result of the McCarran-Walter Act.

It was in this context and with great trepidation that I took a chance and wrote to the US Embassy, Visa Section, in Rangoon. In the meantime, I took holiday leave and traveled to south Burma, visiting Moulmein, where there was still a Christian Hospital. While sitting around the veranda of the hotel one evening, I met

---

[1] An interesting aside: upper-class Eurasians had an easier time establishing themselves in the West; because of the similarity of religious belief and their liberal democratic values they assimilated smoothly into the larger societies of the West.

[2] The June 27, 1952, Act retained the quota system for nationalities and regions. It defined three types of immigrants: those with special skills or who were relatives of US citizens, who were exempt from quotas and were to be admitted without restrictions; average immigrants whose numbers were not supposed to exceed 270,000 per year; and refugees. It was passed over the objections of then-President Truman, who feared that it could discriminate against potential allies that contained communist groups.

[3] Results from the 2020 Census show nearly 5 million South Asians living in the US. *New York Times* Wednesday, August 25, 2021, A14.

an American surgeon. There was a beautiful sunset, a warm breeze coming off the Andaman Sea, and temple bells were ringing. The older American and I struck up a conversation. After a while he suggested that I could seek an internship at an American hospital and encouraged me to apply for one at his hometown hospital in Youngstown, Ohio. "Write to them," he urged, which I did. Much to my surprise, I received a speedy reply from the hospital, on July 31, 1959. It said, in part, "Complete the enclosed application and return it as soon as possible." I returned the application promptly and in the same time period also received a letter from the Visa Section of the US Embassy to set up a date for an appointment. My reception was quite pleasant. The visa officer was a young man—not much older than I. We hit it off. He explained to me the problems of going to the US on a student visa and told me to wait another six months, at which time I could get an "immigrant visa." But I was driven by own fears, of missing an opportunity. Together with the anxiety of not wanting to linger in increasingly depressing Burma, this clouded my judgment, and I moved forward with the student visa (which to this day I regret). With the paperwork in place, I went back to Kengtung to resume work and await further developments. The situation was changing in Kengtung too; there was increased tension between the ruling family and the Burma Army.

George came calling one day and did not appear his usual cheerful self. He had already had a few beers. He said "I think that something bad is going to happen here. You know how we mistrust the Bamar? They are up to something, and it will be bad." I asked him to explain and received an earful. "The Bamar want to take over our kingdom, our riches; they want to replace the present rulers with puppets who would do the army's bidding." He took another a swig of beer, then went on.

> The army is adding more troops; a battalion arrived last week. They are building a new base a few miles south of here. It has been reinforced, and there are rumors that there may be a coup. Our police are feeling the pressure. They want our police to spy on our leaders, want to weed out unfriendly Shan people, want to buy informers. They want to Burmanize everything: replace our names, our language, our customs, and our way of life; steal all our assets, our women especially, and take the extractive resources from us.

THE YOUNGSTOWN HOSPITAL ASSOCIATION
SOUTH SIDE UNIT
Youngstown 1, Ohio

W. J. HITCHCOCK
President
PAUL WICK
Vice President
DONALD J. LYNN
Sec'y-Treas.

D. A. ENDRES
Superintendent and
Ass't Treas.

July 31, 1959

Dr. S. Samuels
41 Mezigome Rd., Kamayut
Rangoon, Burma

Dear Dr. Samuels:

We have received your letter from Dr. [illegible] relative to an Internship at Youngstown Hospital.

Enclosed is a pamphlet which will answer questions you might have regarding the hospital and a copy of the activities in our Graduate Education Program. Also enclosed is an application form which I would like you to complete and return as soon as possible.

Thank you for your interest in us.

Very truly yours,

THE YOUNGSTOWN HOSPITAL ASSOCIATION

William D. Loeser

William D. Loeser, M. D.,
Director of Medical Education

WDL:gb

Enc. - 3

Figure 62. Letter from Youngstown Hospital with application form. Personal collection.

By now he had consumed a lot of beer. I thought he had had too much to drink and was worried that he could not drive safely. He assured me that he was ok, then got on his bike and took off. But this troubled me. I too worried about trouble ahead.

George's words were alarming but true. The despised Burma Army was indeed everywhere, and tension between the ruling class and the army continued to increase. The ill-equipped Shan police were not going to challenge them. This only increased my angst and motivated me to expedite my plans to leave the country. Along with the application, the hospital in Youngstown had sent me a brochure informing me of the work terms and promising to pay the airfare. If after six months I passed the ECFMG exam,[4] I would be allowed to finish my internship and also apply for a residency. It was good news, even though it would be difficult to leave this friendly and hospitable place, where I had found peace and comfort and friendly people. I now worked to disentangle myself from my work and prepare to leave.

As part of the preparation, I started to read up on life in America. I worked on my English, listened to the radio—Voice of America (the soothing voice of Mr. Conover), Radio Australia, and BBC. I listened to jazz music and remembered when Louis Armstrong and Benny Goodman had played at the University of Rangoon: I had been in the front row and experienced a moment of pure joy when I got to shake hands with some of the musicians.[5]

Once again, telling Mother was going to be difficult. The family was divided. While I felt that the best course for the future was to accept modernity, some in the family turned to extreme evangelical Christianity or traditional Indian/Burmese culture. As Mother aged and became feeble, some in the family retreated from engagement with the world. I worried about their future. I did not know how they would get by. Attempting to explain the facts only increased tension among

---

[4] The certificate program established in 1956 by the Educational Commission for Foreign Medical Graduates. It was designed to assure that international medical graduates are ready to enter residency or fellowship programs in the US. It had to be completed within seven years of arrival in the US.

[5] I never had an interest in Indian or Burmese music. Burmese music was noisy and unappealing; the non-rhythmic banging of the drums just turned me off. Nor did I have any interest in Burmese or Indian cinema.

us. I became more distant from my family and prepared to separate from them. I suspect it was my instinct for self-preservation. I was disciplined, tenacious, and willing to better myself. This all saddened me. I promised Mother that I would send care packages. I knew that there would be no marriage till the plans for the future were firm.

Two years after I left, the entire country would be involved in a bloody revolt. Army officers led by the infamous mad General Ne Win[6] staged a coup. He ousted and imprisoned all opposition, incarcerated all the Shan rulers and the political elite, gunned down students at Insein and the University of Rangoon, locked the student union building and—with rebellious students inside—sent in sappers and miners to blow up the building. All people suspected to be against him were sent to Insein for long prison terms. The Burma Army blew up the beautiful Mughal Palace-cum-Club in Kengtung, bulldozed the earth, and erected an ugly Bamar-style hotel on the property. What became of my friend George? Knowing him, he must have had few beers and got boisterous; they shot him in cold blood, I would later find out. I met Noi in Rangoon years later, at their place on Martin Avenue. They were reluctant to talk but confirmed that George had died. For my family and others, for the people of Burma, the long nightmare was just beginning.

[6] Ne Win was the second in command of the Fascist Burmese Army, a cruel and ruthless man. He suspended the constitution, murdered many, and set up a brutal reign of terror.

# Part Three
# Life in America

# Chapter 32
# The Journey to America

Before World War II, the opportunity to study abroad (mostly in England or Scotland) was limited to the well-connected and rich; for others it was almost impossible. This system was said to be "creaky," as many of those selected for overseas study were ill suited for such study and did not do well. In Rangoon academic circles there was little solid information and lots of misinformation, such as "you can get a degree in basket-weaving in America," said derisively about education in the US. In the 1960s there was not much information in Burma about the US.

In my narrow circle of relatives and friends, negative comments abounded. "You will not be able to cope with advanced studies"; "America will not let you work as a doctor"; "Once you get there, they send you out to wash dishes in the kitchen" (I never had to do dishes). I was surprised by the vitriol I had to put up with. Some of it was rank jealousy, but not all. I fended off most of this and kept my focus. But I too had my doubts. I lay awake in the dark of night and worried—about all the tests I would have to pass, about stories of ill treatment of non-white people, about slavery. I knew there were very few people of Indian origin in the US and worried about the Jim Crow laws and bias against non-white people. I followed the horrible story of the young boy Emmett Till—the fourteen-year-old black boy from Chicago who was tortured and murdered in Mississippi, all for whistling at a white woman?—and the frightening series of events underlying his murder. I was concerned also about mob activity; I had just finished reading a book on the mob and found the names of the characters such as Legs Diamond and Kid Twist all too real. I kept my fears to myself, however, and continued my plan and studies. These concerns would not deter me from my pursuit. Being an optimist, I still hoped for the best. The young American servicemen I had met after the war were quite friendly, and at Mawchi I had treated British women and men with little difficulty, so I thought perhaps things would not be so bad in North America.

It was mail day. A letter arrived from the US for me. I tore it open. It confirmed my acceptance to the internship program at Youngstown Hospital in Ohio and gave me instructions for travel. I was ecstatic. I called on the young visa officer again, filled out visa form, and submitted it. He told me again of my options, that I could apply for an immigrant visa but that it would take time. He asked me to change my mind and then with a smile stamped my visa. I followed the instructions in the letter and went to the British Overseas Airways Corporation (BOAC) office on Dalhousie Street, fronting the main railway station. A few days later the BOAC informed me that I had a prepaid ticket from Rangoon to Youngstown, Ohio, USA. It was an exciting time. I wound up my affairs in Kengtung and reassured my mother that this was a great opportunity. I promised I would write to her and went on to prepare for my new adventure. I ordered a couple of suits. Rangoon tailors were notorious: in spite of instructions, they clung to Indian style and created suits with tight sleeves and baggy pants. I picked up the ill-fitting suits, shoes, and a suitcase. I was ready to travel to America.

The late 1950s was the dawning of a new era of air travel. Old war-time planes were being replaced with new aircraft built for passenger comfort: comfortable upholstered seats, more leg room, good food and spirits, and shorter flying times. On the appointed day I arrived at the small, unkempt terminal and walked on the tarmac to the plane. Unlike the converted DC 3s that I had flown on to Mawchi and Kengtung, this was a big four-engine propeller-driven plane. It was clean and smelled fresh and new. The flight to Bangkok took one hour, and there I changed planes. The Bangkok airport was better than Rangoon's, but it was nothing like it is today. Along the side of the runway were shop stalls; it appeared to be busy and more prosperous than Rangoon. I took note of how well things worked here compared to Burma. Soon the plane took off for Hong Kong. I am not certain whether it was a Comet or another model, but it was beautiful, with a shiny metal skin and a plush interior. The British hostesses wore white blouses with dark skirts and high heels; they were slim, young, and beautiful. They greeted me with a smile, seated me, and provided instructions on safety measures. I must have disembarked in Hong Kong, as my passport shows an immigration stamp from Hong Kong immigration (my recollection is vague), and the next leg took me to Tokyo. In flight

I recalled war-time Movietone news clips about the fire-bombing of Tokyo. I expected to see evidence of devastation of the war, but Haneda airport's runways (later they built a new airport at Narita) were long and showed no evidence of war damage. The plane landed safely and taxied, and we were bused to the airport terminal. The terminal was well-kept, clean and modern.

THE YOUNGSTOWN HOSPITAL ASSOCIATION
SOUTH SIDE UNIT
Youngstown 1, Ohio

W. J. HITCHCOCK
President
PAUL WICK
Vice President
DONALD J. LYNN
Sec'y-Treas.

D. A. ENDRES
Superintendent and
Ass't Treas.

March 15, 1960

Dr. Solomon Samuels
41 Mezigone Road Kamayut
Rangoon, Burma

Dear Dr. Samuels:

You have been appointed as an Intern at this hospital for one year beginning July 1, 1960. This appointment is dependent upon your passing the ECFMG examination given in March 1960. Please let me know at once if you will accept.

Very truly yours,

THE YOUNGSTOWN HOSPITAL ASSOCIATION

R. W. Rummell, M. D.
Medical Director

RWR:rm

Figure 63. Letter of appointment as intern at Youngstown Hospital. Personal collection.

FORM DSP-66
7-22-57

DEPARTMENT OF STATE
INTERNATIONAL EDUCATIONAL EXCHANGE SERVICE

Form Approved
Bureau of the Budget No. 47-R144

**CERTIFICATE OF ELIGIBILTY FOR EXCHANGE VISITOR STATUS**

*(Authorized by regulations promulgated under provisions of P.L. 402, 80th Congress, as amended)*

I.

1. NAME OF EXCHANGE VISITOR: Solomon Samuels, M. D.
2. DATE OF BIRTH: October 12, 1930
3. NATIONALITY: Burmese
4. PLACE OF BIRTH: Rangoon, Burma
5. PLACE: Youngstown, Ohio, U. S. A.
6. DATE: June 27, 1960
7. THIS CERTIFIES THAT THE SPONSOR NAMED BELOW HAS SELECTED THE EXCHANGE VISITOR NAMED HEREIN TO PARTICIPATE IN EXCHANGE VISITOR PROGRAM NO. P II - 564
8. DATE OF PROGRAM DESIGNATION BY THE DEPARTMENT OF STATE: April 10, 1951
9. SPONSOR: The Youngstown Hospital Association
10. TIME AND TERMS OF PROGRAM PARTICIPATION *(Length of Stay, Financial Arrangements, Training Objectives)*

Will serve as an Intern for a period of six months beginning July 1, 1960 and ending December 31, 1960. Will receive a stipend of $ 250.00 per month plus complete maintenance. This contract may be extended to one year contingent upon Dr. Samuels' passing the ECFMG examination in September, 1960.

8/8/61

(Dr. Samuel's contract has been extended for one year ending June 30, 1962.)

R. W. Rummell M. D.
R. W. Rummell, M. D., Medical Director

11. CERTIFICATION: *I certify that Exchange Visitor Program No.* P II - 564 *provides the program activities as stated above for the exchange visitor named herein, and that the designation is still valid.*

THE SPONSOR AGREES (1) TO INSURE THAT PARTICIPANT ADHERES TO CONDITIONS UNDER WHICH HE WAS ADMITTED TO THE U.S. AND WILL DEPART FROM THE U.S. UPON COMPLETION OF HIS PROGRAM; (2) TO NOTIFY IMMEDIATELY THE DISTRICT DIRECTOR, U.S. IMMIGRATION AND NATURALIZATION SERVICE HAVING JURISDICTION OVER THE DISTRICT IN WHICH THE EXCHANGE VISITOR IS RESIDING IF HE CEASES TO PURSUE THE PROGRAM OBJECTIVES FOR WHICH HE WAS ADMITTED TO THE U.S. GIVING THE VISITORS NAME, ADDRESS, NATIONALITY, DATE OF ENTRY INTO THE U.S. AND HIS PRESENT ACTIVITIES; (3) TO SUPPLY ALIEN WITH REQUIRED TIME AND TERMS OF HIS CONTINUED STAY SUFFICIENTLY IN ADVANCE OF EXPIRATION OF STAY TO ENABLE THE ALIEN TO APPLY FOR EXTENSION TO THE IMMIGRATION AND NATURALIZATION SERVICE.

IMM. & NATZ. SERVICE
HONOLULU, HI 366
ADMITTED

William D. Loeser
(SIGNATURE OF RESPONSIBLE OFFICER) William D. Loeser, M. D. — Director of Medical Education (TITLE)

II. FOR USE OF IMMIGRATION AND NATURALIZATION SERVICE

| 1. DATE: JUL 16 1960 | 2. PLACE: 8/11/61 | |
|---|---|---|
| 3. ADMITTED: CLASS TO 7-15-61 | | 4. EXTENDED TO: 6/30/62 |
| 5. EXTENDED TO | 6. EXTENDED TO | 7. SIGNATURE OF INS OFFICIAL: B. Buchanan |

Figure 64. Department of State Certificate of Exchange Visitor Status at Youngstown Hospital. Personal collection.

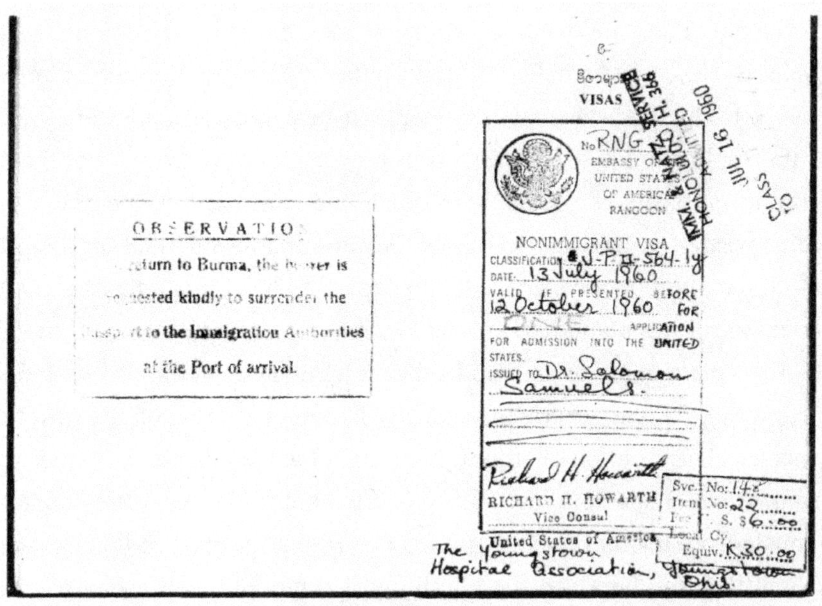
VISAS

OBSERVATION

…turn to Burma, the bearer is …ested kindly to surrender the …rt to the Immigration Authorities at the Port of arrival.

No RNG

EMBASSY OF THE UNITED STATES OF AMERICA RANGOON

NONIMMIGRANT VISA

CLASSIFICATION J-P II-564-14

DATE: 13 July 1960

VALID IF PRESENTED BEFORE 12 October 1960 FOR ONE APPLICATION FOR ADMISSION INTO THE UNITED STATES.

ISSUED TO Dr. Solomon Samuels.

RICHARD H. HOWARTH
Vice Consul
United States of America

Svc. No: 148
Item No: 22
Fee U.S. $6.00
Local Cy. Equiv. K30.00

JUL 16 1960

The Youngstown Hospital Association, Youngstown Ohio.

Figure 65. Immigrant visa from US embassy in Rangoon. Personal collection.

I had many concerns about encountering Japanese, who had been so cruel to us in Burma and whom I had so feared as a teenager. During the war and occupation, I had been instructed not to look at a Japanese soldier or officer; any eye contact with the "master race" was not allowed and would be met with severe punishment. Now I would come face to face with them again. In the terminal, to my shock, I did have eye contact but encountered no hostility. I found the Japanese to be polite and efficient; they smiled and were helpful. I had to pinch myself. Only a few years ago I had been yelled at "Kura Kura" while Japanese soldiers pointed their bayonets and barked at me. Inside, I could not suppress the fear and loathing I had for them. After a light breakfast I picked up the boarding pass, went through customs and immigration, waited for the boarding call, then was bused to the plane. To hear Japanese again had brought back memories of the war and all the fears associated with the war. I was happy to begin the next leg of my journey.

The new Pan Am 707 was a shiny, sleek plane, introduced only two years ago. Inside, it looked and smelled of new leather. No smell of sweat or cordite (as on the DC 3s). The fresh-faced, wide-eyed, Pan Am stewardesses were young and so beautiful; polite and helpful; dressed in powder-blue skirts and high heels they guided me to my seat. The seats were plush and comfortable, the plane was not crowded, it was all orderly and efficient. A minute after I settled in, the pilot announced on the intercom "we are ready to depart." The young attendant made sure I was buckled in, the plane taxied, and we made a smooth take off. At cruising altitude, the captain came on the loud speaker again and announced "our first stop will be Honolulu." I was surprised because I had not seen that on the ticket; it said San Francisco. The mention of Honolulu brought back memories both pleasant and unpleasant. It had a special place in my heart. I could still hear the haunting Hawaiian music from a long time ago, which had filled Rangoon radio after the Pearl Harbor bombing and heralded the bombing of Rangoon itself a few weeks later. The memories of war were still fresh.

Flying was such a pleasure in those days: soon an appetizer arrived, then a little wine, followed by good dinner, all on miniaturized but real (truly) china. This was unique compared to lack of any services in earlier days. We were traveling east with a good tail wind. Gaining time as we went east, we crossed the international date line. After a beer, a little reading, and the onset of darkness, the drone and vibration made me drowsy and sent me to sleep. I do not know how many hours elapsed, but at dawn I went to the toilet, cleaned up, and returned to my seat to find a full American breakfast waiting. I set aside the bacon; it was more than I could finish.

When the captain announced our approach to Hawaii, old Hawaiian music filled the air, filling me with emotion. Stepping on terra firma was surreal. I was overwhelmed by memories of war and my emotions overcame me; tears welled up in my eyes, and although I tried to hide my face from those around me, I finally broke down and cried. By the time I walked to the terminal I gained self-control. It was the port of entry to the US, so Customs and Immigration went through my papers, the health officer took my chest x-ray (yes, back then we had to have chest x-rays), and Immigration took my papers and asked me a number of questions. In those days there were no short cuts; all paperwork had to be in order. After the formalities were over, I walked into the terminal, waved through by a huge African-American man. I encountered Hawaiians for the first time (the girls lived up to the expectation of being exceptionally beautiful). I wanted to linger, but soon there was the first boarding call, so I did a slow walk. I was shooed into gate by another burly attendant. I had a window seat from which I could look down at the runway and wonder what it had been like nineteen years ago.

Headwinds as we approached the US coast delayed our arrival, and we arrived at San Francisco in the forenoon, behind schedule. Setting foot on American soil for the first time was exhilarating. I could see out the large clean windows that it was a warm and balmy summer day with a gentle breeze. I had heard much about the city and its great beauty, and my brief encounter showed that it lived up to its reputation. I took stock and looked for United Airlines counter, where I was told I had missed my flight to Ohio.

I had sixteen dollars in my pocket (that's what the government allowed me to take out of the country). I explained my predicament to the young desk clerk. Contemporary travelers may not believe this, but she smiled and reassured me, "Don't worry; we will put you up at a motel for the night and book you on your flight in the morning." She printed up the new ticket and arranged transport to and from the airport to my lodging. This was the first night I spent in an American hotel. The room was clean, almost sterile, and comfortable; the bed looked inviting. I crawled into bed and tried to pull the sheet over my head to hide from mosquitoes (old habits die hard) but found that the sheet was tucked in too tightly. To my relief, I finally pried enough up to cover my head (I try to do this to this day). The next morning I was taken back to the airport to catch my flight to Chicago and, from there, to Youngstown. Both flights were uneventful.

# Chapter 33
# Youngstown

After a journey of more than 8,000 miles, I arrived at Youngstown Hospital on July 18, 1960. Youngstown, a northeast Ohio town of about 100,000 people, had been founded by John Young in 1797. Ten families came and settled along the Mahoning River. The city grew till it was large enough to be incorporated, which happened in 1802. As growth continued, Youngstown became an important intersection along a number of major railroads, and the railroad connections attracted immigrants—Poles, Italians, Hungarians, and others. It was a steel town, said to be second in the nation in steel production. Republic and Youngstown Sheet and Tube were well-known steel producers. It was here that the Congress of Industrial Organizations was founded, and steel production saw a spurt of growth during World War II. But when I arrived, the heyday of steel was coming to an end; production had diminished, competition from overseas had forced the closure of some mills, and decline was evident. When the steel workers went on strike for seven weeks in 1952, President Truman had ordered the Secretary of Commerce to seize the plants, including Youngstown Sheet and Tube (later reversed by order of the Supreme Court). Youngstown was also an outpost of the Chicago Mafia; the city center was dominated by the mob.

As soon as I arrived, I reported for duty at the North unit, which was my first posting. Because it catered to the upper-class and mostly white population of the city, it consisted of a very appealing building and grounds. I was given my white uniform and had a meeting with the head of education and the hospital administrator. I was given a stack of papers to read and fill out. Then I was directed to the floor where I was to learn. I was greeted there by a big, young, blue-eyed RN. She was friendly, eased my anxieties, reassured me, and helped me get started. With few exceptions I got along with the staff. Later one of my fellow interns told me to enjoy my time here, because at the South unit it would be different: that was the City unit and was a world away. It catered to the poor, immigrants, and the black community. The Youngstown hospital was a microcosm of the great American divide.

Work was intense, and yet I spent much time familiarizing myself with the new surroundings and the American way of doing things. It was a big surprise to note that each patient in the semi-private and private rooms had a different doctor, which meant calling half a dozen doctors to give evening reports. I also spent much time in the medical library and quickly adapted to hospital life. There were many interns and residents from foreign countries, who spoke many languages. I got along with most of the nurses and the staff doctors.

Figure 66. Author at Youngstown Hospital North Unit. Photo taken by a friend.

The senior resident went over the rules for work, namely taking the "history and physical," then calling the appropriate consultant to get the orders and any special tests. Each morning started with quick "rounds" to take care of any immediate patient problems, then on to the operating rooms, which work ended usually in the afternoon or, on occasion, dragged into late afternoon. Out of surgery, I went over the afternoon admissions and then had to be on alert for any emergencies. Most patients came in the afternoon for surgery the next morning. I groaned at the schedule. Some days the number of patients to be "worked up" was reasonable; other days there would be ten patients, and it would take till midnight. After that you crashed and then rose at six in the morning for another long day. Assisting at surgery, some cases were short while others took many tedious hours. This was my second internship (my first had been at Rangoon General Hospital), so I knew what I had to do.

Surgeons came in all stripes: some good surgeons, who went to work without fuss and could perform an appendectomy in twenty minutes. A less competent surgeon would take up to an hour, with a lot of grunting and fussing; and the worst would stumble, take more than an hour, and leave a mess to clean up. Some surgeons were abusive and some friendly, and there was the usual complement of prima donnas. One such was a portly East European gynecologist, a stereotypical Hungarian, who was tyrannical, demanding, and overbearing. He was a crybaby and needed more help than others. While most surgeons were given one assistant, he demanded two; then he complained all through the procedure. There was nothing we could do to satisfy him, and there was little one could do but endure the abuse. In those days there was no avenue for appeal, so he could get away with it. Another gynecologist, an otherwise happy and fair man, took a harsh view of black women: after he delivered black babies, he did a tubal ligation without the woman's knowledge. He would say "It's in their best interest." This was eugenics and was reminiscent of all the horrors of the Holocaust. He probably believed in slavery. That eugenics was carried on in this country was unbelievable.[1] I recoiled

[1] Oliver Wendell Homes had asserted that three children were enough and approved the sterilization of "feeble-minded" women.

at this but could do little. Given my background, having seen human suffering during the war and having endured personal difficulty, I had a certain compassion for human suffering. All I could do was bite my lip and carry on. Aside from complaining to your fellow interns, you just continued on. Keeping on the good side of the senior resident was essential; an angry senior resident who did not like you could make your life miserable. He had the power to go over the surgery list and determine who you would "assist" the next day. After one year I was appointed to a first-year residency at the hospital.

In the medical wards, the procedure was different from that in Rangoon. A weekend of work typically started at 6.00 pm on Friday (after a full day's work) and ended at 6:00 am on Monday (followed by a full day's work), a total of 60 hours. You could not leave work undone. A "weekend off" meant off at noon on Saturday and start early on Monday. On a busy day or weekend, the work load could be grueling, could become overwhelming. Nurses could help or make your life miserable, and fortunately I got along with the head nurse, a very important fact. My proficiency in American English was an enormous help. Like the senior resident, the head nurse could make your life miserable. It was my good fortune to work with a friendly, young blonde RN I will call Sue, although it was not her real name. She helped with the nuances and helped me understand local practices. In the old country you had a hierarchy and a chain of command, with a chief whom you rarely saw, but here every patient had a private practitioner, and so you had many bosses. It was easy to adjust, although I still had plenty of things to learn. For example, reverting to British English I said the telephone was "engaged," which brought giggles from the staff. But I quickly picked up American pronunciation and sounds, adjusted my accent, and understood American slang. Besides, I loved American music, had read newspapers and books since my years spent at the American Center Library in Rangoon. So, what other people found difficult was easy for me, and these facts hastened my adaptation to American culture.

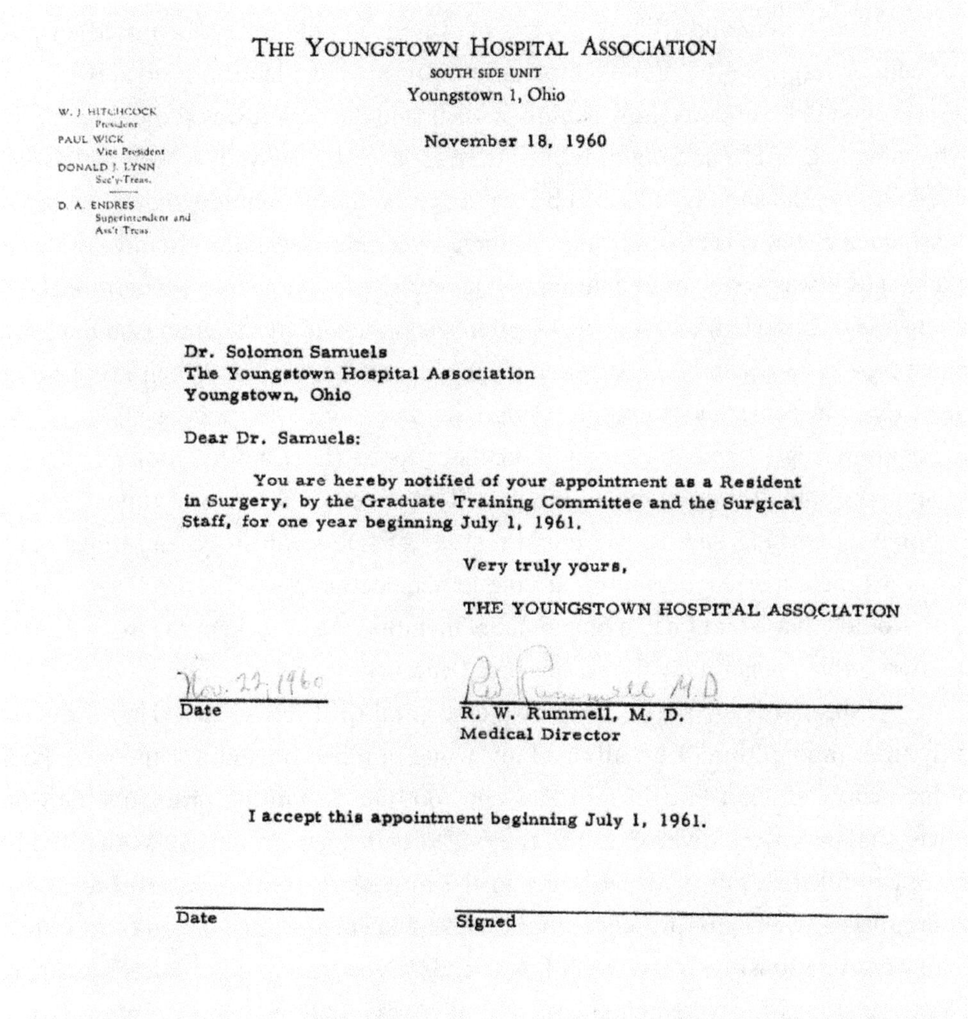

THE YOUNGSTOWN HOSPITAL ASSOCIATION
SOUTH SIDE UNIT
Youngstown 1, Ohio

W. J. HITCHCOCK
President
PAUL WICK
Vice President
DONALD J. LYNN
Sec'y-Treas.

D. A. ENDRES
Superintendent and
Ass't Treas.

November 18, 1960

Dr. Solomon Samuels
The Youngstown Hospital Association
Youngstown, Ohio

Dear Dr. Samuels:

You are hereby notified of your appointment as a Resident in Surgery, by the Graduate Training Committee and the Surgical Staff, for one year beginning July 1, 1961.

Very truly yours,

THE YOUNGSTOWN HOSPITAL ASSOCIATION

Nov. 22, 1960
Date

R. W. Rummell, M.D.
R. W. Rummell, M. D.
Medical Director

I accept this appointment beginning July 1, 1961.

Date

Signed

Figure 67. Letter of appointment to residency at Youngstown Hospital. Personal collection.

There were and still are aspects of American culture that bemused, disappointed, or surprised me. For example, there was always plentiful food at the cafeteria (although I wondered how healthy it was), and the surfeit was sometimes overwhelming to me. The amount of wasted food shocked me as well, especially having lived through the shortages caused by war and rebellion. I mentioned this to a businessman once but was told that "our resources were inexhaustible." In most of these exchanges it was wise not to contradict and argue. I found people's woeful lack of interest in or knowledge of the world, often accompanied by statements about how much they knew, disturbing. My skepticism increased over time. When I first came here, I was insecure about my knowledge, but over time I felt increasingly secure in my knowledge. I had no interest in spectator sports (later in life I took an interest in tennis); football did not excite me. Small talk seemed a waste of time. I found fiction uninteresting and instead pursued study of science, history, and travel; and my war-time experience gave me a unique perspective on the world. My second wife would tell me that I had a phenomenal memory. Reading kept me in my living quarters, which was fine with me, because I enjoyed my private time.

I did not leave the security of the hospital till I felt secure. Then I did so only from time to time. I usually had my white uniform on, and for the most part at the nearby shops I bought toiletries and food items with no problems. Downtown, shoppers were diverse, but in the outskirts, they were mostly White. I was more careful there, even when going to the movies. I was also careful to avoid going places where my presence might cause a scene, such as cheap bars. Other than work relationships, there were few friends. Even among other interns and residents, relationships were ephemeral, and of course there were no Burmese or Indians among them. Instead I developed relationships with interns from the Philippines and South America.

My sojourn at the North unit (the "country club") was coming to an end. As I was preparing for my exams, I was moved to the South unit (the "City hospital"). The difference between the units was as stark as night and day. Emblematic of the times, I was now in the "real America"—a downtown city hospital, which did not have acres of greenery like the hospital in the north but was efficient nonetheless. In the South unit, the patient population reflected the population at large.

While Whites dominated, there were more minorities and poor—middle-class patients along with blue-collar working-class Italians and black Americans. The emergency room was busy and was an eye-opening experience. Like in any ER, there were car accident victims, gunshot wounds, victims of knifings and fights—all were brought here. Not long after I was transferred, I would come face to face with gangsters, members of the mob about whom I had read so much.

Early in the evening a patient with a gunshot wound was brought to the ER. Immediately, a huge crowd gathered outside; it looked like the city's entire Italian community was in the parking lot. Before I went to examine the patient, the head nurse grabbed me, pulled me aside, and whispered, "Handle this patient with care; don't ask too many personal questions, just deal with the injuries." Remembering the book I had recently read about the mob, I took her advice and just went about my business. To get the patient ready, I started an IV, took a blood sample

Figure 68. Youngstown Hospital South Unit circa 1960. Photo by author.

for transfusion, and watched the nurses do their thing. I was eager to admit the patient to the hospital operating room and breathed a sigh of relief when he was transported out of my domain. Later I learned that he was a high-level mobster.

The first thing a house officer does is take the history of the patient. The guidelines for this were well delineated and had a dark side. It had to start with race. A "white person" was listed as such, and black patients were called "Negro." So, in taking a patient's history, one starts with "55-year-old white male" or "55-year-old Negro." I have alluded to this earlier. Black patients were placed in rooms separate from all others. The question of black physicians was contentious. At Youngstown Hospital there were two black physicians, and I was appalled to see how they were treated: there were severe restrictions on them. Even at the charity clinic they were not allowed to see destitute white patients. Ironically, Asian physicians—no matter how dark their skin—could do things that native born "Negro" physicians could not. I never could find a good answer for this.[2] My relationship with the "Negro" doctors was good; it was man to man and doctor to doctor. I did encounter discrimination on a social level, however, as the following incident reveals. I was walking down the main downtown street one day and saw walking opposite me one of the older nurses whom I thought I was getting to know. Instantly I recognized her and smiled and tried to say "Hi." She turned her head and briskly walked away. This was just the first of many instances of the hypocrisy of some Americans. Many of them were friendly, however, and I was invited to the homes of doctors and even to the homes of some non-hospital persons, but in most instances, business relationships were one thing and being social was another. Some American doctors were wonderful, others less so, and we were intensely involved with one another at work in caring for patients. But beyond that, interest stopped, and in this they merely reflected society.

Most doctors were conservative politically, socially, and financially. It soon became apparent that I would have a hard time dealing with the extremism. I had been born into a very conservative religious family, but my life experience—

[2] A recent report notes that just 4 percent of US doctors are Black. *New York Times*, August 20, 2018 (www.nytimes.com/2018/08/20/health/black-men-doctors.html).

—especially the war—changed me forever. In Asia, by the end of the war, there had been revulsion against colonialism, capitalism, and the exploitation of the peoples. I was conservative in money matters but otherwise had difficulty accepting the conservative viewpoint. I would, of course, have to adapt to this carefully and suppress my views. At this stage in life I had not completely formed my political and medical views, but they were developing. The American usage of term "liberal" made me cringe. To me the term represented the "Neo-classical view," that of Locke, Shaw, Mill, Smith, Hume, and Gladstone. I came from a country where the state tried to provide (however poorly) basic medical care for poor people; in the US it was all private, with only a small, mean clinic for the poor (during my time in Youngstown there was still a poor house run by the county, but that soon closed). The long hours, the scut work, and some of the social interactions I observed were demoralizing at times, but all had to be endured in order to advance to a residency and become an attending physician. But it was not all work.

Outside of work there was a wonderful life to live: to read what I wanted to read, and eat what I wanted to eat, and go places I wanted to visit. Early in my stay in America, families invited me dinner, which provided my first introduction to American home life. I respected their solicitude and am grateful for what I learned about family life in the US. This was the era when Americans were competing with the Soviets, so there was much discussion about Viet Nam. Some would say "The war will be won if we could win the hearts of enough of the Vietnamese," but others were more interested in body counts and how much destruction we wrought; that alone, they perceived, could assure victory. Given my experience and view of colonialism, of war, I had my doubts about this colonial war. At gatherings I just nodded and kept my thoughts private to myself.[3]

My first vacation, to the Big Apple, fulfilled the dream of every immigrant. Walking down the street I encountered a friendly man next to me who said "Hi. Good morning." I responded in kind, he complimented on me on my appearance, and observed, "You have brown skin, but you look different. Where do you come

[3] I will stop here on the topic, as I have a whole chapter on the draft and the Vietnam war later in this book.

from?" I told him "I am of Indian descent but was born in Burma." "What do you do?" he pursued, and after I told him, he smiled, wished me well, and took off. In contrast, middle-aged women on the subway would grab their purses and hold them close when their eyes landed on me. I had so many good experiences that gave me a good feeling about the US and myself, but then there would always be an episode that would spoil this good feeling.

Back to the topic of medicine. The debate on health care was intense, and the current (twenty-first century) debate on health care reminds me of the one raging in 1964. After President Johnson succeeded the assassinated President Kennedy, there was much talk about expanding care for the elderly and the poor and much discussion about civil rights. At first I did not have a strong opinion on the proposed Kennedy-Johnson Medicare plan, but when debate began to label care for the elderly and the poor as "Fedicare" or socialized medicine and expressed strong criticism of the British and Canadian systems, I was shocked at the hostility and vitriol. I heard much angry rhetoric in the hospital; almost to a man, the doctors were vehemently opposed to the proposal, prophesying that Medicare heralded the end of good medicine and creeping socialism. "The best medical care in the world," they said "will be destroyed," and they would fight to keep the old system. The AMA (American Medical Association) and most specialists were opposed to the program. The discussion was mostly between the surgeons and the anesthesiologists, but it pervaded the entire establishment. Occasionally one of them would look at me. Were they looking at me because they did not trust me? or looking for my reaction? was it more the latter than the former? I just nodded, looked the other way, kept my opinions to myself, and avoided any discussion. Most of the resident staff was also split: the foreigners kept their opinions to themselves, knowing that the American resident staff favored the private system. I listened to both supporters of Medicare and its critics. After I finished my training, my opinion would synthesize further, but that was in the future; for now I said nothing. Many foreign-born and foreign-trained physicians would fall victim to avarice and greed and take a position to the right of the right wing of American conservatism, and some would pay a dear price for it. The twenty-first century is now embroiled in a debate about "Medicare for All," but I am afraid that a golden opportunity was lost in 1964.

# Chapter 34
# Private Life

Life was not all work; I had to have a private life as well. Internship meant working closely with nursing students, nurses, and RNs. Some were amiable but others bitchy, especially night nurses, who, if they disliked you, could make your life miserable (like make you get out of bed, go to the hospital and up the elevator to the sixth floor at 2:00 am just to sign an aspirin order). Working with young women would naturally lead to some close relationships. My first date was with an LPN (licensed practical nurse) who was quite friendly. She was slightly on the plump side, blonde with blue eyes. During breaks in work she talked to and took an interest in me, asking me if I been to an outdoor movie. I had little time for fun things, but I wanted to go to an open-air movie, which I had heard so much about. When she suggested that "we should go to a drive-in movie" so that we would not been seen downtown, I had no idea how to get about town. I had no car or driver's license. At an agreed-upon place and time she picked me up in her car, and we went to an outdoor movie. Before long, it would lead to the inevitable intimacy. That was my first experience in America.

Less than a year later, emboldened by experience and with a car at my disposal, I would soon meet the first girl whom I really cared about and with whom I would fall in love. She was young, slight, pretty, medium height, with light blonde hair. Her blue eyes at times sparkled. Two years out of school, she worked the evening shift (3:00 to 11:00 pm) as a registered nurse. On evenings when worked slowed, we had time to kill and an opportunity to talk, and it was in this setting that I got to know her. Her name was Barb. Her speech was soft, slow, and deliberate; she appeared vulnerable, frail, ethereal. She was none of those, as I would find out later. She was full of kindness and gentleness. Her parents had migrated from Central Europe (Czechoslovakia) after the war. Coming from post-war Europe and being devout Catholics, they were far to the right in their views about social life. They were anti-communist and very conservative, and she said they "would never approve" of those who did not hold rigid views with them. But that did not deter us from dating. I do not quite know how it started. I think I asked if she would like to go out for dinner. It was a bold move, as in the early 1960s, given my brown skin, there were not many places we could go to. On the busy Market Street downtown were restaurants, among them a Chinese restaurant. We met after work and had supper at the restaurant. We continued to see each other. In the summer she wore flowered cotton dresses, making her very appealing and cute. The first time we held hands, I noticed that she had slender delicate fingers and was quite taken with that. The friendship matured. The interns all lived in an old frame house, and we went in and out, commonly bringing a date. Going places was sometimes difficult, but Barb owned a blue Dodge Dart and was always willing to drive. Some evenings we stopped at the Mahoning River and the Mill Creek pond. It was a beautiful park, with a large pond, a small waterfall, and nooks and crannies where one could find privacy to spend a quiet evening together. There were birds and ducks; I loved watching the ducks because it reminded me of home. At the height of summer, the vegetation was dense, almost tike the tropics. She wanted me to go to her home, then became nervous and changed her mind. We talked at length, and while she was concerned about how her family would react to me, nevertheless the relationship deepened. Then the inevitable happened. At this time, neither of us were ready to deal with marriage. It was a time of anguish while we did not fully talk about the consequences. At age 27 I told her "I love you" (she was my first love), and she reciprocated. We continued to see each other.

## RESIDENCY

Surgical residencies are very structured: you start at the of bottom of the pyramid, and by the third year only two would get the coveted Chief Resident spots. I wanted to get a big city residency. I could have stayed in Youngstown but had a dream to go to a big city. Barb and I danced around the issue, did not talk about marriage; again my courage would fail me. There were many young residents, for the most part American, who were married. But I knew that I had a long slog ahead. It was OK for native-born physicians to marry young; they had families to support them. For foreign residents, on a student visa, marriage came with problems. Timidity and courage existed side by side within me. I was fearful of taking such a big move, of being married. Some surgical chiefs considered marriage to be a disadvantage and frowned on married residents—a far cry from today. Already older than many native-born interns, I was in a hurry to get my education and did not want anything to interfere with my quest to get ahead. I told Barb of my plans, that to improve my chances I had to go to a big city. She agreed but was worried about the long periods of absence. I promised that I would travel frequently to see her.

I found a position in Philadelphia. I had been hoping to land a second-year residency but instead landed a fellowship. I had to do this to advance my career and complete my training. Barb said nothing, but I knew she was saddened. She turned her head and quietly cried. I held her close while she wiped the tears from her eyes. It was a difficult moment for us. "It is not the end, just a good-bye," we agreed, and I promised to come back to see her. I put all my belongings into my Ford Comet and set out to another strange city. I knew nobody, had no friends there, no family or mentors. This nomadic life of going to strange new places every year or so was becoming routine.

Long-distance romance inevitably fails. Time and distance would cool the relationship. Given the brutal work of a resident, it was difficult for me to drive eight hours on a regular basis. In the first year I visited her several times and stayed over. She came to Philadelphia once. But the rigors of training and the long distance would take its toll, we grew distant, and the relationship died. So it would be another sad good-bye.

Many years later I reflected on how my pursuit of an advanced degree came at a high personal price. I sometimes lacked courage, always afraid of making mistakes. We knew it was a risk to wait until after my residency to marry. We had agreed that we would have to face many obstacles if we married. But fear kept me from taking the plunge. In retrospect I regret not having the courage ask her to marry me. Now, looking back decades later at my two beautiful, successful daughters, I muse: Had I married her, I would not have later entered into a marriage that failed. I may have fulfilled my dream of having a big family, grandchildren, and great-grandchildren.

# Chapter 35
# Philadelphia

In 1962, Philadelphia was the fourth largest city in the US. It boasted the longest street—Broad Street, alleged to be 13 miles long. In addition to the Liberty Bell, the city's most dominant feature was the fine Art Museum. The famed Pennsylvania Central Railroad Station was nearby. The Schuylkill River runs through the city and was famous for its sculling and boat races. The city also hosted free summertime "Shakespeare in the Park" and outdoor concerts. The suburbs had strange names like King of Prussia and Germantown.[1] The unnamed suburbs like Little Italy and South Philly were most noted for violence. The University of Pennsylvania Medical School dominated education, along with Temple University and Hahnemann Medical School at 230 N. Broadway. My hospital. It was about two blocks from city square.

My first day at work was a disappointment. I was expecting to work in a big-city hospital and continue my residency, but instead the then-Chief offered me a fellowship in his lab. Inject dogs with various substances, euthanize the dog, process the pancreatic tissue, search for the trigger that causes pancreatitis. There was not much direction. I had completed two internships, and now I was spending an extra lost year in the lab of a big-city hospital. Life was difficult. The hospital pay was low, lower than when I was an intern. Food was available only when working, and no housing was provided. Looking for an apartment in a big city was a challenge: finding something affordable that was safe and not far away from the city center was difficult. Given the civil rights debate and protests, I was seeking a place where I could live without too much discrimination. Most places close to the bus or rail line were in a low-rent district and were little more than a hole in the wall. I finally found a tiny apartment in a mixed neighborhood.

---

[1] Not until I read the history of the French Revolution did I know the difference between the Prussians and the Germans.

Figure 69. Author in front of apartment in Philadelphia. Photo taken by a friend.

I soon tired of the lab and wanted to go back to clinical work. The Chief left the hospital, and I sought a mentor who would help me get a residency for my second year. I found that mentor in the Acting Chief, with whom I worked several years. He was a hard-working young man, with whom I got along well. I worked closely with him, and he was very supportive of me. I worked very hard, enjoyed my work, and got along well with other residents and staff. I was promoted regularly. I thought that I would have money, but reality was different. The Acting Chief sympathized with my circumstances and suggested that I could get a position in the department that would supplement my resident pay. He promised me that he could get me a research grant that would have called for me to do some research and write a report, which I promised to do. The extra money would be helpful. In one year, according to immigration rules, I had to leave the country before I could apply for re-entry and eventual citizenship.[2] The research grant would really help, but that good news did not last long. I also had found a weekend position in Chester, a small city near Philadelphia. The head administrator of the hospital took pity me on and gave me weekend work in the hospital ER.

Fate would intervene again. The hospital appointed a new Chief of Surgery. In a flash, everything changed. My close working relationship with the Acting Chief was severed. The new Chief was of the old world: a very conservative Anglophile. He did not like foreigners. He believed that foreign doctors in training should be grateful for the opportunity to be here to serve and learn, and he felt that being paid a stipend was more than generous, even though the paltry salary that I worked for barely covered essentials. He forbade any attempt to work on the weekends at peripheral hospitals (moonlighting). "You did not come here to get rich," he opined. (That is an irony; you could not get rich on $200 a month, even back in the 1960s.) I suppose he never had to contend with reality. My worst fears were realized shortly, when he changed all promises made to residents by previous Chiefs. He brought his own men and assigned to them all the benefits that had been promised to others. My promised research grant was given instead to his golden-haired boy, the resident he brought with him.

Unlike in Youngstown, no Philadelphia families invited foreign students to their homes. There was little time for private life anyway, as the residency was all consuming. I was surprised by the obsession with sports among the native-born residents; work seemed to be something they *had* to do, and what they seemed to enjoy most was watching and talking about sports. Being without family, I helped married residents who had families by covering for them over holidays and their vacation times. I felt lonely at times, but helping others earned me some friends.

Philadelphia had loads of challenges, and life as a resident at a big-city hospital was more complex than it had been in Youngstown. This was the era of civil rights marches, protests, and sit ins. The city and its environs were deeply divided along ethnic lines. Germans were a strong presence in the city and in the

---

[2] Among some of the older residents there were other foreigners who were trying to evade the immigrant visa requirement by circumventing the rule: prolonging the residency while working to have the immigration status changed, the great quest for the "green card."

outlying areas. South Philadelphia was predominantly Black, and the Italian enclave section was close by. This created many problems. There was constant friction between the two groups as well as with other ethnic groups, to put it mildly. In lucid moments the Italians would say that the Black area should be ringed with artillery and obliterated. Life was rough in big-city ERs; no cake walk, it sometimes resembled a war zone. One episode is etched in my memory. One night when I was on call, a big, strapping black man walked into the ER and said "Doc, they shot me" and then keeled over and dropped to the floor. We had to pick him up, rushing him to the operating room. I called the Chief Resident, who told me go ahead and that he would be at the hospital in fifteen minutes.[3] I fretted that I might find a condition I could not handle, but this night all went smoothly.

Some days when the city went wild with killings and shootings, we started the morning with scheduled surgery and then by afternoon the shooting and stabbing victims were brought to the ER. Case after case was brought to the operating room. One case ended, we took a potty break, drank more fluids, and then back to surgery it was. Often we had 36-hour shifts. Always tired. On November 22, 1963, we were in one of those long 36-hour sessions when the circulating nurse walked in and, in a terrified voice, announced "The president was shot." My Senior Resident, an extreme right-wing Catholic, without as much as looking up, said "Good. Is he dead?" That shocked me, especially coming from an ostensibly religious man.

My term as a resident was ending, and the world had changed dramatically since I had first arrived from Burma. US visa law required that I leave the country. But there was no home to go back to: since the Ne Win coup in Burma in 1962, there was no way I could go home, which had been my original plan. The ugly face of finances came up again. And hunger returned: Food was free in the cafeteria on working days, but not on weekends and non-working days. I was reduced to eating fast food and cheap canned food. Finally, I met with the vice president of the hospital and explained my predicament. He was sympathetic, said he had access to some funds, and that he would look into the matter. He ultimately came up with $3,000, for which I was immensely grateful. I considered my options, where I

[3] My superiors had greater confidence in me than I had in myself.

would go when my visa ran out. One was to enlist in the US Army, which was in need of residents trained in surgery.

## THE VIETNAM WAR, THE DRAFT

I had learned about Vietnam in the old country. When I was in medical school in the 1950s, my study habits were such that I took a break every fifty minutes on the hour, to get some fresh air and listen to the late news. It was on one such break in 1954 that I turned on the battered old radio at 10:00 pm. I brought up a clear and strong signal from Radio Australia. I remember the night well. I was in my third year of medical school. The announcer in somber terms reported: "The general in command of Dien Bien Phu reported to his boss in Hanoi, 'I cannot hold.' General de Castries reported that he was surrendering the fortress at Dien Bien Phu and the Plain of Jars." Later the overseas news of Voice of America confirmed that Dien Bien Phu was lost.

This was essential news to us at the time. At the end of World War II, from the time when the Japanese surrendered in 1945 to the time that French colonial troops arrived to reclaim their former colony, there was a vacuum. In this vacuum, in September 1945, the League for the Independence of Vietnam revolted and seized power. The French pleaded for British help, and, at the request of the British government, the South East Asia Command sent RAF fighters and the 20th Indian Division to Vietnam, to maintain order till French troops arrived. The Government of India, under Nehru, was incensed; he wanted all Indian troops returned home to India, with no more casualties. It appeared that the intervention was a continuation of the war. The press reported fulsomely on the intensity of the fighting and on Vietnamese anger at the Indians for siding with the French colonial power. The Indian troops kept order for a while but were finally withdrawn as the strife continued and Nehru's pressure persisted. The British recognized that colonialism had ended in Asia, but the French would take almost another two decades to come to terms with it.

After I arrived in the US in 1960, I had to register with the draft board (I still have the card). Since I could not go home to Burma, and given all the uncertainties I was facing, it was tempting to join the army. To do so would have given me employment, good pay, and a path to US citizenship. I considered going to a recruiting center to enlist; I had the selective service card and was fully trained. It was a time of great angst for me, living in a tiny apartment, with cockroaches and other vermin. I felt I could better myself by enlisting.

It was also a time of deep divisions in America. At the hospital lunch counter there was much discussion about how to avoid the draft, especially among young doctors. Having survived four years of a colonial war, I loathed the name-calling, slurs such as "gooks." "We killed thirty Gooks today," a report in the press would read. And all the talk of kill ratios, 1 to 14 to 30: they were talking about fellow Asians, and this repelled me. In spite of advances in civil rights, underlying attitudes had not changed much. I was aghast to hear comments from the leading generals, statements like "Life is plentiful, cheap in the orient." The prevailing view was that "the oriental doesn't put the same high price on life as the Westerner." This made me wince. The generals' policy was based on a profligate disregard for human life, the desire to kill as many enemies as possible, with success measured in body counts; anything that moved got killed. Reports of secret bombing of Laos and Cambodia trickled out; later there was the Mai Lai Massacre.

I thought long and hard. My fellow residents at risk for the draft talked endlessly about it. For some it was the Berry Plan and all its permutations.[4] Foreigners could evade the draft as long as they were in training. In those days, immigration enforcement was quite rigid, unlike today. At the end of each year, the immigration service sent a card; it was a simple brown (as all government publications are) form but quite efficient. It asked your status and date of completion of the residency, at which time you were given thirty days to wrap up your affairs and leave the country.

Those who had already served painted a grim picture of Vietnam and an even grimmer picture of the war. The description of the country was not a surprise;

---

[4] The Berry Plan, enacted in 1954, allowed physicians to defer obligatory military service until they completed medical school and residency. They still would need to enter the armed forces after the full residency; or they could enter after the internship or after the first year of residency, with a guarantee that they could complete their education after completion of service.

its topography and climate would be similar to Burma, so I would have no problem with the climate and would in fact be at an advantage. But the war was something else. Up to now I had spent almost one-third of my life in a strife-riven country, and I was tired of war, insurgencies, rebels, ambushes, and post-colonial rebellions. War can change one's life on a dime: if you were in the wrong place at the wrong time, you could die in short order. Of course it would be exciting to be an officer in the military, but that would not outweigh the danger of being in a war zone again. Even so, I gave it much thought. Then I took a break, set aside the war for a while, and turned back to life at hand. I spent time catching up on my reading, feeling a need to read the classics and great literature, native and foreign.

Reports in the press were not encouraging; the war was not going well for the US. The death rate was climbing, and there were many protests against the military draft, in fact daily protests on the streets. The usual refrain was "Hell no, we won't go." In the cloistered halls of the universities and the hospitals, deferral for a variety of reasons was common (Calcaneal spurs was the excuse that President Trump would choose). My choices were limited. I could go to Canada, Australia, or England. There was another alternative: to be a perpetual resident or fellow. This could be done by adding a year or two upon completion of one's primary residency. One fellow (from Iran) aged forty added another two fellowships outside his specialty to evade the draft; some did this year after year. I chose not to go this route.

England and Australia were tempting, but they were far away and, given my financial constraints, would be difficult. Hard pressed for money and unable to buy a ticket anywhere, Canada would be the most pragmatic choice.

THE FOREIGN SERVICE
OF THE
UNITED STATES OF AMERICA

Consular Section
American Embassy
Rangoon, Burma
October 11. 1961.

Dr. S. Samuels
The Youngstown Hospital Association
Youngstown 1, Ohio.

Dear Dr. Samuels:

Enclosed please find one copy of Form FS-497 ( Questionnaire To Determine Quota or Nonquota Status And Application For Quota Registration) and two information sheets. In order to register as an intending immigrant, please fill out the questionnaire and return it to me. The day that I receive it will be the date of your priority.

At the risk of being repetitious, but in order to avoid any misunderstanding at a future date, I would like to point out again that your case will not receive active consideration until you have departed from the United States and have resided outside the United States for at least two years. You may be sure, however, that when you have complied with the foreign residence requirements, your application will receive every consideration.

Sincerely,

Richard H. Howarth
Richard H. Howarth
American Vice Consul.

Figure 70. Letter from the US Embassy in Rangoon informing me that I would need to leave the US for two years and reapply as an immigrant. Personal collection.

THE FOREIGN SERVICE
OF THE
UNITED STATES OF AMERICA

Consular Section
American Embassy
Rangoon, Burma.
August 24, 1965.

Dear Dr. Samuels:

In reply to your letter of August 4, I am pleased to inform you that, under current Foreign Service regulations, your name has not been dropped from the quota waiting list. You are still registered under your initial date of February 6, 1962. Although the nonpreference category in the Burmese quota is heavily oversubscribed, individuals with a registration date as early as yours are now eligible to qualify for their immigrant visas. Thus, we can hope that, after you have satisfied the two-year residence abroad requirement, you will not have to wait after that time to qualify for your visa.

Accordingly, it will be in your interest to keep this office informed of your address and to let us know when you have completed two years of residence outside the United States.

Sincerely yours,

Leo J. Reddy
American Vice Consul

Dr. Solomon Samuels
Chief Surgical Resident,
Hahnemann Medical College,
Philadelphia, PA.

Figure 71. Letter from US Embassy in Rangoon confirming that I would qualify for an immigrant visa after residing outside the US for two years. Personal collection.

# Chapter 36
# Canada

I was not going to break the rules and dodge immigration law to extend my stay. I was going to play by the rules. My choices were limited, and going to Canada seemed the best option. I applied to Canadian Immigration and was surprised at the speed of their response. They assured me that all I needed to do was present myself at the border, where I could pick up my Immigration papers. In preparation, I sold my old small car and bought an old, oversized beater with a small engine (it evoked some laughter), attached a little U-Haul trailer, and took off for the unknown. I knew little about Canada, other than it was part of the British Commonwealth and was cold. Saying goodbye to all the friends, residents, nurses, and other staff was sad; we residents had spent nights on call together in a 10 by 10 room and could tell by smell who was sharing the room! I had lost contact with Barbara but promised myself I would get in touch with her again. In the wee hours of the morning, in the privacy of the room, I cried for girlfriends, friends, and the place. Some emotions were infatuation, some even romantic. My desire to sink my roots and stay in one place was not to be fulfilled. Now it was time to move on.

I looked at the map and memorized the route to the Ambassador Bridge. All the way from Philadelphia to Detroit I had butterflies in my stomach. I crossed the bridge and went through Immigration, where I was pulled over to the check-point; fortunately, I had the appropriate papers. In less than an hour the officials waved me through and I headed to Hamilton, Ontario, where I had a job waiting as a third-year resident. I made only one stop, in Windsor, to fill the gas tank and drove steadily toward my destination. Compared to Philadelphia, Hamilton was a small town. I arrived late on Saturday and checked in at the hospital, then after some questions and completion of paperwork was sent to the house staff quarters. I cleaned up and then, not having eaten all day, went out to get some food. The street in front of the hospital somehow looked the same and different at the same time. The streets were deserted; the city sidewalks rolled up by sunset, and there were no restaurants open. I went to bed tired and hungry. The next morning, I went

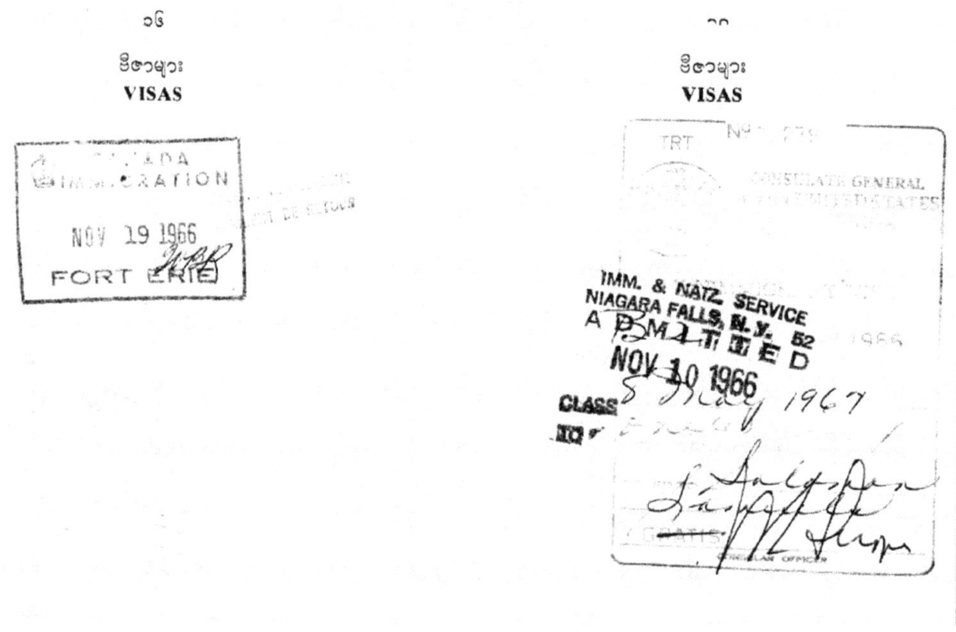


Figure 72. Visa and immigration stamps from November 1966. Personal collection.

out to get some coffee and breakfast and again found the city deserted. I walked block after block, only to find all stores were closed, no fast-food places, all restaurants closed. Finally, I found an old ethnic Greek man sitting outside of his closed shop. I asked "why is every shop was closed?" He looked puzzled, then explained: "It is Sunday" (the blue laws). It was then that I realized life was going different here. The Greek man took pity on me and brought some food out for me.

Prior correspondence from Hamilton Hospital had explained that my residency in the US was not recognized, was not good enough. Nor was my medical degree from University of Rangoon acceptable in Ontario. I could have gone to western Canada, where requirements were looser and my credentials would be accepted, but it was colder than Ontario. So I had swallowed my pride and accepted that—although I had already completed a five-year residency, including a Chief Residency—I had to start all over, at the third-year level. At least I could get a foot in the door. The staff at the hospital were friendly for the most part, but some were cool; being mostly Scottish-Presbyterian and conservative to the core, they were not used to foreigners. They did not think much of non-British, non-Scottish people. Moreover, their attitude towards US training was mixed, that is, they did not think much of US training, especially of non-white doctors.[1] While the Americans grudgingly let you go into practice if you passed all the prerequisites, the Canadians did not give you that option. Listening to them in the surgery lounge, their pejorative language was surprising. It was quite similar to the way white Americans talked about black people, but here it was directed at French speakers. And the same epitaphs were used for people of Asian descent. Talking to other Indian residents, I discovered that the Canadians raised all manner of obstacles, even questioning the medical degrees that were obtained in the third world. This was shocking, as Canada and her foreign policy were said to be the most liberal of all dominions. In fact, views were liberal in the central government with respect to foreign affairs, but the provinces were rigid. The provinces granted licenses mostly to graduates of schools in the UK and other white dominions and in fact discouraged non-white people from even applying. Ironically, the Canadians were always critical of American racism but did not see their own prejudices. They still shared Kipling's view, that the Asians were "half savage and half child."

My first impression of Canada was that it was cold, even in September. The cold winter season was long, which was difficult for me. Canada in the 1960s was a lily-white country (natives were all hidden, like sending Inuit children to faith schools, where they were forbidden to speak their own language), and with the exception of some Chinese immigrants to the west coast, there were few Asians in the other provinces. The mid-section and east of the country had very little contact with former British colonies and in some ways were more backward than the US.[2] The country's treatment of the native and Asian people was in some respects worse than in the US. Hamilton was primarily a small industrial city, with little diversity other than some East Europeans and a few Greeks. There were a few Greek restaurants, but other amenities were lacking. Soon I realized that in

[1] Their treatment of their own native-born "Indians" or indigenous people was the same.

[2] Although Canadians fought for the Empire in World War II, their experience of war was exclusively in Europe, hence their education about the non-white colonies was deficient.

Canada—in spite of all the rhetoric—there was no future for me. Being without family or friends made life even more difficult. Even CBC, the Canadian public broadcast company, was boring most of the time. Too many of the women lacked warmth and were not friendly, and the nurses were the same. I just ignored them. I hear that much has changed, that it is now less harsh than in the past.

My work in the Canadian healthcare system got me to thinking and comparing it to the system in the US. I realized that while I drove from Philadelphia to Canada, I had no insurance. Immediately upon arrival in Canada, I received my Canadian insurance card. The debate in the US was still ongoing about Medicare, and Canadians had a good laugh when they heard stories about the superiority of the American system. The most nonsensical were tales about "interminable waits" for medical treatment, specifically a long delay for elective hernia surgery. In fact, the Canadian system did give top priority to immediate life-threatening procedures and therefore might postpone elective surgery. But delayed elective surgery did not cause loss of life, and surgery was free or required minimal payment. The AMA and lobbyists who opposed Medicare in the US engaged in name-calling, some underhanded methods, and ridicule of the UK, Canada, and other countries. Americans developed unreasonable expectations of medicine.[3] Such resistance surely led to death or prolonged suffering for the uninsured.

The long cold months and loneliness were hard on me. This clouded my judgment and led to poor decisions. To be rational can be difficult in stressful times. Lack of money, the perennial problem, would lead me make a decision that would haunt me the rest of my life. I still thought of going to England or Australia but nonetheless somehow hung on for almost a year. It was getting to be tiresome

---

[3] Many families had expectations beyond what medical care could provide. Years later I would operate on an elderly man, for an incarcerated hernia; given his age and poor health, he soon developed multiple systems failure and was now terminally ill. The family put off the decision about life support until the arrival of a long-forgotten prodigal son from California, and they asked me to keep the patient alive in the interim. When the son finally arrived, we had the family conference. I listed the condition and the organs with system failure including lungs, kidney, and liver. The brash young man, with very little insight into life and death, listened with increasing impatience, then thundered his question: why had I not done a kidney transplant? He had not seen his father in a decade, and now, to assuage his guilt, he was making impossible demands. I chuckled and explained the facts of life.

doing scut work. I then applied to another hospital in London, Ontario. While it was not a jump in either income or status, it was better in one way: I would have no night call or spend long hours in the operating room; the position was in the Pathology department, which was run by an old British-trained gentleman who was a kindly man, which made the transition easy.[4] I had long periods of reflections and reminiscences and longed for Youngstown, fondly remembering my stay there and the friends I had gotten to know. In retrospect I should have considered other venues. When you are in melancholy mood you make the wrong choices. I wrote to the US Immigration and Naturalization Service in 1967 and received a waiver of the foreign residence requirement so that I could apply for an immigrant visa early. I then married for all the wrong reasons—a young woman I had met in Philadelphia at Hahnemann Hospital.

---

[4] Professor Frederick Grant Banting, who was a co-discoverer of insulin at the young age of 32, had worked at this hospital. He and John James Rickard Macleod received the Nobel Prize in Medicine in 1923.

PLEASE REFER TO THIS FILE NUMBER

**UNITED STATES DEPARTMENT OF JUSTICE**
**IMMIGRATION AND NATURALIZATION SERVICE**
**128 N. Broad Street**
**Philadelphia, Pa. 19102**

AMERICAN CONSULATE
AUG 17 AM '67
AUG 8 PM '67

August 2, 1967 A 13 419 483

Dr. Solomon K. Samuels
Staff Residence
Westminster Hospital
London, Ontario, Canada

Dear Dr. Samuels:

This refers to your application for a waiver of the foreign residence requirement of Section 212(e) of the Immigration and Nationality Act, as amended.

Upon consideration of all the factors in your case, it is the decision of this office that the waiver should be, and hereby is, granted.

You should present this letter to the United States Consul when you apply for an immigrant visa.

Very truly yours,

Bertram M. Bernard
District Director

Figure 73. Letter from US Immigration and Naturalization Service granting a waiver allowing me to apply early for re-entry to the US as an immigrant. Personal collection.

# Chapter 37
# Life Back in the US

While in Canada I had written to the US Immigration department to expedite my application for re-entry. Bureaucracy being what it was, it took months and multiple exchanges of letters, but I finally got my re-entry papers. After eighteen months in Canada, now I could return to the US and get my green card.

After fourteen years of training and many years of doing scut work, I could not find a job right away. Settling in the right place is not easy, and I wanted time to make the rounds. After a few weeks I found a "fellowship" in a small hospital in Cleveland, Ohio. It was probably one of my worst places of work. I had thought of applying to get on the staff, but I did not like what I saw: there were a number of procedures that were of dubious value. It disappointed me. My new wife and I were living in an apartment in the big city of Detroit. In 1967, Detroit was not a hospitable place. I was now past thirty, back to living in a small apartment, going back and forth from Detroit to Cleveland; it was all very depressing. Only the weekend brought relief.

Since I was living there, I took the licensing exam in Detroit and passed it, which meant that I could work anywhere in Michigan. The search began. I had been warned by my mentors that finding a position in general surgery, my preference, would be difficult. It would be easier, they counseled, to find one in a subspecialty (i.e., plastic surgery, orthopedics). My passion, however, was general surgery, so I decided to take my chances and seek a position as a general surgeon.

After a long search, I found a place to practice with a three-man group of surgeons in Kalamazoo, Michigan. All were older men who practiced general and industrial medicine. The senior doctor was a retired Lt. Colonel who had started the practice. Industrial workplace injuries formed the bulk of the practice, so there was not much surgery, which disappointed me. I wondered about all the years of high-powered training. I felt as though my training was being wasted on minor procedures, and I still wanted to grow professionally. But I needed a steady job,

Figure 74. First office in Kalamazoo, Michigan, an industrial medicine group practice. Photo by author.

the pay was good ($18,000 in the first year), and it enabled a more stable life, so I hung in there. I had big dreams, however: I wanted my own general surgery practice. After eighteen months I had saved enough money. I borrowed another $10,000 from American National Bank in Kalamazoo and went solo. I worked out a repayment plan and kept to it.

Going solo had challenges. One doctor sent me a welcoming letter and later became a tennis buddy. He gave me my first referrals and continued to do so. After an initial slow start, referrals increased, and after six months I was quite busy. I hired a secretary who managed the office and my schedule, allowing me to concentrate on my surgical skills. I was happy.

My move to solo practice was going so well that I now wanted to build a house. I found an idyllic spot in a new subdivision: a large lot with a stream in the back; on the other side was a small island. I applied for another bank loan but was told I could not get financing for raw land. After two more years of work, I had saved enough money to buy land and made a down payment for a home. A friendly builder helped me acquire the land and build a home in a mostly white neigh-

Figure 75. My daughters enjoying the ducks in the back yard. Photo by author.

borhood. It was a large home for its time. The builder left me to finish the yard, which I took on with gusto. I spent long hours landscaping: I planted flowers, dammed up the stream, and watched it turn into a small pond. The pond in the back would hold long memories, as each Easter I would buy ducklings, watch them grow, and watch the children enjoy them. The finished product was beautiful. It was a lifelong dream. I bought the lot next door so that I could have a larger property. While working long evenings in the back office, I could look out at the yard and admire the beautiful setting. I still keep a photo of the first house in my home.

My firstborn came at 10:00 pm on September 1, 1970. She was a delight. I was present in the room. She had a shock of dark hair, brown eyes, beautiful skin; she was a bundle of joy. Making sure that mother and daughter were going to be fine, I left for home. I had no relatives with whom to share the happy news, so I stopped at the Wayside West bar, had a beer, and went home. Eighteen months later my second daughter was born. I was beside myself with joy and wanted to spend most of my non-working hours with the girls. At Easter I brought more ducklings and placed them in the back-yard pond, and every evening I took the girls to the pond to feed the ducklings. They loved it. I loved the new home and the girls. But the marriage was not going so well.

My wife was not a homebody. Living with her for the first time was revealing. For the first four years of our marriage, while I was in Canada and then working in Cleveland while living in Detroit, it was a long-distance marriage. Now it was becoming apparent that our lifestyles and goals seemed different. I was delighted at this dream come true, but I would come home and find that there was a babysitter. My wife wanted to have the babies bathed, fed, and ready to put to bed when she got home. This began to concern me, and our dreams soon diverged. I was dealing with someone who did not know what she wanted in life, other than money. Her interests lay elsewhere, beyond home and family. Our personalities were different. I looked forward to a quiet dinner, watching the news, and reading. But staying home was not her lifestyle; she always wanted to be out and about. All this weighed on my mind. One week after we moved in, she ordered furniture, curtains, appliances, and other things that go with a new house. With thousands of dollars of bills outstanding, just two weeks after moving into the house, she wanted to go on a vacation. I asked why, she shrugged, said something about boredom, and walked away. I barely got to enjoy the fruits of my hard work. She would go on a spending binge, obtain monies from banks with false signatures, and for my part I was getting increasingly angry at her erratic behavior. One of my fondest goals was to have a large family living on a large compound.

But the worst was yet to come. I felt an urgent need to save. While I tried to save money for the children, she would ask "how many saving accounts do you need?" She had little understanding of money. There was trouble ahead. It was downhill from there. We were arguing constantly.

Society was changing, and divorce had lost its stigma. In fact, she said it was fashionable. One of the problems of living in a foreign land without resources or relatives was being unable to reach out to relatives for advice. And so I did the dumb thing by moving out of the house. It would be the worst mistake I made in life. Courts and lawsuits were some of the most unpleasant parts of life. On a very cold, snowy, overcast day in January, the divorce degree was issued. I felt I had hardly gotten to know the children, and the estrangement from them was most painful. It was harder on the youngest, because she was barely three years old, vulnerable (the eldest was five years old). I feared the impact the divorce would have on the children. My wife was going to raise the children entirely as she saw fit. If I thought the divorce, which she requested, was going to end the rancor, I was in for a big surprise. Indeed, throughout their minority, until the children reached eighteen, we fought over them, over money, and over lifestyle. It was the most painful experience. There were frequent threats of court proceedings that, now looking back, were quite humorous at times. In the medical community all the negativity and gossip would hurt my professional standing in the community, and it hurt the practice. I held my head up, held my counsel, dedicated myself to my practice and girls, and got through these contentious times.

In spite of the acrimonious divorce, weekends with my daughters were mostly contented. We looked at ducks in a nearby park, played a little tennis when they got older, and engaged in other "normal" family activities. I watched more "Love Boat" than was probably good for me, but if the girls were mesmerized, I was happy. I found a dude ranch outside of Traverse City, Michigan, called Ranch Rudolph, and each summer we would spend some weekends and a whole week there. Canoeing, horseback riding, and campfires with marshmallows delighted both girls The staff were very kind to the girls and gave them special horse rides across the river. One time a horse was so eager to get back to its stall in the barn that my youngest daughter, still mounted, was almost knocked off. We still reminisce happily of those adventures. We also took some driving vacations, memorably one trip to Washington DC in an RV: the girls took pride in making me bologna sandwiches for lunch. When she was twelve years old, I took my eldest to Africa for two weeks.[1] When we arrived at the airport in New York, we discovered that our luggage had been delayed from Kalamazoo. My daughter had spilled a soft drink on her shirt and was beside herself over the fact that she could not change her clothes. We would have to spend the night in New York because I had managed to forget to take our passports, which would be overnighted to us. In tears as we were leaving the airport, luggage-less, my daughter heard her name being called

[1] It took forty years before my youngest and I were able to visit Africa as well.

over and over again: our luggage had arrived on another flight and was now available! These mishaps have provided many good laughs throughout the years.

In spite of it all, my first wife was a good mother to the girls. The girls benefited from two families that loved and nurtured them. Now I take pride in the fact that both girls graduated from college debt free and have had meaningful and successful careers. And I give thanks that, for all the friction in their growing-up years, I have a splendid and loving relationship with both my daughters.

# Chapter 38
# Medicine was Changing

The politics of medicine had its quirks, and medicine was changing. In the sixties there had been no safety nets except for poor houses (sometimes called the county house). The poor were taken to these institutions, quietly hidden from society, and larger society carried on living blissfully in ignorance of this. In the US, if you had a good job and money, you could get good care, but if you had neither, you went to the poor house, where conditions were abysmal.[1] The big issue was how much government control there would be in medicine. The merits of government intervention in medicine had been a hot topic when the Medicare program was initiated, and the battle raged on. There were those—like the AMA—who opposed any role for government, and comments frequently were vitriolic. Most advanced countries in Europe have a system wherein the government plays a major role. Back in the 1960s we kicked the can down the road, and now it came to haunt us again.

As early as the 1980s, hospitals were changing. The Hill-Burton act provided funds to modernize hospitals. Old buildings were being torn down, and new buildings were going up, which created all manner of conflict. If a city had more than one hospital, they would go to war to attract patients and money. For example, each hospital in Kalamazoo had a helicopter crew, and sometimes helicopters chased one another for motor-vehicle accident patients. The public watched with opprobrium, looking askance at all this. Not to mention that the costs of maintaining two hospitals in a city of 100,000 were mushrooming. To me, the basic function of a hospital was medical care, not necessarily getting bigger or expanding its influence. This was validated by a lengthy story in one of the leading newspapers that reported that mergers did little to bring down the cost of medical care. Hospitals also were shifting emphasis from general practice to specialized services. To

[1] To correct some of these inequities, Bismarck the German chancellor, set up an old-age pension system in 1899. Germany's would start at age sixty-five, but there was a quirk: life expectancy was 60, so his actuaries predicted that the cost would be bearable.

this end, the hospital administrator supported specialties such as neurosurgery and cardiac surgery to the exclusion of other services. As I was neither, I felt my role was much diminished. When there was talk at the hospital about starting a kidney transplant program, I joined the team. My experience working with a kidney transplant surgeon at Hahnemann Hospital in Philadelphia was valuable. I worked hard to organize the program and harvest kidneys and received a letter of appreciation from the organ transplant association. I continued my involvement with the program for many years until others took up the mantle.

By the 1990s it was getting frustrating. The system was such that only the big-money doctors and doctors' groups got all the extra privileges. While the hospital provided patient care impartially, it was also involved in competition with the other hospital. The quest for power and money was distressing.

Competition was getting comical. The old general practitioners, by now in their mid-sixties, clung to power as much as they could, but specialists were moving into town. The Catholic hospital in town attracted both American and foreign-born doctors, but the other hospital was conservative and was still controlled by the old guard. The Catholic hospital encouraged a number of enterprising cardiologists, neurologists, and other specialists, who brought their up-to-date techniques and set up shop; the hospital provided the facilities and staff to equip cardiac catheter labs, neurological operating rooms and labs, for example. The old guard complained but were on the losing end. For the hospitals, it meant more revenue. My memory was that there was a big new building every few years. One building was completed, and immediately the ground was broken for another. The administrative president now had six VPs whereas he had only three before; the corporate offices now were housed in fourth-floor corner offices along with multiple new large office suites. They were not as easily accessible now. There is a saying that it is unwise to get in between when giants go to war; better to stay away. Modernizing meant covering concrete floors with luxury carpet. The clean but spartan patient rooms now had wall-to-wall carpeting and all the trappings of luxury. This also extended to technology, leading to much duplication of services. If one hospital seemed to have an advantage, the other would go out and spend millions to "catch up." Observation and economic theory suggest that each institution had strengths and a comparative advantage based on location, clientele, and community support, but they went on to spend millions on buying equipment that had little economic value anyway. Modest yet comfortable administrator salaries rose exponentially to compete with Wall Street salaries.

Turf battles were everywhere, were daily occurrences, and were legendary, especially when new technologies were introduced. Any innovation or creative idea, when implemented, would draw a negative reaction, then competition. One such episode affected me profoundly and sticks in my memory.

I had become interested in electronics in the post-war years, had taken a short-wave radio course, and had achieved a technician's license. This laid the groundwork for me to understand later how new technology could allow doctors to make diagnoses of Deep Vein Thrombosis (DVT) through non-invasive means. By the late 1960s, systems were being developed to diagnose medical conditions without the use of needles or the need to inject substances into veins and arteries. Doppler ultrasound could use high-frequency sound-waves to measure the amount of blood flow through arteries and veins and detect early vessel disease. Fourier Transform principles were used to process waveforms into images. In the mid-1970s, duplex scanners were just being introduced and were touted as affording non-invasive vascular testing.

Long before this testing was widely adopted, I searched for centers offering training in such procedures and found one at, of all places, Tucson Medical Center, in Arizona. There I learned how to diagnose blood clots in the major venous artery of the leg (to prevent fatal pulmonary embolism) and how to study arterial flow and diagnose peripheral arterial disease in the legs to detect plaque formation in carotid arteries, which can cause stroke. Back in Kalamazoo, I presented this new technology to the hospital administration, who provided the funds to purchase the equipment, hire and train the technologist to do the testing, and set up a Vascular Lab at the hospital. It was a wonderful challenge to start something new. In time the Lab was up and running, the volume was growing, and it pleased me that I could bring this technique to success. Success, though, brought attention.

Aggressive cardiologists now expanded into areas like peripheral arteries, which traditionally was the purview of vascular surgeons. Radiologists touted that they had been imaging the arteries for many years. Two new vascular surgeons joined a suburban clinical practice in Kalamazoo, and they set up labs in their offices to directly compete with the hospital, siphoning off patients from the hospital Lab. When they examined the Lab's operations, moreover, they now wanted part of it; they wanted to be included in the "reading panel" so that they could increase their revenue. The younger of the two, a short man with a big Napoleonic ego, wanted not only sharing but also control. I received a number of letters[2] from them saying:

> We are writing to you to suggest that we would like to become part of the panel to read the non-invasive tests that are performed in the Borgess Vascular Lab. (Letter dated 9-30-81)

On December 24, 1981 they wrote again:

> By having a more coordinated effort, we could strive to increase referrals many-fold from other Specialists.

Ironically, the doctors writing this had contributed nothing to the creation of the Lab. They were not referring any of their patients to the Lab.[3] They did not support my effort, just wanted to accrete patients to their own labs and ultimately shut down the hospital lab.

Subsequent letters contained negative comments about the Lab and about me. One doctor (who did not work in the field) wrote:

> Many of the procedures that have been performed there are interesting adjunctive evaluation procedures but do not play a significant role in determining the type of procedure to be performed nor do they really affect the indication for appropriate surgery.

---

[2] I have kept all the correspondence and quote from it.

[3] After a number of letters, the hospital conducted a study that found that 55% of the studies in the Lab were done on patients referred by myself and a small number of doctors with whom I worked closely; the rest were referred by family physicians and other doctors.

> I would recommend that these procedures be limited to use in a central imaging department of Radiology as might be appropriate since use of such in the Vascular Lab is limiting the use of the equipment to a very selective group of physicians.

This last statement was not entirely truthful, for when the Lab was opened, an information packet was sent to all physicians on the hospital staff (the letter-writer had been a resident at the time and hence not on the staff). All this would have consequences, which I enumerate below.

Changes were occurring both in medicine and in my personal life. The old guard at the hospital was aging, and the hospital board brought in a team from Pittsburgh—high-powered administrators who came in like a whirlwind, set to sweep the place clean. The new team fired many trusted employees and replaced them with outsiders, with new people. In eighteen months, the new CEO left, but his underlings continued the changes until they also left in relatively short order.

The new vice president appointed the aggressive young doctor to replace me as director of the Vascular Lab. It became apparent that the new director wanted complete control over the Lab; he wanted to replace the entire staff and appoint someone who would be loyal to him. He wrote to the administrator:

> I am disappointed in the present technicians.[4] When I went to the Lab I found the machine was not properly set, and she did not know how to properly adjust it. ... We have had the machine for about four months, even at this point she is not well versed in the basic techniques which are implored [*sic*] in using in using the machine.

This drum beat (of a clean sweep) was to get rid of the trusted staff and bring in someone to do his bidding.

The old rules that I set up were set aside, and short-cuts were taken. The technicians I had trained were let go. The new director had difficultly hiring and

---

[4] For privacy, I will not use their full names. Both were young mothers. Both had been well trained and were skilled technicians.

keeping staff, who tended to resign when they faced the difficulty of getting tests done in a timely manner. The situation went from bad to worse. Soon patients were diverted to labs in which the new director had a financial interest. Doctors expressed frustration with the new director's poor management style. They were concerned about the short-cuts being taken. To assuage the other doctors, the new director finally brought in a new technician but admonished those doctors in a letter dated March 26, 1990:

> I can understand the anger all of you harbor; we have to all recognize that we have to come up with positive suggestions to improve the working of the lab. If we continue to be very negative, then we will not be making any progress in the development lab.

In another letter he argued (quite ironically, as it was he who had jettisoned the guidelines I had established):

> There should be strict guide lines for this panel, which should be decided upon as a group. ... In a very medico-legally oriented society, these tests become a legal document, and the future course of action depends on these studies.

But even the new technician soon found irregularities: No longer was every study reviewed by an M.D.; the technician signed off on the report. Doctors did not do daily rounds, and it fell instead to the tech staff to interpret the studies, while the doctors billed for services.

In 1997 I closed my office and assumed part-time positions at the Psychiatric hospital and the Veterans hospital, performing pension benefit exams. On July 17, 1998, the headline of the local newspaper screamed:

> suit accuses local doctors of false claims. Former employee alleges surgeons, with hospital's knowledge, billed government for ultra sound services they never performed.

At the bottom of the page was my name. I was dismayed and shocked, shocked beyond belief.

The new technician had brought suit against all the physicians associated with the Lab, active and inactive (myself). It was a huge multi-million-dollar suit involving millions in claims and using an "old" civil rights era law. It was filed under the False Claims Act.[5] At first it appeared that we as individual members would have to bear the brunt of the cost and share in the payout to the plaintiff. It could have been devasting for me; this was not how I envisioned ending my career. Lawsuits have a way of hanging one out to dry. It was a relief when the hospital took responsibility and agreed to defend us. The lower court ruled in our favor, it was appealed to the appellate court, and finally went to the supreme court. On or about the 28th of that year I received a letter from my lawyer saying that "the plaintiffs' petition has been denied. Congratulations."

It was a relief when I heard that my name was dropped and that the lawsuit would be dismissed. And it was some vindication to learn that guidelines (as I had established when I first set up the Lab) were to be re-instituted. But it was still distressing that something I had created for the betterment of patients had resulted in litigation. Greed and cutting corners had its hazards. For hospitals, profit and return on investment was now paramount, often trumping patient care. The hospital tried sometimes to sort out turf battles among doctors, but with little success.

Solo practice was difficult even beyond turf battles. It meant being on call 24/7, taking little time off, even on weekends. This was problematic, particularly when the children were young. Case in point: I had operated on a young girl who had severed her brachial artery. Repair was not common in those times, but I had taken additional training and had successfully repaired it. I had custody of my daughters that weekend, when at 2:00 am I got the dreaded call from the hospital, that the patient had lost the pulse, indicating occlusion. I had to think quickly. I could not call a babysitter at two in the morning, so I took the still-sleeping children to the hospital and prevailed upon the night operator in the lobby to keep an eye

---

[5] The False Claims Act is a statutory scheme that imposes liability on persons who make fraudulent demands for payments on the United States Government. It is also known as "Qui tam," meaning "who brings the action for the king as for himself."

on them. I ran upstairs to the bedside and carefully took the pulse; fortunately, it was present, it had been an overreaction on the part of the night nurse. I thanked the night operator profusely and took my children home to put them back to bed. I had to wait till the next day to tell the children what had transpired.

# Chapter 39
# A Powerful Urge to Travel

*At the Paris Peace Treaty, 1919, the talk turned to the Middle East and the Arabs. An "American expert" told the British P.M. Lloyd George about the American Indians: "Their temper is passionate, resentful, revengeful, intriguing and treacherous, they make good soldiers but poor leaders, they are avaricious, utterly selfish, shameless beggars, and have a great propensity to steal."*

My practice was successful enough and my daughters visited only on weekends. I took classes (ham radio, power squadron, medical continuing education) but still had time and inclination to learn more about the world in which I lived. I decided to travel and explore the West. I wanted to see the country for myself. I had heard many stories of conflict between the Whites and Native Indians. How accurate were Hollywood movies (it took me years to de-construct the falsehoods especially about life in the West)? I prepared by reading books of the West, especially on the Indian wars, not the usual tourist attractions. I armed myself with books and bought more along the way; one that impressed me was *Bury My Heart at Wounded Knee* (1970, by Dee Brown). I bought myself a sports car (my history with British sports cars)—a used E-type Jaguar, one of the most beautiful cars of all time. The young man brought the car to a parking lot near my home. It was biscuit colored. I checked it out and decided to buy it. It was five years old. The young man told me that he had raced it, but denied ever damaging the car. I did not check it out for body damage. I was going to drive this car to see the West, and check the veracity of Hollywood's version of history. For me this was a voyage of discovery, and I read up on the idiosyncrasies of British cars, especially Jaguars. The luggage compartment was small; it held no more than a duffle bag and a lady's hand bag, so I put a luggage rack on the boot, topped off the fluids, packed some tools, and took off.

My first stop was at the Wisconsin Dells, then I headed westward. The country was beautiful and for the most part bereft of traffic; there were long

Figure 76. E-Type Jaguar on Pine Ridge Indian reservation. Photo by author.

stretches of empty road and land, which was just as well. I finally arrived at the Pine Ridge (Sioux) Indian reservation. It was as though I had crossed an invisible border to a place on a different planet. I was shocked at its bleakness, degradation, and the level of abject poverty that are seen in the most desperate places on the planet. It was like a third world place.

I stopped the car in front of the small battered café. There was no specific parking area. I got out and walked around, noting how different the place was. It does not take a doctor to see the effects of alcohol abuse. It was just past noon, yet a number of young men loitered nearby, obviously inebriated. It bothered me that outside the reservation, people in the same state seemed to have a higher standard living. A sense of guilt overcame me.

I did not encounter any hostility as I did the usual tourist things: walked around, asked questions, ended up at the café, ordered coffee, and waited. In due course a grizzled old Indian man, probably an elder of the tribe, came over. I asked him if he would join me for a cup of coffee, after which he slid into the chair and struck up a conversation. "Who are you and what are doing here?" he asked bluntly, looking sidewise at the car; "you do not look native." "I am an immigrant, from Burma," came my reply. He looked puzzled, did not understand, did not know where that was, so I explained further and drew a map. "My parents were East Indians from India, and I domiciled in Burma." That he seemed to understand. He asked "what I did," and I told him I was a doctor. There was a long pause, and a quizzical look passed over his face; after a while he said "but you are not one of 'them' (meaning white doctors)." I shook my head and he questioned further: "You treat white patients?" When I responded "yes," he shook his head in disbelief. I tried to tell him it was different out there, but I am not sure that I convinced him. I asked him about care here. He paused and said, "we have to drive a long distance, to see white doctors." "Are you sure you are a doctor?" he asked again. I assured him. "I have a license to practice in Michigan and as a matter of fact am working there." He asked me if I would like to work here, but the coffee arrived and we let that question go. It was a window into a different world, hidden away from the rest of America; tourists rarely go there. We engaged in more small talk over coffee, I said goodbye and took my leave, but not before he warned me, "you are living dangerously; be very careful here." He paused and said "the police arrest Indians for no reason. Be very careful; if you do violate any rules, the police will pounce on you." I promised to drive carefully. I reflected that he was offering advice based on his own life on the reservation and based on the Lakota Sioux tribe's experience.

Reservation life was dismal. There were no property rights, no jobs, much privation, poor housing, subpar medical care, and poor education. I was struck by the starkness of life of the original peoples. Their kind had lived here for 14,000 years, lived freely, hunted and roamed as they pleased. Now robbed of their lands, they had been reduced to dependency on the "kindness of white conquerors." Your average American would not accept that kind of life. Any thoughts of working on the reservation were disabused quickly. I drove out of the reservation with much sadness, headed further west.

I was a glutton for punishment and headed next to the battlefield at Little Big Horn. While still in Burma I had gone to the cinema often; it was the only recreation there, and most of movies shown were Westerns. I remember the movie version of the battle well. Errol Flynn played General Custer, with his long, blonde, flowing hair and riding his favorite horse the (the real General Custer was not handsome at all; his features were craggy, rather crude). Miriam Hopkins played his partner. The movie version depicted General Custer setting out from the army post at the head of the 7th cavalry, his partner looking on with tears of sadness flowing like torrents from her eyes. Indeed it was a tear-jerker: man going off to war while the family cried. In those days back in Burma, the natives were depicted as bloody-thirsty savages, and I rooted for the General. Later I had read of the assault by the US cavalry against the unarmed women and children of the Sand Hill Creek tribe and re-read the official version of the battle. I had studied the battle firsthand, their chiefs Crazy Horse and Sitting Bull and White Cloud. Now I was off to see for myself what it was all about.

The park grounds were impeccably maintained, the battlefield well kept by the park service. I walked the battlefields and read all the signs. Another eye-opener: I began to realize how distorted the Hollywood version of history was. This battle actually was won by the Indians with their great leadership. As I stood on the ground where they made their last stand, I realized that the battle had been nothing like what I had seen in the cinema back in Burma.[1] It was the beginning of my deconstruction of the Hollywood version of History—not just about local affairs or the Indian wars but also about stories of World War II, movies like *Objective Burma* or *The Purple Plain*, which had caused mirth, laughter, and sometimes riots in India and Burma.

I still remember the American film actor Randolph Scott (portraying Philip Sheridan) saying "the only good Indian is a dead Indian" in another western. Sheridan supposedly uttered those words more than two centuries ago, but nothing has changed. The American treatment of Native Americans was hypocritical; they got a raw deal. Their land was seized, even though it was protected by sovereign treaty, their medical care was second class, their children were taken from them and educated by white Christian teachers who forbade them to speak their own language, and I could go on.

---

[1] Recently a team of archeologists went to work on the battlefield, digging up shell casings and noting where they were located. Their findings led them to rewrite the details of the last stand, as the evidence showed that it differed in many ways from how history was written.

I was curious about Glacier National Park, its remoteness, its location off the common tourist routes. I set out to answer why this park, so out of the way, existed. The story is that after the Battle of Little Big Horn, Sitting Bull fled north and with his tribe joined with the Nez Perce tribe (who lived on both sides of the Canadian border). Together they fled to Canada, thus escaping capture and confinement to the rustic stockade for life. Sitting Bull's greatness was finally recognized, and he returned many years later to tour the US as a celebrity.

My first long vacation out of the US was to Tahiti and Bora Bora. Resorts had not yet been fully developed, and there were not many tourists. It was fantastic. Not only did I learn about the history of Polynesia, about the true story of the Mutiny on the Bounty, but also was reminded of Southeast Asia by its climate and the availability of fruits and vegetables that I had not seen since I had left Burma.

Other international travel followed. The Nazca Lines (huge geoglyphs made in the soil of Peru's southern Nazca Desert sometime between 500 BC and AD 500) enthralled me. I ascended Machu Pichu. I still have a vicuna rug and a lama blanket that I purchased there. From Peru I went to the Galapagos Islands, which reinvigorated my lifelong fascination with evolution and, later, genetics. After an initial trip to Kenya, I visited three more times; I loved the country and the wildlife immensely. There were also many trips to Europe, Asia, and the Caribbean to follow, to the point that my colleagues would tease me about my wanderlust.

In the 1980s, after I was allowed to return to Burma and after my second marriage, most of our travel was to Southeast and South Asia: Burma, Thailand, Cambodia, India, Sri Lanka. In the new century, many family and friends in Burma had passed on, and we no longer needed to buy inventory for our gem and jewelry business (see next chapter), but we continued to travel: to Europe again, Australia, Russia, Greece, Costa Rica, and elsewhere.

I saw the world, learned about myself and a multitude of cultures, had adventures too numerous to recount, established connections with far-flung family on four continents, visited countless museums and libraries and historical archives, and collected hundreds of books not available in the US. Travel was one very important aspect of my life.

# Chapter 40
# Going Home

Back in 1962, when I was still in Youngstown, Burma's independent government had been overthrown in a coup by General Ne Win. Having left the country just two years prior, I was not welcome back in the country. I had not been allowed to return to see my aging mother and the rest of the family or friends for nearly twenty years. As the years passed, I also felt a certain a certain nostalgia. I had been trying for years to get a visa, but the xenophobic government of Burma just ignored my letters. However, in late 1979, much to my surprise, I did get a response from the Embassy, and a visa.

So much has been written about "going back home" as troubling and disappointing, even in stable countries and in the best of times. I had learned through letters from home and friends that the country had become a dreadful place, but nothing was going to stop me. Finally the day arrived. After eighteen hours of flying, I arrived in fast-developing Singapore. Unlike other Southeast Asian countries, Singapore had made much progress economically; even in 1979 the streets were clean, the hotels were new and up to Western standards. I stayed at the Shangri-La Hotel, a five-star hotel (the same hotel where President Trump met Kim Jong Un). Singapore was in the midst of a recession, which was good for me, as I paid the equivalent of just $70 for a suite of rooms. After resting and enjoying the good food and the banter of British doctors who had come to attend an event, the next day I boarded the plane bound for Rangoon. It was a short flight. As we approached the city, I heard the Burmese language for the first time in years and was surprised at how much I understood (and how quickly I would pick it up again). The airport terminal was seedy; not much had changed since I had left and in some ways was much worse. The grand arrival and departure halls still featured beautiful teakwood walls, benches, and balconies, but birds flew freely around the cavernous rooms and left droppings everywhere.

I dreaded the customs and immigration procedures, and going through customs was as onerous as I suspected. They went through everything but a rectal exam; they searched me thoroughly. I had to fill out reams of paper; they even counted pocket change. I had to declare all money as well as all watches and cameras. I was given a currency form on which every purchase I would make would need to be recorded and authorized, and all would be cross-checked upon departure. Sweating profusely when it was over, I took a deep breath and drank some cold juice.

I hired a "taxi." I could not roll down the windows, and there was no air conditioning. The trip to the hotel left me speechless. Rangoon was even more decayed now than it had been twenty years ago. The cars were old, beaten, vintage vehicles; the only "taxis" were tiny, battered Toyota trucks imported from Singapore that smelled of oil and whose tail pipes spewed black acrid smoke. Passengers sat on planks in the bed of the truck. There were few stores, and the streets and occasional sidewalks were rife with cracks, potholes, and upheaved concrete. Most troubling was the strange reaction of the people: they looked downward, avoided

Figure 77. A Burmese taxi circa 1984. The government did not allow free movement through the country at that time, so we hired a guide so that we could traverse the city. Photo by author.

eye contact, appeared fearful. I checked into the hotel and the next day took a trip to the city. All the old restaurants were no longer there, replaced by small, pitiful street vendors. Their savories smelled good, but I was afraid to eat any for fear of catching "Rangoon Belly." It is surprising that you cannot eat food that you ate twenty years ago. There were few stores; those previously owned by Indians were all gone, again to be replaced by street vendors who spread their wares on a blanket set on the sidewalk. This was heartbreaking. The military had stepped into the vacuum and entered into many businesses; the "Diplomatic store" was one such entity. There they sold dry goods, British-made products like Milo (chocolate malt powder), Horlicks (sweet malted drink), and biscuits. Payment had to be in US dollars, which meant only a few people could afford these products. Moreover, the prices were exorbitant. I bought chocolates, Milo and Horlicks, and other British canned food for Mother (she would be quite pleased with them, although some of it would be pilfered and sold for a profit).

When I arrived at the old family home, I was shocked beyond belief. It is commonly said that returning home is emotional, both sad and happy, but time, rebellion, oppression, and a failing economy changes the landscape in unbelievable ways. I did not recognize the surroundings, except for the house itself. The changes were so profound it was improbable. I had lived here as a young boy and young man, and the house had been the bulwark against violence and upheaval; it had been a place of refuge and solace for much of my life. Now I was to find that most of the neighbors I had known were no longer there. The old man next door was barely recognizable. Huts were everywhere (squatters escaping the beggary caused by the war), filling the open space between our house and the railroad station. Decay was present all around. I soon turned my gaze away and saw my mother waiting at the door. I hugged her, and she hung on for a long time, finally breaking away only reluctantly. I presented her with the Milo, Horlicks, and other goods. She was overjoyed—both to see me and the foods that she had not had for thirty years. I learned that my beautiful sister Kamala had died from hepatitis at age fifty-five, leaving her young children motherless. I remembered her as the best looking and most beautiful of my older sisters. Her husband had potential but never exercised it; he was a bookkeeper at the American Embassy and, compared to the local salary, was paid well. But he quit his job and took to drink, neglecting his children while their mother cared for them.

After I settled in, I walked to the room where I had spent so much of my youth. It appeared much smaller than I remembered it. It took a little while to sink in, that what shocked me was that the room was bare. I noticed my long wooden box was missing–made especially for me in Kengtung, it housed all the special gifts and collectibles I had acquired: Japanese emblems from the war, gifts from my Shan friends George and Rosie, gifts from my patients and friends. But all were gone, as were my treasured medical books! I took a deep breath and asked my sister Merlyn about it; she looked down said "your friend (an unfamiliar name) came and took all the books away." "Who gave permission?" There was no reply, but she implied that I was remiss in not leaving instructions. It was the most amazing answer. I felt she was lying to me, which she did with such ease. It was obvious that my younger brother Jason had stolen everything and sold it all to pay for his gambling debts. What irked me most was that they had made no effort to stop him. All the irreplaceable items were sold for a fraction of their worth. That the sisters looked the other way and made no attempt to stop him was angering. He won them over by sharing some of the money from the loot, and they saw no fault in such behavior. Well, he was to pay dearly for this. When he could not pay his debts, his debtors had chased him through the jungle and beat him up. He had suffered traumatic brain injury, and for a while was confined to the mental hospital. He ended up with Traumatic Brain Encephalopathy and went mad.

Disappointed and angry as I was, I set aside those feelings. Wanting to brighten their lives, I ordered food from a restaurant for all the family, including my James cousins. We celebrated with a grand feast: chicken, mutton curries, and heaping plates of rice, and flat breads. The family had not been able to eat like this for years. After the main meal there was French pastry, yes French pastry, a relic of colonial times. The family filled me in on the sad news: my half-brother had moved to England and died soon thereafter, as had many of my cousins with whom I had grown up. All my school buddies had moved out. The Christian cemeteries had been dug up, obliterating the graves of Father, Margaret, and Uku. The family told me of the foreboding, terrible times of the bloody Ne Win coup, the blood that was shed. Still two decades later, Rangoon was a fearful place to live.

I went for a walk. It all seemed strange. The train station was filthy and littered with debris, the ticketing booth was shabby and ugly, the tracks were showing their age. The man who had made wonderful pastries, the one-legged man and his shop, was gone. Another evening I took a walk toward to the rail line but had to turn back half way; I could not take it any longer. The bucolic scene behind the home, the green meadow with lush grass, had been replaced by ugly squatters' huts packed cheek by jowl. The squatters were fresh out of the back country—*Tawtha* (forest dwellers), as the Burmese called them. It was chilling. Looking back, I felt lucky to have escaped the times of terror and deprivation.

Over the next several days I went about the city looking at old places by myself and reminiscing. It is said that it comes as a shock to see your home town as it is now, totally different from the image in your memories. As I walked the streets of downtown Rangoon, one memory came to mind. It was immediately after the war in 1946, and there were many bombed-out buildings. I remember a big subedar (an NCO in the Indian Army) approached me and promised me some chocolate if I followed him into bombed-out building. As I got closer, I got nervous, fearful, and ran away.

It is said that some emotions are repressed and that you will take them with you to the grave. For me, one such episode was Father's death. I dealt with it myself and have been able to talk about it, but some stories you cannot tell; they are so deeply suppressed that it is hard to reach down to the depths. In old age, when you cannot sleep, you lie awake thinking about some of those long-suppressed memories. There will be omissions, but at some point, you say "enough." I have memories of the rape of one of the sisters, but I cannot bring myself to talk about it.

But some good came of the trip. In this otherwise dismal state of affairs, the buzz was all about the fabulous gems of Burma, the rubies, sapphires, and spinel for sale at government auction. I was interested, made some enquires. Each year Ne Win's (the mad General) government held an auction, called the Gems Emporium, of rubies, sapphires, pearls, and jade. Burma was famous throughout the world for its colored gems, especially rubies. I was told that world-renowned dealers came here to examine and bid on the great gems. I visited the Museum Shop (open to the diplomatic corps and select tourists) and was astounded by the display of beautiful gems and jewelry. The display cases were surrounded by Chinese women from Singapore who were singing the praises of 3-carat sapphires and 1–2-carat rubies selling for only a few thousand dollars. I had not come prepared to buy jewelry or gemstones but queried the officials and got an application form. After I returned home to the US and resumed work, after recovering from jet lag, I started to plan. I knew I wanted to go back and take my soon-to-be new wife with me the next time I went back. Much to my surprise, many months later, I was sent an invitation from the Ministry of Mines. Along with the invitation came a visa, with special provisions, such as red emporium luggage tags that eased the customs experience at a special desk to expedite the entry process.

The next step was obvious: I had to learn more about the trade and science of gemology. I wrote to the Gemological Institute of America and received a swift response. I immediately started a correspondence course in colored gems and jade, and then diamonds. I would receive the material by mail, learn and practice, and send back the exams. I would keep this up for about three years and in 1985 was awarded the Graduate Gemologist Certificate. But even early in my studies, I was ready to dip into my savings and look into this fascinating business.

## THE STEALING OF PATRIMONY

Before I tell the tale of the gems emporium, I feel compelled to include a short history about the stealing of patrimony. Western imperial powers have a long history of stealing the precious gems, jewelry, and art of third-world nations—and aggrandizing to themselves the glory of those nations' history. Case in point: Some time in the 1970s I traveled to Machu Picchu, Peru, the city built by the Incas. I picked up a postcard of the famed mountain city. The note on the back of the card reads, "The site is surrounded by precipices a thousand feet sheer. Founded (7-24-1911) by Dr. Hiram Bingham." I will let the reader judge the veracity of this statement for himself. In fact, the Incas founded Machu Picchu in the twelfth century.

In 1911, Yale University sent Professor Bingham to study and bring back some artifacts from the site for further study. Yale received many artifacts, but Mr. Bingham kept many more to himself.[1]

Much of the fabulous art that can be seen in the great museums of Paris, London, New York, and Los Angeles was smuggled or stolen. Auction houses in the US and Europe are selling Indian and Mughal jewelry from the collections of the emirs and kings of the oil-rich states, most of it obtained by dubious means or smuggled out of India.[2] The British have no clear provenance for many items on display in their museums. When asked why the British Museum had not returned the Elgin Marbles to Greece, the former Prime Minister responded that (I paraphrase) "If we returned all the art work to the original owners, the British Museum would be empty." This manner of stealing patrimony from third-world nations continues even to this day.

Most of India's great diamonds were spirited out of the country, including the blue Hope Diamond, now in the Smithsonian in Washington, D.C. The provenance of this diamond is sketchy. It supposedly was purchased (from the Kollur mine in Golconda, Andhra Pradesh, India) by the less than honest merchant Jean Baptiste Tavernier. He in turn sold it to King Louis XIV of France in 1668. It was stolen, re-surfaced, was re-cut and re-set over the years, and was ultimately donated in 1958 by Harry Winston Inc., New York, to the Smithsonian. The Kohinoor Diamond, "the Mountain of Light," likewise was probably mined in Golconda before it was stolen by an agent of the East India Company[3] and presented to Queen Victoria. This magnificent gem is part of the British Crown Jewels and now resides in the Tower of London. This story was replicated manifold times.

---

[1] Dr. Bingham on two visits excavated thousands of artifacts: ceramics, tools, jewelry and human bones. Peru allowed him to take the artifacts to Yale for study on condition that they would be returned to Peru upon request. Yale, however, claimed permanent possession and for nearly a century refused Peru's request. Only in 2010 was their return to Peru negotiated.

[2] People of the currently constituted Middle East have no skills in this industry.

[3] On May 4, 1850, the *London Times* announced that the Kohinoor would soon be "riding the high seas aboard the good ship HMS Medea. ... All of London buzzed with excitement and speculation." Dale R. Perelman, *The Mountain of Light* (Winona, MN: Apollo Books, 1984), 164.

Much is made in the Western gemological press of the British East India Company. Names like Robert Clive and Jean Baptiste Tavernier are revered. But a new reading of history suggests that this reverence is unwarranted, that many of the merchants responsible for the presence of gems in the West were unsavory and unscrupulous characters. William Dalrymple describes the British East India Company as

> a dangerously unregulated private company headquartered in one small office, five windows wide, in London and managed in India by a violent, utterly ruthless, intermittently unstable corporate predator—Clive. India's transition to colonialism took place under a for-profit corporation, which existed entirely for the purpose of enriching its investors.[4]

New young Indian investigators are making discoveries that shed light on the history of these notable gems.

As in India, so in Burma. Throughout its thousand-year history, Burma's fabled ruby mines produced untold numbers of rubies. These were purchased (by trade) by rich maharajas of India, by French traders, European royals, and wealthy collectors. All this came to an end in 1962, when the Burmese military staged a coup. When General New Win closed Burma's borders in 1964, the free flow of cut and uncut rubies abruptly came to an end. But this does not mean that the outflow came to an end. If you were an ethical trader, you could be invited by the Ne Win government to the Emporium, now the only authorized source of rubies. Traders with wobbly ethics, however, developed a new system for smuggling rubies of great beauty out of Burma. American and European gem dealers set up trading houses in Bangkok, from which they dispatched buying agents loaded with hard currency to the Thai–Burma border, to cities like Mae Sot or Chanthaburi. There the agents would buy goods smuggled from central Burma by gangs, at cheap prices. The gems would be taken to Bangkok, then smuggled again out to cutting

---

[4] William Dalrymple, *The Anarchy: The Relentless Rise of the East India Company* (London: Bloomsbury, 2019), xxv.

shops in Europe and America.[5] This business was so thriving that a big firm in Europe could order uncut rubies of a specific size. Of course, there is no record of which mine produced the ruby, who found it, how it got transported to the Thai border, etc.[6] Scientific evidence can identify place of origin, but the detailed provenance (record of ownership) of such gems is murky. Stories abound of smuggling rings assembling great mule trains, loaded with contraband gems before setting off from the Mogok ruby mines. On their way to the Thai–Burma border, they would pay off the Burma Army (and Karens and others) at checkpoints; at the border, throngs of eager buyers would pay the smugglers, sometimes fighting over the most prized stones. Some notable rubies acquired in this fashion have been sold at auctions for a princely sum. At a 2015 Christie's auction in Hong Kong, for example, one of these rubies (15 carat) fetched $18.3 million; another (10.05 carats) fetched HK $78 million in 2016.

---

[5] The US penal code states that buying and receiving stolen property is a violation of the law.

[6] From the moment a gem is extracted from the bowels of the earth, to the point where a famed gem house cuts it, thence to the jewelry house where the gem is set, there is no "history." The gems are typically dug out of the earth by poor miners, sold for a paltry sum to middleman, who smuggle the gem out of Burma. No names are listed. Many gems are stolen from miners, middlemen, or smugglers who have no legal recourse. Who the agent was who bought the gem is not recorded. Some notable writers in the gem trade today contributed themselves to this unseemly trade.

# Chapter 41
# The Gems Emporium

*The Emporium, the yearly auction of Rubies, Sapphires, and Jade*

In 1981 I made my first visit to Rangoon as a bona fide gem merchant. Notwithstanding all the rumors of KGB-like surveillance by the Military Intelligence, I was surprised at the ease of travel. Going to Burma as a guest of the Emporium had its advantages; wearing the Emporium badge opened doors that were closed to the average tourist. Another privilege was the opportunity to examine hundreds of great rubies, sapphires, and jade. One could examine every lot offered for sale, thousands of some of the most beautiful and much-coveted gems, and could touch and feel hundreds of rubies, sapphires, spinel, peridot, and jade. Over my thirty years as a gem merchant, I examined thousands these gems, using modern tools.

Buyers from Britain, France, Italy, Japan, Thailand, and Singapore—from all around the world—came to the annual Emporium to examine and bid on the gems.[1] The Emporium committee set up tables with microscopes and other tools of the trade to examine the gems. The equipment was not much used by Asian dealers. Most buyers in that era relied on government guaranties and so dispensed with the microscope, but I saw it as an opportunity to learn. I learned fast. Armed with the knowledge I had gained from my studies with the GIA, I would settle in at a table with a microscope, and the attendants would bring virtually every lot of stones to me for examination. I was able to examine the gems, look into the interior of exotic gems. With my ability to speak Burmese, I could glean additional information from the attendants and discuss inclusions with them. I learned about the local lore and romance of the historical gem trade. I made notes of weight, inclusions, facets, and value of each gem. Sometimes they were poorly cut, as in their

[1] In later years, the Ministry of Mines hosted two Emporia each year, and the military began to host their own auction.

zeal to preserve weight the cutters did not adhere to the international standards of faceting. Over the years I collected and kept this raw data, which enabled me to compile information that I would ultimately use to write three books: one on rubies, one on jade, and one on a rock that is not seen much in America and Europe: Maw Sit Sit.[2]

My second wife accompanied me on subsequent trips, and we both chuckled at the stares we received from locals and other gem merchants alike. An East Indian gem merchant, able to speak Burmese, married to a white American woman, and visiting not only tourist sites in the city but also private (family) residences.... Everywhere we went, an awestruck, hushed whisper followed in our wake: "Burma-born! Burma-born!"

The number and quality of jewels that were on display was astounding, as were the comparatively reasonable prices. There were some excellent values, but, as usual, I was short of capital. I did not mix my medical practice with my gems business. All purchases had to come from savings. I was able to buy medium grade material initially; after some private sales I could buy finer material. Raising additional capital was not easy, but I established an S-Corp, with plans to sell at trade shows in the US. This was difficult when both my wife and I were working full time, but we persisted and eventually developed networks with other dealers. In the end, the item in which we invested the least (Maw Sit Sit) turned out to be our best-selling item! The years of study were quite a difficult slog, the long travel to Burma was grueling, and the deprivations of life in Burma were onerous, but in the long run it paid off by bringing in extra income in the retirement years, which was especially welcome when Wall Street hit the skids. The experience of holding such prestigious gems was a rare privilege that I will long remember and will always cherish.

My trip in 1985 was very sad. I noticed my mother's health had declined. She was eighty-one years old and had lived a difficult life, caring for a large family after Father's death. Now it was the end of the line. After I came out of her room,

---

[2] *Imperial Jade of Burma and Mutton-fat Jade of India: Mining, Trade, and Use from Antiquity to the Present* (2014); *Rangoon 1941. A Novel Based on True Events* (2013); *Jade and Maw Sit Sit of Burma* (2004, 2009); and *Burma Ruby. A History of Mogok's Rubies from Antiquity to the Present* (2003).

I just looked at my family members gathered around. It was the same dilemma that had faced my Uncle Rao when I had asked him how bad my father was; Uncle had looked with sadness but said nothing. Now it was my turn. I said little. My family may have thought I was heartless, but from a long history of caring for patients, I knew there are few words that can console. Just two months later I received a call that she had died, but there was little I could do; Burma would not give me another visa, so all I could do was attend a memorial service arranged by my sister in Washington, DC.

After 1988, Burma began to open a little to the outside world, and I got an opportunity go to the ruby mines at Mogok and traveled also to the jade mines of Burma, from whence came the much-coveted imperial jade of Burma, widely admired and costing a king's ransom to obtain a piece of the velvety green semi-transparent gem. The mine is located up in the wild north country in the land of the Kachins (Jingpaw, as they called themselves). There we met the owner of a mine who allowed us to hold and examine a piece of jade valued at half a million dollars—something most will not experience. Some imperial jade specimens at the Emporium were valued at millions of dollars; one offered in 2007, weighing 171 kilograms, was listed for 80 million Euro. Because of my ability to speak Burmese, we were also able to visit a small spinel mine near the town of Namya.

Most of the precious gems from Burma in the past would become the crown jewels of some great kingdom, such as the Bourbons. The majority of the precious gems sold today will be rarely seen, as most of them end up in the private collections of the rich and famous. Not royalty and not rich and famous, I nonetheless have been able to give many gems and jewelry pieces to my daughters and my wife.

Figure 78. Myitkyina. On our way to the jade mines. Photo by author.

Figure 79. Kachin damsels in festival parade just outside Myitkyina on our way to the jade mines. Photo by author.

Figure 80. In the 2000s, the military began hosting its own gem auction (UMEHL), and I was also invited to those emporia. Personal collection.

Figure 81. Imperial jade boulder offered for auction at Myanmar Gems emporium 2007. Weighing 171 kilos, it had a reserve price of 80 million euros. Photo by author.

# Gemological Institute of America

*Awards this Diploma to*

## Solomon K. Samuels

*who has successfully met the exacting requirements*

*of this Institute by completing the examinations, research, and assigned projects,*

*thus earning recognition as a*

## Graduate Gemologist

*Issued by the Board of Governors upon recommendation of the faculty*

*together with all the rights and privileges thereunto appertaining.*

October 25, 1985

DATE

CHAIRMAN, BOARD OF GOVERNORS

PRESIDENT, GEMOLOGICAL INSTITUTE OF AMERICA

SECRETARY, EXAMINATIONS BOARD

Figure 82. Graduate Gemologist diploma from GIA. Personal collection.

# Chapter 42
# Life Beyond Medicine

With the passage of time, the science of medicine progressed, but the politics of medicine got worse. Litigation, onerous rules, and turf battles made practice difficult. Solo practice had always been grueling because it meant being on call all the time, perhaps arranging coverage with a colleague for emergencies or vacations. Paperwork, billing, and coding added to the expense of running a solo practice and took up time that could have been spent on patient care. States demanded fifty hours of Continuing Medical Education (CME) credit each year, and medical seminars charged astronomical fees. My first malpractice suit had occurred just five years into practice, for reasons that I had no control over. It was devastating to have that happen so early in my professional life, but it led me to [wisely] practice defensive medicine for the rest of my professional life. Malpractice insurance kept rising in price as lawyers were becoming more strident, making it difficult for physicians, especially those of us in solo practice. The problem was systemic. Doctors blamed lawyers, lawyers blamed the insurance companies, and people continued to engage in destructive behavior like smoking and overeating and not working out. All this meant that expectations were not only high but almost impossible to meet. Solo practitioners were becoming dinosaurs as the complexities of billing codes, the expense of proprietary scheduling and billing software, and the proliferation of HMOs forced doctors into group practices. I was now beginning to tire of the system, was suffering burnout, had difficulty concentrating, and wearied of going to medical conferences that consumed time away from the practice and increased costs. While in the guise of imparting knowledge, some conference organizers and speakers were also lining their pockets and promoting ineffective drugs.

My medical practice was changing as well. Due to advances in medical specialties, what had previously been treated by surgery was now treated with new medical devices. Historically, the mainstay of any general surgical practice was surgeries for stomach ulcers and cancer of the stomach, but the new discipline of gastroenterology—along with new medicines and the discovery of the bacteria H pylori (a bacterium which was now successfully treated by pills)—whittled away at the need for such surgery. Worse, you lose your skills if you perform only a few cases a year. I had not yet reached my financial goal but saw my surgical practice declining while expenses were rising. Finally, my referral base was shrinking as old friends and colleagues retired and new physicians referred among themselves. I started to become increasingly disenchanted with the establishment and, at times, with myself. I knew I had to supplement my income in the short term and had to decide what I would do in the long term, after active practice.

First, in the short term, I began night work at the State Psychiatric Hospital and later at the Veterans Hospital. In a way it was scut work all over again, but it also added to my knowledge base and allowed me to gain new skills. I also did part-time compensation work for the Social Security Disability program. Working with new patient groups gave me insight into segments of American society that I had not been familiar with previously.

Second, I stepped up my education about finances. I had always believed that education and business knowledge were essential in and of themselves and also would be a great help in retirement. In my fifties I took more rigorous courses on money, banking, and credit. I was determined to learn the arcane science of economics and of investing. I attended an all-woman's college that now offered a Master's course in Management to a wider student base.[1] I was surprised to learn how economists viewed medicine and doctors—it was not flattering. Many economists were predicting that the way things were done in medicine could not last. They drew pie charts, used graphs and statistics, and described the arcane details of economic theory. Their theory was that demand was driven by what patients demanded and what doctors provided. My medical colleagues would scoff at economics and would aver that they did not know or care much about the discipline. At the coffee table, one portly ethnic doctor expounded, "who cares if we spend six percent of GDP; we need to spend any percentage that would provide care to patients." Doctors did not know much of the "dismal science."

---

[1] I received my Master's degree in 1999.

I also took many classes at the Chicago Mercantile Exchange. The Chicago Board of Trade offered day- and week-long courses in the basics of investing, in the bond market, in stock picking, and in futures and currency. These courses gave me confidence that I could now manage my own assets. I transferred my IRA account to a well-regarded financial management company, took more interest in growing it, and actively managed my account. I felt I had set the stage to consider a date for retirement. I made plans to wait to retire until the IRA portfolio achieved a set amount before I would cease all medical work. I needed to feel confident that I had sufficient funds to retire and could depend on income from my portfolio as well as additional income from the small gems business enterprise that I had set up.

I highly recommend that everyone have a side business to augment one's fixed income in retirement years. Once the gem business was established, I continued to build on it. Early on, in 1984, I had obtained a Master's degree in Biological Sciences from Western Michigan University, which further helped me understand the formation of gems and their attributes. I would later write three books on gemstones and gemology, which has brought additional income. Since retirement I have continued to study: physics, electricity, magnetism, light. I soon realized how the theory of light can be applied in the identification of gemstones. I keep a copy of Faraday and Charles Maxwell Clark in my library. Even after suffering losses in the stock market, I continued to earn extra income from the gem trade.

Developing confidence and expertise in managing finances was only one of several endeavors that I pursued outside of medicine. Along with the gem business, financial acumen was a way to assure that my retirement would be financially comfortable. Other endeavors were designed to add to my intellectual breadth, and still others resulted from longstanding passions.

My passion for British cars started early in life, at age nine, when Uncle Rao's Wolseley car was seized. Then, after he returned to Burma after the war, he bought another new car: a beautiful Hillman. My first opportunity to own a British car myself came in my first year of practice. I bought a yellow MGB from a local dealer in 1972. It was a dream come true. I drove it to work and enjoyed caring for it. As is well known, British cars require lots of tender care, and owning a British car meant that you must know something about cars. I learned how to check oil, fluid levels, and other basic maintenance. Over the years I added to my collection of cars: a 1969 E-type Jaguar, a 1932 MGJ2, and a 1951 MGTD among others. I bought a ten-acre parcel outside of town on which there was a large pole barn, and there I restored these cars and others, which I sold as another side business. To learn restoration skills, I took advantage of schools offering evening classes in repair and body work on cars and in electronics. For me it was an endeavor that would bring me much pleasure and satisfaction for the rest of my life (I am still working on my 1969 Jaguar). I went to school with young men who were making up classes to get their GED. At roll call I was the oldest man. I got a lot of teasing from my fellow students, but it was all in good humor. I took lessons in welding, soldering, and body work with paints. Over the years I fully restored three cars.[2]

Figure 83. Portion of classic car collection. From back: 1937 Humber, 1969 E-Type Jaguar, 1932 MG J2, 1951 MG TD. Photo by author.

---

[2] I had to sell my treasured MG-J2 after the market collapsed in 2001 and banked that money in a separate savings account to make up for the loss of so much money. It was wise indeed. I also sold gold bullion, silver, and, of course, gemstones to argument the stock losses. We lost almost half of our nest egg, which led me to become ever more wary of all the financial experts. We landed on our feet because we had diverse assets and ways of earning income even in retirement.

"If you want to succeed," a fellow resident once advised me, "you should participate in the other half of American life, namely sports; its builds character and strength." I knew nothing about baseball or football, so my colleague bought me a ticket to a football match. It was boring, and something I had no desire to ever repeat.[3] But I was increasingly aware of how important it is to preserve one's health and wanted to begin an exercise regime. I had started lifting weights at a neighbor's house in Kamayut when I was sixteen but had to give that up through all the troubled times. After I established my medical practice, I joined West Hills Tennis Club in Kalamazoo and started to work out regularly, then took up tennis. I had first picked up tennis at the beautiful mountaintop club in the remote mining city of Mawchi.[4] I fell in love with the game. At West Hills I hired a pro who taught me the fundamentals. "Practice, practice, practice," he admonished. It was easier said than done. I would get up early, two hours before surgery, go the club and practice at the indoor club. At the end of the building was a wall that was painted to simulate a net, and the point was to hit the ball over the net. "High; three feet over the net," the pro would say. I took up the cudgels and went to work. Early on I could not hit the backhand; it would take years to acquire that skill. Over the years I went to tennis clinics in Florida and California, and gradually my game improved to the point that I could hit a backhand to surprise my opponents. This takes years to develop. I derived great pleasure at being able to hit a down-the-line backhand and watch the ball sail over the net to the complete surprise of my opponent. It is important to learn not just the strokes but also the most important factor of physics. My club pro went over the facts. First was just making contact with the ball in front and forward of the knee, off the left knee for the forehand and off the right knee for the backhand. I practiced and practiced. The one-handed backhand is a classic and is harder to master than a two-handed backhand, as M. Steinberger wrote in the *New York Times*: "The one-handed backhand is the last redoubt of

---

[3] The only activity that interested me was the half-time show: the music and the cheerleaders. When I told him this, he grew silent. I did not know that he was highly religious. He never spoke to me again.

[4] I soon learned why the balls went over and fell into the 4,000 foot gorge below: I was not holding the racquet correctly. There was no pro, however, in a British club in the middle of the remote jungle.

artistry." The stroke is also technically challenging because it requires synchrony between hips, trunk, and arms; the two-handed backhand requires less precision. I was satisfied I had the basics. I could hit a single-handed backhand cross court and an inside-out backhand. On vacation I took my racquet and played wherever I went, even in Cusco, Peru. After moving to Arizona, for many years I played twice each week with a pro, increasing my power and accuracy and running down the balls like a forty-year-old. It was very satisfying.

# Chapter 43
# Skin Color, Discrimination, and Immigration

*Color and racism have been the cause of much hate and violence. Many societies in human history have (and still do) preferred pale skin, seeing it as a sign of high social status (the poorer classes worked outdoors and therefore got darker skin). In the colonial period, dark-skinned people were considered uncivilized and inferior and therefore rightfully subordinate to lighter-skinned invaders. During the slavery era in the US, lighter-skinned African Americans were perceived to be more intelligent and cooperative than darker-skinned African Americans, who did not get educated and worked in the fields.*[1] *In North America, skin color became associated with factors beyond social status, for example intelligence and beauty. Even after the abolition of slavery, skin color in North America remained associated with factors such as beauty and intelligence, the preference for fair skin remained, and racial stereotypes have persisted in virtually every aspect of life. Modern genetics pays no heed to any of these racial theories. Science and scientists believe that there is only one race, Homo sapiens. Homo sapiens originated in Africa, so the first humans were dark skinned.*

People living close to the equator are heavily pigmented, an evolutionary process that protects against high levels of ultraviolet (400 nm) radiation and helps to prevent skin cancer. Those living at the poles are lightly pigmented. Scientists have tried to explain why the amount of pigmentation is important, but there is little interest—even resistance—among the general public in learning about evolution, pigmentation, and genetics. Instead the general public tends to embrace outdated perceptions of "race" and deny the science of genetics. My encounter with race and genetics started near the beginning of my life in medicine. In my early years of practice, one of my white colleagues (a cardiologist), asked me to enroll in the ongoing Farmington Study. All went well until I was

---

[1] Slavery ended in France in 1794 and was abolished in England through the Slavery Abolition Act in 1833. Slavery persisted in North America long past that period.

asked to submit biographical data; several weeks later I was notified that I would be dropped because the study required only "white" people; it included Jews but excluded all others. At the time there were two primary scales used to classify human skin color: (a) Felix Von Luschan's chromatic scale developed in the early twentieth century; and (b) the scale developed in 1975 by Thomas Fitzpatrick.[2]

While in Youngstown, I experienced firsthand how racial divisions played out in America. I was invited to homes by well-meaning American families and groups that were working for better understanding between Asia and America. I admired these efforts, even though there was also talk about maintaining white privilege. It was a time of hope, although change was slow to come. Although my early experience in the US was positive, there was always prejudice: usually subtle but sometimes open and hostile. At the Youngstown hospital where I worked, there were two "Negro" doctors (as they were called then). The two doctors worked at the county poor house and were allowed to attend sick patients at the hospital in the surgical clinic—but only black people; they could not attend white patients. In contrast, I—a young brown-skinned doctor from a foreign country—could attend all patients, both white and black. This was disturbing.[3] Who are the minorities on the planet? If one counts all the white people of Europe, the Levant, the US, and a percentage of the South American white population, they would add up to less than one billion people. With a world population of seven billion, that means only one in seven is White, will be classified as White using American standards.

In the 1960s, the south remained rigidly segregated. On the evening news, TV screens were full of strikes, sit-ins, and marches; speeches by Martin Luther

---

[2] Both scales described six variations of pigmentation:

1. Very light or white; Celtic
2. Light or light-skinned European
3. Light intermediate, or dark skinned European
4. Dark intermediate or "Olive skin"
5. Dark or "brown"
6. Very dark or "black."

[3] I observed this same pattern at the US embassy in Rangoon, where there were two black Public Doctors, sent by the USAID, to assist public health; they were not accepted by the Burmese.

King, bull-whips and dogs attacking protestors, and Bull Conner. I feared travel to the south, even to southern Ohio, which was closer to the Dixie South. The language there was the same as in the deep south. In 1964, after the Civil Rights Act, much progress was expected, and progress was indeed made. Attitudes were changing, but not quite as rapidly as hoped for or expected. In the hospital there was little change in race relations, and crude racial jokes persisted. When my colleagues got together at the lunch table, for instance, they insisted "you cannot legislate morality," meaning you can pass laws but you cannot make us like them. It was always "us" and "them." There was a lot of public talk about morality, but in private there was little change of attitudes—and that is true to this day. Many are determined not to have civil rights rammed down their throats. People who call themselves Liberals[4] were not so adamant, but a die-hard segment of people could not accept the premise of the civil rights movement. Overtly, in public places, civil rights were grudgingly accepted as legal mandate, but outside of the legal system, people's attitudes hardly changed at all. In the workplace they would work together, but once outside the workplace there was hardly any social interaction at all; white staff rarely visited their "colored" co-workers' homes.

Asians have their prejudices too. In the early 1960s I took my first trip outside Ohio, stopping in Pittsburgh. I had been given the address there of a small group of Asian interns and residents, and I stopped to join them for coffee, tea, and talk. After a while we turned to the topic of the problems we faced in this country. I was shocked by the attitudes of the (mostly Thai) interns; they were so biased it astonished me. They proclaimed boastfully that there were no "Negro doctors" on staff at their hospital, and they said it with pride. It may come as a surprise to most Americans that there was also a pecking order in Asia, based on skin color. My views were influenced by experiences formed during the war: cruelty, disease, hunger, starving people (experienced myself); it was hard to forget those days. I felt empathy for all people and had found it hard to see pain inflicted on innocent people by the Japanese "master race."

---

[4] American usage of "Liberal" implies "tax and spend." My view is a neo-classical English interpretation of "liberal" as described by Locke, Shaw, Mill, and Huxley.

Through the years I experienced my share of racial prejudice. At one jazz club I talked to a young African woman who said "Why do you come here? You could go almost anywhere," the operative word being "almost." Another night I was invited by a woman to a honky-tonk bar (I had stopped at this place before); a pimply faced boy who could barely read or write, who probably walked in the swamp barefoot, refused to serve me. I felt contempt for him. In my second year of training at Youngstown I had my first encounter with hostility: my senior resident warned me that a patient who did not have any insurance insisted that he not be examined by a "non-white" physician. The senior resident informed the patient that he had no option, and then told me to be extremely careful. Thankfully the episode passed without incident. Immigrants in any country tend to always travel in groups, but since I did not fit into any group, I went alone. I took a boat trip down the Colorado River and shot the rapids in a craft large enough to accommodate about ten people. On the fourth day, two Texans came over and heaved me over into the cold water of Lake Powell. I clung to the raft in desperation. When it was all over, they simply shrugged, "We did not know you could not swim." This did not endear me to southerners. Once I took my beautiful twelve-year-old daughter to Washington DC. While walking around, I stopped to take a picture of her; a stranger walked up to her and asked her if she was "alright." After that she was upset and angry. An Italian colleague cautioned me about having children: where they would fit in? Having lived in Asia and having seen many mixed marriages I knew that marriage between South Asians and white people produces remarkable offspring. My older daughter is a tall, beautiful, gregarious, smart young woman who is professionally successful and moves in the white world. My younger daughter is a beautiful, smart, tough, and disciplined young woman who has achieved success in a white man's world of law enforcement. I talked to my daughters at length about their experience at school; their experiences were positive; they were not bullied and did well at school, although I realize that this was not universal. Many school-goers had unpleasant experiences. I think what helped my daughters were the facts that they had English names, they spoke well, they had a Christian background, and they were pretty and well groomed.

My generation was the first group of Asian immigrants in the post-war years to come to the US. We laid the groundwork for later generations. My generation of immigrants was influenced by the disasters of the most destructive war: merely surviving the war and getting an education was a struggle, and to get on with life was in itself a blessing. Most South Asians never lived under Japanese rule, never endured Fascism; their experiences had been different than mine. Some immigrants who came later made contributions, but some also brought disrepute. One persistent theme that I have observed is that many immigrants bring their views and believe that their tribal customs, if adopted by America, would solve America's social problems. Many of them singularly abhor the habit of dating, and some have carried this to the extreme of killing their daughters "to protect the family honor." This discussion can get pretty interesting. One time I asked one of them if genital mutilation would be good. There was silence. Some immigrant doctors came with dollar signs written all over them. The notion that one could get filthy rich while "serving" people was repulsive. I wanted only to make enough income to live comfortably and to save a portion of that income not only for myself but for the family. I have lived in this country for fifty-six years, except for a sojourn of eighteen months in Canada. If you want to be a billionaire, go to the market and become a bond trader, not a doctor.

How Americans views immigrants: I divide Americans into three groups, based not on any statistical studies but my own observations and experiences.[5] About one-third are, in one form or another, not sympathetic, sometimes hostile. About another one-third are indifferent but not offensive, accepting of diversity. The last one-third are friendly, even encouraging, with a live-and-let-live attitude or even a keen interest in learning about other parts of the world.

---

[5] My assessment is entirely anecdotal. I am not quoting any statistical data, only my own observations. The business elite and the neo-cons have hardly shed their imperial past; they work to preserve and expand white privilege. Historically, from the conquest of Hawaii to the acquisition of Alaska, business has financed many colonies and promoted strife. America progressed and benefitted from the Monroe Doctrine, which allowed the US President Andrew Jackson to grab land from the desperately poor "natives" and allowed President Polk to take advantage of turmoil in Mexico to expand America's borders in the south. The Monroe Doctrine manifested itself in the post-war years as the US asserting its "leadership of the free world."

For immigrants: It makes a difference where one is born, what culture one is born into. Different immigrants bring different perspectives, respond differently to America, and adjust to American life in different ways. It is quite dependent on country of origin, culture, and religion but also the person you are. If you like Americana, pop music, jazz, classical (Western) music, bikinis, girls in summer dresses, Western literature, Shakespeare, books, cars, and gadgets you can have a head start. Those who do not have that commonality tend to seek out only people like themselves, who cannot appreciate America for what it is. For them, life is difficult the minute they step out of the house in which they have re-created the environment of their home country. My experience was different. I was of South Indian ethnicity but not from the subcontinent. I was not a Hindu. I had embraced Western music and culture from an early age. I was well educated. Language can also be a tool for prejudice, and I had worked to speak English well, with no accent.

For every person born overseas, the search for a place in America can be wrenching. Almost always, immigrants—at least those from non-European countries—gravitate to where like-minded people from countries similar to their own congregated, at least initially.[6] What happens then depends on how quickly the immigrants embrace America. If you are a "sports nut," for example, obsessed with spectator team sports, you can immerse yourself in it and find like-minded Americans. Figuring out where one "fits" can be agonizing, even for someone like me who came well equipped. I have encountered many different ways of handling this emotion. The reaction of some immigrants is denial. One of my colleagues who was as brown-skinned as I averred that he had "never encountered any discrimination." I thought it was a bit of tunnel vision; he wore blinders, like many others. Others take to extreme forms of withdrawal and protection; they hate being here and resort to violence against those whom they perceive to be against them. In between is a vast spectrum of immigrants from all manner of countries who are comfortable in their cultural identity and in their adopted country; they see the

[6] I had not looked for community, as there were very few Burmese communities in the US then, and besides, being of Indian ethnic origin and being raised a Christian, I had little commonality with either community.

good and bad of both places; and they know that they are different but accept that difference.

Those who had achieved a high level of education before coming to the US or who completed higher education in America have an easier time coping with the complex life of an immigrant. I have heard many excuses by the young for not getting an education: how difficult it was. That is the easy way out. What I faced at the end of the war was daunting—lack of money, lack of family support, lost years of schooling, general despair. Confronted with these difficult circumstances, it would have been easy to give up and join the multitude, to go get a low-level job and muddle through life. Instead, I dealt with the vicissitudes that were placed before me and proceeded to follow my dream. The best time for life preparation is while you are young. Youth passes surprisingly quickly, and if you have not prepared, then you join the long line of the disaffected, casting about for excuses and blaming your misfortune on others, and probably giving in to passion and hormones to marry an unsuitable woman at an early age. Instead, you should finish a Bachelor's degree at twenty-two; get a well-paying job at age twenty-five; maybe obtain an advanced degree; then go to work, and by the time you are thirty-five you are set. By age forty-five you think about retirement and start thinking of ways to assure a comfortable retirement, maybe augment your income; and by age fifty-five you should have a plan to keep your mind occupied and learn new things.

Many Christian immigrants sought comfort in churches, especially the Catholic church, but not all churches are welcoming, particularly in the south. A bitchy nurse once told me "if you are brown skinned, you go to a black church." The reception can be warmer in the Catholic church because of its widespread presence throughout the world, but you have to fall in line with all their rigid teachings to be embraced by the church. I was a doubter very early, even an agnostic at age sixteen. I was greatly influenced by natural sciences. My first lesson in physics impressed me immensely. The "demonstrator" brought in a small basin of water, took out a small cube of sodium, told us to stand back, and then, no sooner than he placed the cube in the water, the little piece of sodium took off like "greased lightning." I was hooked on science from that moment on. I read reams and piles of books to learn about physics and cosmology and other sciences. That investment brought me new knowledge and new perspectives on the world. It was exiting, and I learned facts that were useful in everyday life. Immersing myself in science rather than in a church community had no adverse effect on me.

# Chapter 44
# Racial, Ethnic, and Religious Conflict

Racial, ethnic, and religious conflict is pervasive all over the planet, on all continents. It crosses religious and ethnic lines. The Tutsi and the Houthi have been at war, slaughtering one another, for decades. When Muslim Pakistan was split off from secular India, Hindus slaughtered Muslims and vice versa. The ethnic conflicts in the Balkans rose to a crescendo in the 1980s but still persist. The Middle East today is riven by conflict between Saudi Arabia and Iran, Sunni and Shi'a Islam, not to mention persecution of the Sufi subgroup. Less murderous but nevertheless destructive is discrimination based on race, ethnicity, or religion—commonplace in American life.

Americans tend to lump all Asians[1] together, hardly able to tell the difference between them: Han Chinese, Japanese, Korean. Despite discrimination and bans on immigration in earlier centuries, the twentieth century saw greater acceptance of immigrants from East Asia. This was due in part to the belief that "Asians" were equal to or superior to "Caucasians" in math and science. In some ways they were envied, even. With a good education and money, they could live almost anywhere, except in the toniest neighborhoods. After the Vietnam war, the Southeast Asian Vietnamese boat people were given the benefit of the doubt, largely out of a feeling of guilt; few of them faced the kind of discrimination faced by native-born African Americans. The same cannot be said of South Pacific Islanders. This is due to both cultural and educational factors. Their tiny island nations have no great centers of learning.

As a rule in the US, people from the Middle East face more religious discrimination than color discrimination. Light-skinned Lebanese Christians, for example, assimilated and were accepted quite easily into America. In contrast, men

[1] Asia is divided (not by geographical lines) into Northeast Asia (Japan, China, Korea), Southeast Asia (Cambodia, Malaysia, Thailand, Burma), and South Asia (India, Nepal, Pakistan, Sri Lanka, Bangladesh).

and women who don the trappings of conservative Islam (hijab, full beard, skull-cap) are often shunned as possible terrorists. This is especially so since 9/11.

South Asians (including India, Nepal, Pakistan, Sri Lanka, Bangladesh) generally vary from light to darker skinned; those with light skin did well, many of them going on to high academic positions or even becoming CEO of Microsoft, Google, and other technology companies. But South Indians, typically darker skinned, evoked different responses. In contrast to the British, who had colonies throughout South Asia, Americans had little understanding of the people from South Asia and so reacted mostly on the level of pigmentation and phenotype (outward appearance). In recent years there have been attacks on and murders of turban-wearing Sikhs, as ill-informed Americans equated turbans with the Middle East and terrorism.

Many good things came out of India—yoga and meditation for instance; also secular democracy. But South Asian immigrants brought much baggage with them when they came to the US. Many high-caste Hindus came here with the notion that because they were light skinned they were therefore equal to Whites; they tend to not make eye contact with darker-skinned Indians. In this the Indians brought with them all the biases and prejudice from the subcontinent. When questioned about the persistence of the destructive caste system in India, they make all sorts of excuses, in part blaming the British, which is laughable because it was the British who put an end to Hinduism's more egregious practices, like the dreadful practice of *suttee*, where a widow was made to jump onto her husband's funeral pyre. Or the notion that it is acceptable to attack Untouchables.[2] Hindu groups try to sanitize the evils of the caste system and desperately try to redo the bad image of Hinduism. Some groups have gone so far as to try to change the content of textbooks to deny that Hinduism is responsible for the dreaded caste system. Groups such as these are more interested in protecting the "good name of the Brahman and upper caste Hindus" than searching for and eradicating evil practices, or

---

[2] An anecdotal story: if perchance you are invited to a Brahman's house and are not a Brahman, you may have to wash your own dishes. Caste rules make any vessel that has come into contact with the saliva of another person contaminated, and no person whose status is higher than that of the eater can handle the vessel. See www.nytimes.com/2016/10/13/opinion/indias-eternal-inequality.html.

upholding the truth. Sometimes this desire shades into arrogance, scorn for American behavior, "loose" morals, and lack of "family values."

Some Hindus are embarrassed about their customs but still practice arranged marriages within a small population, which leads to genetic diseases.[3] Some immigrants from the subcontinent brought greed and avarice, which cast a dark, negative shadow on all South Asian immigrants. There are a great many good Indian doctors, but there are also some bad apples who tarred us all. Some second- and third-generation Indians now are faced with the fact that, despite all the advantages that their parents came here find, they are no better off than the cousins they left behind.

Skepticism, fear, and resentment of immigrants have many sources. One is all the conflicts in the Middle East—the nature of our involvement in the Israeli–Palestinian conflict, for example—as well as our support for despotic Arab rulers rather than the common people. After 9/11 and the senseless Iraq war, the situation worsened. The change progressed slowly at first but inexorably. The progress that had been made over the last thirty years was dissipating fast, as America became less friendly and the anti-Muslim rhetoric became more corrosive.[4] The veneer of stability that we thought was present (in the 1960s and 1970s) began to fray, exposing raw and savage emotions. This is not an indictment of all Americans, but relationships in general were getting worse. Whereas hostility was not expressed openly in earlier years, now it came out in the open and is sometimes frightening.

## THE CHALLENGES OF ASSIMILATION

Manners: For some, life in the tropics, in the third world, is vastly different from life in the developed world. Western manners are a mystery and, to most uneducated immigrants, pose many problems. Hardest to learn can be simple facts such

[3] The Reddy clan of south India is a textbook example. Due to interbreeding, this clan developed an inability to recover from anesthesia, specifically muscle relaxants. Until this was recognized, they had a high incidence of death during surgery. So much for marrying within the clan.

[4] While touring Arizona, I recall stopping at a site where the Japanese Americans were interned during World War II. It was incomprehensible that America would treat its own citizens in this way.

as not to interrupt while others are speaking. In the East, a discussion was sometimes chaotic, with everybody talking at the same time. No Roberts Rules of Order. The American practice of calling strangers by their given name is abhorrent to many people in Europe and throughout Asia. The use of the given name is simply unacceptable and is considered disrespectful. In Germany it is "Herr Doctor" or "Herr Professor." I still cringe when people, especially younger people, call me by my first name, but I put up with it because I know this is the norm here. I learned that the reason for this widespread practice stems from the business schools and the business world, which believe that to be on a first-name basis is a way of breaking the ice and disarming the conversant, thereby allowing for a more friendly atmosphere. This may be the received wisdom in America, but in the rest of the world it is considered ill mannered.

Adopting American personal habits and manners facilitates acceptance. I wore a clean shirt, a good suit and tie, and polished shoes, not casual wear that might pass for acceptable in the third world. In recent years the notion of a dress code has broken down, and that adds a new dimension in attitudes toward minorities. Small talk has always been difficult for me. I dislike it and detest racial jokes, whether they were about Blacks, Poles, or Asians. I slowly withdrew from casual conversations in the doctors' lounge or cafeteria. I was not reclusive but became quite reserved.

In the early years, when walking into a restaurant or a mall or any public facility, I was always aware of the eyes following me. I was never accosted but wondered: were they looking at me because I was different? Or were they hostile? I will always be the outsider looking in, and I have come to revel in it, in not accepting everything American but forging my own hybrid life. I like drinking tea (sweet tea) with a dash of milk; cooking with spices such as turmeric, chilis, and papaya; taking a nap at noon. In the early years, yoga was derided in America, although it has been practiced in South Asia for centuries. I find it an excellent way to remain limber and have a quiet moment in what are still busy days. In retirement I have made time to read books, three at a time: a chapter at noon, one before dinner, and another late at night—at least three hours a day.

Of course I brought my own prejudices with me to this country. I disliked American intervention in the affairs of other countries. I saw that the desire of the American establishment for regime change in elected governments in third-world countries actually back-fired and created chaos. For example, when the Egyptian president was overthrown, a leading neo-con boldly stated that the most important policy issue was that "American interests have to be taken care of first." That is the kind of statement that is offensive to people overseas.

Given my war-time experience, I am acutely aware of shortages, am committed to protect the environment, try to treat animals with kindness (they have their own lives to lead), and because I care about humankind, I remain interested in humanism and human progress. It is hypocrisy for America to preach to other countries about civil rights when we do not address the problems that we have in our own country, and they seem to be getting worse. In my early years in this country I lived without fear; now I have moments when I am wary and concerned. On the whole, however, being an outsider has been fine, it suited me well. I could still be patriotic in my own way and be faithful to this country's great institutions. I follow politics closely and know I have the right to question policies. I embrace much of Americana, the essential goodness of the country, its people; but I never rule out the questioning of lapses in policy. Being of independent bent, I have chosen no party affiliation, calling myself independent or internationalist or humanist.[5] I could be dispassionate, not self-righteous. I could look at both sides of an issue and reach my own conclusions. To quote Cicero: "I am neither an Athenian nor a Corinthian."[6] I am passionate about keeping my pride in my family, my parents, my origins, my singular identity, and my self-worth. To do so does not conflict

---

[5] Since the early years of my residency, I have worked in an environment that was mostly rich and conservative. Not that there is anything inherently wrong with conservatives, but I found some of the discussions difficult. Sometimes the tension between the various staff members was palpable, and I found it wisest to keep my own counsel.

[6] Marcus Tullius Cicero (Roman statesman, orator, lawyer, philosopher; 1st century BCE) observed that the later years of a man's life could be embraced as an opportunity for growth and completeness at the end of a life well-lived. Michel de Montaigne (16th-century French philosopher) observed: "Withdraw into yourself, but first prepare yourself to receive yourself."

with being a good citizen, a good father, and a husband. I always want to preserve my identity.

# Chapter 45
# Change

*"Time and tide wait for no man"*

*—Geoffrey Chaucer*

One of life's greatest ironies is change. Just as one gets used to a way of life, it changes. There have been more goodbyes in my life than I care to remember, more than I care to count. Saying goodbye sometimes rips you inside, is painful. I left home at twenty-three, and a year later I walked up to the mountaintop to say goodbye to the staff I had worked with and to the acting manager. Full of sadness, I remember pausing to look at the scene, the flowers growing at the building entrance. I turned to look at the tall mountaintop and recalled the many evenings that the manager and I had sipped gin in its shadow. It was a remarkably beautiful place. I did not want to be a nomad, but less than two years later I said goodbye again to friends and staff in another beautiful setting, Kengtung. When I left Burma and my family, I did not think it would be permanent, then it was. Youngstown, Philadelphia, Hamilton, London, Detroit, Kalamazoo, Arizona; group practice, solo practice; marriage, divorce, remarriage. Change was a constant in my life and affected me profoundly. Even small changes can still affect me with a sense of loss: saying goodbye to watching Jay Leno each evening caused me great sadness.

## Remarriage and Retirement

Seven years after the divorce, a friend arranged a blind date with a woman who eventually became my new partner—a woman with two Master's degrees and working on a PhD at the time. We were together through the years of establishing the gem trade, acquiring academic degrees, restoring cars, sending two girls to college and seeing them launch their careers, and traveling to Southeast Asia sometimes several times a year. As we planned for retirement, we went looking for a suitable place. Neither of us cherished the thought of spending winters in cold Michigan. I am cold intolerant, and my desire to get out of the cold weather was overpowering. After a years-long search we chose Tucson, AZ. We found a 3+-acre parcel of land and a house plan that appealed to us. We put a lot of effort into planning our new home, a beautiful home larger than any that I previously owned. Since my days in Burma I had a long love affair with teakwood and natural stone and for years had imported teak, marble, and granite flooring from Burma and Thailand. Our home truly is our castle and is a constant reminder of my origins and our travels.

One advantage of our property is that I could make a small track to test-run the cars. The land was quite dissimilar from Michigan: it was desert, full of cactus, surrounded by mountains, with beautiful vistas, but it had some unpleasant surprises. Wildlife flourishes in Tucson—some unusual and some deadly. Coyote, rabbits, mule deer, and a wide variety of birds range through our property. But so do destructive javelina, deadly rattlesnakes, and large poisonous lizards (Gila monsters). One small rodent was to prove most destructive: the pack rat. It is the most vile, destructive, and elusive animal. It lives in large burrows under cactus, decorated with bright, shiny objects. They loved my cars, to eat the brightly colored wires and take them into their burrows.[1] They ate the wires of the E-type Jaguar, which took a long time and much money to repair. They ate through wires in my new everyday car one night. If you leave your car outdoors, you have to pop the engine hood and put a light under the engine.

## FINANCIAL CRISIS

The year 2001 was tumultuous. I was in the process of moving from Michigan to Arizona and was on the road, cut off from news, when the dot-com bubble hit and

---

[1] Pack rats, little known outside the southwest, are more destructive than the bigger predators. An apocryphal story from war-time Europe: The German Wehrmacht in its retreat left a company of tanks in the field, well camouflaged, so that in spring they could return and ride them into war again. But when the German Army unit during came back in the spring, they found that the tanks would not start. To their chagrin, they discovered that the wiring had been destroyed by pack rats.

the market collapsed.[2] I would spend days out of touch with my broker. In the hinterlands of this country, financial news is difficult to obtain, and even these few days would prove very detrimental.[3] What I learned the hard way was absolutely shocking: how fast money disappeared from the portfolio. It was terrifying and frightening. We were bruised and battered but survived the crash, albeit much poorer. I, along with many people, am still angry and mystified that nobody took the blame for it or went to jail for it. After the drubbing I took, I began to question all the propaganda Wall Street and the banks and others connected to the financial world spewed out on a daily basis. Too many of them used their wiles to prey upon unsophisticated investors or said one thing in public but worked behind the scenes to enrich themselves.

But the 2001 crash was hardly the worst; it was only the beginning. There was much talk of a housing bubble, but so many "in the know" debunked it. Banks kept acting irresponsibly, for months, then it hit and was devastatingly brutal. In 2007 Bear Stearns was sold, and then Lehman would go bankrupt, another disaster, and the portfolio would take another hit. All the talk about the "goldilocks economy" and resilient markets vanished when it happened again in spring of 2008.[4] So many people lost their homes and their life savings. I became even more deeply suspicious of the financial press and never again trusted the banks or Wall Street. Wall Street became the Street of Shame.

I would strongly recommend diversifying. My diversifying was a lifesaver. It did not protect completely, but it mitigated the losses in the markets. Yet 2008 took an emotional toll: many of the friends we had made at the fitness club dropped their memberships; my favorite tennis coach was let go by the club (with two young children, she had a hard time and moved home to live near her mother); several of the programs there ended. From a bustling place it became quiet. Beyond

---

[2] I was in Amarillo, Texas, when the market crashed. I went looking for the *Wall Street Journal* but could not find it anywhere. Most clerks laughed hilariously when I asked for it. My daughter ended up working there in later years.

[3] It may now be hard to believe, but in 2001, smart phones and cable news were not at all ubiquitous. The *New York Times* and *Wall Street Journal* were simply not available in small towns.

[4] Billions of dollars were lost, yet nobody was held accountable for it.

that, university programs were cut and employees let go; some public schools closed; roads were left to decay; many businesses went bankrupt; and storefronts stood empty. It was a years-long rolling disaster from which many did not recover. The economy would never be the same again.

# Chapter 46
# Medical Challenges

Moving to a distant place in retirement is an experience by itself. Much as we love our home and are happy to have escaped the cold climate, there were downsides to our move to Arizona. One was the length of the ragweed season and with it the cross-reacting weeds; another was health care. My allergies worsened, and finding a competent allergist proved elusive. Other than my allergies I was in relatively good health. I had always been active and ate wisely. But age caught up with me, and I soon needed more than routine medical care.

Removed from family and friends and starting all over again to find medical care is a challenge. It is not the same as calling on colleagues whom you have known and worked with for years. It is strange and difficult, when a doctor gets sick, to be on the exam table with your own doctor sitting on the other side. In the heyday of my practice, it was such a pleasure to sit across the table and talk about what ails the patient, and after that was done it was their time to talk about their family and life. With some patients who had survived the war, we exchanged our experiences and stories. One had the feeling that your patient was part of the extended family. Now the relationship between doctor and patient has become distant, frigid, impersonal; there is no warmth. Doctors look at and tap at their computer screens while firing questions at the patient; one always senses that the doctor has to rush off to the next patient. As solo practices fade and medical groups grow ever larger, the back- and front-office personnel move like automatons; phone calls are not returned; messages get lost; patients are pushed to patient portals that are not updated; and it can be a fight to truly communicate with the medical professional who is overseeing your health. Case in point: The mere act of carrying out my doctor's orders for a test at the hospital imaging department recently took two months, multiple phone calls and faxes, and a letter to the hospital CEO. My doctor did not get the results for weeks after the test was done.

In Michigan the allergy season is short, the worst time for people allergic to ragweed being from August to September. I had no knowledge of how different Arizona was: the ragweed season was long (starting in April and ending in November) and very antigenic. There are three species of ragweed.[1] Soon the allergies affected my lungs. I was on the road back to Kalamazoo one summer soon after retirement when my symptoms worsened. I was coughing was so badly that I was getting light headed and was afraid I would lose control of the car. In Kalamazoo I made an appointment with a former colleague. He examined me and alerted me to the fact the my Fev1 was depressed; and he gave me a prescription for an inhaler, which I used as prescribed when I arrived back in Tucson. I then started to look for an allergist.

The allergist I chose ended up being not very helpful, and his neglect would ultimately lead to permanent damage to the lungs. The first interview did not go well. He was not interested in any testing, like the usual skin test, chest x ray, not even blood work; he just wanted to put me on steroids. As a transplant surgeon and knowing the long-term effect of steroids, I refused, continuing the inhaler. I had to prod him to run skin and other tests. Finally, after years of allergy shots and this ineffectual treatment, I developed a lung infection. I was coughing and expectorating copious amount of yellowish sputum. All this time the allergist told me this was caused by gastric reflux. It went on for a number of years, until June 2013. I did some traveling to get out of the antigenic environment of Arizona, and when I came back, it got even worse. I developed pneumonia, shortness of breath, and night sweats. The allergist never ran any tests like culture of the sputum until finally, at my insistence, he bitterly consented to a sputum culture and a week-long course of Azithromycin (which was ineffective). The tests results shocked me. They showed that I had four organisms in my lungs, any one of which could be fatal.[2] I found a pulmonologist (lung specialist) to take over my care. He asked

---

[1] There are seventeen different species of flowering plants in the genus Ambrosia. Each plant can produce a billion particles of pollen, which are highly antigenic and cause severe allergies in those susceptible to its pollen.

[2] Nocardia, Pseudomonas Aeruginosa, Haemophilus Influenzae, and Nontuberculous Mycobacteria. When I kept the appointment, if he did look at the results, he angrily told me to put six-inch blocks

why I was seeing these doctors (a question I should have asked myself, earlier) and told me that my infections were serious. After multiple cultures he put me on an old sulpha drug (which is quite toxic) for the most serious infection and a combination of other antibiotics. After eight months the two deadliest infections were finally brought under control, although the medications took their toll on the lining of the stomach. I had two subsequent episodes and finally developed Bronchiectasis, which permanently damaged my lungs. I debated whether I should sue the allergist, but unfortunately, not wanting be accused of being greedy, I chose to lodge a complaint with the Arizona Board of Medicine. Other than the material I sent to the board, they never asked me to appear, nor did they seek additional information. In retrospect I should have sued. The Arizona Board of Medicine was only interested in sexual predation and drug addiction.

My personal experiences as a patient are not very flattering to the medical profession. Soon after our move to Tucson there were reports in the newspapers of the near chaos in the medical degree program and hospital at the University of Arizona. Lurid details emerged about infighting between the doctors and the university regents. To keep up with medical education, I attended medical "grand rounds," and the scuttlebutt gleaned at those meetings painted an even more disturbing picture—of medical groups working against one another and all seeming to work against the university administration. After years of battle, the university sold its medical facility to a private healthcare company, a rare occurrence. Typically, only services such as radiology services are sold to private corporations.

Given all this information, when I needed cataract surgery, I sought out an ophthalmologist who did not practice at the University Medical Center. I had met him at grand rounds, and he came well recommended. He accepted Medicare. The surgery went well, but when the bill came, it was three times what Medicare paid, and he billed me for the difference. I disputed the bill, and he ultimately adjusted it, but I should have reported the matter to Medicare. All my years of practicing

under the bed posts at the head of the bed and come back and see him in a month. This was malpractice. I could have died of the multiple infections. I angrily walked out.

medicine had been patient-centered, and I simply was not prepared to meet doctors who cared less for the patient and more about getting money.

Some years later I had ringing in the years. I consulted with an older ENT doctor about the tinnitus and about my sinuses. He looked at an old x-ray and told me "if you look at one hundred people off the street you will find many with the same finding. Try nasal rinse." As symptoms got worse, despite using a nasal rinse, I went to see a young otolaryngologist, who took time to examine me. He told me there was pus and that my maxillary sinuses were full of fungal balls. There were other issues that could only be redressed by surgery. He performed surgery successfully, which improved my quality of life immensely. Doctors such as this give me hope that all is not lost in medicine.

It pains me to write about this breakdown in the doctor–patient relationship. There are many good doctors who are ethical and old-fashioned doctors, with notions of service, the love of science, and the love of progress, but given the system we have, such doctors have become increasingly rare. This does not bode well for our future or that of our children. The relationship between doctor and patient has become distant frigid, impersonal, without any warmth, and it hurts both the physician and patient. It took me a long time to find a group of physicians with whom I could work and who would consult with one another.

It also pains me to observe the sorry state of medical care in this country. The high cost of drugs, the willingness of the government to be a supplicant to money from medical companies who pay more attention to the bottom line than health outcomes, the desire of the president and congresspersons to gut patient protections while catering to drug companies to fund re-election campaigns—these are truly enraging. Lobbying is one of the baleful forces that prevent solutions to many of these problems.[3]

The relationship and experience with hospitals is no better. In late 2020 I had typical symptoms of the flu. I did the usual: took Tylenol, ASA, fluids, and my doctor prescribed antibiotics. I felt better for a while but then began to decline

---

[3] I am aware of the right to petition the government. We, however, have taken it to such an art form that it produces more negative than positive consequences.

again. One morning in February 2021, I felt intense shortness of breath, extreme fatigue, and serious brain fog. After consultation with my doctor, my wife drove me to the hospital emergency room. My first encounter was with a male nurse who was burly, angry-looking, aggressive, and abusive. I am cold intolerant, and while waiting for some tests, I started to shiver and asked for a warm blanket. That request went unanswered. The EKG technologist tried to perform the EKG test, but I was shaking so hard that there was nothing but scatter on the tape. The poor man tried three times and ultimately got a short strip, saying "that's all I can do." I complained again about the intense cold, but the male nurse again ignored me. My condition made my memory foggy. I cannot remember all the words exchanged. Nevertheless, I remember the abuse and negligence. After more than five hours I was finally admitted—to the COVID ward!—for observation. The room's ugliness shocked me. It was dirty and unkept, with large vacuum tubes, obviously for negative pressure. The red tape surrounding the tubes had fallen halfway down. It was noisy, again bitterly cold, and wildly depressing. This encounter made me agitated. I worried about the care I was about to receive and that I would die in such bleak surroundings. Fortunately for me, my physician visited very early the next morning. He was visibly upset at the way I had been treated and made immediate demands that I be removed from the hell-hole. He started an intensive regimen of antibiotics and various other therapies, to which I gradually responded (temperature came down, breathing improved). A few days later, tests showed that I had no COVID but did have community-acquired pneumonia. I was transferred to the main ward. Here I encountered helpful, compassionate, hard-working nurses who took good care of me and communicated regularly with my wife. In about two and a half weeks, and after two surgeries to drain fluid from my lungs, I was still in pain but recovered enough to be transferred to a long-term care/rehab center.

My first encounter at the rehab center echoed that which I had at the hospital. The first room I was put into was frigidly cold. A little Japanese nurse assistant to whom I complained showed total indifference, reminding me of the callous Japanese whom I encountered during my youth. After multiple complaints and increasingly urgent and strident requests for a blanket, the staff admitted that my room did not have heat and finally transferred me to another room where the systems worked. My wife has additional horror stories about getting the brush-off from desk personnel and no contact with a care facilitator about a care plan. I had many bad experiences in both institutions. It is not the place in this book to talk about all the inadequacies. That will be dealt with in a separate essay. Suffice it to say that the facilities, the processes, and the personnel left much to be desired.

Progress in medicine comes in fits and starts, sometimes at glacial speed. Many of the discoveries we have made have been slow and incremental. In the early 1600s, William Harvey estimated that the amount of blood present in the left ventricle of the heart is passive diastole. Keeping his calculations conservative, he speculated that only a fraction of the blood "roughly a drachm in weight" would be ejected every systole. He computed that in a single hour—during which the heart beat, at low estimate, roughly 2,000 times—approximately 2,000 drachms would be expelled by the organ. This meant that over the course of one day, a little less than 50,000 drachms of blood would be ejected into the arteries. Harvey simply could not believe that the liver was capable of producing so much blood; nor did he think it possible for men to consume the amount of food required to generate such an enormous quantity. He could not understand why the arteries did not swell or even "burst with too much intrusion of blood" from the contracting heart, or how the muscles and tissues and organs of the body could absorb it all in the space of a few hours; the body would surely become flooded with so much liquid, he thought.[4] Harvey failed to discover the connection between the artery and the vein. It took until the middle of the seventeenth century until Marcello Malpighi discovered the "capillary" and the connection between artery and vein and, hence, the modern concept of circulation.[5] There was a time when we used medication even though we did not know how it reacted with the body. Genetics, biology, and drugs have advanced the treatment for many diseases and conditions and, in some cases, have been able to prolong life, but this comes at enormous cost. Too many people in the twentieth and twenty-first centuries have too high expecta-

[4] Thomas Wright, *Circulation: William Harvey's Revolutionary Idea* (London: Chatto &Windus, 2012), 133.

[5] The dates are somewhat confusing, as Malpighi lived in Italy and Harvey in England. There was an absence or at least a considerable lag in communication.

tions, and the logistics of medical practice have not kept up with scientific developments.

It would be unfair to emphasize the negative aspects of Arizona and not point out the good. The state has a low income-tax rate, and property and home prices tend to be more affordable than in the northeast. The climate allows for year-round outdoor activities such as hiking and birdwatching and supports many tropical plants common to Southeast Asia. Having a pool allowed me to gain confidence in my ability to swim and a pleasing way to relax. The area has a rich history of Native American culture, and we have visited many sites that foster knowledge and understanding of the various tribes. While the state has a reputation for being hostile to immigrants, Tucson is a tolerant and peaceful oasis that welcomes diversity and values fairness. Each year Tucson hosts a huge Gem, Mineral, and Fossil Showcase, lasting four weeks, that has provided a terrific venue for sale of our gems, jewelry, and books as well as multiple opportunities to attend seminars taught by world-renowned gemologists and develop firm collegial relationships. The University of Arizona has a world-famous program in tree dendrology and is a leader in optics and astronomy. Its sister university in Tempe, Arizona State University, has world-class physicist and scientist Lawrence Kraus in its Origins department.

# Epilogue

I remember being a happy boy when I was about ten years old. I used to sing in the bathroom, go up on the rooftop and sing, and put putty on the zinc sheets on the roof. In spite of financial difficulty, I was pretty happy. I could make friends: I had Muslim friends, Christian friends, and later had young Hindu men with whom I got along. Like all young men I told off-color jokes.[1] But the war, the war's aftermath, the hardship of medical school, the dangerous life working in rebel-infested areas, and the difficulties of settling in the US would take their toll on me. I had horrifying dreams to which my second wife can bear witness. Some nights I would have paralytic sleep dreams, and early in our marriage I awakened her with my moaning, shaking and later screaming; she gently took me by the shoulder and eased me up. She calmed me down, sat by my side and said nothing for a while, then turned on the light and asked what happened. In a nutshell I told her of my recurring dreams. This one had involved two hooded cobras who had pursued me up a dead end; the Snake Community had tried me and condemned me to death for all the killing of snakes I had done in the war years. I was paralyzed, and all that noise was me trying to escape them. Her soothing voice and firm grip of my shoulder were reassuring and comforting. The story line was different for each subsequent dream. There were many themes, like bombers or fighters that were targeting the home, my effort to run to the shelter being thwarted by my paralysis; whatever the theme, the dreams all have the horrifying paralytic moment, and then I wake up shaking. I finally learned that this was a REM disorder, and medication has reduced their incidence.

I left Burma in 1960, having survived snake bites, scorpion stings, four years of deadly bombings, robberies, and deaths and having witnessed a whole range of atrocities and a deadly ambush. I came to this country with a medical degree and $16 plus change in my pocket. I did two internships, one residency, several fellowships; fourteen years of "education" in all in Burma and the US and

---

[1] When later I told jokes in the operating room, I found they were not well received, so I made few comments other than to say what I needed; I became less open and more reserved.

finally ran my own medical practice for thirty-four years. I built a nice home (homes) and educated my two beautiful and talented daughters, who finished school debt free and on time and who have been continuously employed after graduating from college. My eldest daughter brought her first home at age twenty-eight, followed by my second daughter buying her home eighteen months later.

My older daughter's friends are very diverse; she is fully integrated into mainstream American life and society. Her work and the environment allowed this happen; her gregariousness facilitated her success. She married at twenty-eight, and I hoped that I soon would have grandchildren. She has such a kind heart that I had expected her to raise a family. I was seventy-five when she told me she was not going to have any children. It crushed me. I almost crashed the car. I had a hard time accepting her decision, and she was not willing to talk about it. I did not want to sever our relationship, so after a period of distance and coolness, we reconnected after a year.

When she was just fourteen, I knew my second daughter would not have any children. She turned vegan at that age and has remained so. She obtained her baccalaureate at age twenty-two, then a Master's from Loyola University. She now works for the Federal government, in law enforcement. I am proud of her dedicated hard work, which has been recognized by meritorious awards about every two years.

I have a well-read and well-educated wife with two Masters degrees and a PhD; I enjoy talking to her on a variety of subjects. She has built a strong and loving relationship with my daughters and has given generously to extended family members, all while pursuing her own education and career. For myself, I read avidly. I am quite certain of who I am and quite comfortable in my skin. I have seen much and endured much throughout my life and came to enjoy being the outsider. While being true to America, I also look at the rest of the world and try to understand the problems that other countries face; I never want to lose my essential humanity. There is a peculiar notion in this country that courage, patriotism, tenacity, and ferocity in conflicts is unique to America and that these words do not apply to other peoples and nations on the planet, even to those who suffered all the horrors of war and privation. This attitude diminishes America. Much is said of "American exceptionalism," which implies that we are somehow inherently superior to the rest of the peoples of the world. I respectfully beg to differ. We remain human (homo sapiens sapiens), connected to the rest of humanity. My beliefs are firmly rooted in the Magna Carta: free expression and personal rights. I still view America as the bastion of freedom.[2] Considering the genocide that is ongoing in my home country of Burma, I consider it a gift and a privilege to live in America.

Nearing the end of my life, I have had to ask myself three questions that I think all of us need to settle or ask ourselves:

1) Did I achieve my goals? I am proud of having overcome many obstacles to achieve my education and medical credentials. I am proud also that I was able to establish and run a successful solo medical practice for many years, help to develop a kidney transplantation program at my hospital, and establish an important Vascular Lab at the hospital. I criticize myself that I did not think big; I should have aimed higher.

2) Did I assert myself forcefully enough in the world, in my profession, in my relationships? I realize that my early life experiences rendered me too fearful at times, too reluctant to initiate change. I often ask myself if life would have different and better had I forged ahead rather than give in to those fears. For example, I should have asserted myself more forcefully and earlier with my allergist.

3) Did I achieve all I could in life; did I live life to its utmost; did I leave this world a better place than I found it? Here I can answer an unequivocal "yes." Sometimes I am amazed to look back on the adventures I had in life, the places I have traveled. In my travels I was always generous to people who helped and guided me and was richly rewarded with insights and information not shared with other tourists. Through our years in the gem business, we formed true friend-

---

[2] A claim is made by one of the congressmen from Iowa that "non-white people did not contribute much to knowledge or science or math." Of course, the Chinese invented paper, dynamite, built the great wall. Much in science, biology, and math were discovered before 1777. Arab mathematicians made important contributions to astronomy; the Mesopotamians built great temples; and the Egyptians built the pyramids. Indian mathematicians followed: in the fourteenth century, Madhava discovered the sine, cosine, tangent, and arctangent; he is purported to have discovered Pi long before Leibnitz.

ships with many gem dealers in Burma and from around the world and again was richly rewarded with experiences, information, and photos not available to others in the profession. In my medical practice I held myself to a rigorous standard of ethics and saw my patients as fellow-humans, not potential income, and was always heartened to have them or their offspring recognize and greet me warmly in later years. I continue to provide supplemental support for the education of grand-nephews and grand-nieces in the US and in India, knowing that education is the key to success and wanting to give to them what was so difficult for me. Given the hand I was dealt with, I did the best I could and am proud of the legacy I leave.

# Afterword
# Observations on the Current Situation in Burma

*My personal story has ended. As so much misinformation appears on social media and in the press about Burma, I felt it prudent to comment on the ongoing conflict there: the Rohingya crisis that began in 2017 and the coup of 2021. No book making mention of Burma can be complete without discussing these issues.*

*Burma is an enigma to many people. This arises from its checkered history. The military, once it took power, made it a policy to curtail and control the flow of information into and out of the country. Part of the reason for this plan to isolate its people from access to the world was the desire to carry out the military's oppression of the ethnic peoples. The army resorted to every subterfuge to keep the nature of its dreadful atrocities form becoming known to people of the world.*

*It started in the 1960s with the psychotic, xenophobic, superstitious, semi-literate, mad general Ne Win's "Burmese Way to Socialism" and his authoritarian rule. Every general that succeeded him has followed his mad policies. The 2015 political victory of Aung San Suu Kyi's National League for Democracy in Burma was but slight window-dressing. It had little chance for success in the face of military power, as detailed in the following pages.*

*These observations provide simply a snapshot in time, when this book was written. Developments continue to unfold.*

# Rohingya Genocide 2017–

*In the background the flimsy homes were burning and people were fleeing. When asked by a reporter why the homes were burning, the toothy Burmese colonel with reddish juice*[1] *dripping from the side of his mouth said: "We don't know why these people were throwing their babies into the creek, setting fire to their homes, and running away."*

This is a most egregious, laughable, and preposterous statement about human behavior, one that will go down in history as such. Humans do not burn their homes. That would be like setting yourself on fire. Home is where humans seek shelter from the fear that darkness brings, home provides shelter from predators, a place to cook, eat, sleep, and sustain life. Psychoanalysts will say that musings such as intimated by the colonel above and by his military cronies are alien to humans. But the Burma Army is strange in so many ways: it has no rules of engagement, obeys no international laws, plays by its own rules, is a rogue army. Its elimination will make the world a better place.

According to the government there are 135 races in Burma. That is nonsense. The illiterate, untutored generals have no concept of modern genetics, their interpretation of how mutations work and how they influence the way people look (phenotypism). The generals are not informed about the new genetic studies, about how we now see race and ethnicity. According to the Burmese authorities, Rohingya are not part of Burma's "races." The ongoing genocide is predicated on this interpretation that "they" are not part of "us" and so can be forcefully removed (by intimidation, rape, burning of homes, mass killings, murder) from the country, even though they have been living there for more than one hundred years.

[1] Caused by chewing the pan and beetle nut.

## GEOGRAPHY AND GEOLOGY OF THE ARAKAN[2]

When the India plate collided with the Southeast Asia plate sixty-five million years ago, that event left a gaping suture right through the middle of Burma. Eventually, as this suture began to close, it would become an inland sea and then in time would silt over; the sea would contract, forming the Irrawaddy River basin. That chasm filled up and become the Irrawaddy River.[3] To the south the land fades into the ever-changing delta. To the west of this suture is a chain of low hills, about 4,000 feet high. It is not the height of the hills nor their ruggedness that matter as a physical barrier; it is not a formidable high range. But in all other aspects the barrier is deadly. The hills are called the Pegu Yomas (mountains) and in every respect are a hell hole. The area is home to every biting, stinging, blood-sucking insect imaginable, most of them disease-carrying vectors. There are blood-sucking leaches as big as a thumb, stagnant water holes filled with cholera bacillus, shigella dysentery, and rats as big as cats (bandicoots) infested with plague-carrying fleas. Ferocious Burmese tigers and leopards roam freely. There are two mountain passes through the Arakan range: the "Ann" and "Toungup" passes. In peacetime it took days to travel; in wartime it took weeks. This barrier separates the peoples of the Arakan from the Bamar people. Their origins are different and contentious.

## WHO ARE THE ROHINGYA?

Almost every society has an origin story. The Japanese have the Sun God liaising with a human and thus creating the Japanese race. Christians have the story of Adam and Eve. Burmans claim: "We belong to the Sykya-muni," meaning "we are

---

[2] The British called this area of Burma the Arakan; the Burmese name for it today is Rakhine State. I use both terms interchangeably.

[3] The remnant of this is the great Sagaing–Namya fault, along which many earthquakes occur. The government does not mention the earthquakes, but I have seen the ruptures in the land, fallen pagodas, and landslides.

descendants of Gautama Buddha," who was born at Limbu, in Nepal, to a princely Indian family.[4]

The Rohingya are a non-Mongolian Muslim people who have lived for hundreds of years in Burma's Rakhine State. There is endless argument about who were the first people who lived here. The most reliable reference is by the historian and British Commissioner of Pegu, Sir Author Phayre; his *History of Burma* (1883) provides some clues. But it is complicated. He notes that peoples from Bihar state in India migrated from India and adopted the Buddhist faith. The *Chronicles of Arakan* say that the first kings (of Arakan) reigned from Bihar (India) and that the king sent his first-born son (named Benares) to Arakan to rule as king. He reigned in a city called Ramawati, supposed to be near the present town of Sandoway, in Arakan. A fair number of writings from the time of British rule establish these facts and attest that the Chandra dynasty (Bengal) of India (1020–1050) helped the Burmese king Anoarahta (present spelling Anawrahta) found the first kingdom (1044). This is how Buddhism came to Burma.

Bengalis (for want of a better term) are Caucasians "with diverse haplotypes." There was much gene flow between the northern groups of India (the so-called Aryans) and the southern Indian groups. The claim by some groups that they are pure Aryans is fiction, incorrect, and nonsensical; there is no pure race. There is little or no information about the Burmese subgroup, no information on their Y chromosome and mutations (except for Karen women). So, to classify who is Burmese and who is not is a daunting task. It must wait until such studies are conducted, which in all probability will take years. One statement is clearly erroneous: the Burmese are not Tibeto-Burmese but are genetically close to the Nancho of Yunnan China.

---

[4] Gautama Buddha may have been born in Limbu, close to the India–Burma border, but he was born of a princely Indian family. Hence he was genetically Indian. Phenotypically, he had Indian features (sharp nose, round eyes, lighter skin) as seen in sculptures all over western India and Afghanistan. The Bamar claim to be descendants of the Buddha's "race" are fatuous. Burmese features are Mongolian (sloe eyes, flat face and nose, and darker skin). Burmese typically refer to Indians as "Kalas," which in current usage is a pejorative term. The people in Limbu were more peaceful and non-violent, progressive and liberal, than the Bamar.

Prior to 1784, Arakan was ruled by the Arakan kings. The kings of Pegu (Mon kingdom) invaded Arakan in 1784, deposed its leaders, and looted artifacts including the Mahamuni Buddha, which now resides in Mandalay. That quest to steal the famed Buddha image was key, an all-powerful incentive for the invasion. It is said that unusual vision, great powers, will accrue to those who pray and make offerings to the Buddha; they will be richly rewarded and have their wishes granted. The image is venerated throughout Burma. One sign of veneration is to press small squares of gold leaf onto the image.[5]

In the late eighteenth century, Mr. Michael Symes of the East India Company went up the Irrawaddy River to explore and expand trade. His mission was successful. When the Irrawaddy Flotilla Company was formed in 1865, the Scottish company recruited people from Chittagong and environs to man their boats because the Chittagonians were excellent seafarers and knew the Irrawaddy like the back of their hand. After the Third Anglo-Burmese War in 1885, when the British annexed Burma, they folded the Arakan into Burma proper and removed all barriers to immigration. In the colonial era, the British allowed Indian labor to work in the docks, on road building, and performing other menial tasks that the Burmese in their arrogance would not do.

The Burmese assumed that all people from the subcontinent were poor; never mind the fact that it was Indian money that built the Rangoon tram and owned much of the land and the buildings in Rangoon. The Burmese to this day bear hostility and hatred toward the Indian money-lending class, as Burmese farmers would borrow money and then be unable to pay back the loans, thus losing the rich farm lands. If you are not "Bamar" (true Burmese), you are a "Kala," a pejorative akin to "Negro" as used in the sixties, used still today for people of the subcontinent (non-Mongolian in appearance). It also applies to people of the Middle East and elsewhere. If you do not look Mongolian, are not Buddhist, and are not light skinned, you are not part of the so-called "Burmese master race."[6] You are a

---

[5] The original features were Indian, but years of pressing gold leaf onto the statue have obliterated those original features.

[6] See, for example, U Maung Maung, *Burmese Nationalist Movements, 1940–1948* (Honolulu: University of Hawaii Press, 1990).

"Kala" and have no rights in Burma. The current government only recognizes as citizens those people with "Burmese phenotype and skin color" (not that many Bamar are so much lighter than the Rohingya; Bamar skin color does not differ much from that of other people of the region, using the modern Luschan's classification).[7] This despite the fact that some peoples from the subcontinent are lighter skinned than the Bamar and have refined and sculptured features. The Burmese hill tribes are definitely light skinned.

For the Bamar (excluding the other minorities), the argument as to who inhabited this land is moot.[8] Facts from antiquity were misused or lost in the discord, heat, and anger that consume this land. The conflict is ethnic, racial, religious, and political. The effort is directed toward making Burma a Buddhist country, 100 percent homogeneous, and obedient to the Bamar ruling class. In this mythical country, the minorities will be subsumed. The goal is to control all the people within the country's current geographic boundaries. Thus citizenship and all the rights were changed willy-nilly, the constitution was changed, and rights that were once given to the Rohingya immediately after World War II were revoked, at least twice.

This region has suffered violence since 1941. During World War II, after the British retreated from Burma in 1942, various attempts to recapture Burma were mounted, most of them in or bordering on the Arakan: the Arakan Campaign 1942–43 (a disaster), the First Arakan Offensive, 1943–44 (almost successful), and the Arakan Campaign 1944–45 (successful). After Independence in 1947, U Nu sent the demonic Ne Win and his 5th Burma Rifles to "cleanse and stabilize the region." Military operations have continued off and on ever since.

The Burmese Army had a long-term planning operation to confiscate and aggrandize property and resources to themselves, knowing that there is wealth in the Rakhine State. The current "clearing operations" were long in the making. The army colonel in charge of the operations said to the villagers, "We can take away

---

[7] Scientists of questionable repute will claim that a difference of one or two shades lighter confers greater IQ.

[8] Francis Buchanan, *A Journey from Madras through the Countries of Mysore, Canara, and Malabar*, 2 vols. (Cadell and Davies, 1877), 1:22, 29; Sir William Wilson Hunter, *A Statistical Account of Bengal*, 16 vols. (London: Trübner, 1877), 11:41, 79.

all your property rights and even kill you."[9] In 2017 the army launched multiple "clearing operations" supposedly in response to an attack on a police and army post by a ragtag band of young Muslim men. This was an elaborate ruse (like the Marco Polo Bridge incident staged by the Japanese and the staged attack on Nazi soldiers that provided the excuse for the German Army to invade Poland). Few Burmese soldiers were hurt in the raid by the young Muslims. But it provided an excuse to execute a well-planned clearing operation, which started the current genocide. The scale and fighting strength of the battalions involved in the government "response" suggests that there had been elaborate planning. The "response" was not a police action but a pre-planned, full-scale military operation against unarmed civilians, women and children. The resulting violence, rape, and murder on a mass scale has resulted in the displacement of 700,000 Rohingyas to Bangladesh, countless rapes and killings; an estimated 140,000 deaths.[10] Yet the Bamar people accept the government's version of events.[11]

Especially Burma's Buddhist monks embrace the military actions, as testified by the following anecdotes. A group of thugs in 2017 captured some young Muslim boys, forced them to sit down, and summarily executed them. The method of this extrajudicial execution, whether by gunfire or sword, was not specified. In the same year, a group of Muslim boys sits in the dirt while a Bamar man goes about beating them mercilessly. He was supervised by a purple-yellow-robed monk who egged him on. Finally, not satisfied with the pain being inflicted, the monk picked up the stick and went about savagely beating the hapless boys, whose

---

[9] Jon Emont and Niharika Mandhana, "'We'll Turn Your Village Into Soil': Survivors Recount One of Myanmar's Biggest Massacres," *WSJ*, May 11, 2018.

[10] These numbers vary. The United Nations Refugee Agency (UNHCR) has combined numbers, but reliable statistics are hard to come by, as Burma's Suu Kyi government prevented independent observers and interested groups from conducting studies.

[11] The events point to the fact that these operations were planned, not a spontaneous response to a random event; there is evidence of long-term, in-depth planning, as proven by the rapid use of air power and artillery. When torching of homes began in the mass clearing operation, one Army Colonel said, "we do not know why they ran away, why they threw their children in the river, why they set their houses on fire and ran away." Suu Kyi echoed those same sentiments publicly, as widely covered in the international press. Psychologists scoffed at this analysis; only the Burmese could come up with such nonsense.

only crime was that they happened to be non-Buddhist. The young monk in question had earlier in the day taken his begging bowl, walked barefoot (lest he inadvertently kill something live) through the streets to collect curry and rice dished out by believers, gone back to the monastery to enjoy the meal, then lounge around. Perhaps in the afternoon he was seeking some activity, maybe some bashing. Buddhism as practiced by many in the world is peaceful. The Bamar Buddhist, in contrast, craves cruelty, violence, and murder and has no remorse.

Figure 84. Rohingya village burning. Public Domain. Facebook.

Despite the fact that Burma's government tried to deny access to foreigners, various NGO adventurers, journalists from the *New York Times*, the *Wall Street Journal*, and the *Guardian* newspapers and CNN have documented these atrocities. They report that Suu Kyi consistently blocked a UN fact-finding mission tasked with investigating allegations of human rights abuses. The International Criminal Court, UN officials, human rights groups, and governments have found evidence of wide-scale human rights violations, including extra-judicial killings, gang rapes, arson, and infanticides, which the Burmese government dismisses as exaggerations. Part of Suu Kyi's nature is to rebel and tilt at windmills; her dalli-

Figure 85. Rohingya refugee mother and child [https://commons.wikimedia.org/wiki/File:0G2A6012.jpg], Saahmadbulbul, CC BY-SA 4.0, via Wikimedia Commons. Public Domain.

ance with President Orban of Hungary is a case in point. In actuality, human-rights group have released satellite images that show about 1,250 Rohingya houses in five villages burned down by security forces. The media and human rights groups have frequently, over many years, reported intense human rights violations by the Myanmar military.

One of the most telling reports appeared in the *Wall Street Journal*, which I summarize here (to post others would occupy many chapters).[12] In Chut Pyin, a village in the contested area, the twenty-five-year-old village leader, Ahammed Hossain, says he hid in the pond for four hours. Around him, he recalled, there was gunfire and the cries of men, women, and children trying to outrun the deadly force of the Myanmar 33rd Light Infantry Division. "More than 350 people died that day," Mr. Hossain said, "which would be one of the largest massacres by Myanmar security services since the military initiated its campaign against the minority group last year." At a meeting called by the Myanmar Army (Aug. 22) at the school house, recalled Mr. Hossain, "the 33rd Division's regional commander, *Aung Myo Thu* (a potential war criminal), told the leaders that if they disobeyed his orders, their villagers would be destroyed." He continued, "*Killing is nothing to us. So we will kill you, too, if you don't follow what we say.*" Dil Mohammed, the Rohingya leader of a nearby town, reported that the commander said "We'll turn your village into soil." Hasina Begum remembered how she and her family fled to the forest only to be met with soldiers carrying rifles

[12] Emont and Mandhana, "'We'll Turn Your Village Into Soil.'"

and machine guns who intercepted everyone who fled. According to Ms. Begum, the soldiers marched fifty of the men, "including Ms. Begum's husband, toward the Buddhist side of the village. They haven't been seen since. A village shopkeeper, a disabled man in a wheelchair, was shot in the head. The thieving Burmese soldiers grabbed valuables from the women—earrings, nose rings, bracelets and phones," according to survivors. Then the women were divided by age. Younger women were told to hand their children to older women or be shot. Ms. Begum gave her baby to her mother-in-law. The younger women were ordered to a nearby village. There, Ms. Begun remembered, "approximately 100 men—including soldiers and police—crowded outside a classroom. Inside, she said, three men used her head scarf as a blindfold, bound her hands with rope and forced her onto the concrete floor, where she was raped by several men." Several men who were hiding in a bamboo hut along with women and children reported that "after about fifteen minutes, the soldiers began to shout, 'burn the houses!' Moving through the village, north to south, soldiers doused houses in flammable liquid and then set fire to the bamboo thatch. ... Other troops fired rockets that exploded buildings." The villagers in the bamboo hut fled in various directions, and some escaped unnoticed. "Another woman ran with her 2-year-old son toward a graveyard where others were hiding. After a few steps, she and the child were shot and killed."

## SUU KYI'S ROLE

There was great hope when elections were held in Myanmar in 2015; great expectations that change was about to happen. After the election, Suu Kyi made great promises about peace and progress. Given her long resistance to Burma's ruling junta and her Nobel Peace Prize, it was thought that her election would auger well for Burma. It was not to be. As a matter of fact, after the election she drew closer to the generals and supported the clearing operations.

In this Aung San Suu Kyi was disingenuous, vague, and evasive, saying that news reports are untrue, that no atrocities have been committed. She resorted to the time-honored principle of blaming the West, charging that the Western press was hostile to her and her country for "unknown reasons." She blamed the West for conspiring to destabilize Burma, to seize Burma's "enormous extractive wealth" (which is preposterous). Burma does not have much wealth any more. By her silence and evasion and also by her uttered words, Suu Kyi backed up army claims that the genocide was a police action. The world responded to her position with indignation and rejection.

While the Nobel committee has not yet commented on stripping her of her Nobel prize, Oxford University has revoked her degree.[13] St. Hugh's College, Oxford, removed her portrait, and the city of Oxford revoked her Freedom of the City award (residents of Sheffield submitted a petition to withdraw that city's Freedom of the City award from her as well). The gist of their reasoning is that "Aung San Suu Kyi and the Burmese government need to make it very clear that the military action should stop." European Union countries also have removed honors that they conferred on her in the past, and more countries and cities are revoking the honorary degrees and keys to the cities they had formerly bestowed on her. The Holocaust Museum and multiple organizations within the European Union have all labeled this genocide, and the London-based Public International Law & Policy Group called it genocide. Nearly all these studies call for sanctions and a trial by the international criminal justice court, at the Hague. The *Wall Street Journal*, the *New York Times*, and CNN have extensively covered this subject, with grisly photographs and sordid other details. Suu Kyi's recalcitrance is easy for me to understand: it is part of the inherent Bamar character, in line with the long history of violence towards Burma's minorities and toward British and Indian soldiers, during World War II and in the post-war years.[14] There is not a promising future for Burma.

Suu Kyi is not truthful. She is stubborn, intransigent, lacks empathy, and is unable to cope with reality. She has no administrative experience and depends on untutored advisors. The Burmese economy is stagnant; her dream of attracting foreign direct investment (FDI) has not worked. Foreign exchange reserves are

---

[13] She went to school at Oxford, earning a BA in Philosophy and Politics. In 2012 she was celebrated with an honorary doctorate from Oxford University.

[14] The Burmese ransacked the Hindu village of Payagi, massacred the people, and destroyed the Hindu temple.

low. Part of her problem is that she never provided leadership to a not-so-literate Buddhist population, who have peculiar notions of who they are. The politicians, the Thakins, had imbued the common people with the notion of their superiority, which is hard to eradicate. Suu Kyi could have provided leadership by publicly educating her people about the truth of the matter and appealing to them not to resort to violence. However, she could not overcome her fears, that if she pleaded for tolerance, she would appear weak, which could be exploited by her opponents. This is the new world, wherein the Bamar society has fallen backwards. They have to accept the new world and get along in the changed world. After closely observing seventy years of misrule, I conclude that if one were to profile Burma's rulers they could be said to have come directly out of a lunatic asylum.

# Coup of 2021

On February 1, 2021, the diminutive general Aung Ming Hlaing staged a coup. The ostensible reason given for the dastardly coup was that there had been fraud (ha ha) in the previous election. The army had expected to win by a large margin but, much to its surprise, it did not. We are getting ahead of ourselves. Given Burma's convoluted history, the coup was inevitable, as was what was to follow. It did not have to be bloody, but it was. History repeats itself. The outline as to how the coup was carried out was pre-ordained.

## Legacy of Violence and Authoritarian Rule: Aung San

Min Hlaing thinks he is somewhat like Napoleon, who was not just a great general but also was an intellectual and was of great stature. This shrimp of a general is no Napoleon. Collectively, the IQ of the Burma generals is either average or below average. Take the leading general circa 1940–41, Aung San. He got an easy degree from the University of Rangoon, went to Japan as a political hack with no military background to study at the infamous Nakano school, and in six months became a major general. In the Bamar language there was no word for "general" so they created one: "gyoke." Voila, he became a major general.[1]

Aung San is often described as an "Independence Hero." Where did this description come from? Certainly not from the British, nor from the Karens, Kachins, or Shans of Burma. It is entirely a myth perpetrated in Burma and then picked up and perpetuated by Americans, like the Indian rope trick.[2] This myth was based on tea-shop talk among "Bamar historians" (pseudo-historians) who assert

---

[1] In the standing armies of the world, to become a general would take many years; after boot camp or a military academy it takes more than twenty years of leadership to lead 12,000 to 16,000 men.

[2] John Elbert Wilkie of the *Chicago Tribune*, reported on an Indian father and his son who performed the rope trick wherein the father would flip a rope, the son would climb the rope and then vanish briefly, only to re-appear in the crowd of onlookers. This brought much attention to Wilkie and the *Chicago Tribune*. Of course it was all an illusion. The physics of this was explained, and then thoroughly debunked; go to Wikipedia to read the story.

that Aung San first threw out the British (including the 17th Division, BurCorps, and the Burma Brigade), then threw out the Maung Pu (a derogatory term for the Japanese), then threw the British out again. In truth, the Burma Defense Army (BDA) was formed by the Japanese on August 26, 1942[3] with 3,000 core troops *of questionable competence*. The idea that Aung San could singlehandedly defeat the British is preposterous.

As noted in several places earlier in this book, the Independence movement, including the BIA and BDA led by Aung San, was willing to collaborate with the Japanese army and to engage in murderous actions in pursuit of their goal.[4] British Intelligence at the time was very much aware of Aung San's tendencies, even though post-war Burmese "history" whitewashes his thuggery. I went to the British archives and retrieved the following, just a small sample of British perceptions of Aung San:

1

Telegram No 57 the 7th November 1945, to Secretary of State for Burma, London, from Buroffran, Rangoon.

"There is a possibility that evidence may be forthcoming to lay charge against Aung SAN of murder committed in 1942. While I realize that news that investigation is being made might lead Aung SAN to adopt definitely hostile attitude I am sure you will agree

---

[3] From the dregs of the Burma Independence Army or BIA, which the Japanese had formed on December 31, 1941, then disbanded in July of 1942 after the initial campaign to attack Victoria Point and march toward Rangoon. A British observer noted that the BIA was "run by upstart youths [Aung San, Ne Win] who had no experience or training and who in many cases used their newly found authority to pay off old scores, to feather their own nests, throw their weight about and to become thoroughly objectionable. They were unpopular with both the Japs and the Burmese people." See *Burma During the Japanese Occupation* 58–59.

[4] Postwar Burmese generals set up a Japanese-type academy in the former British School of Jungle Warfare in Maymyo. The entire crop of "generals" produced would carry out the Japanese type of warfare—ruthless, cruel, and barbarian, with no rules. This is now the type of war that the Burma Army is conducting against its own people.

that investigation must proceed. It will of course be conducted as unobtrusively as possible."

2

Draft paragraphs to follow reply recommended by C.O.S. on purely military aspects [3 June 1946].

The political consequences of your support of resistance movement and degree of recognition of it and its leaders accorded thereby, may be most far-reaching ... the section which now contemplates action ... is led by persons who have previously been actively pro-Japanese and actively hostile against us. Support of this element, therefore, may well be misunderstood by and give offence to less active but more dependable elements, particularly if the support of the ex-collaborationist resistance movement is such as could be interpreted as indicating that we regard them as in any sense the liberators of their country, with a consequent claim on other elements of their allegiance and a claim on us for preferential treatment. It is essential, therefore, that they should not get the idea that we attach undue importance to their contribution and that they should be reminded more clearly than you propose that they have a lot of lee-way to make up as ex-collaborators with Japanese both in our eyes and in the eyes of their co-patriots who have suffered at [their] hands.

3

In a top-secret memo from SEAC Headquarters to 4 Corps and 33 Corps headquarters, April 1945, British Intelligence laid out two principles that needed to govern any coordination with the Burmese National Army under Aung San (whose whereabouts were, at the time, unknown):

(a) No written recognition of services or testimonials must be given.

```
        (b) No payment must be made to them as soldiers of the B.N.A.
This does not, however, exclude monetary or other reward to indi-
viduals for special services, from intelligence funds, nor the pro-
vision of JAP currency necessary to the performance of their oper-
ational role.
```

As can be seen, the "hero" honorific is not based fact but is entirely spurious, yet every American writer has succumbed to this artifice.

## SUBSEQUENT RUTHLESS LEADERS

The Burma Army generals have never had a propensity to listen to advice, no matter how well meaning. In the late 1940s, Indian Prime Minister Nehru strove to get the Burmese government to negotiate with the Karens and Karenni so that it could deal with the menace of communism. Convinced that a simple military solution would not work, he pointed out to Burmese Prime Minister U Nu that the powerful and well-equipped British Army had not made headway against a similar group of "freebooters" and self-styled communists, despite eight months of effort. U Nu refused, however, and the situation in Burma further deteriorated. Communists refused to lay down their arms, bands of insurgent PVO men (young thugs) refused to join the national army and revolted.[3] Min Hlaing's current refusal to accept ASEAN help echoes U Nu's intransigence.

In 1947, after the University was reopened, I used to walk to the main campus from my home for some classes. The 1.8-mile route: Thuka Road dead-ended at the Rangoon–Insein Road. There was a soap factory behind the road. A footpath took me around the north end of the building then connected to another footpath leading north. The first half of the trail was lonely, and robbery was frequent. Just past the halfway mark, the footpath became wider and dead-ended into Rangoon-Prome Road, now called Parami Road. Parallel to the road was the bund, which the British had built by damming Inya Lake. In peace time it was a nice

---

[3] Bayly and Harper, *Forgotten War*, 464.

place to go for an evening walk. But during the Ne Win coup of 1962 and in the brutal suppression of the 1988 independence movement, this was the staging area for the troops that demolished their opposition. Many were killed.

Figure 86. Sein Lwin, the "Butcher of Yangon." President for just seventeen days in 1988, succeeding General Ne Win. Public Domain, Wikipedia.

In 1962, Sein Lwin was Ne Win's henchman, the general who carried out Ne Win's orders. His troops bolted the doors to the two-storied student union building, and with thirty-nine students in the building, he ordered it blown up. Mad Ne Win had been plotting such action for a long time and now imprisoned the Prime Minister U Nu and established a government that was almost exclusively run by the military. Carnage ensued in the city and its suburbs. How many he killed is not known. The country was plunged into a twenty-plus-year nightmare of economic stagnation, political oppression, and widespread fear.

On August 8, 1988, Sein Lwin used the same technique again in assembling his troops to quash the growing independence movement. Using Japanese-built trucks, he positioned troops from the Mogul Street jail to Phayre Street. As students and young men began to assemble around Sule Pagoda Road, just about four blocks away, the troops would cut off their avenue of escape. Standing on an army vehicle, Sein Lwin waved his hands around and around and unleashed a most deadly slaughter. Automatic gunfire erupted, and protestors were gunned down as they fled the city. No reliable statistics are known, but this episode alone is said to account for ten thousand deaths. My sister gave me an account of the events. As the hapless students fled into the narrow streets, they were chased and gunned down. At times, gunfire hit homes of people living alongside the narrow lanes.

Sein Lwin died in April 2004. He was reported to have died penniless and on public dole. This practice of leaving all worldly possessions to the family and abandoning the family in order to go into a monastery, there to die penniless, is a common feature of Burma's Buddhists. The practice is meant to cover up all the sins that one committed during one's lifetime. The retiree spends all day repeating mantras and praying, and in this phase they do not communicate with the outside world. It is noted that during this period of penance, from sun up to sun down, one goes into a trance-like meditation, hoping that all the misdeeds will be forgiven. By so doing, the Burmese Buddhist hopes to be absolved of all the mayhem, blood, and murder he has caused in the world and expects to be reborn a human with good Karma. It is a wonderful way of Buddhist life. *This of course begs the question to what end, that one's most dastardly deeds are forgiven (by whom) and one can be reborn a good human. Butchers the likes of Ne Win, San Yu, Sein Lwin, Khin Nyunt, Than Shwe, and the rest of the Mad-dog butchers of Burma are forgiven and allowed to come back as human, to repeat the cycle all over again?* It is perhaps this belief that has caused the violence for more than seventy years. If that be the case, then there will be no end to the Buddhist cycle of violence in Burma.[4]

## INDEPENDENT THINKING LEADS TO INDEPENDENCE

As long as the populace is uneducated in or disbelieves in science, it remains vulnerable to manipulation and propaganda, whether from the army or the monastery. An anecdotal story told long ago by a British official who was visiting a lay school in Burma one day: "... I was talking to one of the pupils, a very intelligent boy. I asked him about the shape of the earth and so on. He had it all pat, the conventional proofs included. I said, 'Now, you know what the Pongyis teach, which do you believe—what you have learnt here, or in the monastery?' He replied unhesitatingly, 'what the Pongyis tell me, of course.' 'Why then,' I asked, 'did you say the earth was round and went round the sun?' 'Oh,' he said, 'I must say that or I should not pass the examination; but I believe the other.'"[5]

In the 1960s, on visits to Washington DC, I met Burmese who spoke to me in hushed whispers about goings-on in the home country. Even in this tiny

---

[4] The universe we experience isn't designed for us ... our existence is a cosmic accident. See Lawrence M. Krauss, *The Greatest Story Ever Told—So Far: Why Are We Here?* (2017; New York: Atria Books, 2018), front cover.

[5] Sir Charles Crosthwaite, *The Pacification of Burma* (1912; Frank Cass & Co. Ltd., 1968), 340.

group they suspected each other, worried that one might be a spy, so comments were brief and vague. Today discussion is widespread and open. Three million people from Burma live outside their country, and most of them are not fearful of talking about conditions in Burma. Of the three million, virtually all are opposed to Min Hlaing. With cell phones, Facebook, and Twitter, word spreads instantly to negate government propaganda. This poses a great handicap to the regime, as their propaganda has little effect.[5] Moreover, many of the expats contribute money if they can. This means funding for the freedom fighters will increase while the parlous state of the government purse will worsen.

I write this eight months since the coup occurred in February 2021. In the whole scheme of things, this is not a long enough time for a coup to succeed. To date, the organization that keeps track says 800 people have been arrested, often tortured. Their brutalized bodies have been returned to the family or just vanished; more will die. I have been told that the military has camped out in hospitals so as to arrest any resistance fighters who are brought to the hospital wounded, which of course complicates treatment for patients showing symptoms of COVID-19. On all counts, the stats are often misleading. My contacts say that many more than the government acknowledges have been hospitalized, killed, or have fled.

The depths of cruelty and the lengths to which this government will go are beyond the pale. The Associated Press reported (Sunday, July 18, 2021): "The military has declared war on health care—and on doctors themselves, who were early and fierce opponents of the takeover in February.[6] Security forces are arresting, attacking and killing medical workers, dubbing them enemies of the state. With medics driven underground amid a global pandemic, the country's already fragile healthcare system is crumbling." *What madness is this?* It takes seven years to

---

[5] A *Wall Street Journal* article, however, recently underscored that the UN had concluded that Myanmar's military turned Facebook into a propaganda tool for genocide against their own people. Ignorant of various dialects spoken in Burma, Facebook allowed posts to advocate violence against a persecuted ethnic group. Reported in the *New York Times*, Monday, September 27, 2021, B7, "Does Facebook Need to Be Everywhere" by Shira Ovide. Additional charges have been made that Facebook allowed Burmese Buddhist monks to advocate violence against non-Buddhists. As this book goes to press, a whistleblower has documented Facebook's malfeasance in the Burmese debacle.

[6] More than sixty doctors were under arrest by July 2021.

complete a degree, more additional training to be a full-fledged doctor. When this insanity is over, who will be there to care for the people? The military officers will go to Thailand; the rest will die for lack of care.

Figure 87. Flyer from Amnesty International clearly spelling out Min Aung Hlaing's responsibility for genocide. Personal collection.

I see subtle differences between the present situation and previous revolts in Burma. Overseas Bamar no longer talk about Bamar superiority and the Bamar master race. The freedom fighters are not interested in Bamar arrogance and denigration of ethnic peoples but are more interested in winning their freedom. They are comprised of a more diverse group and have joined forces with ethnic forces battling the government. The outcome of the present strife is uncertain. The army is on a world-wide hunt for advanced weapons. Even if such weapons were obtained, the clueless privates (recruits) first class and NCOs in the Burmese army do not have the education or skills to handle and maintain such weaponry.

Figure 88. Protestors in Rangoon, 2021 [https://commons.wikimedia.org/wiki/File:Protestors_marching_Yangon_15.png] by Maung Sun, CC BY-SA 4.0, via Wikimedia Commons.

## OUTCOMES

Burma's economy has historically been based on extractive industries (see Table 1). About every decade there is an economic crisis, as is well documented by Sean Turnell.[6] The early years of excitement over the opening of Burma's economy in 1988 and its enhanced growth was based on growth and development in these

[6] Sean Turnell, *Fiery Dragons: Banks, Moneylenders and Microfinance in Burma* (Nordic Institute of Asian Studies Press, 2009).

industries. Gems and jade account for less than 8% of Burma's GDP, yet some writers dwell on this sector endlessly. Both agricultural products and forest products (timber, rice, and pulses) constitute a far larger percentage of Burma's GDP than gems and jade. The largest sector today is oil and gas.

**Table 1. Export Structure of Myanmar 1993–94**

| Sector | Percent of GDP |
|---|---|
| Agricultural Products | 32.2 |
| Forest Products | 32.1 |
| Marine Products | 8.7 |
| Minerals and Gems | 8.6 |
| Other | 18.4 |
| Figures based on information provided at a business conference in 1994 hosted by InFocus Group. | |

Today, human capital and creativity are still minimal. Apparel manufacturing has increased over the past twenty years. Tourism began to flourish after 1988 and gave a boost to GDP, but it has declined dramatically as a result of the Rohingya genocide and the current coup. Multiple studies have shown that, given the state of civil conflict, foreign investment and growth in Burma will be almost nil as a result of the coup and current conflict. New resources cannot be discovered or exploited. Sale of present resources is hampered by sanctions imposed by many Western countries. Hence the outcome is dismal for the Burma army and government. In contrast, the rebels are increasing their income from expatriates.

The Burma Army gives lip service to national unity and solidarity. These are unlikely to be achieved, however, as the majority of the non-Burman and most of the Bamar people are against this. People in general are fed up with such propaganda. The opposition today is well informed compared to the sixties and seventies. They have cell phones and all the accouterments to receive and inform the freedom fighters of the tremendous support from people outside the country.

Reading between the lines, there is dissent in the upper echelons of the Burma Army. Min Hlaing has a deadline: he must defeat the rebellion before his term expires next year. That is unlikely to happen. The biggest obstacle the army faces is financial. The Burmese kyat has become volatile for the umpteenth time.[7] Its value has dropped precipitously, and the number of kyats it takes to buy foreign exchange has gone through the roof. Inflation is rising and rising fast. Burma is experiencing hyperinflation like Germany did during the Weimar Republic. Foreign reserves are declining just as fast. Information is that food, cooking oil, charcoal, medicines, and other necessities are in short supply. The poor are desperate. They borrow in the morning (from money lenders), agree to usurious rates, and repay by sunset, otherwise the next day they have to pay even higher usurious rates. Starvation and deaths will grow. I am told that withdrawals from banks are limited to small amounts each day, forcing people to queue at ATMs early each day before money runs out.

Ms. Suu Kyi is still respected both within and outside the country, but she is aging and fading fast. She has endured many vicissitudes, which have a bearing on how she can stand up and lead the party. Among some, especially abroad, she has been tainted by her lack of forceful response to the Rohingya crisis. Her party, the National League for Democracy (NLD), has to find younger, more vigorous and charismatic leaders. I would like to see the younger set shed their traditional Burmese attire and dress and conduct themselves more like people elsewhere in the world. Given the opportunity, they will do so. The zeal and endurance of the men and women fighting against the military is astonishing. They are in the game to stay. They want to be like their neighbors—free to travel, think, eat, and express themselves freely. It is a noble goal.

Countless crimes are being committed by the junta on a daily basis—heinous crimes too numerous to detail. It would fill a book to include all of them. The rulers are thieves and robbers, corrupt thugs. They expropriate the natural resources for themselves and, using their ill-gotten gains, buy homes in tony places in London, the USA, and various flesh pots of the world. Actually, the poor and near poor of Burma were better off under colonial rule.

My prediction is that the conflict will come to a head by 2022. If the army fails to suppress the freedom fighters (after 70 years the army's chances are slim),

---

[7] The value of any country's currency is dependent on stability and growth.

there is little chance that they can do it now. The freedom fighters are gaining in strength. Hitherto the army sustained no losses; now they are subject to IEDs, daily bombings, and frequent casualties. The army also has a morale problem.

Due to the parlous state of the economy, it is likely that the banks and the economy will collapse, that Burma will become a failed state. I have been monitoring the value of the kyat. It has become volatile, weak, and has been losing value. Over a three-week period, its value dropped from 1500 kyats to $1; to 2000 kyats to $1; to 2700 kyats to $1. At this rate, the predicted economic collapse could come sooner than previously thought. The World Bank reports that Burma's GDP fell nearly 10% in 2020 and will fall further in 2021.

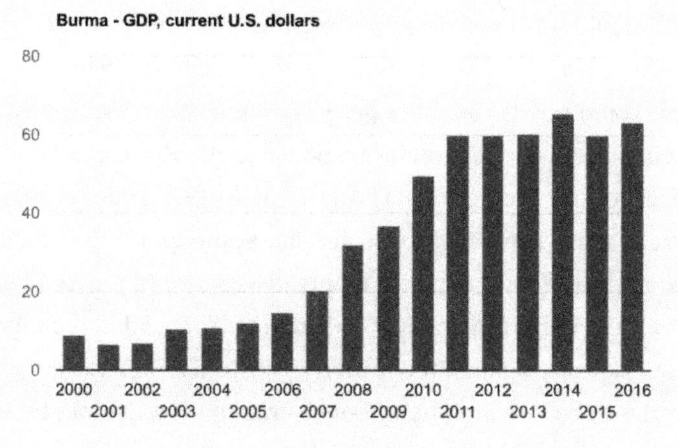


The Shans, Kachins, Chins, and Karens will try to form some type of federation, which will give the resistance space to succeed. The outcome is a toss-up. It will depend on how well the opposition stays together and how the world powers react. As always, American policy-makers as well as American writers will want stability over all else (to counter China's power), a policy that has been an abject failure. The UK, Western Europe, and the rest of the world should avoid America's failed policies of the past and support a more equitable and all-inclusive society (politically and economically). Not only the generals but also the monks who support the military should then be tried as war criminals.

# Index

*This is a very basic index of pertinent places, names, and Burmese words [with brief definitions]*

C

T

www.ingramcontent.com/pod-product-compliance
Lightning Source LLC
LaVergne TN
LVHW081601100826
845153LV00004B/431

* 9 7 8 0 9 7 2 5 3 2 3 5 8 *